ADORNO'S PRACTICAL PHILOSOPHY

Adorno notoriously asserted that there is no 'right' life in our current social world. This assertion has contributed to the widespread perception that his philosophy has no practical import or coherent ethics, and he is often accused of being too negative. Fabian Freyenhagen reconstructs and defends Adorno's practical philosophy in response to these charges. He argues that Adorno's deep pessimism about the contemporary social world is coupled with a strong optimism about human potential, and that this optimism explains his negative views about the social world, and his demand that we resist and change it. He shows that Adorno holds a substantive ethics, albeit one that is minimalist and based on a pluralist conception of the bad – a guide for *living less wrongly*. His incisive study does much to advance our understanding of Adorno, and is also an important intervention in current debates in moral philosophy.

FABIAN FREYENHAGEN is Reader in Philosophy at the University of Essex. He is co-editor (with Thom Brooks) of *The Legacy of John Rawls* (2005), and (with Gordon Finlayson) of *Disputing the Political: Habermas and Rawls* (2011). He has published in journals including *Kantian Review, Inquiry, Telos*, and *Politics, Philosophy & Economics*.

MODERN EUROPEAN PHILOSOPHY

General Editor

WAYNE MARTIN, *University of Essex*

Advisory Board

SEBASTIAN GARDNER, *University College London*
BEATRICE HAN-PILE, *University of Essex*
HANS SLUGA, *University of California, Berkeley*

Some recent titles

Frederick A. Olafson: *Heidegger and the Ground of Ethics*
Günter Zöller: *Fichte's Transcendental Philosophy*
Warren Breckman: *Marx, the Young Hegelians, and the Origins of Radical Social Theory*
William Blattner: *Heidegger's Temporal Idealism*
Charles Griswold: *Adam Smith and the Virtues of Enlightenment*
Gary Gutting: *Pragmatic Liberalism and the Critique of Modernity*
Allen Wood: *Kant's Ethical Thought*
Karl Ameriks: *Kant and the Fate of Autonomy*
Alfredo Ferrarin: *Hegel and Aristotle*
Cristina Lafont: *Heidegger, Language, and World-Disclosure*
Nicholas Wolterstorff: *Thomas Reid and the Story of Epistemology*
Daniel Dahlstrom: *Heidegger's Concept of Truth*
Michelle Grier: *Kant's Doctrine of Transcendental Illusion*
Henry Allison: *Kant's Theory of Taste*
Allen Speight: *Hegel, Literature, and the Problem of Agency*
J. M. Bernstein: *Adorno*
Will Dudley: *Hegel, Nietzsche, and Philosophy*
Taylor Carman: *Heidegger's Analytic*
Douglas Moggach: *The Philosophy and Politics of Bruno Bauer*
Rüdiger Bubner: *The Innovations of Idealism*
Jon Stewart: *Kierkegaard's Relations to Hegel Reconsidered*
Michael Quante: *Hegel's Concept of Action*
Wolfgang Detel: *Foucault and Classical Antiquity*
Robert M. Wallace: *Hegel's Philosophy of Reality, Freedom, and God*
Johanna Oksala: *Foucault on Freedom*
Béatrice Longuenesse: *Kant on the Human Standpoint*
Wayne Martin: *Theories of Judgment*
Heinrich Meier: *Leo Strauss and the Theologico-Political Problem*
Otfried Höffe: *Kant's Cosmopolitan Theory of Law and Peace*

ADORNO'S PRACTICAL PHILOSOPHY

PHILOSOPHY

Living Less Wrongly

FABIAN FREYENHAGEN

University of Essex

CAMBRIDGE
UNIVERSITY PRESS

CAMBRIDGE
UNIVERSITY PRESS

University Printing House, Cambridge CB2 8BS, United Kingdom

Cambridge University Press is part of the University of Cambridge.

It furthers the University's mission by disseminating knowledge in the pursuit of education, learning and research at the highest international levels of excellence.

www.cambridge.org
Information on this title: www.cambridge.org/9781107543027

© Fabian Freyenhagen, 2013

First published 2013
4th printing 2014
First paperback edition 2015

A catalogue record for this publication is available from the British Library

Library of Congress Cataloguing in Publication data
Freyenhagen, Fabian.
Adorno's practical philosophy : living less wrongly / Fabian Freyenhagen.
pages   cm. – (Modern European philosophy)
Includes bibliographical references.
ISBN 978-1-107-03654-3
1. Adorno, Theodor W., 1903–1969.   2. Ethics.   I. Title.
B3199.A34F74   2013
193–dc23
2012046972

ISBN 978-1-107-03654-3 Hardback
ISBN 978-1-107-54302-7 Paperback

Additional resources for this publication at www.cambridge org/freyenhagen

To those who taught me

CONTENTS

ACKNOWLEDGEMENTS

In completing this project, I have been greatly assisted by both institutions and individuals, and I hereby want to express my deep gratitude.

First of all, my thanks extend to a number of institutions which have supported me financially during the completion of my PhD, a now distant predecessor to this book: the Arts & Humanities Research Council; the *Studienstiftung des deutschen Volkes*, the pension fund of the *Nordeutscher Rundfunk* (NDR) and the *Bundesrentenanstalt für Angestellte* (BfA); and the University of Sheffield. I would also like to thank the *Adorno-Archiv* (and, in particular, Michael Schwarz) for granting me access to its treasures. Moreover, I would like to acknowledge gratefully the Senior Fellowship awarded by the Deutsche Forschungsgemeinschaft (DFG) project *Justitia Amplificata* (directed by Stefan Gosepath), hosted at the most congenial surroundings of the *Forschungskolleg Humanwissenschaften* in Bad Homburg during the Summer Term of 2010.

I owe an enormous debt to my two PhD supervisors, Bob Stern and Leif Wenar – especially for their assistance during my studies at Sheffield, but also afterwards. In tandem, they gently pushed me forward, reassured me when I needed it, challenged me on every turn of the argument, and pointed me to many invaluable ideas and resources as well as contributing tirelessly to making my texts clearer and more accessible. I cannot thank them enough for all their endeavours. I would also like to express my gratitude to the Department of Philosophy at Sheffield for its stimulating and helpful environment, and in particular for the opportunity to teach a course on my PhD topic (and to the students of this course). Many others at Sheffield had a hand in the beginnings of the project – let me particularly highlight Thom Brooks, Gerry Hough, David Liggins, and Doug Ryan. Conversations about Adorno with Gordon Finlayson date back to this time too and those about Kant's practical philosophy with Jens

Timmermann further back still – I learned a great deal from both over the years.

At Essex, I have experienced a wonderfully supportive and intellectually rich environment. I have benefited greatly from discussing ideas and drafts with my colleagues Peter Dews, Timo Jütten, David McNeill, Patrice Maniglier, and Dan Watts, as well as various students and post-docs (such as Nick Joll). Béatrice Han-Pile and Wayne Martin have contributed in a variety of invaluable ways – as critical and constructive interlocutors in numerous discussions, in reading and commenting on drafts, as supportive Heads of Department/School, as mentors, as running partners (in Wayne's case), and, last but certainly not least, as friends. Indeed, Wayne has also contributed in another capacity yet: as editor of the series in which this book appears (and a principled and thorough one at that!). In this context, I would also like to thank Hilary Gaskin and especially two anonymous referees, whose detailed and thoughtful reports have helped to improve this manuscript in many ways.

I count myself extremely fortunate to have a second intellectual home – the *Forschungskolloquium* initiated some years back in Cambridge. Its co-members – Raymond Geuss, Richard Raatzsch, Jörg Schaub, Christian Skirke, and, later on, Manuel Dries, Martin Eichler, Michael Hampe, Robin Celikates, and Lorna Finlayson – patiently read, discussed, and forcefully criticised various drafts over the years as well as generally contributing to my *Bildung* in innumerable ways and being wonderful friends. (Raymond Geuss deserves special mention not just for all of the above and more, but also for working closely with me on editorial matters, helping me to turn the completed PhD – a rather unwieldy beast of a text – into something closer to a book manuscript.)

Moreover, my gratitude extends also to various other individuals (and audiences of talks), with whom I have discussed ideas and drafts. My recollection is incomplete, but let me at least mention Amy Allen, Kenneth Baynes, Seyla Benhabib, Jay Bernstein, James Bowman, Maeve Cooke, Rainer Forst, Katrin Flikschuh, Jane Heal, James Ingram, Hallvard Lillehammer, Alasdair MacIntyre, David Owen, Peter Niesen, Lubomira Radoilska, Martin Saar, Till van Rahden, Lea Ypi, and especially Rüdiger Bittner, Axel Honneth, and Brian O'Connor. There are many others who contributed more indirectly – say by proofreading drafts (T. J. Day and Edward Pile), by introducing me to ideas and books (for example, Lothar Müller and Tim Nevill), or by going walking with me and being an amazing friend (Simon Schulz). Indeed, the dedication of this book is meant to be understood broadly – to refer not just to those who taught me in formal, academic settings, but to all from whom I learned.

Those closest to oneself contribute to one's endeavours in so many ways that it is impossible to delineate – be it rather mundane matters (such as proofreading or finding a book in a German library) or existential ones. They are also likely to be those who endure more of the pain and anguish than anyone else surrounding authors. Moreover, it is even more difficult to describe the deep gratitude felt towards them than is the case with the others to whom one is indebted. This occasion is no different. All I can do is note my endless appreciation of all that both my mother, Christine Freyenhagen, and my wife, Sabine Laemmel, have done for me and continue to do every day.

ABBREVIATIONS

Works by Adorno

Apart from references to Adorno's lectures and some of his radio programmes, all references to his works are to the *Gesammelte Schriften* (Adorno 1970–86; henceforth GS), stating the volume number followed by the page number. The first page number is from the German text, the second of the English translation, if there is one. Some references to *Minima Moralia* are to the aphorism number only. In case of the unpublished lectures, the references are to the page mark assigned by the *Adorno-Archiv* (preceded by 'Vo', as customary with references to this source). The following abbreviations are used:

CM	*Critical Models*, trans. H. W. Pickford. Adorno 1998a.
DE	*Dialektik der Aufklärung* (with Max Horkheimer) [1944, 1947]. GS, 3.
	Dialectic of Enlightenment, trans. J. Cumming. Adorno and Horkheimer 1972.
EA	'Erziehung nach Auschwitz' [1967]. GS, 10.2: 674–90.
	'Education after Auschwitz', trans. H. W. Pickford. CM, 191–204.
HF	*Zur Lehre von der Geschichte und der Freiheit* (1964/5). Posthumously published in 2001.
	History and Freedom, trans. R. Livingstone, 2006. Adorno 2001.
LCoIS	'Spätkapitalismus oder Industriegesellschaft?' [1968]. GS, 8: 354–70.
	'Late Capitalism or Industrial Society?', trans. R. Livingstone. In Adorno 2003a: 111–25.

MCP	*Metaphysik: Begriff und Probleme (1965)*. Posthumously published in 1998. *Metaphysics: Concepts and Problems*, trans. E. Jephcott, 2000. Adorno 1998b.
MM	*Minima Moralia* [1951]. GS, 4. *Minima Moralia*, trans. E. Jephcott. Adorno 1978.
MTP	'Marginalien zu Theorie und Praxis' [written 1969]. Posthumously published in 1977. GS, 10.2: 759–82. 'Marginalia to Theory and Praxis'. CM, 259–78.
MWTP	'Was bedeutet: Aufarbeitung der Vergangenheit' [1959]. GS, 10.2: 555–72. 'The Meaning of Working Through the Past'. CM, 89–103.
ND	*Negative Dialektik* [1966]. GS, 6: 7–412. *Negative Dialectics*, trans. E. B. Ashton, 1973. Adorno 1966. [When indicated, the 2001 translation by D. Redmond is used instead.]
P	'Fortschritt' (1962). GS, 10.2: 617–38. 'Progress'. CM, 143–60.
PMP 1956/7	*Probleme der Moralphilosophie (1956/7)*. Adorno Archiv Vo1289–1520.
PMP 1963	*Probleme der Moralphilosophie (1963)*. Posthumously published in 1996. *Problems of Moral Philosophy*, trans. R. Livingstone, 2000. Adorno 1996.
S	'Gesellschaft' [1965]. GS, 8: 9–19. 'Society'. Adorno 1989: Ch. 22: 267–75
SO	'Zu Subject und Object' [written 1969]. Posthumously published in 1977. GS, 10.2: 741–58. 'On Subject and Object'. CM, 245–58.

Works by Kant

All references to Kant's works are to Kant's *Gesammelte Schriften*, edited by the Deutsche (formerly Königlich-Preussische) Akademie der Wissenschaften (Kant 1900–), stating the volume number followed by the page number. The one exception is the *Critique of Pure Reason*; here page numbers refer to the first (with the prefix 'A') and second edition (prefix 'B'). The following abbreviations are used:

G   *Grundlegung zur Metaphysik der Sitten* [1785]. Kant 1900– , 4: 385–463.
         Groundwork of the Metaphysics of Morals, trans. and ed. M. J. Gregor. Kant 1996: 41–108.

KpV   *Kritik der praktischen Vernunft* [1788]. (5: 1–163)
         Critique of Practical Reason, trans. and ed. M. J. Gregor. Kant 1996: 137–276.

MS   *Die Metaphysik der Sitten* [1797]. Kant 1900–, 6: 203–493.
         The Metaphysics of Morals, trans. and ed. M. J. Gregor. Kant 1996: 363–603.

R   *Religion innerhalb der Grenzen der inneren Vernunft.* [1792–3, 1794]. Kant 1900–, 6: 1–202.
         Religion within the Boundary of Mere Reason and Other Essays, trans. A. Wood and G. di Giovanni. Kant 1998: 31–191.

Other works

NE   Aristotle, *The Nicomachean Ethics* [*c*.350 BCE]. Barnes 1984, Vol. 2.

INTRODUCTION

Pessimism and optimism often come as a pair. In Adorno's case, his deep pessimism about the contemporary social world is coupled with a strong optimism about human potential. In fact, it is the latter which explains his negative views about the contemporary social world and his demand that we should resist and change it – or so I argue in this study.

Adorno's combination of pessimism and optimism finds perhaps its best expression in a discussion with the anthropologist and sociologist Arnold Gehlen. There is much to be said about the relationship between Gehlen and Adorno,[1] but it suffices here to note that Gehlen and Adorno share a number of views – specifically, a negative, pessimistic evaluation of much of the modern social world and its culture – but they also disagree strongly: Gehlen is a conservative, a former member of the Nazi party, and is a firm believer in institutions and order as the only way to prevent chaos and to protect individuals from their own mistakes; Adorno, on the other hand, is a Hegelian Marxist, who went into exile in the 1930s and who – as we see in detail later – does not believe that modern institutions could save us, but rather that they are part of the problem and need to be overcome. They got on surprisingly well personally and in the 1960s they engaged in a series of public disputes about their respective positions. Their disagreements notwithstanding, they took each other seriously, and each thought it necessary to take on the other, if not to convince him (there is little evidence of that going on), but at least to demonstrate to third parties the superiority of their viewpoint.

Of these disputes, one is particularly revealing. It took place in 1965 and contains the following key passage:

---

1 See, for example, Müller-Dohm 2005: 340, 377–9, 390–1.

ADORNO: Ethics is surely nothing other than the attempt to do justice to
the obligations which the experience of this entangled world presents us
with. Yet this obligation can equally take the form of adjustment and
subordination, which you seem to emphasise more here, and also the
form which I would emphasise more, namely, that the attempt to take this
obligation seriously consists exactly in changing what stops human beings
in contemporary conditions – and I mean stops all human beings – from
living out their own possibilities and thus realising the potential contained
in them.

GEHLEN: I did not exactly understand. How do you know what potential
undirected human beings have?

ADORNO: Well, I do not know positively what this potential is, but I know
from all sorts of findings – including the particular findings of the
sciences – that the adjustment processes, which human beings are
subjected to nowadays, lead to an unprecedented extent – and I think that
you would admit this – to the crippling of human beings. Take for
example an issue about which you have thought extensively, namely,
technical talent. You tend towards saying – and Verblen also held this
thesis – that there is something like an instinct of workmanship, thus that
there is a kind of technical-anthropological instinct. Whether or not this
is the case, I find difficult to decide. But what I do know, is that today there
are uncounted human beings, whose relationship to technology is, if I
may use a clinical term, neurotic, that is, they are tied non-reflectively
to technology, to all sorts of means to control life, because [their]
purposes – namely, a fulfilment of their own lives and of their own vital
needs – is largely denied to them. And I would also say that just the
psychological observation of all of those uncounted, defective human
beings – and defectiveness has become, I might almost say, the norm
today – that this [observation alone] justifies us in saying that the potential
of human beings is being wasted and suppressed to an unprecedented
extent by institutions.[2]

The way this passage encapsulates Adorno's practical philosophy
only becomes apparent as this study unfolds, but let me – by way of
anticipation – summarise some of the main points it raises.

The first striking aspect of this passage is that Adorno talks in a way
that suggests that he has an ethics – something that some commentators
deny.[3] While one passage will never be conclusive, it is telling that he
speaks in the first sentences about an ethical demand. He says that our
experience of our situation ('our entangled world') gives rise to certain

2 Adorno and Gehlen 1983 in Grenz 1983: 246–7; my translation.
3 See, for example, Tassone 2005; for critical discussion, see Freyenhagen 2009.

norms. In particular, he thinks that it gives us the obligation to resist our social world and to change it (rather than – as Adorno summarises Gehlen's alternative position – to react to it by subordinating oneself to the institutional order). Thus, we are confronted here with evidence that Adorno accepts that there are ethical obligations, that they arise from (our reactions to) certain states of affairs, and that they consist in negative prescriptions (to resist and overcome our social world).

The second striking aspect of this passage is that Adorno links ethics to human potential, specifically to its denial by the present social world and its institutions. The reason why we should resist these institutions and world is that they cripple human beings and waste our potential. While talk of human potential is actually very widespread in Adorno's corpus, it has not been properly recognised as an explicit and central normative category operative in it (I return to this later). It is here that Gehlen's challenge emerges: how does Adorno know what potential undirected human beings have? How can or does he support this pivotal premise of his critique of modern social structures?

The third interesting aspect of the quoted passage is that it contains Adorno's answer to this challenge – or, at least, the elements of an answer which requires further development and elaboration (which I provide in this study). What Adorno is saying reveals something – at least in my view – absolutely central about his thought: he says that we do not know positively what the human potential is; we only know something indirectly concerning it – by realising when things are going badly, both individually (as when people suffer from neuroses) and collectively (for example, in economic crises or breakdown of civil order, but also when groups engage in racist discrimination and violence). The pathologies of the social world point to the crippling of human potential, and they do so without our having to know what the realisation of this potentiality would positively entail.

What we encounter here is a specific kind of *negativism*.[4] Generally, negativism can take various forms – it can be methodological, epistemic,

---

4 It is no small irony that in psychology and psychiatry 'negativism' can be a symptom of (mental) illness or disorder. (In this case, it is understood – as the *Oxford English Dictionary* has it – as 'active or passive resistance to producing the expected response to a stimulus, command, request, etc.; negative or oppositional behaviour or thought'). Adorno would admit that the fact that the bad is realised and the good unknowable to us in our current predicament is a sign of the illness of our time, but he would refuse to accept that his negativism (now understood in the non-psychological sense of the *OED* as 'the practice of being or tendency to be negative, critical, or sceptical in attitude while failing to offer positive

and substantive.[5] According to *methodological negativism*, the way to find out about something positive (say the human good or health) is to look at where things go badly, where the positive element is missing or being denied. For example, it might be the case that in order to find out what it is to be healthy, one must study first what it is for people to be ill. This might, however, be merely a methodological procedure to acquire knowledge of the positive element in question. Once we know what illness is, we can conceptualise and define health, either as the absence of illness or more positively (in terms of well-functioning). Many thinkers adopt a methodological negativism, both within the Frankfurt School tradition (apart from Adorno, another clear example is Honneth's work, with its focus on the grievances of marginalised groups as an indicator of misrecognition) and beyond it (such as Canguilhem's famous study *The Normal and the Pathological*).

However, there is also the stronger thesis of *epistemic negativism*. Here, the claim is that we can only know the wrong, the bad, illness, etc.; we cannot know the good, the right, what health is. It is, thus, a claim about the limitations of our knowledge – at least in our current circumstances. The latter qualification of epistemic negativism is important in the context of Adorno's work: on my reading, he is an epistemic negativist, but only within a certain historical context – specifically, he (like Hegel) thinks that we cannot know what the good life is prior to the realisation of its social conditions. These conditions are given neither in any pre-modern society, nor (*pace* Hegel) in our modern social world.

Finally, one can be – and Adorno is – a *substantive negativist*, where this means affirming the thesis that the bad is not just knowable, but instantiated, realised in the social world (including its thought forms or culture). This world is fundamentally wrong, bad, even ill and patho-logical. This is a substantive claim about the (moral) nature of this world.[6] It can be connected to epistemic negativism. In fact, in Adorno's case it is thus connected: according to him, we cannot know

suggestions or views') is pathological. If anything, the craving for constructive criticism and positive alternatives would be that (see, for example, 10.2: 793/CM, 287–8).

5 It can also be *meta-ethical* – here the thesis is that knowledge of the bad (or parts thereof) is sufficient to account for the normativity of claims based on it. I come back to this later.

6 It is also a substantial claim about the nature of morality. I comment later in the chapter on Adorno's meta-ethical negativism and discuss it in more detail in Chapters 7–9. However, I only indirectly deal with constructivist and relativist challenges to his objectivism: by defending Adorno's views on the fact of reason and on normativity and justification more generally (Chapters 4–5 and 7–9). Much more could be and would have to be said on these issues – the focus here is, primarily, on showing that Adorno's project is not self-defeating, but instead a serious contender for our allegiance.

what human potential and good is *because* this world realises the bad and suppresses this potential.

The passage from the Gehlen–Adorno exchange provides clear evidence for ascribing a methodological negativism to Adorno: the way to find out about human potential is to look at instances where it is suppressed and human beings are crippled. This passage also suggests that he is an epistemic negativist: he tells us that we cannot know positively what the human potential is; suggesting that we can – for now at least – only know the bads that cripple human beings. Finally, the passage also points to Adorno's view that the modern social world and its institutions systematically stunt and suppress human potential and, as such, realise the bad – in short, his substantive negativism.

In fact, this final point is also supported by another noteworthy aspect of the quoted passage – his claim that defectiveness, illness, has become the norm. Adorno expresses this in a typically conditional and cautious way ('I might almost say'). Still, he actually subscribes to the view that individuals, as a norm, are damaged.[7] In a wrong world, no one can be healthy, live well or even rightly. Also, in such an ill state of affairs, reacting as if everything was normal is pathological and can only be upheld by inner or outer repression. Part of the claim here is that we often do not recognise bads as such any more because they have become so prevalent, so much part of normality. In this way, Adorno's substantive negativism has a further epistemic implication – this time, that the very widespread nature of the bads makes recognition of them difficult. Also, society forms a delusional system, such that the bads it systematically produces are often not directly in view. Instead, they manifest themselves in most people's experience only indirectly – such as in psychological conditions (notably neuroses) to which they become subject as a consequence of their repressed lives, or in the sense of powerlessness they feel in relation to social forces. Thus, the fact that we live in a pathological world and suffer from the way our potential goes to waste requires careful unearthing, despite the fact that at some level everybody senses it.

Here a final aspect of the quoted passage becomes noteworthy. The passage points to the fact that, for Adorno, the *explanatory success* of his critical theory vindicates the negativistic conception of humanity

---

7 As is, for example, evidenced throughout *Minima Moralia* – aptly subtitled 'Reflection from Damaged Life' – but most explicitly expressed in Aphorism No. 36.

embedded in it. If this theory succeeds better than rival theories in explaining (1) certain social phenomena and developments (such as the high incidence of paranoia and neurosis in the modern social world); and also (2) why its rivals fail to explain these phenomena adequately, then its underlying conception of humanity is as redeemed as it could be. This strategy relies on the claim that any theory, whether acknowledged or not, contains normative presuppositions, whose legitimacy is directly tied up with its explanatory success – in a word, theorising is inextricably partisan. This fits well with Adorno's and Horkheimer's own conception of theory: for them, understanding and critique are one and the same project.[8] Thus, we should not think of the normative part of the theory as separate from the explanatory one. In other words, Adorno rejects the nowadays widespread view, according to which we engage in purely normative theorising and then bring our results together with the results of purely descriptively conceived social sciences. This is simply not a possibility and those who claim otherwise are either deluded or try to mislead us. Instead, we can only confront normative-laden explanatory theories with each other in order to establish which one of them is the best, including in terms of its normative content.

In these ways, the quoted passage encapsulates a number of important aspects of Adorno's thought – aspects we revisit throughout this study. However, it also encapsulates one of the key challenges which is itself connected to a wider set of problems. Thus, the epistemic challenge that Gehlen poses (the problem of how we could know what the potential of undirected human beings consists in) is part of a wider question as to how Adorno can account for the normative claims he makes. Does Adorno undermine his own position by taking an ultra-negative and uncompromising critical perspective? Does it not lead him into a performative contradiction such that his substantive theses, if they were true, would make it impossible to engage in the kind of critical theorising that is required to develop and support these theses? Even if Adorno could avoid entangling himself in contradictions, what would justify or vindicate his critical theory? Would it not be just be the expression of the idiosyncratic tastes of a certain elite, lamenting the coming end of civilisation while still enjoying its luxuries to the exclusion of the wretched of the earth?[9]

---

8 See, for example, MCP, 101–2/64; see also Horkheimer 1972: 216, 229.
9 Such worries are not restricted to those unsympathetic to the Frankfurt School, but were also crucial to the reorientation initiated by its second generation (see, for example,

Let us denote this set of problems the 'Problem of Normativity'. As we just saw and also see in more detail later, it takes on various specific guises, but for now I want to elaborate the general issue that pertains to all of them. In order to get a clearer grip on this problem and on possible responses to it, I adopt the following more formalised way of capturing it:

A Adorno's philosophy contains normative claims (it involves standards ('norms') of judgement and is meant to give rise to reasons).
B In order to justifiably make normative claims, one needs to provide an account of the normativity in question.
C Accounting for normativity requires appeal to (and knowledge of) the good.
D Within Adorno's philosophy no such appeal (or knowledge) is possible. [Adorno's Epistemic Negativism.]
E From (B), (C), and (D), Adorno cannot justifiably make normative claims.
F From (A) and (E), Adorno is not entitled to make the normative claims his philosophy contains.

Let me comment more on each of these premises as well as – first of all – on the sense of 'normative' with which I operate. By 'normative' I mean to denote those considerations that provide us with reasons – not just reasons to act (such as a moral obligation to help others in need, or a prudential consideration to stop smoking now in order to live longer and avoid future health problems), but also reasons to believe (such as the presence of a trace in the cloud chamber pointing to the existence of a sub-atomic particle) or reasons to admire (such as the fine workmanship of a craftsmen or the beauty of a painting). To make normative claims is to invoke standards of judgement, and these standards are (part of) the account we give of the reasons we have. Thus, if I make a normative statement (such as that you ought to keep your promises or that *War and Peace* is a masterpiece), I at least implicitly invoke a standard (be it a moral standard about what I owe to others, or what makes a novel a masterpiece) and this standard is directly connected to certain reasons (say, it gives us a reason to keep our promises, or to read *War and Peace*). This is, I take it, an ecumenical understanding of normativity – restricted as it is to a minimal core.

Habermas's 'Theodor Adorno: The Primal History of Subjectivity – Self-Affirmation Gone Wild', in his 1983b: 99–110, esp. 106).

With this clarification in mind, we can turn to the premises. We have already seen textual evidence to support premise A – the Gehlen-Adorno exchange quoted at the beginning of the chapter indicates that Adorno makes normative claims (such as that the social world cripples us) which invoke normative standards (that such crippling ought to be resisted) and imply reasons for, and guidance of, action (we should resist the social world because of the way it suppresses our potential, and one important element in doing so is to study the various pathologies to which we are subject). While the ascription of normative claims to Adorno remains disputed, there are other passages that support it. Consider, for example, the following passage:

> If philosophy is still necessary, it is so only in the way it has been from time immemorial: as critique, as resistance to the expanding heteronomy, as what might be the powerless attempt of thought to remain its own master and to convict of untruth, by their own criteria, fabricated mythology and a conniving, resigned conformity.[10]

Here we see that he conceives of philosophy as a critical enterprise. If you combine this with the further claim that any critical enterprise is a normative endeavour (that it invokes standards of judgements and aims to provide us with reasons of various sort),[11] then it would follow that his theory – or indeed any philosophy worthy of the name – is normative. Consider further:

> Hitler has imposed a new categorical imperative upon human beings in the state of their unfreedom: to arrange their thoughts and actions so that Auschwitz will not repeat itself, so that nothing similar will happen.[12]

This passage raises all sorts of interesting questions – some of which we consider later (especially Chapter 5) – but for the current purposes the main point is that it provides further evidence that Adorno thinks that there are ethical claims on us (including a particularly strong moral claim: a categorical imperative). This also shows that Adorno's theory is normative.

As to premise B, the thought here is that whenever one makes normative claims – whenever one invokes standards of judgement that are meant to give rise to reasons – one owes others (and perhaps even oneself) an account of these claims. There are several issues at

---

10 10.2: 464–5/CM, 10; translation amended.
11 For doubts about the claim that all critiques are normative, see Geuss 2005: Ch. 9.
12 ND, 6: 358/365; translation amended.

stake here – both epistemic issues of the sort Gehlen raises about Adorno's claim to know that our human potential is suppressed and questions of justification, of the right and authority to invoke certain standards – and we look at these in detail when considering the more specific forms of the general problem I want to draw attention to here. It turns out that much of the controversy surrounding the Problem of Normativity depends on disputes about what it would be to account for normativity (and whether we do need to do so at all). The critics of Adorno often presume it would have to involve grounding our normative claims (in the sense of justifying), but whether or not this is required or appropriate is very much part of the dispute (see especially Chapter 7).

Still, there is one overarching theme to such debates: accounting for normativity (whatever that turns out to be) has to invoke positive goods or ideals (the right, the good, health, etc.). This is often an implicit premise. In fact, as far as I know, not one of Adorno's critics argues for it, at least not explicitly or directly. The underlying thought can, however, be reconstructed as follows: whenever one, for example, criticises a sculpture, one – at least implicitly – does so with reference to what a good sculpture would be. One appeals to the perfect exemplar and relies on one's knowledge of it. This sort of consideration might lead one to accept the claim that accounting for normativity requires appeal to (and knowledge of) the good – i.e., to accept premise C.

We now begin to see more clearly the problem that Adorno seems to face. His theory is premised on the claim that we cannot know what the good is (i.e., on epistemic negativism). This would suggest that – if premise C is true – it lacks the resources for an account of its normative claims. I have already pointed to one passage that supports the ascription of epistemic negativism to Adorno, but let me muster some further evidence. In *Negative Dialectics*, he speculates that 'In the right situation everything would be ... only the tiniest bit different from what it is', but goes on to say that even so 'not the slightest thing can be conceived as how it would then be'.[13] And later on, he reaffirms this standpoint, emphasising how society is an objectivity which has 'supremacy [*Vormacht*]' over the individual and blocks any view beyond itself, even by the imagination:

---

13 ND, 6: 294/298; translation amended.

> Whoever presents an image of the right conditions, in order to answer the
> objection that he does not know what he wants, cannot disregard that
> supremacy [which extends] also over him. Even if his imagination were
> capable of representing everything as radically different, it would still
> remain chained to him and his present time as static points of reference,
> and everything would be askew.[14]

In sum, the realisation of the bad prevents us from knowing the good
directly – we cannot just read the good off from its manifestations in
social institutions and practices, for there are no such manifestations;
nor can we read it off from the rational potential of these institutions
and practices, for they are too infected by the bads even for this. The
realised badness even undermines other routes to knowledge of, or
acquaintance with, the good: it taints even our attempts to think or
imagine something beyond it. Still, none of this means that we cannot
know the bad, the inhuman:

> We may not know what absolute good is or the absolute norm, we may not
> even know what man is or the human or humanity – but what the inhu-
> man is we know very well indeed. I would say that the place of moral
> philosophy today lies more in the concrete denunciation of the inhuman,
> than in vague and abstract attempts to situate man in his existence.[15]

Indeed, Adorno claims that the false is index of its own untruth, that
it 'proclaims itself in what we might call a certain immediacy'.[16] If,
however, Adorno is an (epistemic) negativist, then it seems that he is
not entitled to make his normative claims. Adorno seems to face a
dilemma: he would have to give up either his negativism (but this
seems to be central to his philosophical position) or his normative
claims (but, again, they seem to be at the core of his theory).

My proposal in this study is to steer between both horns of this
dilemma by rejecting premise C. In particular, I argue that we can
account for normativity even in the absence of knowing the good, the
right, or any positive value – in short, I advocate *meta-ethical negativism*.
This is, in part, quite independently of Adorno's philosophy – he agrees
with this thesis, but I think we should do so, even if we rejected his
overall theory. On any justifiable sense of account of normativity, the
bad is normatively sufficient on its own, and it is only by implicitly – and
I argue illicitly – assuming otherwise that the Problem of Normativity

---

14 ND, 6: 345/352; translation amended; see also HF, 72/47.
15 PMP 1963, 261/175; see also 8: 456.   16 Adorno 2003b: 49/28-9.

gets going. The critics overlook the extent to which Adorno is a negativist – they fail to realise that according to him, we can only know the bad (or part thereof), not the good, in our modern social world, and that this knowledge of the bad is sufficient to underpin his critical theory (including his ethics of resistance).

This is a novel strategy to defend Adorno. There are various other authors who read Adorno as a negativist in the methodological, substantive, or even epistemic sense (although they might not put it like this).[17] However, none of them – to my knowledge – takes the extra step of seeing Adorno as a meta-ethical negativist and developing (and defending) an answer to the Problem of Normativity. Moreover, none of them draws the link – already indicated in the brief consideration of Adorno's discussion with Gehlen – between objective happiness and despair, on the one hand, and Adorno's conception of humanity and inhumanity, on the other. Yet, it is this link which provides the backbone of his own view. Accusations of inhumanity levelled at the modern social world are a constant thread running through his writings, often as criticism of the way it has turned human beings into objects or appendages of the machine.[18] What might be surprising is that Adorno builds here on elements from Kant's philosophy. In *Negative Dialectics*, he writes:

> The 'principle of humanity as end in itself' is, despite all ethics of conviction, not something purely internal, but an instruction to realise a concept of humanity, which [–] as a social, albeit internalised, principle [–] has its place in every individual. Kant must have noticed the double meaning of the word 'humanity', as the idea of being human and as the epitome of all human beings.[19]

According to Adorno, the gap between human beings as they are now – damaged, reduced to appendages of the machine, lacking real autonomy – and their potential – their humanity yet to be realised – provides the normative resources for a radical critique of our social world. Indeed, what is suggested here is a substantive conception of rationality:

---

17 See Schweppenhäuser 1993; Kohlmann 1997; Bernstein 2001; and Cook 2011.
18 See, for example, 8: 582; 8: 390–1/Adorno 2003a: 109–10; 20.2: 464; see also MM, 'Dedication', Aphorism No. 96, 131; S, 8: 18/275.
19 ND, 6: 255/258; translation amended.

> The preservation of humanity is inexorably inscribed within the meaning
> of rationality: it has its end in a reasonable organization of society, other-
> wise it would bring its own movement to an authoritarian standstill.
> Humanity is organized rationally solely to the extent that it preserves its
> societalized subjects according to their unfettered potentialities.[20]

Insofar as the current social world hinders, even represses, the development of these potentialities, it is irrational and deserves to be resisted
and transformed.

When this interpretation and defence first dawned on me, I was
myself surprised, but returning to the text I found it increasingly
confirmed. In optimistic moments, it now seems to me to orientate all
the different pieces of the puzzle that Adorno's work presents to us like a
magnet – with the broadly Aristotelian conception of normativity at
hand, we can make sense of Adorno's ethical outlook, his negativism,
and his (implicit) rejection of the Problem of Normativity. Still, I am
aware that it takes much to convince people of this (not least myself on
more pessimistic days).

While I ascribe to Adorno a relentless pursuit of a (secular) *via
negativa*, for the defence of my interpretation I take a different approach
in this study. Instead of detailed critical engagement with other interpretations,[21] I present positively what my interpretation allows one to
say on Adorno's behalf (including by way of reply to various objections)
in the hope that the result of this speaks for itself. In the words of
Adorno's 'Essay as Form', I hope to interweave the various aspects into
a sufficiently dense texture to demonstrate the fruitfulness of the interpretation.[22] I support my interpretation with extensive references to
Adorno's texts and (discussion of) detailed quotations from them. This
is not to say that I can comment in this study on every passage in which
Adorno seems to help himself to the good or some other positive notion
in a way that violates negativist strictures. I do not deny that there are
passages that give this impression. My claim is that they are better
interpreted in a negativist way. For example, Adorno states that
human beings should no longer be governed by their own creations
(be it the capitalist economic system or state socialism's vast bureaucracy); that there should be an end to human misery and hunger; that
events like those that took place in Auschwitz should never be allowed to

---

20 10.2: 775/CM, 272–3; see also 20.1: 147–8.
21 Elsewhere, I have criticised two of the main alternatives; see my 2009 and 2011a.
22 See 11: 20/Adorno 1984: 160.

happen again; that people should be freed from the enormous pressures that workplaces put them under; that they should even be freed
from most of the kind of work which capitalism requires people to
undertake; that they should be allowed to be different without fear,
not pressed into categories of abstract equality; and even that there is
something brutalising in the fact that casement windows and door
latches have been replaced by sliding frames and turnable handles.[23]
As I see it, nothing in these statements commits Adorno to operating
with a conception of the good. They should be understood as merely
negating the evils of modernity and, indeed, of a long history of
domination. The key point is that – according to Adorno – we can
identify many of the negative aspects of our social world and demand
that the whole social world should be overcome simply on the basis of a
conception of the bad.

However, I should briefly mention a different strategy for defending
Adorno. Here, the proposal is to view his critique of the modern social
world as a form of immanent criticism[24] – that is, Adorno tries to
uncover the contradictions and tensions within a given position (or
social form), rather than judge it against some external or transcendent
standard. On this interpretation, Adorno appeals to certain positive
values used in the defence of this social world – such as freedom;
democracy; individuality; happiness – and shows that this world does
not and could not live up to them.[25] There is no question that Adorno
often uses immanent critiques of this sort, but I am doubtful that he
would (and could) *only or mainly* rely on them. This is partly because of
two general problems with immanent critiques. Firstly, even if one
successfully mounted an immanent critique of our current social
world (say, conclusively showing that real democracy cannot be
achieved within it despite its presenting itself as realising this ideal),
such a critique could only demonstrate the cost of holding on to a value
or ideal (to stay with the example, one might have to admit that the

---

23 See MM, Aphorism No. 19, 66, 100; ND, 6: 275, 358/278–9, 365; and in Grenz
   1983: 234.
24 For a recent example, see O'Connor 2012: esp. Ch. 2.
25 This strategy would either be compatible with negativism (insofar as the positive values
   would not be endorsed as such, but only for the purpose of the immanent critique) or
   involve a different strategy to respond to the Problem of Normativity – namely, to deny
   that Adorno needs to account for the norms to which he appeals at all: they are not his
   own, but those of the defenders of this social world and, if anyone has to account for
   them, it is the defenders, not Adorno.

current social world cannot be fully democratic). However, this still leaves open a variety of responses, not all of which are to be welcomed – such as giving up on the ideal of democracy altogether or suppressing those that mount successful immanent critiques. Secondly, in certain contexts, we might be able to criticise a social or thought system internally, but would not want it to realise its aims – perhaps, the Nazis failed sometimes to live up to their ideals (say, because of weakness of will among some of them), but it would be rather problematic to criticise them internally for that (instead of welcoming the discrepancy). Moreover, there are also textual grounds for thinking that Adorno does not rely merely on immanent critique. Specifically, he does not think that immanent critique can be wholly immanent,[26] and he accepts that certain standards of critique hold true *whether or not* they are affirmed by those who are criticised.

Let me expand on this interpretive claim. Adorno became increasingly sceptical about the possibility of immanent critique of the current social order. In *Minima Moralia*, he points out that confronting bourgeois society with its moral norms might merely have the effect that these norms are dropped, not that there will be a social transformation to realise them.[27] In fact, in a later aphorism within the same collection, he seems to think that the norms and ideals used to justify our social world have already been largely dropped, so that it is no longer possible to confront reality with the claims it makes about itself. He writes: 'There is not a crevice in the cliff of the established order into which the ironist might hook a fingernail.'[28] In other words, there is no longer a discrepancy between what the social world presents itself to realise (its ideals) and its actual reality. Without such a discrepancy, immanent critique cannot get going. Even where immanent critique is still possible, Adorno is not only concerned with demanding the realisation of what the bourgeoisie had promised.[29] Rather, the current state of the world is bad for Adorno, whether or not it cloaks itself in positive claims. We

---

26 See, for example, ND, 6: 183/182; see also 10.1: 23, 28/Adorno 2003a: 156, 160.

27 MM, 4: 105/93.

28 MM, 4: 241/211; see also ND, 6: 271/274; 10.1: 29–30/Adorno 2003a: 161–2. What Adorno says of 'ironist' would, presumably, also hold for the critical theorist.

29 See Kohlmann 1997: 184–5. At one point, Adorno states that it would constitute real progress if what the bourgeoisie had promised were actually realised (10.2: 792–3/CM, 287). Still, this should not be understood to suggest that such a realisation would be all that is required for a free society or the realisation of the (human) good. Rather, Adorno is making a more limited point here: he is reacting to the demand that a critique of society should always be able to offer positive practical improvements. In response to this

know inhumanity and misery by themselves,[30] and by themselves they demand their own abolition.[31] In fact, in order to undertake adequate immanent critiques we have to be guided in them by knowledge of the bad and of the fact that our current society realises the bad.[32] Otherwise, immanent critiques just turn into instances of false consciousness.[33]

Hence, Adorno does not and cannot rely on immanent critique alone. Either this form of critique is altogether impossible today, or, insofar as something like immanent critique is still possible, Adorno is guided by normative assumptions brought to it from the outside – knowledge of the bad and an interest in its abolition.[34]

One real difficulty – albeit one facing anyone trying to understand Adorno's texts – is the nature of his arguments and their presentation. Adorno suggests that we should write in such a way that each sentence is equidistant to the centre of the subject matter under discussion,[35] and he often seems to come close to this ideal. As a consequence, one finds little argument that is developed along one continuous, linear path – if

demand, he argues that critics can always answer that if a society lived up to its own norms, then this would already be such an improvement – one need not present fully worked-out proposals for a different society just to be able to criticise the current society. This response is compatible with Adorno thinking that a free, post-capitalist society would go beyond the realisation of bourgeois norms. In fact, this *is* what Adorno thinks. For example, he says that it would be an improvement to realise the capitalist ideal of free and fair exchange of equivalents, but such a realisation would then allow the transcendence of exchange altogether (ND, 6: 150/147).

30 See, for example, PMP 1963, 261/175.   31 See ND, 6: 203/203.

32 See 10.1: 27–8/Adorno 2003a: 160. Jaeggi suggests that Adorno undertakes immanent critique at its limit (2005: 82) – that is, he proceeds immanently as much as possible, but also realises that this procedure does not yield strict contradictions, but, at best, inadequacies. Also, by giving up on Hegel's optimism of history as the unfolding of reason, Adorno has no longer a warrant for thinking that the long series of individual immanent critiques adds up to progress. Instead of trusting the process of immanent critique, Adorno needs objective criteria of success brought externally to the critical enterprise. In my interpretation, these are part of his negative Aristotelianism (see Chapter 9). As such they are immanent in another sense – they are not positive ideals that transcend our wrong life.

33 Similar considerations apply to ideology critique (that is, the critique of a theory or set of beliefs for misrepresenting reality in a way which benefits the established social order). According to Adorno, there is the danger that ideology critique just becomes the blanket accusation that all theorising relies on particular interests (or that it is in some other way biased). Hence, without a critical stance towards society, employing it would just lead to general relativism (see 10.1: 23–4/Adorno 2003a: 157; see also ND, 6: 198/198).

34 This also means that using immanent critiques does not absolve Adorno from providing an account of normativity.

35 See MM, Aphorism No. 44.

anything such a procedure is rejected as inadequate,[36] not least because
the object of enquiry (the modern social world and its thought forms) is
itself antagonistic and as such resisting 'continuous presentation'.[37]
Often, it seems as if arguments are lacking altogether and we are just
faced with striking and suggestive conclusions, leaving it to the reader to
construct arguments in support of them.[38] Also usually lacking is a
general discussion of background assumptions, although they, or brief
comments on them, sometimes crop up in subclauses of sentences on
other matters. Moreover, I have already mentioned that Adorno often
engages in immanent critique. This complicates the task of interpreting
Adorno's own views (and adds to the semblance of contradictions within
his own work), since what Adorno says in the course of an immanent
critique need not represent his own views at all, but merely serves the
purpose of this critique. Similarly, as part of immanent critiques,
Adorno often uses the complex terminology and ideas of the authors
he discusses (such as Kant, Hegel, or Heidegger), which then require
their own decoding, a task made more difficult by the fact that Adorno
transfigures the terms and ideas in the course of the discussion. In
general, Adorno denies that philosophical ideas can be captured in
neat definitions that provide necessary and sufficient conclusions.[39]
He also eschews examples whenever they remain completely external
or inconsequential to what they are meant to illustrate – whenever they
are mere illustrations.

Fortunately, more recorded lectures of Adorno have become
available since the mid 1990s and his spoken word differs markedly
from the written one, despite the fact that he used the former as early
drafts for the latter. The assumptions and premises are spelled out more
frequently and explicitly; Adorno discusses objections more often and
directly (instead of assuming, as in the published texts, that the readers
will see for themselves how these objections are answered) and proceeds
more slowly and developmentally. Although he still refrains from giving

---

36 See, for example, ND, 6: 44/33.   37 11: 24/Adorno 1984: 163–4.
38 In a revealing passage, Adorno comments on one of his essays in a way that might
   be emblematic for his work as a whole: 'Not only did I give the usual references and
   the scholarly apparatus a miss entirely, but also the nexus of justification
   [*Begründungszusammenhang*] that one expects by rights [*billigerweise*].The attempt was to
   consolidate [*verdichten*] the results of the reflections, not to provide the reflections
   themselves. A vindication of this procedure is only to be expected, if the relevance of
   the questions and some of the answers speak for themselves' (8: 569; my translation).
39 See, for example, 11: 19–20/ Adorno 1984: 159–60.

examples which are mere illustrations, there are more case studies in which he actually works towards his more abstract conclusions by way of analysing concrete objects of investigation (see, for example, his discussion of Ibsen's *The Wild Duck* in lecture 16 of his 1963 lectures on moral philosophy, which I take up in Chapter 4). In many ways, the recorded lectures of Adorno are like the lecture notes (often called 'additions') accompanying Hegel's published lecture outlines: they concretise and expand on the abstract lines of thought contained in texts so tightly constructed by the authors.[40] While I often draw on the lectures in this study, I back up interpretive claims, wherever possible, with references to the published texts. (Admittedly, this support sometimes derives from the already mentioned subclauses expressing background assumptions within Adorno's complex sentence constructions.)

In this study I have recourse to Adorno's lectures to decode and defend his (practical) philosophy. Indeed, I also proceed much more like the lectures Adorno gave than his published works. Thus, the reflections that do or could support Adorno's conclusions are developed along with the latter. The study is an attempt to think through Adorno's claims, to immerse myself in them, to teach them to myself.

This brings with it dangers. Firstly, from Adorno's own perspective, there is the danger that my adopting the looser approach of the lectures might not do full justice to the object of enquiry. Indeed, his detailed views about how to write a philosophical text and his opposition against publishing his spoken word would reinforce this worry.[41] For Adorno, questions of presentation and of content cannot be neatly separated.[42] Trying to present the same content in a different form is bound to fail: 'Essentially ... philosophy is not expoundable [*referierbar*].'[43] Moreover, the difficult work of interpretation which his texts require is part of their educational, even ethical nature – what this work does to us is of at least equal, if not greater, importance than the explicit theses contained in the texts. I do not have a conclusive answer to this worry, but I submit that Adorno might have been wrong (or exaggerating) when he rejected all bridging concepts.[44] Indeed, his own practice of publishing talks and lectures betrays his opposition to publishing his spoken

---

40 One difference is that the texts of Adorno's lectures are (largely) based on tape recordings, while we have to rely on the diligence of students in note-taking in Hegel's case.
41 See, for example, 20.1: 360.   42 See, for example, ND, 6: 29, 44, 61–2/19, 33, 52.
43 ND, 6: 44/33; Redmond translates '*referierbar*' as 'reportable'.
44 MM, Aphorism No. 44.

word. In the preface to one such published lecture series, he accepts the likelihood of greater dissemination at the expense of having a more worked-through text, since it introduces people to his work who would otherwise be scared off.[45] Similarly, my hope is that my way of reconstructing and defending Adorno's philosophy might make it less likely to be misunderstood and ignored. Most importantly, perhaps, a way of publicly thinking through his theory might still serve certain educational purposes – if only as a chance for others to disagree with my interpretation, to show what has been lost in it and to put matters right.

A second danger is that the exposition of Adorno's philosophy is too uncritical, (partly) as a consequence of this procedure of immersing myself in it and thinking it through. I openly admit shortcomings of this study in this regard. I attempt where I can to indicate possible objections and weaknesses, trying to weave them into the reconstruction and defence. Still, I have not always succeeded in doing so. In my defence, it is difficult to write about an author who keeps so many elements at play at once, including engaging in immanent criticism of other authors and transfiguring (their) concepts as the texts unfold, while at the same time not overloading the reader (and the author!). *Let the reader be warned then* – when I present something without objecting to it, it should not be taken as an indication that I find nothing wrong or puzzling about it. All too often I cannot articulate worries that naturally arise, but have to suspend judgement in order to continue the development of the thought at issue. Some worries get addressed (at least in part) later or elsewhere in the study, but others escape the net altogether.

A third danger is that my approach systematises Adorno's thought more than it can or even should be. His works aim to be an anti-system. They are animated by what is incommensurable, what cannot be subsumed under categories or pressed into schemas, what cannot be expressed – in short, by the non-identical. He highlights aporias, contradictions, and antagonisms, and this places constraints on how we can present his work. Turning Adorno's thought into a system would, thus, be to miss its point.

However, the first thing to note is that whatever coherence I present Adorno's thinking as having, it is of a different sort from the coherence he rejects in criticising philosophical systems. I am not proposing to derive all elements of his thinking from fundamental premises – just the opposite: I follow Adorno in rejecting discursive grounding (see especially

---

45 See 14: 171.

Chapter 7). In fact, I even refrain from making the notion of the non-identical central and pivotal to the whole endeavour – partly because of worries about turning it into the kind of master concept to which it is supposed to stand in opposition (and partly because it plays less of an explicit role in his practical philosophy). Admittedly, I present Adorno's thinking as not ridden by aporias to the extent that it exhibits no structure, coherence, or binding argumentative force, but as compatible with (defensible) demands of argumentative stringency.

Thus, to object to my approach one would have to accept a stronger thesis – one which Adorno does not endorse, and neither, I think, should we. The stronger thesis would consist in saying that we can only be true to Adorno by writing in aporias, by flouting the rules of logic, by infinitely deconstructing and erasing every step as soon as it is taken, perhaps ultimately only by writing poetry or engaging in other artworks. This is committing the opposite mistake to the kind of systematisation that Adorno objects to: it proposes that once one rejects discursive grounding and the idea that the world can be captured in a top-down deductively organised conceptual framework, one loses stringency, exactness, clarity, bindingness, structure, and the like altogether. In this way, it actually shares a common premise with its opposite: that these qualities can only be had at the expense of a system. Yet, it is this premise that Adorno rejects, not the rules of logic or the demands to be clear and binding in one's thinking – as, for example, his comments on the essay (his favoured way of writing) attests:[46]

> For the essay is not situated in simple opposition to discursive procedure. It is not unlogical; rather it obeys logical criteria in so far as the totality of its sentences must fit together coherently. Mere contradictions may not remain, unless they are grounded in the object itself. It is just that the essay develops thoughts differently from discursive logic. The essay neither makes deductions from a principle nor does it draw conclusions from coherent individual observations. It co-ordinates elements, rather than subordinating them; and only the essence of its content, not the manner of its presentation, is commensurable with logical criteria.[47]

---

46 See also the interesting comments by Reginster in the similar context of his taking a systematic approach to Nietzsche's work (2006: 2–4, 290 n. 24). Reginster also brings out the fact that rejection of philosophical systems (specifically the ambition to derive all knowledge from fundamental premises) is compatible with systematically thinking about a problem.

47 11: 31/Adorno 1984: 169.

Similarly, negative dialectics is not an anti-system in the sense of being contrary to logic, but in the sense of breaking the sway of modern systems of thought and living '*by means of logical consistency*'.[48] Just as (musical) composition involves, for Adorno, not mere stabbing in the dark, but stringency and its own logic, so does thinking, even where it turns against its own tendencies to petrify the world and our experiences into rigid systems.

There is, however, one element of truth in the objection at hand: Adorno does, indeed, admit that some contradictions in thought cannot be resolved. However, the reason for this is that these are (or at least correspond to) real antagonisms in our social world (for example whether or not to punish individuals for evil deeds; see Chapter 3). A theory which papered these over or even denied them would be problematic; instead, theories need to reflect them (and on them). Yet, this does not mean that we should accept any contradictions or inconsistencies in our theories – just the opposite: the passage quoted earlier provides us with a criterion for which contradictions ought to be preserved: 'Mere contradictions may not remain, *unless* they are grounded in the object itself' (emphasis added). In other words, only those contradictions that really are antagonisms in our social world need find their way into our theories. Moreover, even these contradictions are not to be celebrated – to the contrary, their existence points to what is wrong about this world (see also Chapter 2).

A final danger in my approach that I want to briefly discuss is that it might be accused of downplaying or even denying the utopian dimension of Adorno's thought. By insisting on Adorno's negativism, his urge to see beyond the wrong totality of our social world and its thought forms might be lost. Again, I think that this rests partly on a misunderstanding. On my reading, Adorno is a thorough negativist – such that he denies that we can currently know what the good is, but need not do so in order to object to what we have now. Yet, I am not thereby denying that his thinking is utopian in the sense that he holds on to the possibility *that* things could be different. What I am denying is that he can tell us *how* things would then be – what utopia would consist in positively speaking (that is, other than the avoidance of the bads he can identify). Indeed, he denies that he or anyone can say these positive things – as we have already seen from the textual evidence for his (epistemic) negativism provided earlier. If anything,

48 ND, 6: 10/xx; my emphasis.

trying to spell out what utopia would be is not just bound to fail, but actually sabotages its realisation.[49]

There are certain limitations to my approach that I would like to own up to at this point. Firstly, my reconstruction of Adorno's (practical) philosophy operates mainly at the level of content rather than the history of ideas. Thus, as already briefly indicated, in many of his writings Adorno works through and criticises (more or less) immanently someone else's theory (for example, Kant's account of freedom) and, in the process of this, he draws on the history of this theory's reception. Making the various influences explicit and filling in some of the background to them is often a good way to unpack and decode what he is saying. Even in his less text- or person-focused works, it often helps to consider whom Adorno has in mind in saying certain things (for example, his common targets are the positivists and Heidegger), or on whose work he is drawing (the main ones include Kant, Hegel, Marx, Kierkegaard, Nietzsche, Freud, Weber, and Benjamin). Indeed, sometimes one cannot make sense of a sentence or paragraph at all, without knowing to what or whom Adorno is alluding. In this way, discussion of Adorno's work particularly benefits from tracing the ideas and works that form the context of its development and content. It is, however, also particularly difficult in his case, with such an array of (often conflicting) influences. Be that as it may, this study is limited in its references and exploration of the background.[50] Partly this is because I could not thread in all the various influences which are identifiable

49 See, for example, 10.2: 798/CM, 292–3. In a radio conversation with Bloch in 1964, Adorno adopts what he describes as 'the unexpected role of being the advocate for the positive' ('Etwas fehlt ... Über die Widersprüche der Utopischen Sehnsucht', in Bloch 1978: 350–68, here 364; my translation). He insists that we have to hold on to the idea that things could be different. Moreover, he suggests that we should describe, as much as possible, what concretely the current level of the forces of production would allow us to do. Nonetheless, he is adamant also in this conversation that we cannot know what a free society would be like *positively*. Hence, he, presumably, means that we should detail what steps could be taken to avoid bads we are acquainted with – notably hunger, inhuman work conditions, etc. In this context, his comment in *Negative Dialectics* that self-preservation has become 'virtually easy' after eons of being 'precarious and difficult' (ND, 6: 342/349) is also noteworthy. It suggests that what he might be thinking of in the conversation with Bloch is a kind of technical account of how self-preservation could be organised differently, such that no one goes hungry and human labour-time expended on material production can be reduced radically. Indeed, he says that neither he nor Bloch is competent to offer the concrete description in question (in Bloch 1978: 363) – perhaps because they lack the required technical expertise.

50 Similarly, it is limited in exploring parallels with other thinkers – whether near-contemporaries of Adorno or later ones. One particularly interesting comparison,

without making the study even more unwieldy than it is; and partly it is because if I had pursued all the possible leads and connections, I could not have finished this book for at least another twenty years (if at all) and it would have grown even more out of proportion by then. Again, perhaps others (or my future self) can fill in the blanks.

Similarly, Adorno's writings and lectures are treated here almost as if they formed a co-present theoretical totality, rather than tracing the development of Adorno's thinking. This is less objectionable than with other authors. Historical and other developments certainly left a mark on his thinking (not least the experience of fascism, exile, and all that came with them). It also took some time before he developed his own distinctive ideas and way of thinking. Still, there is already a remarkable continuity and consistency in his work from the early 1930s onwards and especially from the 1940s. Also, Adorno makes no claims about having awoken from a dogmatic slumber, left philosophy, or undergone a fundamental *Kehre* regarding this period (but only makes such comments regarding his academic apprenticeship preceding it). Moreover, my interpretation is such that I have no reason to identify particular periods in his work, or downplay part of it (in contrast to, for example, Thyen, whose interpretation of Adorno's conception of experience forces her to postulate a break between the *Dialectic of Enlightenment* and *Negative Dialectics*). Nonetheless, I openly admit that the reconstruction offered here could have benefited from a study that traced the chronological unfolding and enriching that Adorno's (practical) philosophy underwent over the years.

I should also disclose upfront that what I present in this study is preparing the philosophical ground for Adorno's interdisciplinary research programme, not yet carrying this programme out. In particular, my defence of Adorno's theory mainly addresses the accusation that the theory is self-defeating. As part of my answer, I argue that once it is understood as an explanatory project, which aims for vindication in the sense of being able to explain better the social world (and its ills) than alternative theories, then it is not self-defeating at all, but a project we ought to take seriously. However, if I am right about this, then such a vindication requires a *comparative* study of various explanatory frameworks that demonstrates the superiority of Adorno's theory. This is not

---

which has been largely neglected so far (with the exception of Butler 2003), would be with Foucault's work.

something I can provide in this study, and anyway not something that one can hope to complete alone or in a book-length treatment.

Finally, I would like to acknowledge yet another lacuna. Critical theorists, Adorno included, may have firm convictions – they may be partisan in opposing suffering and oppression – but they also aim to be relentlessly self-reflective and critical, including in respect to their own role as theorist and author. In some sense, this challenge of accounting not just for what one says, but also for how one can say it (and how one can have the relevant and necessary insights in the first place) is impossible to meet, especially if one holds a view, such as Adorno's, the truth of which seems to undermine the very possibility of its articulation. Different authors propose different strategies for managing this challenge or containing the problems it raises – Kierkegaard's use of pseudonyms is just one such example (albeit a pertinent one, given the influence of his thinking on Adorno). I considered various options of how I could account for the possibility of my being able to reconstruct and defend Adorno in the way I propose in this study – such as including a self-reflective investigation of my life and intellectual development in the hope of being able to disarm any debunking accounts of why, say, early childhood experiences (for example, of the separation of my parents) led me to the interpretation and claims at hand (such as negativism). In the end, I could not settle on anything other than simply to acknowledge the problem.

Perhaps, there is some comfort in what Robert Nozick (an unlikely ally!) once wrote:

> I believe that there is also a place and function in ongoing intellectual life for a less complete work, containing unfinished presentations, conjectures, open questions and problems, leads, side connections, as well as a main line of argument. There is room for words on subjects other than last words.[51]

He then goes on to say that, although many works of philosophy are written as if the authors believe that what they say is both absolutely true and final, they actually know that it is not, and are often too keenly aware of the weak points. To create the impression of a completed picture, there are a lot of 'notable distortions, pushings, shovings, maulings, gouging, stretching, and shipping ... not to mention the things thrown away and ignored, and all those avertings of gaze'.[52] Still, to mention

---

51 Nozick 1974: xii.   52 Nozick 1974: xiii.

these issues is not to take anything back, but to 'propose to give it all to you: the doubts and worries and uncertainties as well as the beliefs, convictions, arguments'.[53]

With these preliminaries in place, I can briefly comment on the structure of this study. After a chapter introducing Adorno's theory (including the general picture of modern society and thought forms with which he operates), the discussion turns to his practical philosophy. In Chapter 2, I consider what implications this general picture of modern society and thought forms has for the way we, as individuals, can and should live. I bring out the fact that according to Adorno we are destined to live the wrong life in two senses: it will neither be a real form of living, nor a good and morally right life. The quite well-known, but deeply puzzling, claim that 'there is no right life in the wrong life' is then further decoded and scrutinised. Firstly, in Chapter 3, I show that, for Adorno, our social world leaves no room for autonomy, but only for negative freedom of resistance.[54] I also discuss the implications of Adorno's conception of freedom and autonomy for moral practice and responsibility. This is followed, in Chapter 4, by a reconstruction of his critique of (modern) moral philosophy, specifically of his main objections to Kant's moral theory and, albeit much briefer, to alternatives to it. Then we turn to Adorno's own ethics – his guide on how to live less wrongly. In Chapter 5, I present one of its central planks – the new categorical imperative – and, next, in Chapter 6, the other elements of his often neglected minimalist and negativistic ethics. We, then, ascend in Chapter 7 to more abstract heights, discussing Adorno's views on justification in (practical) philosophy, before I mount a defence of (meta-ethical) negativism in Chapter 8, in part for reasons independent of Adorno's own views. Finally, and in lieu of a conclusion, Chapter 9 brings together the various aspects of Adorno's practical philosophy in the process of unearthing an Aristotelian conception of normativity in his thinking. In the Appendix, I discuss an important background consideration (that willing is constitutively somatic), which provides additional support to a number of argumentative moves in the main text.

This study is meant to offer something both to those not yet familiar with Adorno's thought and to those who have already grappled with it.

---

53 Nozick 1974: xxiii–xxiv.
54 That Adorno allows for negative freedom of resistance is mostly overlooked in the literature, but crucial for his practical philosophy as a whole (see also Chapter 6).

Some of the chapters are more accessible than others – apart from the introductory Chapter 1, these are Chapter 2 (on why there is no right living), Chapter 3 (on society as an obstacle to freedom and autonomy), Chapter 5 (on the new categorical imperative), Chapter 6 (on Adorno's ethics of resistance) and, at least in part, the concluding Chapter 9. Various threads run through this work which come to the foreground at different points – Adorno's critique of Kant's practical philosophy (in Chapters 4–5 and the Appendix); his substantive ethics (in Chapters 2, 5–6, and also 9); and wider issues about normativity and justification (Chapters 5–9), to name three important ones. You, as a reader, might want pursue them independently or in a different order, but, ultimately, they belong together.

1

THE WHOLE IS UNTRUE

One of Goethe's best-known poems, '*Der Zauberlehrling* [The Sorcerer's Apprentice]' (1797), tells the story of a sorcerer's apprentice who, when his master is away, decides to use magic to bewitch a broom to fetch him water for a bath. It all starts off well, with the broom growing legs and swinging into full action, bringing bucket after bucket at lightning speed. However, predictably perhaps, it then all goes horribly wrong: when it comes to stop the broom, the apprentice has forgotten the necessary spell and instead of a relaxing bath, the apprentice ends up fighting his own creation, albeit only to make things worse (for he splits the broom in two and the flooding of the house is accelerated further). Seeing the master return, the apprentice cries for help: '*Die ich rief, die Geister / Werd' ich nun nicht los* [The Spirits that I summoned / I cannot now get rid of]'.[1] The master saves the day (and the house) by restoring the broom to its original state (while at the same time asserting his own authority by reminding the spirits that it is only to him that they should respond).

This poem captures nicely two of Adorno's key claims about humanity's current predicament. Firstly, it suggests that the means we choose to achieve our purposes can take on a life on their own and even come to govern us. In particular, Adorno thinks that we are driven fundamentally by the aim of self-preservation and have developed powerful tools in its pursuit – sophisticated conceptual schemes to cognise the world, natural sciences to explain and predict it, and technological means and organisational forms to transform it. However, like the broom in the poem, our creations do not in the end obey our commands any longer. Instead – and here I move beyond the poem – we end up serving our own creations.

---

1 Translation by D. Luke amended; Goethe 1964: 177.

Secondly, the poem highlights the danger that our creations take on a
life of their own: if the master sorcerer had not arrived in time, disaster
would have struck and even then, we can imagine the apprentice spending long hours putting things in order under the watchful eye of the
master. For Adorno, the difference is that there is no master sorcerer to
come to humanity's rescue (at least, if – as I do – one rejects messianic
readings of his works). Yet, the danger of disaster is no less real. In fact,
if Adorno is to be believed, the catastrophe has already taken place and
the modern social world has an inbuilt tendency towards permanent
catastrophe.

In this chapter, I present Adorno's fundamental claim that the
powerful means we developed in the pursuit of self-preservation have
taken on a life of their own and that this has led to disaster. I begin with
introducing Adorno's controversial thesis that the events for which the
name Auschwitz stands epitomise the radical evil of the modern social
world and demonstrate that this evil is not accidental to this world, but
intimately connected to it (Section I). I then expand on the fundamental claim further by looking at Adorno's critique of modern society
(Section II) and modern thought forms (Section III) – both of which
are implicated in the evil. In the next chapter, I begin to engage with
Adorno's more explicit practical philosophy by mapping out the difficulties which living in a radically evil world present to us individually.

I Auschwitz, radical evil, and failed culture

Whoever reads anything by Adorno cannot but be struck by how much
his thinking stands in the shadow of the events to which he refers simply
by the name of the most infamous of extermination camp complexes,
Auschwitz. For example, he famously claims that one could no longer
write poetry after Auschwitz[2] – which, whatever else he might mean by it,
brings out the rupture which these events represent for him.

However, for Adorno, Auschwitz was not a unique set of events, standing out from history and unlike anything which came before or after.
In many ways, almost the opposite is the case for him: Auschwitz is an
exemplification of the general tendencies of the age.[3] In particular, it is
an extreme example of two (interrelated) central tendencies of modern
social reality: (a) the elimination of all individuality to the point of

---

2 10.1: 30/Adorno 2003a: 162; see also ND, 6: 355–6/362.
3 See, for example, ND, 6: 355/362.

indifference towards individual life (which includes the objectification and depersonalisation of human beings); and (b) the inversion of means and ends (which includes the subordination of human beings to their own creations). The victims of Auschwitz were not just murdered but the perpetrators also attempted to erase any sense of being a unique, irreplaceable individual in them. In Primo Levi's words, the aim was 'to annihilate us first as men in order to kill us more slowly afterwards'.[4] The actions of the perpetrators thereby mirrored something fundamental in the workings of modern society and rationality (according to Adorno): the elimination of particularity, such that everything and everyone becomes fungible – just another instance of a general category; one which can easily be expended or discarded, since others could take its place. Those actions foreshadowed a tendency, according to which differences matter, if at all, as inefficiencies or stopgaps to be eliminated. Auschwitz expresses also the inversion of means and ends typical of modern society (and thought forms), albeit in an extreme form: the modern means of industrialisation, transport, and bureaucratic administration (as well as technical-instrumental rationality) are not just decoupled from human ends, but actually turned against the most basic of such ends, survival. Notably, capitalism has replaced human ends and needs with its own *telos* – production for production's sake or (what comes to the same thing for Adorno) the maximisation of profit – and satisfies these ends and needs, if at all, incidentally and even then in a distorted and incomplete manner.

In this way, the events for which the name 'Auschwitz' stands were not something which went against the trend of civilisation. Rather, these events were intimately connected to some of the main tendencies of the path which civilisation has taken and to the structure of modern society and thinking in particular. The lesson of Auschwitz – at least, according to Adorno – is not that culture was replaced by a momentary fallback into a barbaric state; the lesson is that culture itself failed.[5] If Auschwitz was possible in a country with an advanced economy and high culture ('a land of poets and thinkers', as Germany is known); if it happened despite the fact that moral theories reached into the minds of perpetrators (in the way Eichmann claimed that he had lived his whole life according to Kant's categorical imperative of which he seemed to

4 Levi [1958] 1996: 57; see also 47, 60, 127–8, 156; and Marrus 1989: 23, 131.
5 See ND, 6: 358–61/365–8; see also Adorno 1971: 128; MCP, 184–7, 200, 201/118–19, 127–8, 129.

have a decent grasp);[6] if it was carried out not so much by monsters, but ordinary men (and women);[7] if they thought of themselves not as acting against morality and civilisation, but as men of integrity who have taken on a heavy burden to protect them, remaining in their own eyes, with few exceptions, decent and respectful of human life (as Himmler described the work of the SS in his October 1943 speeches at Posen); and if it was not the act of a small group of people, but if a whole society contributed, in one way or another, to it;[8] then it seems not altogether far-fetched to come to Adorno's pessimistic conclusion that Auschwitz was not an accident, but an indication of a deep-seated problem of modern society, civilisation, and culture. If this view is defensible,[9] then it suggests also another conclusion: as long as our modern culture – its thought forms and the social world underpinning it – continues unchanged, the reoccurrence of events such as Auschwitz remains a real possibility.[10]

It is thus unsurprising that Adorno speaks about the modern social world in very negative terms. In fact, one way to capture his views is to say that for him late capitalist society is 'radically evil'. It might seem strange to apply the description of radical evil to a social form. After all, it is a traditional religious notion and is normally applied to individuals, rather than ways of life as whole. In particular, the connection to responsibility would seem to be lost, if we start applying the term 'radical evil' to a social form, since this does not seem to be the right sort of entity to be a bearer of responsibility. Moreover, this term is potentially misleading or even dangerous in that it is often used to oversimplify matters and create clear-cut oppositions when in fact there is much more complexity – one only needs to think of its recent usages in the

---

6 Arendt [1963] 1994: 135–6.   7 See notably the seminal study by Browning 1992.

8 Marrus, summarising the historical research on this matter, writes: 'To achieve the task of comprehensive mass murder the machine called not only upon the cold-blooded killers in the SS, but also remote officials of postal ministries, tax and insurance adjusters, bankers and clergymen, mechanics and accountants, municipal officials and stenographers. The clear implication is that murder on such a colossal scale involved the entire organized society to one degree or another and depended on a measure of support elsewhere' (1989: 83).

9 For a defence of the Adornian thought that the Holocaust indicates a general problem with modern society and culture, see, for example, Bauman 1989. For criticisms of Adorno's view of Auschwitz and anti-Semitism, see Bahr 1978; Jay 1980; Rabinbach 2002; and Benhabib 2009.

10 This connects with the new categorical imperative – 'to arrange their thoughts and actions so that Auschwitz will not repeat itself, so that nothing similar will happen' (ND, 6: 358/365) – to which I return in later chapters (esp. Chapter 5).

political discourse (such as 'axis of evil').[11] Nonetheless, 'radical evil' is an apt term to capture Adorno's views (see also Chapter 5, where I take this objection up again). For him the modern social world is radically evil, firstly, because its evil is particularly grave and, secondly, because it is evil in a way which is systematically connected with its existence (it is evil to the root). Moreover, the fact that the use of the term radical evil raises questions of responsibility is also apt, since it is one of the key challenges within Adorno's theory to explain why and how we allowed things to go so badly wrong and how we could break with this pattern. (I take up the issue of responsibility in Chapters 3 and 5.)

To illuminate this issue further it is necessary to look in more detail at Adorno's views of both (a) modern society and its workings and (b) modern thought forms. Both are directly implicated in the radical evil of the modern world and, as I show now, they are so implicated in partly similar ways.

II The whole is untrue 1 (modern society)

Basically, Adorno has a Marxist understanding of modern (capitalist) society insofar as he thinks that it is structured fundamentally by the 'law of value'. Strictly speaking, within Marxist theory, this law just concerns the equivalence of the value of commodities with the socially necessary labour-time required to produce them. Yet, Adorno seems to use it as a placeholder for a much more general phenomenon: the (initially) market-mediated drive to maximise surplus-value within capitalism.[12] For Adorno, this drive is itself the outgrowth of humanity's coping with its natural environment. Capitalism is just the latest and most advanced socio-economic system in a series of such systems which resulted from the pursuit of self-preservation. Like the broom of Goethe's *Der Zauberlehrling*, these systems take on a life of their own and come to dominate their creators. In the case of capitalism, this tendency

---

11 For a detailed discussion of this and other problems raised by appeals to evil, see Dews 2008, especially Introduction and, in respect to Adorno, Chapter 6.

12 Adorno understands surplus-value in the Marxist sense. It arises from the surplus which can be produced by human labour once a certain level of technical and organisational development has been reached. At that point, to produce the goods (or their equivalent value) required to restore the workers' labour-power does not take up the total labour-time which the full use of their labour-power (their labour) makes available each day. If the labourers are nonetheless put to work for longer, then they produce surplus goods and the value of these goods is surplus-value, which, under capitalism, is largely appropriated in its monetary form, that is, as profit.

has reached its peak: human purposes, including self-preservation, are only taken care of, if they are taken care of at all, as a by-product of the pursuit of surplus-value maximisation. In this sense, capitalism is the ultimate form of a means-ends reversal: what developed as a way of securing human needs has become an end in itself, using human needs (both real ones and those capitalism artificially creates) for its own purposes. Moreover, capitalism has produced technological and organisational advantages which, although they could potentially liberate humanity from the most strenuous forms of securing self-preservation, can instead be employed as means of destruction to an extent which the pre-modern world had not seen before, as Auschwitz and Hiroshima demonstrated.

The market-mediated drive to maximise surplus-value affects all areas of life in a number of ways. Firstly, there is the increasing *commodification* of all aspects of life. According to Marx, what makes exchanges of goods possible is not the value they may have for individual persons, which can vary considerably from person to person (this value Marx calls 'use-value'); rather, all goods need to have something in common which makes them commensurable and enables their exchange (hence dubbed 'exchange value' by Marx).[13] This exchange value, Marx argues, consists in the average human labour-time expended to produce the good in question. Even though the actual price of goods may vary from the exchange value (at least in the short term), the latter determines their real market value. Capitalism's drive to augment surplus-value leads to the transformation of an increasing number of objects into commodities to be exchanged – for commodities are the vehicles by which profit and thereby surplus-value are realised. As a result of the pressure towards commodification, more and more objects are seen in terms of exchange value, thereby abstracting from their intrinsic qualities and the importance we attach to them individually. This in turn has the consequence that objects are only (or largely) seen in terms of their quantitative, exchange-salient properties. Moreover, as commodification spreads, it also affects human beings (as bearers of the commodity labour-power) and their relationships. For example, what people value is affected so strongly by the increasing commodification of the lifeworld that people start to value exchange value for its own sake (rather than realising that it is a means to facilitate the exchange of what people genuinely need).

13 See *Das Kapital*, Vol. 1, Hamburg: Meissner, 1867; *Marx and Engels Werke*, 1956–90 MEW, XXIII/ *Marx Engels Collected Works*, 1975–2005, MECW, XXXV, Ch. 1.

They attach status and prestige to certain luxury items representing exchange value.[14] Moreover, they start thinking of each other and their mutual relationships in terms of exchange-value properties – for example, they ask themselves whether they get enough out of a friendship to make it 'worth their while', given the 'investment' of time and energy it requires. Finally, human beings start increasingly to think about themselves in terms of commodities – be it that they consider selling some of their body parts or the use of their body, or be it that they talk about their annual salary in terms of 'how much they are worth'.

Secondly, there is the *alienation* aspect connected to capitalist economic production. The main idea here is that workers, in selling their labour-power, cannot identify any longer with the fruits of their labour and thereby become estranged from the products and even themselves. While any labour process involves an externalisation and objectification of the producers' capacities and energies, the externalised product need not become alien to the producers, if they have full control over it and the production process. In capitalism the labourers have for the most part control of neither area – the capitalists tend to dictate the conditions of production and appropriate the fruits of their labour, paying the workers only what it takes to reproduce their labour-power (if that), not the full value which the use of their labour-power in the production process yields. Moreover, it is one of the features of capitalism that production processes are broken up into increasingly smaller tasks, so that lack of control is especially important in the second area, the production process. The workers are increasingly unable to relate to the whole product, given that they each only contribute one highly specialised element in its production. This also means that the workers use only a very small part of their capacities in the production process (which often makes their work repetitive and monotonous). The production process increasingly moulds the workers; they become like parts of the machine (as is illustrated in the famous scenes of Chaplin's *Modern Times* or Lang's *Metropolis*). Apart from negative effects on our physical and emotional health, being moulded by the production process is also bad insofar as it leads to a reduction of our ability to interact with people and to experience the world around us.[15]

---

14 LCoIS, 8: 362/Adorno 2003a: 117–18.
15 Adorno, for example, suggests that rudeness and brutality between people is, in part, due to the fact that technology has become so dominant in our lives and the workplace (see MM, Aphorism No. 19).

Hence, Marx and, following him, Adorno claim that labourers (and humanity as a whole) are turned into mere 'appendages of the machine', and this is another manifestation of the means-end reversal – instead of the production process serving humanity and its needs, human labour takes on the form of serving machines and processes. Instead of using the technological and organisational advances of capitalism to lighten the burden of work and reduce human labour-time, these advances are only employed for increasing surplus-value, irrespective, and often to the detriment, of those who produce it. Moreover, by standardising work, it does not just become impoverished as an activity, it also can be carried out by almost everyone. This means that each labourer and each person becomes (potentially) replaceable. Structurally similar to what the Nazi machinery was designed to do with its victims, the individual is reduced by the capitalist system to a mere instantiation of a general property (in the latter case, bearer of human labour-power). Similar considerations apply to the consumption sphere. As consumers, human beings are as replaceable as each other and the satisfaction of their needs is just a means to the maximisation of surplus-value.[16] In most cases, and for obvious reasons to do with economies of scale, this also means that the products are standardised and replaceable. Yet, even where individuality seems to be catered for or even targeted – such as when a jeans company offers to produce a jeans according to the exact measurements supplied by its customers – this is just a more sophisticated way of trying to maximise surplus-value and, more often than not, comes at the expense of people's real needs.

While the sense of alienation or estrangement is the experiential reflection of the badness of the capitalist production process, it is important to note that the capitalist production process and the alienation accompanying it are – at least for Marx and, to some extent, also for Adorno – a necessary step in human development, in the process of advancing the forces of production to a point where human beings would be almost completely freed from the necessity of engaging in material production. Thus, neither Marx nor Adorno would welcome going back to, for example, the craft production process.[17] Rather, the hope is to go forward to

16 In one of his lectures, Adorno says of people in the modern social world: 'Even in the sphere of consumption – significantly, this term has displaced what used to be called enjoyment – they have become appendages of the machine. Goods are not produced for their sake and their consumption satisfies people's own desires only very indirectly and to a limited extent. Instead they have to make do with what the production line spews out' (HF, 12/5–6).

17 In relation to Marx, see Cohen 1988: 183–208.

the point where the division of labour makes radically reduced working hours possible and thereby loses its 'horror of shaping the individuals throughout'.[18] Thus, to some extent the capitalist development of the production process and the estrangement from the working process are also a liberation, since they make it possible for humans not to identify themselves with their traditional, narrow roles and eventually to sever their self-conception completely from the production process (and thereby the natural drive of self-preservation). This could lead to a world in which human beings could concentrate on developing their own potential as creatures beyond the drive of self-preservation.[19]

Still, even if the capitalist production process is a necessary step in human development, it has significant bads associated with it. Beyond those already noted is the basic Marxist idea that capitalist relations are *exploitative*. The basic idea behind the Marxist concept of exploitation is that the labourers only get back what is necessary in order to reproduce their labour-power, not what its use produces (which – according to Marx – is, on average, more than the former). Thus, while on one level the exchange of labour for a wage is just in that equal value is exchanged, on another level it is unjust (by capitalism's own logic of identity) in that (as Adorno puts it): 'Since time immemorial, the main characteristic of the exchange of equivalents has been that unequal things would be exchanged in its name, that the surplus value of labor would be appropriated.'[20] The capitalist ideal of free and just exchange hides beneath it a violent history (such as in the process of so-called primitive accumulation of capital), the coercion of the (labour) market and the unequal power of the two parties (capitalists and workers), the appropriation of

---

18 ND, 6: 275/278–9.

19 Adorno sometimes objects to talking of self-estrangement (or alienation) on the grounds that this idea would seem to imply (wrongly) that, prior to capitalism and the alienation it produces, human beings were already themselves, had already realised their humanity (ND, 6: 274/278; see also ND, 6: 216/216). For this reason, Adorno gives credit to Marx for dropping the term 'alienation' from his later works – but both hold on to the key idea that the capitalist production process (and society) have taken on a life on their own that turns human beings into mere appendages of the machine.

20 ND, 150/146. Like much of the rest of this discussion, I can provide here only a high-altitude sketch of Adorno's position within a contested and complex terrain. For example, even among Marxists, the claim that exploitation is unjust (by capitalism's own logic of identity) is not generally accepted, but, for our purposes here, what matters is, first and foremost, that it captures what Adorno says about exploitation. Importantly for our context, Adorno's appeal to fair exchange is here an immanent criticism of capitalism, not his endorsement of a positive ideal. (On this and immanent critique more generally, see also Introduction.)

the surplus-value, and 'the naked privilege of monopolies and cliques'.[21] Moreover, there is a clear sense in which this evil is systematically linked to capitalism. Without the appropriation of surplus-value, capitalism could not sustain itself – it would cease to be capitalism. Equally, in at least one sense capitalism is more exploitative than that which preceded it, although, admittedly, the appropriation of surplus-value in, for example, feudal times was much more linked to direct personal domination and violence (to which neither Marx nor Adorno advocate that we should return). Yet, when it comes to the injustice of economic exploitation considered by itself (rather than what other injustices and badness are involved in enforcing it), then capitalism is the biggest culprit. The extent of exploitation is far greater in capitalism, since its technological development dramatically reduced the value required to reproduce labour-power and thereby dramatically increased the surplus-value appropriated.

Marx anticipates that both commodification and subordination of human beings to surplus-value maximisation will come to structure all areas of life, but for Adorno this process is close to completion. The result of this process is that society, according to Adorno, becomes completely governed by forces not controlled by those affected by it. This domination is not a form of personal domination (as was the case in feudal or ancient societies), but works just via the economic process.[22] Everyone – whether consciously or not – fulfils functions that sustain and expand the existing capitalist system (and those who do not fulfil functions in this way have to fear and struggle for their survival). In fact, even though there are always people administering capitalism, they are ultimately themselves governed by the structures of capitalism,[23] which has developed its own independent dynamic. For example, should a capitalist entrepreneur want to deviate from the trend and implement, say, Nietzsche's value of nobility, he or she would either have to give up this ethical project soon or just end up bankrupt.[24] The fundamental problem is not what individual capitalists do and intend (though this can be problematic too), but the capitalist system itself.

However, the 'emancipation' of society from its members and their interests is not easily noticeable. Society's dominance has become so all-encompassing that there is (almost) no aspect of life that is not touched by it and which would allow an outside perspective on it. As

---

21 ND, 150/146; see also P, 10.2: 636–7/CM, 159.
22 LCoIS, 8: 360/Adorno 2003a: 116.
23 See, for example, HF, 12/6; see also Chapter 3.   24 PMP 1963, 256–7/173.

Adorno puts it at one point, 'all social phenomena today are so completely mediated that even the element of mediation is blocked [*verstellt*]
by its totalising nature'.[25] Put differently, when everything is mediated
economically, then this mediation is no longer clearly visible, because
(a) market forces are often not seen as social relations (and hence not
seen as the social relations of domination which they are);[26] and (b) there
is no external standpoint any more from which the mediation could be
detected. In this way, society forms an all-encompassing whole, a totality.

One way to express what Adorno means to say is by drawing a parallel to
Hegel's philosophy: Hegel claimed of spirit [*Geist*] that it will encompass
everything, and something like this has indeed become reality, but in a
different way from what Hegel envisaged: it is not spirit but society that is
the whole, and instead of constituting absolute truth, 'The whole is the
untrue.'[27] It is untrue both (a) in the sense that it appears different from
what it is, constitutes a 'delusional system [*Verblendungszusammenhang*]';
and (b) insofar as it, despite being factually true (part of reality), lacks
actuality in that it is the very opposite of what a human society essentially
aspires to be (a context for the protection of genuine human interests and
for the unfolding of human capacities and potential).[28]

Capitalism forms a totality, but it is nonetheless not free from antagonisms and contradictions. For example, there is a tension in the very drive
for maximising surplus-value itself. This maximisation requires that the
capitalists reduce the value given to the labourers to the smallest amount
possible, but at the same time, capitalism needs to keep (a sufficient
number of) the labourers alive for the system to sustain itself. Surplus-
value for Marx (and Adorno) arises because the average labour-time
required to reproduce human labour-power is less than the time-span it
can be put to use for. This means that surplus-value can be increased
only either by reducing the value given to the labourers to reproduce
their labour-power (i.e., by reducing their wages) or by working them
longer or harder. It is, however, in the long-term interest of capital not to
overdo this, since it cannot have surplus-value, unless human labour is
constantly reproduced – which is endangered by too low wages or by over-
working the labourers. Thus, there is an in-built tension within capitalism
between the conditions of augmenting surplus-value and the conditions

25 LCoIS, 8: 369/Adorno 1984: 124; translation amended.
26 See, for example, S, 8: 14/271.
27 MM, Aphorism No. 29, 4: 55/50; translation amended; see also 5: 325/Adorno 1993b:
      87–8; 1974: 262–3.
28 See S, 8: 17/273–4; 10.1: 21/Adorno 2003a: 154–5; MTP, 10.2: 775/CM, 272.

for surplus-value production generally. Moreover, this tension is aggravated, since labour itself fights for a bigger share of its produce. In other
words, it is aggravated by the class conflict definitive of developed capitalism, namely, the class conflict between the representatives of labour and
capital.

There are also other tensions, conflicts, and antagonisms inherent
in capitalism. For example, there is the competition-spurred drive to
develop the forces of production. In the short term, surplus-value is
increased for the individual capitalist who uses a new production technique and so can lower the prices for the item produced to capture a
market.[29] This prospect of extraordinary economic rent (and the
connected danger of being shut out of a market) is, hence, a powerful
incentive to constantly innovate in terms of technology and organisation
of production. The downside of this is, however, that more and more of
the produced value has to be used for capital costs, thus reducing profit
in the long term. Moreover, the rapid development of the productive
forces leads to a point where a different use of them, one determined by
the satisfaction of individual needs, becomes possible. The potential
immanent in the productive forces of society comes into conflict with
the relations of production, the ownership and administrative relations,
which continue to be structured by the demands of capitalism.

It is on this point that Adorno's conceptions of history and of modern
capitalism differ from Marx's conceptions (or, at least, from those which
Adorno ascribes to Marx). Adorno does not think that when the forces
of production come into conflict with the relations of production –
i.e., when the latter become fetters on the further development of the
former – capitalism will necessarily collapse and the class representing
the future relations of production (the proletariat) will prevail in its
class struggle.[30] In fact, capitalism has proved to be remarkably resilient,
despite having – speaking in terms of the development of the forces
of production – outlived itself. There are a number of reasons for this.
Firstly, capitalism has been able to distribute some of the fruits of the
massive technological development it spurred on to raise the living
standard of the majority of the population (albeit only in a number

29 To explain further: the innovative capitalist can produce and sell the items below the
    average labour-time necessary to produce them until the average labour-time has settled
    on (or close to) the time necessary given the new technology. It settles there either because
    the competitors react and also adopt the new technology, or because the innovator gets to
    dominate the market to the extent that she or he is the main or only producer.
30 See LCoIS, 8: 363–2/Adorno 2003a: 119.

of economically developed areas of the world). People have, consequently, more to lose than their chains, and Marx's prediction of an
ever-increasing impoverishment, which would have necessitated a revolution at some stage, has largely failed to materialise (at least as far as
the economically developed world is concerned).[31] Secondly, capitalism has become much more administered than Marx anticipated,
cushioning some of the system-internal shocks (for example, via
Keynesian demand management). This has also contributed to its survival. Important factors for Adorno in this context are the formation of
monopolies and the intervention of the state apparatus in the economy
(both disrupt or mitigate some of the internal tensions of capitalism,
since these are often driven or at least exacerbated by the operation of
the (free) market). Thirdly, and most importantly, capitalism has been
able to completely reach into the individuals who unwittingly sustain it.
Via social mechanisms, like the family, state-run schools and, crucially,
the 'culture industry' (the highly administered cultural sphere that,
according to Adorno, is increasingly controlling and homogenising
people's experiences), capitalist society constitutes individuals as well
as their interests, their needs, and their ability to make sense of the
world. This has dramatically increased the deceptive powers of capitalism. Thus, while modern humans think they follow their interests and
own choices, the very way they come to form these interests and choices
is guided by society's interest (in particular, the production and maximisation of surplus-value), but the individuals do not tend to realise this.
They have internalised their domination to such an extent that they
have become voluntary slaves to their own creation, i.e., modern capitalist society. The result of all this is that the capitalist system has evolved
into a second nature to its members – its existence and mechanisms are
seen and accepted as the way the world is, as the unchangeable backdrop of human existence. This evolution itself took place as if through a
natural process (namely, blindly and over the heads of the individuals),
and this is why Adorno, following Marx, speaks of it in terms of 'natural
growth [*naturwüchsig*]'.

   In sum, according to Adorno, we have become almost totally dominated by our most sophisticated 'tool', capitalist economic production.

---

31 According to Adorno, the theory of increased immiseration has not proved true in
   respect to economic impoverishment (in economically developed countries), although
   it has been confirmed in terms of the growing unfreedom and loss of power (see LCoIS,
   8: 360/116).

Modern society built on this basis is in some sense more rational than what went before it – the technical means at our disposal are much more developed than at earlier times, we use them more efficiently, and our ability to explain the world has also reached unprecedented levels with the rise of modern science, which developed along with the unfolding of capitalism. Yet, at the same time, capitalism is the height of irrationality with its means-ends reversal and its disregard and distortion of individual needs (as well as its disregard of non-human nature).

Following even here in Marx's footsteps, Adorno does not offer us a worked-out alternative to capitalism. Any such proposal would be too coloured by the current wrong state of affairs. However, Adorno does make some scattered remarks, based on the analysis of what is going wrong with capitalism. Firstly, it would be necessary to end structural domination (and, indeed, personal domination). For this, humanity would have to actually control its own fate. Given the complexity and interdependence of our lives, this would require at least some forms of collective governance. However, this in turn should not take the repressive form it took in the Soviet Union and the other nominally socialist regimes.[32] Secondly, the technological and organisational developments made possible by capitalism have to be put to the service of human beings and their needs. This means, first and foremost, that no one should go hungry any more.[33] Yet, it also means an end to the pursuit of ever-expanding production and a radical reduction of labour-time[34] – freeing people from the pressures of work and production for production's sake (as well as protecting nature from the all-consuming human juggernaut). Finally, exchange relationships would have to be transformed[35] – away from the distorting effects of making incommensurable things commensurable, but also away from the underlying exploitation implicit in what is only at the surface level an exchange of equal things – and yet we should also not return to the old injustice of direct appropriation. Solutions to these three challenges cannot be theoretically anticipated (least of all within the wrong life of capitalism), but would have to be practically solved, guided by what history has told us about what to avoid – which includes, according to Adorno, the deeply problematic world of modern capitalism.

Adorno's conception of modern capitalist society is controversial, to say the least. The elements from Marx's economic theory it presupposes – such as the labour theory of value and surplus-value – are often criticised as

---

32 See, for example, ND, 6: 279–80/284.   33 See MM, Aphorism No. 100.
34 See also ND, 6: 242/244.   35 See ND, 6: 150/147; P, 10.2: 636–7/CM, 159.

mistaken, even by commentators sympathetic to Marx's work.[36] Similarly, one might question the truth of Adorno's negative views about capitalist society, which go beyond Marx's own views. This is largely a question to be answered in economics, politics, or sociology, although philosophical issues would probably also be relevant.[37] It is also a difficult question to assess because it is unclear what exactly would be required to either prove or disprove Adorno's claims. If society is as delusional as Adorno suggests (if it is a '*Verblendungszusammenhang*'), then perhaps any theories to the contrary have fallen prey to the delusion they were meant to analyse. Yet, this difficulty also cuts the other way: for if society is so delusional, how can we know about it? In fact, Adorno himself admits that it becomes increasingly difficult to comprehend society and its workings.[38]

These are difficult and weighty matters, and I cannot do justice to them here. Instead, I invite the reader to suspend judgement about them for the time being and to follow me along the path of seeing how far Adorno's views can be sustained on his own terms. Many critics doubt that his theory is defensible *even* if we granted him his conception of the capitalist social world – indeed, they would claim that his theory is indefensible *especially* if we granted the truth of this conception because it is self-defeating (see Introduction). To show that these critics are mistaken would be an important result in itself. Moreover, it is necessary to get his full view on the table and judge it as a complete entity, instead of dismissing it from the outset and thereby prematurely. Admittedly, even at the end of this study, only a partial picture of Adorno's theory emerges, but the reader will then be in a better position to judge whether suspending judgement earlier was merited. Thus, I want to propose that the possibility of his being right deserves to be taken seriously and examined on its full merits – not least because faced both (a) with the way our production processes threaten the very basis of our survival and (b) with a world of abundance in which almost half of humanity none-theless lives in extreme poverty, Adorno's claim about the irrationality of our socio-economic system seems not completely off the mark.

In this section, I have talked about Adorno's views of modern *capitalist* society and this might wrongly suggest that Adorno would have endorsed the nominally socialist regimes that still existed during his lifetime (and

36 See, for example, Elster 1985; Wolff 2002.

37 For example, Rosen argues that the idea of society as a self-sustaining entity commits one to very strong metaphysical views which are never successfully defended by the propo-nents of this idea (see Rosen 1996: esp. Ch. 7 on Adorno).

38 See, for example, S, 8: 9–12/267–70.

of which a very small number still linger on). It is true that Adorno, for various reasons, concentrates his analysis on capitalist societies, including the reason that he lived and worked in them – something which is itself indicative of what he thought about the Soviet Union and other such regimes. In his view, the nominally socialist regimes are worse versions of the liberal-democratic regimes of the West – for they deny its members even the formal freedoms that the latter recognise and in their repressive character have affinities with other totalitarian regimes of the twentieth century. Indeed, Adorno does not even think that the nominally socialist regimes have freed themselves from the capitalist imperative of production for production's sake – they are just even more bureaucratised and clique-dominated versions of the mixture of state-involvement, (near) monopolies, and culture industry that replaced the liberal phase of market-driven capitalism during the early parts of the twentieth century in the West. They continue, even heighten, the means-end reversal and the subordination of individuality characteristic of capitalism – deeply tarnishing in the process the Marxist alternative, which promised to summon spirits that finally would obey the human command, to build a society that would not come to govern its members but be governed by them and in their real interests.

III The whole is untrue 2 (modern thought forms)

However, it is not just capitalism (and its nominally socialist rivals) which are wrong for Adorno – modern thought forms are also problematic.[39]

Adorno paints a basically Kantian picture of modern thought forms. Thus, he suggests that empirical cognition is a composite of concepts and sensory input, such that the latter is subsumed under the former. This process of synthesis involves bringing something specific and particular (the manifold given to us via the senses) under something general (concepts). In effect, cognition becomes thereby a process of identification, of assigning the particular to a general class into which it falls.

---

39 It is unclear whether this is for Adorno just a reflection of the economic base, or an additional evil, or even, in a reversal of Marxist theory, the root of the problem. On my reading, Adorno's view is that identity thinking and commodity exchange are equiprimordial (see ND, 6: 149/146; see also 168/166) and mutually reinforced each other in their development. This interpretation is compatible with Adorno's Marxist materialism, since both identity thinking and commodity exchange presuppose a change in the way humans (re)produced their life – namely, the introduction of a division between manual and non-manual labour (see 14: 405).

This means that we never cognise the thing in itself as such, but only how it appears to us, mediated by our spatio-temporal frame of reference (Kant calls this our 'forms of intuition') and our conceptual scheme (that is, in Kant, the twelve categories).

However, unlike Kant, Adorno does not think of this conceptual scheme as unchangeable or a priori.[40] Instead, he historicises the Kantian idea (following the work of the early Lukács).[41] For Adorno, as for Horkheimer, the conceptual schemes with which we operate are what might be called 'historical a priori' – given the historical and social setting we grow up and live in, we approach the world and think of it in certain ways.[42] Society is always already inside human beings and their experiences.[43] Both the object of experience and the way we experience it are shaped by the society we inhabit.[44] These ways of structuring our experience take on a necessary and universal character within a social world, but, at least historically speaking, human beings have been subject to a series of incommensurable frameworks, such that Kant's claim to a stronger form of necessity and universality comes out false.

Kantians would reply that our conceptual scheme is not just a reflection of a particular society or stage in human history, but inherent in thought and experience as such. Perhaps human societies differ in terms of certain specifics – in their empirical concepts – but certain basic categories are necessarily operative in each of these variations. I cannot resolve this disagreement here, but merely note that, even if Adorno is right and our conceptual scheme is not necessary in any transhistorically strong sense, this does not mean that we could do without any conceptual scheme whatsoever. Adorno himself notes that to think is to use concepts and thereby to identify,[45] and, hence, 'identity thinking [*Identitätsdenken*]', of which Adorno speaks frequently and critically, seems to be the only thinking there could be.

However, what Adorno means by talking about identity thinking is more than just emphasising the inevitable fact that thinking is conceptual.[46] While all thinking has this latter characteristic, only some

---

40 Also, Adorno, *pace* Kant, thinks that space and time are not forms of intuition, but concepts (see, for example, 5: 151/Adorno 1982: 146–7).

41 See Lukács [1923] 1971a: esp. 'Reification and the Consciousness of the Proletariat' and, within it, the second part 'The Antinomies of Bourgeois Thought'.

42 See SO, 10.2: 747–8/250; see also ND, 6: 172–3, 378–9/170–1, 386.

43 SO, 10.2: 748, 750/250, 252.   44 See also Horkheimer 1972: 199.

45 ND, 6: 17/5; see also 152, 156/149, 153.   46 See also Wellmer 2007.

forms of thinking – albeit the dominant ones in the modern world – are
based on the assumption that the synthesis performed by subsuming
the sensible manifold under concepts actually captures this manifold in
full (or in its essential properties). We need to be careful here. Adorno is
not just worried about which concept is used in a particular case – it
might well be that we often do not use the most suitable concept in a
given case and that this has to be corrected. (Perhaps Pluto is actually
not a planet, but better conceptualised as an asteroid, despite a long
tradition that thought otherwise.) What Adorno complains about is
something more fundamental. It is the thought that any subsumption
under concepts, even the most apt one, misses something about its
object and if this mismatch is not reflected upon, then thought does
injustice to the object.[47] Instead of saying what something is, 'identity-
thinking says what it falls under, what it is an example or representative
of, what it consequently is not itself'.[48]

What is missed in the object is called variously 'the non-identical' [*das
Nichtidentische*] or 'the non-conceptual' [*das Nichtbegriffliche*] by Adorno.
This central idea in Adorno's work is difficult to make sense of. This
is partly for philosophical reasons – that which escapes our conceptual
schemes is inherently and unsurprisingly hard to grasp. Given that language is based on concepts, we struggle to express it. Still, some of the
difficulty also stems from having to interpret Adorno's texts and statements on this issue, which are far from easy and often give the impression
of presenting a contradictory or otherwise problematic picture.

The way to unlock some of these difficulties is to consider the following puzzle. If all thinking uses concepts, which are general rules, under

47 This way of putting the objection to identity thinking – one that Adorno frequently adopts –
    is no longer strictly speaking internal to Kantian epistemology, at least not on a two-aspect
    interpretation of it. As the empirical object is constructed in the synthesis, we cannot say –
    within the Kantian view – that we do injustice to it in this process by not fully capturing it
    (there is no prior object to capture fully or incompletely). We might want to say that we do
    injustice to the thing in itself because we cannot fully capture it, but (a) Kant acknowledges
    that we cannot fully capture it and, hence, the objection would not have succeeded in
    showing what Kant's view is missing; and (b) on a two-aspect reading, it would be mislead-
    ing to speak of the thing in itself as a separate object from the empirical object (rather than
    of two different perspectives on, or aspects of, the 'transcendental object = x'). Perhaps,
    Adorno is objecting that something in the sensible manifold is lost in the conceptual
    construction of (empirical) objects (this would fit well with his concerns that experience is
    currently too restricted). Still, in claiming that identity thinking does not do justice to the
    object, he transfigures what is meant by object in a way that is no longer strictly Kantian (at
    least not on a two-aspect reading).
48 ND, 6: 152/149; Redmond's translation used.

which particulars are meant to be subsumed, then it is an open philosophical question how genuine experience of these particulars is
possible. After all, the particular objects we encounter in experience
are not concepts or mental entities (or at least we tend to presume that
they are not) and how can something completely different in character –
thought – have access to them? Call this the 'Problem of Missing
Affinity'. This problem is probably as old as philosophy and Adorno is
very well aware of this and the traditional philosophical answers to it.
His thesis is that these traditional answers all tend towards idealism –
even where they are avowedly materialist – in the following sense: they
all work on the basis of the assumption that we can capture the world
in the conceptual framework we bring to it (or, at least, the best version
of it, once we have worked that out). Putting it in terms of Hegel's
philosophy, traditional philosophy thinks that the world is rational, as
long as we look at it in a sufficiently rational way.[49] The danger in this
assumption is, however, that instead of cognising the world, we cognise
only what we bring to it – instead of knowledge of something other
than thought and its categories, we might be settled with a big tautology.
Empirical cognition would be like recognising that bachelors are
unmarried men. In this sense, Kant's talk of the inaccessible thing in
itself at least acknowledged the problem, while Hegel's absolute idealism extinguished all traces of it.[50]

Thus, the mistake of identity thinking is not that it involves identification and concepts – all thinking does this inevitably – but the mistake is
that it rests on the assumption, whether explicitly or not, that the world is
fundamentally accessible in full to thought.[51] This assumption is problematic because it loses from view that there might be something in the
object (or even the object as a whole) which is incompatible with, or
inaccessible by conceptual thought. It does not sufficiently attend to the
fact that identifying always involves disregarding what is non-identical
and incommensurable in the particular object of our cognition. It
thereby violates a commitment inherent in its conception of concepts
itself: concepts are directed towards capturing what they are not; in

---

49 See Hegel [1837, 1840] 1975: 29.
50 Again, Adorno follows here the early Lukács's discussion of Kant and Hegel (see n. 41 of
    this chapter).
51 See ND, 6: 25/13–14; 5: 152/Adorno 1982: 147. Adorno denies the full accessibility of the
    world to (identity) thinking as early as his inaugural lecture (see 'Actuality of Philosophy'
    [1931], 1: 325/1977: 120 and *passim*), albeit not quite in the same terms as in his mature
    works.

Adorno's terminology: concepts, incarnation of identity, aim at the non-conceptual, the non-identical.[52]

There are a number of objections that spring to mind, of which I will take up two. One could reply to Adorno's claim that the world is inaccessible to identity thinking by saying that disregarding what cannot be conceptualised is not problematic, since what is left out is not essential about the object, but accidental, fleeting, or otherwise inconsequential to it. True, when I identify an object as a leaf with certain properties it shares with other leaves and objects, something particular and specific about this leaf may slip through my conceptual net or, even, the best of all conceptual nets.[53] Perhaps, it has a unique shade of colour or its shape is particularly unusual; perhaps, the way it fell of its tree differed slightly from the way the other leaves fell off. Still, why think that the specificity lost here is of any importance? After all, for most or even all of human purposes, I know what I need to know about the object in front of me, once I identify it as a leaf with certain properties.[54]

---

52 ND, 6: 19–20, 23, 44, 141, 152/8, 11, 34, 137, 149; see also 159/156–7.

53 While the leaf example is originally from Nietzsche (see 'Über Wahrheit und Lüge im außermoralischen Sinn' [1873], reprinted in 1980: Vol. 1, 879–80/translated in Nietzsche 1979: 83), he uses it in the opposite way from the one I use here – to attack, not to defend (what Adorno calls) identity thinking. In relation to this issue – and the section as a whole – I have benefited greatly from Dews 1995. (I also draw on Jay 1984; Thyen 1989; Jarvis 1998; O'Connor 2004; and Cook 2011.)

54 A telling exception is art – here some of the individual characteristics might matter. This is telling, since Adorno thinks that art involves a mimetic, rather than conceptual grasp of the object and so differs from (identity) thinking. Still, art is, for Adorno, a not unproblematic avenue by which we can come to see the world as it really is without doing violence to it or the objects within it. Art involves shaping the material and, in this way, does violence to it to a certain extent (7: 80/2004: 65). In fact, it relies on the techniques that human beings developed in the pursuit of self-preservation and which are means of domination over nature, and this original sin implicates their use in art too. Similarly, our sensible intuition and imagination are formed by the millennia of our misleading way of engaging with the world and, more specifically, by the particular social and personal circumstances in which we grow up. Moreover, art by itself is as blind as Kant thought sensible intuition is – it requires conceptually mediated interpretation to uncover its truth content. As a result, art – just as much as philosophy – cannot overcome the dualism of sensible intuition and concept, but instead constantly reproduces it. At best, art (like metaphysical experience) can tell us about the fact that identity thinking and the administered world are not all there is or could be. It does not provide us with a truthful representation of a different way of engaging with the world and each other – no such positive picture or conception is available, according to Adorno (see Introduction here). Art is always 'semblance [Schein]' (see ND, 6: 396–7/404–5), but not less important for that: for unlike a mere illusion or mirage (such as a Fata Morgana), it represents the real possibility that things could be different (see also Chapter 8, here).

This objection assumes a certain picture of what is essential about objects and about the ways this is accessible to us. However, Adorno questions this picture too. There might be good evolutionary reasons for thinking that what is essential is permanent, general (or at least, generalisable), and accessible to conceptual thoughts – for example, this way of approaching the world might be a good strategy to cope with it.[55] Yet, this by itself does not show that essential reality has this nature. It might just be a useful fiction.

Still, what reason do we have to presume otherwise? Adorno's answer here consists in a combination of objections to the equation of truth with immutability, permanency, persistence, or solidity;[56] wider critiques of identity thinking (of which this equation is one characteristic); as well as an appeal to certain kind of experiences (what he calls 'philosophical' and 'metaphysical' experiences).[57] For example, at one point Adorno argues as follows. It is part and parcel of identity thinking that whatever is cognised is (essentially) something fixed and enduring – otherwise, it would be difficult to speak of identity at all. Yet, experience disconfirms that the objects cognised are of such nature. The example Adorno gives is our experiences of our own selves: a mere look back at our own life experiences reveals that the self is not something fixed, but is changing and has evolved.[58] While the accumulation of experiences makes the self the unique individual he or she is, these experiences also reveal the non-identity in this: for example, my childhood wish to become a film director of Westerns is both very much part of my biography and alien to me now.[59]

Another argument presented by Adorno returns to Auschwitz as the rupture of modern culture. He claims that 'The murder of millions through administration' changed the meaning of death in such a way as

55 How could this be, if the world itself is fleeting? Adorno's thesis seems to be that by thinking of the world as permanent and accessible to conceptual thought, we to a certain extent shape the world to be like this – we force it into moulds which then 'confirm' our conceptual models. This is empowering, but also has negative consequences, both for the world and us (see, for example, P, 10.2: 627/CM, 152).

56 See, for example, 5: 25–7/Adorno 1982: 17–20; ND, 6: 48–50/37–40.

57 On 'metaphysical experience', see especially ND, 6: 366–8/373–5; MCP, lecture 18; see also Bernstein 2001: Ch. 9.

58 ND, 6: 157/154.

59 This argument by itself does not settle the matter. (What argument does?) For example, Kantians would reply that any experiences of what they would call 'empirical self' rely on the formal unity of apperception without which there can be no experiences whatsoever. Adorno, in turn, is critical of this Kantian idea and a fuller defence of his views would have to consider this debate.

to reveal that supposedly eternal ideas are in fact not indifferent to time and history, but formed and altered by them.[60] What the earthquake of Lisbon did to Voltaire, Auschwitz has done to all of us: shattering the idea that the most fundamental truths and concepts are eternal and unaffected by history (as well as the idea of positive meaning in the world or history).[61] In fact, there is a more general point here, according to Adorno: the experience of suffering reveals that identity thinking and its presumption of fixed, enduring essences should be rejected. Even 'The smallest trace of meaningless suffering'[62] is an indictment of the way we cognise and approach the world, and there are not merely traces of such suffering: the modern social world and thought forms cannot but produce it.

As a second objection to Adorno's account, one could maintain that to deny that the world is accessible to (identity) thinking is a claim that stands in need of justification, especially as this denial might open the door to scepticism about the external world. If reality cannot be fully captured by identity thinking, then perhaps we cannot capture it fully at all and we are exposed to the nagging doubt that what we take for reality is actually just an incomplete or even distorted picture of the world. So, unless Adorno provides good reasons to abandon a more optimistic view, we are ill advised to believe his claim about the inaccessibility of reality.

In reply, Adorno would muster a great number of considerations that he employs against the views of particular philosophers (such as, most notably, Kant, Hegel, Husserl, and Heidegger) and particular philosophical positions (such as empiricism, rationalism, or positivism).[63] He would also return to the argumentative moves already hinted at earlier: the thought that our very conception of concepts points beyond the conceptual.

Still, more important at this point is another argumentative move he employs: identity thinking, while increasingly dominant in our modern world, is not the only way to relate to the world. While reality might never be fully captured by human cognition, we have at our disposal more means than just subsuming particulars under concepts. Firstly, there are various forms of experience that are not fully conceptualised, but

---

60 ND, 6: 355/362; translation amended.   61 See also MCP, 162–5/104–6.

62 ND, 6: 203/203.

63 For helpful discussion of (some of) these considerations, see O'Connor 2004; and also Jarvis 1998.

more immediate.[64] Adorno speaks of them variously as 'philosophical' or 'metaphysical' experiences, and suggests that (a certain kind of) art can trigger or express them. Such experiences provide impulses for thinking that not everything has been captured in identity thinking and for the otherwise immanent criticisms of it.

Secondly, Adorno argues that thinking itself, at least when it frees itself from the grip of the orientation towards identity, can capture more about the object than mere subsumption ever could. In fact, if what is essential about objects is not their enduring or fixed character, but rather their changing, historical one, then the way to cognise them has to mimic this to some extent. One way to do so is to employ a multitude of concepts and bring them into what Adorno (following Benjamin) calls 'constellations' (or, sometimes also, 'force fields' or 'thought models'). One example of this idea is provided by Jay's characterisation of Adorno's own view, which he locates in the tensions and relations between five forces or 'stars': Western Marxism, aesthetic modernism, mandarin cultural conservatism, Jewish theological impulses and self-identification, and proto-deconstructivist impulses.[65] Whether or not one agrees with the details of Jay's proposal, this way of characterising Adorno's view fits well with his way of thinking differently about objects: as historical and deeply connected to their genesis, as changing and inherently tensional, and as dynamically connected to other objects, not isolated particulars. By employing constellations, we can capture what is left out in the subsumption of the particular under a concept.[66]

---

64 That Adorno would have recourse to immediacy is surprising, since he often emphasises the Hegelian thought that everything is mediated (see, for example, ND, 6: 172–4/170–2) and criticises the suggestion of having recourse to something immediate in philosophy (see, for example, ND, 6: 26/15). Still, the text is quite explicit: 'there actually is a mental experience – fallible indeed, but immediate – of the essential and unessential, an experience which only the scientific need for order can forcibly talk the subjects out of. Where there is no such experience, knowledge stays unmoved and barren. Its measure is what happens objectively to the subjects, as their suffering' (ND, 6: 171–2/169–70). However, there is a sense in which even these 'immediate experiences' are mediated: the ability to have them depends on certain social and biographical conditions, which – in our current social world – are largely missing, so that those who have them only do so as a matter of luck (see, for example, ND, 6: 51/41). Also, as I argue in later chapters, the experiences are mediated in another sense for Adorno: they are expressions of what we have reasons to do and believe as the specific human animals we could eventually become.

65 Jay 1984: 15–23. This example is merely illustrative – as this study reveals, I would replace some of the 'stars' Jay chooses with other ones. An analogy Adorno provides to illustrate his approach is thinking in the way encyclopaedias are written (ND, 6: 39–40/29).

66 'Solely constellations represent from without what the concept has cut away within: the "more" which the concept is equally desirous and incapable of being. By gathering around

Moreover, Adorno would emphasise that what we experience is not, in fact, the kind of chaotic manifold that identity thinking often suggests.[67] If it were, then scepticism about the external world would, indeed, follow – for then we would not be able to capture the objects of our experience at all (but, once again, only to capture what we put into them). As Adorno writes at one point, Kant does not realise 'that we can synthesize only what will allow and require a synthesis on its own'.[68] Given that thinking will involve conceptualising and hence always be a too blunt instrument, there will always be a mismatch between the determination and coherence in the objects and the determination and coherence that comes out of the subjective synthesis: 'While doing violence to the object of its synthesis, our thinking heeds a potential that waits in the object, and it unconsciously obeys the idea of making amends to the piece for what it has done.'[69] Such making amends would require a reflection on thinking itself and the problematic nature of its orientation towards identity (what Adorno sometimes calls a 'second reflection [*zweite Reflexion*]' or also '*Selbstbesinnung* [self-reflection/coming to one's own senses]'). It would require a reorientation of thinking, away from fitting the world into conceptual schemes constituted by the subject towards giving the object priority.[70] Indeed, in *Minima Moralia*, Adorno even speaks of adhering to a 'morality of thinking' (Aphorism No. 46); elsewhere of doing 'justice to the object's qualitative moments'.[71]

the object of cognition, the concepts potentially determine the object's interior. They attain, in thinking, what was necessarily excised from thinking' (ND, 6: 164–5/162; translation amended; see also 62/53 and his discussion of 'models of thinking [*Denkmodelle*]' on 39/29).

67 See ND, 6: 142/138–9; see also 5: 27/Adorno 1982: 19–20.

68 ND, 6: 142/138; see also MCP, 104/66.   69 ND, 6: 30–1/19.

70 The main argument underpinning the 'preponderance [*Präponderanz*]/priority [*Vorrang*] of the object' would require much more careful discussion, but is roughly as follows (see ND, 6: 184–7/183–8; see also SO, 10.2: 746–7/249–50): the cognising subject depends essentially on objectivity – for it always already is an object (most notably in virtue of its embodiment); on the other hand, objects are dependent on subjects only for being cognised, not for their very existence. Admittedly, this is not true of all objects – cultural artefacts in a sense are dependent for their every existence on human subjects (even if the existence of the material used to make them might not be dependent on human subjects). Also, if thought entities are objects, then what Adorno says cannot be true about them. Still, the main point might still hold: at least if we deny idealist or religious worldviews, then material objectivity precedes human subjectivity and is not existentially dependent on it. Moreover, once created, even cultural artefacts and perhaps thought entities take on some of this priority of the object, at least in respect to individual human subjects.

71 ND, 6: 53–4/43. Doing justice to objects would be to realise Hegel's idea of 'freedom to the object' – something 'yet to be achieved' (ND, 6: 58/48). Before then, such freedom

This move to the priority of the object – of which Adorno speaks sometimes in terms of a second Copernican revolution[72] – is not the denial of the necessity of the subject's contribution to cognition. Rather, it is a way of correcting the tendency of philosophy to read too much into this contribution,[73] namely, either the Idealist tendency to view the subject as constituting or constructing the world, or the post-Idealist (positivist) idea that the object is the residuum which remains if all subjective experience is abstracted from it.[74]

In fact, on Adorno's view it is only through the external intervention of the subject that objects can fully unfold their potential. Whatever is contained in the objects themselves requires human subjectivity to be voiced.[75] This cannot merely consist in copying the object or perceiving it. Objects require interpretation and this, in turn, requires the subject to move beyond them – not to the fixed categorisation of identity thinking, but to the more fluid forms of (the already mentioned) constellations or force fields of concepts.[76] In this way, the subject can help to unlock the historical, dynamic, and relational character of the objects they cognise.[77] Still, there are no guarantees here: interpretations can miss their object or fail to be illuminating; only the successful ones realise the difficult balancing act of achieving 'bindingness [*Verbindlichkeit*] without system'.[78] Along with the rigid nature of identity thinking, certainty has to be given up too, and fallabilism takes its place.[79]

This lack of certainty is particularly acute within late modernity: within a wrong social life and against the background of the dominance of identity thinking, the objects themselves are deformed and cannot reveal their true nature.[80] Instead, we have to engage in 'negative dialectics', that is, we have to engage in constant questioning of our thought forms and the confrontation of them with the experiences of non-identity. Such a dialectics is negative in the sense that it incorporates the denial of two assumptions: (1) the denial of the assumption that identity of our conceptual scheme with the world can be achieved; and (2) the rejection of the assumption that the conclusions of dialectics can move beyond

remains indeterminate and cannot orientate us. Similarly, justice to objects can be conceived for the time being only negatively: as the absence of disregard and coercion, and the pain they typically cause (by forcing nature – both inner and outer – into forms that serve unreservedly the purpose of unhinged human self-preservation).

72 SO, 10.2: 746/249; see also ND, 6: 10/xx.   73 SO, 10.2: 747/250.
74 For comments on the latter, see SO, 10.2: 750–1/252–3; ND, 6: 187–90/186–9.
75 See ND, 6: 184–7/183–8; see also 6: 38–9/27–8; and SO, 10.2: 746–7/249–50.
76 ND, 6: 165/162.   77 ND, 6: 62/52–3.   78 ND, 6: 39/29.
79 See ND, 6: 25/14.   80 See ND, 6: 54/44; see also 156/153.

the wrong state of the world and the wrong thought forms dominating within it.[81] Negative dialectics is a reflection of this state and these thought forms, and if they were eventually overcome, then it would come to an end too.[82] In that sense, it is not an eternal truth or orientation either.

IV Conclusion

This chapter is (an attempt at) a high-altitude sketch of Adorno's extraordinary thesis that we have become governed by our own creations and that the pinnacle of this development is the radically evil modern social world and its thought forms – an ill state of affairs, an unfolding catastrophe. Much of the detail (and the objections it raises) had to be left out of this broad-brush picture – it resembles, in many ways, more a caricature than the real thing. Still, the introductory sketch provided here puts us in a better position to examine Adorno's practical philosophy, his view of how we could and should live in this wrong world. The best place to start on this journey is his absolutely crucial claim that 'There is no right life within the wrong [life]'.[83] It is to this claim that I turn next.

81 See ND, 6: 398/406.   82 ND, 6: 22/11.
83 MM, Aphorism No. 18, 4: 43/39; translation amended.

2

NO RIGHT LIVING

Let's be honest. Despite the specific failings we might each admit to, we probably think of ourselves as actively leading a life and, moreover, as leading a morally acceptable life. Admittedly, there are all sorts of pressures that we feel ourselves under – perhaps mainly in our working environment, but also beyond it – and all sorts of things we readily admit that we cannot control – the financial markets, the weather, or whether the one we love loves us back. We probably acknowledge that our social and natural environment shaped us from the very beginning of our lives. Still, we think that most of the time we are determining our lives in the light of our own values, beliefs, and ideals. And, yes, sometimes we lie or do not treat others in the way they deserve, but in most cases these lies are small, white lies, often actually told in the best interest of the other person. Similarly, in most cases, when we treat others wrongly, this originates from good intentions or, at worst, was a momentary, but utterly forgivable failure. While we could do more to make the world a better place – volunteer, give more to charitable organisations, take better care of our loved ones, and so on – we normally meet at least the threshold of morally acceptable, decent behaviour. Or so we think.

But what if we are wrong about all of this? What if right living is not possible, both in the sense that we really and actively shape our lives and in the sense of living a morally acceptable life? One of the reasons why Theodor W. Adorno's work is so interesting and challenging is that he thinks that there is no right living in both the senses just indicated. He wants to shake us out of our complacency and make us realise how precarious our modern social world and our lives within it are.

The text that forms the basis of this chapter contains the first statement of Adorno's notorious thesis that there is no right life within our modern social world.[1] It is part of a book called *Minima Moralia*, in which Adorno collected aphorisms and short essays that he wrote during the 1940s in exile. He initially presented this collection to his friend, Max Horkheimer, with whom he wrote *Dialectic of Enlightenment* during the same period. *Minima Moralia* is a very rich and fascinating book. It contains both some of the most accessible writing by Adorno and some of the most difficult passages. The aphorism I want to focus on here is Number 18, entitled 'Refuge for the homeless [*Asyl für Obdachlose*]'. It concludes with the famous claim. Explaining this claim and why Adorno makes it will be the topic of this chapter.

Both the claim and the aphorism in which it is originally stated are difficult to interpret. Fortunately, Adorno comments on the claim again in later works (such as in *Negative Dialectics* and his 1963 lectures on moral philosophy). Thus, we have both the original context of Aphorism No. 18 and later clarifications of the claim available to us. These clarifications help in the task of interpreting and translating the claim in question. The latter task is far from straightforward and much depends on the interpretation adopted. However, Adorno's claim is best translated, in my view, as 'there is no right life within the wrong [life]'. I have to postpone a full justification of this until after the discussion of this claim. For simplicity's sake, I speak of the claim under consideration as the 'No Right Living Thesis'.

In what follows, I focus mainly on the original context of the claim, bringing in Adorno's later comments only for clarification or elaboration. Altogether, I highlight five interconnected elements contained in the No Right Living Thesis and then return to the issue of translating it. I conclude the chapter by discussing some objections to this thesis.

I 'Refuge for the homeless': a summary

Aphorism No. 18 starts off with the claim that we can learn something important about the state of private life today by looking at where it takes place, our homes and dwellings. This approach is typical for Adorno's methodology. He often tries to analyse something general (such as here, private life) by undertaking what he calls 'micrological studies' of an instance of it (such as here, dwelling, meaning 'living in a particular place'). By bringing out the tensions inherent in this particular issue, we can learn something about the more general theme

---

1 MM, 4: 43/39.

with which we started. One of Adorno's background assumptions seems to be *holism*: at least as far as our social world is concerned, each element within it is connected to all the other elements, so that analysing one will bring the others into focus too.[2] His aim in these micrological studies (and especially in the aphorisms) is to effect a perceptual shift: they are not meant to work as linear deductive arguments, but are meant to make the reader see something – notably how intolerable or miserable our life and the modern world is. Adorno's micrological approach is controversial and stands in contrast to top-down procedures that often predominate in theories about modern life. The justification for Adorno's alternative procedure is directly tied up with the question of whether or not it produces fruitful results (whether or not it succeeds in producing a perceptual shift), and this question is best answered by actually looking at examples.

Adorno's claim is that dwelling has become very difficult indeed, or even impossible. The available housing stock is either too functional to allow its occupants to develop a genuine, person-specific relationship with their living spaces; or too kitsch or tied up with 'musty family interests' to be an appropriate place to make oneself at home in.[3] Everywhere lurks the danger of getting lost in trying to make oneself at home. For example, this can happen by concentrating all one's efforts on furnishing and keeping up one's home – such as being preoccupied with getting the newest household and (nowadays) entertainment and communication devices. Being preoccupied in this way is dangerous, since one thereby risks sacrificing reflection and critical awareness, and they ought not to be sacrificed in this way. Thus, instead of spending enormous amounts of energy and time on decorating and redecorating or equipping one's dwelling, one should, for example, question the pressures of today's consumer society that make us feel bad about not being part of the new trend or make us take something

---

2 For our purposes here we need not settle whether Adorno is a holist only in respect to the modern social world (say, because he thinks that it forms a totality – a systematic whole) or whether he also thinks a holistic approach is appropriate for other objects of enquiry (such as past and future societies).

3 Surprisingly perhaps, Adorno here includes modernist architecture in his worries about inappropriate dwelling places. Even modernism has become kitsch: 'Purely functional curves, having broken free of their purpose, are now becoming just as ornamental as the basic structures of Cubism' (MM, 4: 43/39). This is one piece of – admittedly inconclusive – evidence that Adorno might not be the modernist mandarin as whom he is often portrayed.

ultimately unimportant (such as brand names) to be of the utmost importance. Yet, the alternatives are not promising either. Those who can live in a hotel or rent furnished accommodation make a 'prudential' (*lebenskluge*) norm out of the problem of making oneself at home – they do not face up to the problem, but pretend that it is actually advantageous not to make oneself at home. Those who cannot choose have the worst deal, living in slums, or something which by the next day might no longer provide them with shelter.

All these reflections culminate in a kind of paradox: we both should not, but at the same time need to, make ourselves at home. This paradox concerns not just dwelling, but our relationship to property generally. Private ownership has become obsolete, since we could build a society where there would be enough for everyone, so that no one would have to protect his or her holding from others by way of a legal system. The (legal) regime of private ownership is, nonetheless, necessary in the society we currently live in, since without it we risk ending up destitute or precariously dependent on the good will of others or social institutions. Indeed, whenever the legal regime of property temporarily or locally breaks down within our social world, people and things tend to be disregarded and their survival is severely endangered. Still, when people point to the fact that without property they would struggle to survive in today's world, then in most cases this is just an excuse to hold on to their possessions which vastly outstrip what is required to live comfortably. In sum, we could not (and should not) simply endorse one of the two conflicting standpoints and drop the other – in this sense, we might, following Kant, talk of an antinomy here, that is, an irresolvable conflict between two sides with an equal claim to being justified (albeit with the Adornian twist that the conflict is only irresolvable within our current social world – I return to this complication shortly). Having presented this antinomy, Adorno concludes with his famous claim, the No Right Living Thesis.

Insofar as this claim seems to be the conclusion of the aphorism, it embodies what we have learned about private life from looking at where it takes place and the way we dwell. Moreover, the No Right Living Thesis is not just any claim about private life, but rather a claim about the ways in which private life is problematic. In fact, Aphorism No. 18 and its conclusion, the No Right Living Thesis, are programmatic for Adorno's general thesis that life is damaged in modern society. This comes out clearly when we consider the details of the No Right Living Thesis.

II The antinomical structure of our lives

The first particular way in which private life is problematic is the following. As we have seen, Adorno argues in Aphorism No. 18 that we are faced with a practical paradox, or antinomy, in respect to our property and living arrangements. Presumably, this is meant to imply that private life in general is characterised by practical antinomies. That Adorno thinks that this is a general problem is confirmed in other passages in which he directly links the No Right Living Thesis to practical antinomies.

Most notably, each of us faces a practical antinomy when choosing which of two fundamental ethical frameworks we should adopt as our personal moral outlook.[4] On the one hand, we could adopt an 'ethics of disposition [*Gesinnungsethik*]', that is, an ethics which makes moral worth depend only on intentions. On the other hand, we could orientate ourselves with the help of an 'ethics of responsibility [*Verantwortungsethik*]', that is, an ethics which places the main focus on actual consequences.[5] These two moral outlooks are in competition, but for Adorno the problem is that neither side is in the right against the other and that a reconciliation of the two positions is also currently unavailable.[6] The details of why Adorno thinks so, need not interest us at this point (we return to this later in this chapter and in Chapter 4). What is important for our current purposes is that whichever of the two moral outlooks we adopt as our personal morality, we go wrong, according to Adorno. Indeed, he concludes his discussion by saying that 'There is no right way of living the wrong life, for a formal ethics [of disposition] cannot underwrite it, and the ethics of responsibility ... cannot underwrite it either'.[7]

This brings out well the first element of the No Right Living Thesis, the *antinomical nature* of private life. We are faced with conflicts which are practical antinomies in the sense that neither side can give an adequate grounding for (morally) right living. We get here the first

---

4 PMP 1963, 241, 246–7/162, 166.
5 Adorno here uses terminology introduced by Weber in his 'Politics as a Vocation [*Politik als Beruf*]' ([1919] Gerth and Wright Mills (eds.) 1948: Ch. 4).
6 Adorno sometimes speaks of a third type of ethics, an 'ethics of goods [*Güterethik*]'. However, he also thinks that this third type of ethics is equally problematic (on this see Bernstein 2001: 56–7). Thus, strictly speaking, in choosing our private moral outlook we are faced not with a dilemma, but a trilemma.
7 PMP 1963, 246–7/166; translation amended.

indication why Adorno is a critic of both moral theory and practice. Moral theory cannot help us out of the practical dilemmas in our current predicament, and the fact that we face these dilemmas means that moral practice is precarious – whatever we do, we will act wrongly in one way or another. Adorno's scepticism about moral theory and practice does not apply to all social circumstances. Firstly, he differentiates the modern social world from the closed societies of the pre-modern past. The latter were characterised by much higher levels of certainty and agreement about moral theory and practice, such that people within these societies took themselves to know what was morally required of them.[8] Still, Adorno thinks that no right living was possible in these past societies either – for individuals would be truly capable of practising morality only in a free society,[9] and these past societies were not free (I return to this later). The difference between past and modern times, in Adorno's view, is rather that modern times are characterised by a higher level of complexity, a greater number of antinomical structures, and more uncertainty, which make moral theory and practice precarious in a way they used not to be. This is a contentious claim, but it is important to note that Adorno is not saying that pre-modern times were completely free of moral complexities and antinomies (any Greek tragedy would tell against such a claim). Instead, his claim is that these challenges have typically become more pervasive and intense in modern times. Secondly, and more importantly, Adorno does not exclude the possibility that morally right living might finally materialise properly (in a free society), and that as a consequence moral practice would become *less* precarious – no longer undermined by inner and outer repression; no longer afflicted by antinomies (to the same degree); but instead enabled by a more transparent and collectively controlled social structure.

As we see throughout this study, there are numerous other practical antinomies that Adorno claims we face in our modern social world – concerning, for example, the responsibility and punishment of individuals (see Chapter 3); the fact that we are faced with moral demands, but do not seem to be able to discharge them (see Chapters 3 and 5); the choice between liberal democratic societies

---

8 See, for example, ND, 6: 241/243; PMP 1963, 146–8, 166–8, 174/98–9, 112–13, 116. On this, see also Menke 2005. There are parallels here to the work by MacIntyre 1985 and Williams 1993.

9 See, for example, ND, 6: 294/299.

in the West and nominal socialist regimes in the East; and the pitfalls of compassion. By way of further illustration, I here briefly take up the latter – the practical antinomy in respect to whether or not one should be compassionate (see also Chapter 4).

According to Adorno, compassion mitigates existing injustices, but does not change them. Rather, it (often) inadvertently helps to cement them. Hence, it might seem that we should not be compassionate, but rather expose the injustices for what they are and try to overcome them once and for all. However, if we are not compassionate, then there will be more suffering, at least in the short-run, and we would be guilty of the moral failure of not showing a proper regard for those affected by such suffering, many of whom could not be helped in time even if we were to succeed in changing social structures so as to eradicate poverty and its consequences in the future.

Consider humanitarian aid as an example: when faced with a humanitarian disaster (say a crop failure and subsequent famine), it seems natural to extend all the aid one can muster to help people in need. However, the problem is that such intervention often has negative effects on the local economy and on food production (such as changing people's diets and undercutting the livelihoods of local farmers), so that, for example, famines and humanitarian crisis become more frequent, requiring repeated intervention and leading to dependency.[10] Similarly, the structural causes of the famine – unaccountable governments, conflict and war, global institutional arrangements, production of cash crops at the expense of staple food items due to unequal property relations and market power, and so on – are left untouched or are even reinforced. On the other hand, many of the people facing the humanitarian disaster need help immediately and might not survive, unless it is delivered now. So, we are torn between not helping those in dire need and preventing future disasters and occurrences of dire need.

The difficulties involved in practical antinomies, such as the one regarding compassion, are not just due to a lack of imagination or planning, but to the social structures in which we find ourselves. In fact, while Adorno would admit that tragic conflicts exist in all societies, he would argue that at least some of the antinomies we face today only occur because of the social world we live in. Indeed, returning to the example of famine, it could be argued that the problem often originates

---

10 See, for example, de Waal 1997; Maren 1997; Rieff 2002; Terry 2002; Kennedy 2004; Easterly 2006; Bolton 2008; and Moyo 2009.

from the absence of accountable political structures and that their absence in turn is connected to certain unjust features of the international order.[11] Adorno might accept such analyses but argue that the absence of accountable political structures and the existence of an unjust international order are not accidental to, but engendered by and, ultimately, unavoidable in our current social world. This world has produced the technical means and know-how (in Marxist terms, the forces of production) that would allow us here and now to eradicate all hunger, but its social, political, and economic structures are such that this eradication is neither a priority, nor in fact feasible without radical transformation.[12] As indicated earlier, this contrasts with both closed societies of the pre-modern past, which did not face (as many) conflicts of this sort, and a possible free society of the future, in which the practical antinomies that block right living today would not exist. Thus, the pervasive existence of practical antinomies in modern society is the first reason why life in this social world is wrong and why right living is blocked.[13]

III False consciousness and guilt context

The No Right Living Thesis encompasses at least four other elements. To see what the second element is, recall the (purported) fact that without private property we face need and dependency in the current world. Adorno accepts that this is a fact about our current social world. At the same time, he thinks that whenever this fact is actually employed in a defence of holding on to one's possession, then it becomes ideological. By this, Adorno means to say the following. The fact that we currently need ownership rights to survive is used either, at the individual level, to justify holding on to our possessions substantially beyond the level necessary to survive (such that holding on to them would need a different justification, especially in the face of other people's lacking the necessities of life); or, at the social level, to justify the very property system which makes it both the case (a) that those who

---

11 See Sen 1981; Pogge 2008.
12 See, for example, 8: 347/Adorno et al. 1976: 62; see also 10.2: 564, 618/CM, 96–7, 144.
13 Moreover, while the emphasis in the preceding paragraphs is mainly on right living in the sense of morally right living, the existence of practical antinomies also suggests that good living (either in the narrow sense of living happily or in the wider sense of living well, where this includes moral considerations, not just prudential ones) is also blocked – I return to this in Section IV 'Life does not live'.

can survive within it need ownership rights to do so and (b) that many of
the people who could survive and even flourish under a different
system are excluded from the goods necessary to do so. There is again
a general point here: Adorno suggests that we inescapably get entangled
in ideological claims when trying to get on in our social world – this is
the second element of the No Right Living Thesis that I want to
highlight.

Roughly, to say that we are prone to being caught up in ideologies
is to say that we are prone to hold a set of beliefs, attitudes, and
preferences which are false or distorted in ways that benefit the established social order (and the dominant social group within it) at the
expense of the satisfaction of people's real interests. The structure of
our social world is such that by defending our behaviour or social
position, we have to defend what should be criticised, namely, this social
world or central elements thereof (such as its property system). Even
where we do not attempt to justify our way of life, we tend to fall prey to
ideological distortions, so that we accept social arrangements as they
are, instead of changing them as we should (this is often true even of
those who are most disadvantaged by these arrangements). In fact,
everything can become ideology in the wrong life – even what is the
right thing to think and do, if viewed in isolation, turns into false
consciousness when employed, under the pressure of social structures,
for particular purposes or interests.[14] Thus, either by endorsing or by
unreflectively accepting distorted truths or half-truths, we entrench the
social *status quo* that ought to be changed radically. To return again to
the example from Aphorism No. 18: if we only look at what is necessary
within our current property system, it turns out to be true that having
private property is necessary for survival; at the same time, this claim is
false, if we take a wider view, which does not just assume our current
property system.[15] However, according to Adorno, our social world is
such that this wider view is difficult to take – this world presents itself as a
self-contained, natural order and incentivises people to present
half-truths as the whole truth or to suppress the truth altogether.

That our social world tends to produce false consciousness confirms
that right living cannot be achieved. The problem is, thus, not only that
we face practical antinomies, but also that we get caught in ideological

14 See PMP 1956/7 (unpublished), Vo1324; 10.2: 492/CM, 34.
15 Unsurprisingly, one is reminded here of Hegel's treatment of property in relation to
   Kantian ethics (see, for example, *Phenomenology of Spirit* [1807] 1977, especially §§430–1).

claims. Not seeing the world and our place in it for what they are is not conducive to right living, not least because it helps to perpetuate the conditions which sabotage it (such as our particular property system; see also Chapter 3).

These considerations point to the third element contained in the No Right Living Thesis. As Adorno brings out in respect to dwelling in Aphorism No. 18, we are so much part of the social system, that whatever we do, we almost inevitably perpetuate it. In finding a place to live, we sustain manifold exchange relations, and in trying to make ourselves at home, we are likely to fall prey to the fetishism of consumer goods, which also props up the social system. Yet, were we to refuse to do these things, our survival would be threatened (by not being sheltered, by lacking a job which enables us to acquire the means of subsistence, etc.). Thus, we have very strong incentives to cooperate, and most people do so even beyond what is necessary for mere survival. Whether social critic or unthinking conformist, we have to buy into the social system at least to the extent of surviving, and by doing so, we maintain it, however unintended this may be. In this sense, the social world is self-perpetuating – we inevitably maintain it in almost all that we do and refrain from doing.

Yet, as we saw in the previous chapter, this social world is deeply morally problematic, even radically evil – at least according to Adorno. If our social world really is radically evil, then the fact that we sustain it means that we cannot avoid being implicated in its evil and, hence, there can be no (morally) right living within it. As Adorno puts it elsewhere, 'The individual ... participates in guilt, because, being harnessed to the social order, he or she has virtually no power over the conditions which appeal to the ethical [*sittliche*] *ingenium*: crying for their change.'[16] Since it is almost impossible for us not to sustain what should be changed, namely, our radically evil social world, our moral credentials will always be tarnished by whatever we do, or refrain from doing. We are implicated in a 'guilt context [*Schuldzusammenhang*]'.[17]

---

16 ND, 6: 241/243; translation amended.
17 See especially MTP, 10.2: 769–70/CM, 267–8; MCP, 175–7/112–13. A noticeable feature of this third element is the notion of guilt and moral responsibility at play. In liberal contexts we are mostly familiar with moral (and criminal) responsibility for intended actions, but negligence and other forms of omission are normally also counted among those 'acts' for which we are accountable. Adorno's notion of guilt and responsibility has affinities with the latter, but is to some extent more radical (building on Hegel or Sophocles, for whom our doings morally implicate us irrespective of intentions or even of our ability to do otherwise). He is not accusing us of intentionally committing atrocities

This connects with the previous element. One reason why we tend to be caught up in ideologies is just this guilt context. Within it, we cannot fully justify our behaviour – being implicated by evil undermines any legitimacy to which we might lay claim in our behaviour. As a consequence, any justification we do offer will be ideological, at least in part. Indeed, this also brings out why – just as in Marx – it is non-accidental ('necessary') that people get entangled in false consciousness: if we live in a wrong world, in a guilt context of coldness that predominates us, then it is no surprise that right consciousness is hard to come by;[18] that, if it can be attained at all, then it will be only by 'unwavering exertion of critique', not by default.[19]

The third element also connects to the antinomical nature of life in the modern world (the first element highlighted): one of the reasons practical antinomies arise is because our situations are already so prefigured that whichever option we choose, we contribute to the survival of a radically evil social system – in this way, antinomies are the expression of this predicament. For example, we cannot choose an ethics of disposition because the social system does not guarantee that good dispositions result in good consequences; we cannot choose an ethics of responsibility either, however, since this would make morality unduly dependent on the consequences in an evil world.[20]

IV 'Life does not live'[21]

Thus far, I have mainly concentrated on bringing out why there is no *morally* right life for Adorno, but there is also another way to look at the claim at hand, the No Right Living Thesis. Thus, its fourth element is that the life of the individual is so deformed and distorted that it cannot be truthfully said that living is taking place. There are two related aspects to this.

---

or of knowingly perpetuating a radically evil social world where we could easily avoid doing so (this accusation would be reserved to those few who are actually guilty of such acts). Instead, we are guilty of, however inadvertently, sustaining this social world and failing to change it. Moreover, even this act and omission are not something of which we are *directly* guilty *qua* isolated individual, but *qua* member of a collective, humanity. I return to these issues in Chapters 3 and 5.

18 10.2: 591–2/CM, 120.   19 10.2: 593/CM, 121.
20 See PMP 1963, lecture 16; for further discussion, see Chapter 4.
21 MM, 4: 20/19; this quotation by Ferdinand Kürnberger is the epigraph of the first part of *Minima Moralia*, which contains Aphorism No. 18.

On the one hand, life in modern society lacks the richness which would be necessary to mark it out compared to mere existence. 'What the philosophers once knew as life', Adorno writes in the dedication to *Minima Moralia*, 'has become the sphere of private existence and now of mere consumption, dragged along as an appendage of the process of material production, without autonomy or substance of its own.'[22] While human life used to be conceived as encompassing all aspects of human existence, it is increasingly narrowing down to only two aspects: consumption and production. We might not always experience it as such, but, according to Adorno, our lives – whether it involves play, love, doing philosophy, craftwork, gardening, religious devotion, or whatever else – get increasingly structured by the patterns of (capitalist) consumption and production. This is a strong claim, although when considering how hard it is to avoid the influences which Hollywood cinema, TV, social media, and Valentine's Day celebrations have on intimate relationships, it seems less like a rhetorical exaggeration than when one initially encounters it.[23] In fact, however, the claim is stronger still: even the consumption aspect is not something free-standing (as constitutive of or instrumental to human happiness), but, ultimately, has its purpose and limit in the material reproduction of (capitalist) society.[24] Society needs us to consume (and produce) the goods which are the carriers of surplus-value, and permits consumption of the kind and to the extent that is required for its reproduction (which is not of the kind and extent most suitable for human interests). For this reason, human life, despite its sorry state, survives, is dragged along. Our lives become more and more standardised, which further facilitates our functioning in the roles to which we become largely reduced: consumer and producer. Moreover, our forms of experiencing the world become increasingly impoverished – we only take note of what is already familiar, or what can be easily conceptualised within rigid thought systems. Influenced and directed by a dominant society and the culture industry within it, life in an emphatic sense (that is, something beyond the mere material reproduction of individuals

22 MM, 4: 13/15.   23 I return later to the role of exaggeration in Adorno's texts.
24 See, for example, S, 8: 16–17/273–4; see also Chapter 1. While Adorno holds that something structurally parallel applies to the nominally socialist regimes, he mainly concentrates in his analysis on Western, capitalist societies, and this is reflected in my summary here, both because the summary would otherwise become too cumbersome and because nominally socialist regimes are no longer a live option nowadays. For brief discussion of Adorno's views on nominal socialism see Chapters 1 and Freyenhagen 2012 (unpublished).

and society) is not available. Despite the surface impression, human lives are by and large empty of substance and diversity. For Adorno, this is true even of that small part of humanity which can make full use of the goods and opportunities afforded by capitalism. While limited as analogy, one way to think about this claim is as follows: if Adorno is right, then reality TV, despite its obvious absurdity and manufactured nature, actually depicts real life with greater accuracy than its critics realise – for most of our lives are as sad an existence, as devoid of real meaning, and as manufactured and constructed as is captured on the TV screen. What is shown there is not so much a distortion of real life, but an allegory of the distorted life that is reality.

On the other hand, when Adorno claims that life does not live, then what he means is that individuals are not *actively* leading their lives. Individuals are just surviving, or getting by, but they do not direct or determine their lives. As the ability to direct one's life has traditionally been described as autonomy (or positive freedom), one might reformulate this point by saying that individuals lack autonomy. Adorno follows this usage when he asserts elsewhere that individuals are not autonomous or positively free.[25] Individuals might think that they are autonomous – they might think that they choose their own projects, ends, and values – but they are wrong to think so.[26] Society restricts our options so much that any choosing or life-planning, of which individuals are still capable, is insufficient for ascribing self-determination to them. Even in what look like choices contrary to society (when people behave, say, in an overly self-interested way), the individuals are actually just the 'involuntary executioners' of the law of value and thereby of capitalist society.[27] In other words, Adorno turns Adam Smith on his head: instead of making possible a prosperous and moral society, capitalism's invisible hand mechanisms enable a radically evil society that depletes natural and human resources to sustain itself.

This fourth point is bound up with the earlier points; faced with practical antinomies and destined to get caught in ideology, leading a life is not an option. Similarly, the two aspects of the fourth element are related: one reason why life does not live (in the emphatic sense) is that human beings are not capable of actively leading a life in this social world.

---

25 See ND, 6: 222, 230–1, 239/223, 231–2, 241; PMP 1956/7 (unpublished), Vo1289; see also here, Chapter 3.

26 ND, 6: 259/261–2; see also 218–19, 271ff., 292/219–20, 275ff., 297; and here, Chapter 3.

27 ND, 6: 259/261–2; see also 292/297.

V Living less wrongly

However, and this is the fifth and final element, there are not better and worse forms of living for Adorno. In Aphorism No. 18, he comments:

> The best mode of conduct, in the face of all this, still seems a non-committal, suspended one: to lead a private life, as far as the social order and one's own needs will tolerate nothing else, but not to attach weight to it as to something socially substantial and individually appropriate.[28]

Adorno recommends a suspended way of living; and, thus, he seems to be committed to the view that there continue to be evaluative differences between ways of living. Even if the wrong life cannot be lived rightly, it can be lived *more or less wrongly*. (I take this up in more detail in Chapters 5–6.)

In summary, Adorno's thesis '*Es gibt kein richtiges Leben im falschen*' is a claim about the problematic state of private life. It expresses the view that within this sphere we are faced with practical antinomies which are irresolvable in the current social order. It also expresses the view that however we justify our personal behaviour we will get caught in ideologies. Moreover, the No Right Living Thesis contains the further claims that (a) we continuously reproduce the badness of the world around us, and (b) that one cannot really speak of 'living' in respect to our lives (because they are so impoverished as forms of existence and because we are not capable of autonomously directing them). In this way, neither the good, nor the right life, nor any genuine living is possible within our social world. Yet, Adorno's thesis that there is no right living leaves open the possibility that there are forms of living the wrong life which are preferable to others.

It is important to note that the No Right Living Thesis is both descriptive and evaluative in nature.[29] It is descriptive insofar as it expresses Adorno's analysis of the manifold ways in which (right) living has become problematic for individuals. It is evaluative (or normative) in a twofold sense: (a) it is morally wrong that right living is blocked, and (b) some forms of living are less bad than others.

---

28 MM, 4: 43/39; translation amended.
29 I am pairing 'descriptive' with 'evaluative' here, rather than with 'prescriptive', because the latter has nowadays taken on the characteristic of entailing an imperative, and I do not want to suggest that all of Adorno's evaluative and normative statements take the form of imperatives – as we will see later (see Chapter 6), some of his normative commitments are better characterised as ideals.

Moreover, the descriptive and evaluative aspects are inextricably linked: it is *not* necessary to add a moral premise in order to read off the moral implications of what Adorno is saying. Rather, the analysis is at once descriptive *and* evaluative; by describing how right living is not possible for us, Adorno condemns our current forms of living and he prescribes striving to live less wrongly to us.[30]

We are now in the position to clarify how one should translate the original German for No Right Living Thesis (and thereby to justify the translation proposed at the beginning of this chapter). The first thing to note is that Adorno did not choose the pairing '*gut*' and '*schlecht*'. This is noteworthy because this pairing would seem to be the most natural one, given the traditional philosophical notion '*gutes Leben*' ('good life'), of which Adorno must have been aware. That Adorno refrained from using the pairing '*gut*' and '*schlecht*' speaks against using their English equivalents, 'good' and 'bad'. Moreover, while Adorno might agree that 'there can be no good life within the bad one',[31] this does not capture exactly what he is saying in the No Right Living Thesis. It might be a consequence of the fact that right living is blocked that the good life is blocked too, but this is to some extent a separate point. Alternatively, one might suggest pairing 'false' with either 'correct' or 'true'.[32] However, this also seems inaccurate in that it does not capture the ambiguities of '*richtig*' and '*falsch*' as well as their English counterparts 'right' and 'wrong'. As we saw, Adorno does not just want to say that there is no true living any more and that life cannot be lived truthfully, but also that morally right living is blocked and that whatever we do, we are implicated in evil. While 'right' and 'wrong' can capture the first two elements along with the latter points, neither 'false'/'true', nor 'false'/'correct' can fully account for the moral aspects of the No Right Living Thesis. Yet, any translation has to convey the richness in meaning of this thesis as well as possible and to bring across both its descriptive and evaluative aspects. Consequently, the closest to capturing what Adorno is saying in the literature is perhaps Jephcott's rendering, 'wrong life cannot be lived rightly'. However, the most literal translation would be 'there is no

---

30 I defend this (broadly Aristotelian) reading of Adorno's conception of normativity in later chapters (esp. Chapter 9).

31 This is how Livingstone translates the No Right Living Thesis (see, for example, PMP 1963, 246/166 and *passim*).

32 These are the suggestions of Finlayson (2002: 1) and Brunkhorst (1999: 64) respectively.

right life within the wrong [life]',[33] and it is this translation which I have adopted here.

Aphorism No. 18 throws up a number of questions that we will take up later: what conception of freedom and autonomy does Adorno use when he denies that we can autonomously shape our lives within this social system? What can individuals do to live less wrongly? Could moral theory provide us with a canon of the right life, so that even if we do not achieve this ideal here and now, we know what we should aim for? Can Adorno account for the normativity of his strongly evaluative claims?

However, before exploring these (and indeed further) questions, there are a number of more immediate objections that it might be good to address already.

VI No golden past and insufficient material progress

A number of formulations in Aphorism No. 18 might suggest that Adorno thinks that being at home had been possible in the past – 'Dwelling, in the proper sense, is *now* impossible'; 'traditional residences we grew up in have *grown* intolerable'; 'independent existence, *defunct* in any case'; 'the house is *past*'.[34] Similarly, the already quoted passage about 'What the philosophers *once knew* as life'[35] also sounds as if what Adorno objects to is the loss of some rich forms of life in a golden past. This impression would fit a picture often painted of Adorno – namely, a picture of Adorno as the elitist, European mandarin inhabiting his Grand Hotel Abyss, in which he laments the loss of even greater luxury that he was used to in the past. And this picture is rather objectionable – for even if he and Horkheimer grew up in traditional residences which now have allegedly 'grown intolerable', most people did not, but instead were cramped together in often unsanitary conditions, working in the 'satanic mills' of early capitalism (not to mention pre-modern societies and living conditions then for the average person); and even if Adorno dislikes profoundly functional modern habitations, these offer people clear advantages, not just shelter from the elements, but access to modern plumbing and appliances that make life easier, healthier, and more enjoyable (in most people's

---

33 The inclusion of the second 'life' in brackets is supported by the fact that Adorno reverses the order of the sentence which states the No Right Living Thesis in one of his lectures: 'in wrong life there is no right life [– *es im falschen Leben eben kein richtiges gibt*]' (PMP 1963, 241/162; translation amended; see also PMP 1963, 248/167; ND, 6: 356/364).
34 MM, 4: 38–9/42–3; my emphases.   35 MM, 4: 13/15; my emphasis.

view). Thus, Adorno seems guilty of a dual distortion: glorifying the past and understating the advantages the modern social world has to offer.

A full reply would take us too far here, but let me at least sketch some of its elements. Firstly, Adorno does not think the pre-modern world constituted a golden past to which we could return. Indeed, he *denies* both *the reversibility* of history (the possibility of returning to past social forms, whose economic, social, and technological conditions no longer obtain);[36] and, more importantly, *the desirability* of doing so. As little as it is possible to reconstruct the primitive stage of humanity, the evidence we have suggests that it was a 'wretched existence'.[37] Similarly, Adorno emphasises how historical conditions tend to be glorified only in retrospect and often for ideological purposes:

> The meaningful times for whose return the early Lukács yearned were as much due to reification, to inhuman institutions, as he had only attributed to the bourgeois age. Contemporary representations of medieval towns usually look as if an execution were just taking place to cheer the populace. If any harmony of subject and object prevailed in those days, it was a harmony like the most recent one: pressure-born and brittle.[38]

Indeed, Adorno reiterates the final point about the coercive nature of the pre-modern world repeatedly.[39] He even suggests that it perished because its coercive nature had become unbearable when its legitimation strategies could no longer bear the weight of critical scrutiny.[40] Indeed, he goes as far as to purport that many past epochs lacked not only the concept of freedom but also its reality completely.[41] Even in those societies in which some measure of individual conduct of life was possible (such as in antiquity), it was a matter of (rare) privilege on the back of other's unfreedom (notably the slave population). Adorno notes that, in contrast, even an elderly cleaning lady (i.e., those at the bottom of the social ladder) enjoy today 'the licence to be an individual, a right to individuality' and presents this as an advance over the pre-modern world (notably antiquity), even considering

---

36 See, for example, 10.1: 293, 295–6.   37 HF, 79/53.

38 ND, 6: 192/191; translation amended.

39 See, for example, 10.1: 293, 295–6; HF, 288/208.

40 10.1: 293. Williams indirectly acknowledges this aspect of Adorno's thinking when he gives credit to the early Frankfurt School for calling into question the legitimation of past societies by asking whether the acceptance of the legitimation may not have been merely the effect of the power it was supposed to legitimate (1993: 166). He later formulated his 'Critical Theory Principle' on the basis of this idea (see Williams 2002: 225–32; 2005: 6).

41 ND, 6: 217/218.

'however little she is able to avail herself of [her right to individuality] and convert it into reality'.[42]

Moreover, Adorno does not think that freedom can be realised other than through the coercion exerted in the history of civilisation.[43] This coercion is wrong, but still necessary for human survival, the development of their productive and other capacities. As he puts it in one of his lectures:

> Without evil ... there would be no good; without this rift [between individual and society] to provide mankind with its substantial security within a given society, the idea of freedom and with it the idea of a condition worthy of human beings would not exist. This insight is swiftly joined by the suspicion that what were said, even in Hegel, to be substantial ages in which the individual lived in harmony with the collective of which he was a member, were in reality far from providing the settings for a happy and harmonious existence. More likely, they were ages characterized by repressiveness that was so powerful that what has come down to us from them is merely the end result, namely, the triumph of the universal, without our being able to give an account of the excess of suffering and injustice without which these so-called meaningful times ... would not have existed.[44]

Not least because of the excess of suffering and injustice which Adorno mentions here, but even because of their non-excessive instances, Adorno disagrees with those – including Hegel and Marx (as he reads them) – who in a consequentialist manner would view the coercive aspects of civilisation (at least the non-excessive ones) as justified because they were necessary for human survival and development. In a rather Kantian manner, he does not think that the gains accruing to some now and to a freed humanity in the future redeem the pains of those in the past and present – these are separate persons and even if we could accept that the developments under which they suffered were required for the species, and even to some extent unavoidable, this does not suffice to make them right. If Auschwitz teaches us anything, it is that this kind of transhistorical off-setting of suffering – be it by way of traditional theodicy or secular consequentialist calculus – is impossible and morally inappropriate. We cannot and should not squeeze 'any

---

42 HF, 126/85.
43 ND, 6: 150/147; P, 10.2: 630/CM, 154; HF, 72, 82, 287–8/47–8, 55, 207–8.
44 HF, 287–8/208.

kind of sense, however bleached, out of the victims' fate';[45] to attempt to
do so would be to wrong them, to add insult to injury.

Crucially, Adorno does not deny that the modern social world brings
material advances. Instead, his criticism is twofold. Firstly, he objects
that these advances are not rolled out to everyone (with almost half of
humanity lacking sanitary conditions, suffering from often extreme
poverty, and dying of easily preventable causes at the rate of 50,000
a day);[46] and that this is – as already indicated – not something that is
either accidental to capitalism, nor something that could be changed
within its structure (nor indeed within nominal socialist societies).
Instead, the material advances are largely limited to a privileged
minority of humanity, which enjoys its material comforts often at the
expense of the rest of humanity (be it by fuelling resource conflicts in
its insatiable demand for consumer goods; by relying on the labour of
others under terrible conditions to make these goods affordable; or
by degrading the environment and climate, the effects of which are
disproportionally felt by the poorest). Indeed, this affects even the
'happiness' derived from the material advantages by those who have
access to them:

> Precisely because famine continues to reign across entire continents
> when technically it could be eliminated, no one can really be so delighted
> at his prosperity. Just as individually, for instance in films, there is resent-
> ful laughter when a character sits down to a very good meal and tucks in
> the napkin under his chin, so too humanity begrudges itself the comfort it
> all too well knows is still paid for by want and hardship; resentment strikes
> every happiness, even one's own. Satiety has become an insult a priori,
> although the sole point of reproach about it would be that there are
> people who have nothing to eat; ... [47]

Secondly, Adorno also objects on other grounds to the way the material
advances are delivered – namely, by claiming that the standardisation of
production, products, and consumers is problematic (by making people
less able to have unrestricted experiences, by making them less discern-
ing and less sensitive to things and to each other, etc.) and that this

---

45 ND, 6: 354/361.   46 See Pogge 2008: 2.
47 MWTP, 10.2: 564/96–7. The 'happiness' derived from material advantage is not just
    tarnished by the fact that 'the comfort ... is still paid for by want and hardship', but also
    by the further fact that people in our social world have a distorted relationship to goods
    and, partly as a consequence, to themselves and others (see Chapter 1 here and recall
    Adorno's comments on the neurotic relationship to technology quoted in the
    Introduction).

could, at the current stage of the development of the forces of production, be avoidable while maintaining (and spreading to everybody) the acknowledged material advances of capitalism. In other words, he laments the soullessness of much of our consumer world, *not* because of nostalgia for the past and *not* because he does not appreciate the material advances of the present, but because he thinks we could have these advances without the soullessness, if our social world were changed in its orientation towards the satisfaction of real human needs and away from surplus-value production for its own sake.

If there is a nostalgia in Adorno's writing, then it is a nostalgia for the missed opportunities of the past – for the way in which early (liberal) capitalism made possible both some individual freedom (albeit mainly of a privileged class, the entrepreneurs and captains of industry) and the elimination of hunger, but then became fossilised into an administered world that denies us most of the individual freedom that it used to make possible, along with damaging the full development of the human potential of all (not to mention blocking the elimination of hunger). As beneficiary of this liberal phase, it is true that Adorno is looking at the world from a privileged perspective (both in the sense of socio-economic position and in terms of the freedom and education he enjoyed). However, it is not the case that he laments the (threat of a) loss of his privilege, snobbishly sneering at modern functional flats and furniture as well as at those who prefer these to living in slums or servants' quarters. Rather, he objects to the fact that though the privilege could be extended to all – upon which it would not be a privilege in the sense of special entitlement enjoyed in contrast to, and often at the expense of, others – it is not so extended and will not be until our social world and its thought forms are radically transformed.[48]

VII Exceptions to the rule?

There are a variety of other objections one might want to make against the No Right Living Thesis, and I want to take up one more in this chapter. Specifically, one might worry that Adorno flattens the moral landscape too much. Even if it were true that the average member of economically developed countries is complicit in and complacent about the way his or her life depends in myriad ways on unjust property relations or disproportionate use of the planet's resources, this does

---

48 See MTP, 10.2: 768/CM, 266–7; see also MM, Aphorism No. 6; 11: 674–5.

not yet show that there is no right living for a family of subsistence
farmers, or someone who carves out his existence in a sweatshop to
feed his family and send his kids to school, or even someone in the rich
North who, say, works with refugees and campaigns for a greener and
more just planet in her spare time – not to mention Mother Teresa, or
Nelson Mandela.

One way to respond here would be by way of concession: Adorno
explicitly admits using a technique of hyperbole in his work, 'following
the maxim that today only exaggeration per se can be the medium of
truth';[49] and perhaps the claim that there is no right living should, thus,
be read as an overstatement, as allowing for the possibility that some
people somewhere are capable of right living even in the radically evil
modern social world.

However, we need to tread carefully here. Not all of what Adorno says
is meant as an exaggeration – or put the other way around: even the
claim 'only exaggerations are true' is one. At the very least, Adorno
wants to say that our social world has a tendency towards making right
living (increasingly) impossible – this would allow for a sense in which
the No Right Living Thesis is exaggerated, but still suffices for Adorno's
purposes of indicting the social world that contains such a tendency.
There might be extraordinary individuals who are still capable of right
living, but they are rare and their numbers are dwindling for reasons
directly connected with the structure of this world.

Moreover, if we recall the various elements of this No Right Living
Thesis, then we can even make a case for its literal truth. On Adorno's
view of the matter, a subsistence farmer or sweatshop worker would not
be examples of right living, for it is not even clear that they are living in
any sense more emphatic than mere survival. They are certainly not
living well and also lack autonomy (not that they are to blame for
either) – and in this sense already it would be misleading to speak of
right life in respect to them.

Perhaps, the more difficult case is the example of people who devote
themselves to fighting suffering and injustice. Adorno would probably
argue that they lack autonomy – merely reacting, as they do, to injustice,
not really determining their lives in the absence of it – and also lack
what it takes to live well – they might be too absorbed in their fight for
justice, or too depressed and worn down by it, for them to be happy or

---

49 MWTP, 10.2: 567/99; see also DE, 3: 139/118; MM, Aphorisms Nos. 29, 82; 8: 319/
    Adorno et al. 1976: 35.

live a good life. Moreover, they are faced with practical antinomies, are likely to subscribe to some false consciousness, and also cannot but maintain society, the guilt context, at least in some way or at some level.

Still, one might think that such people's contributions outweigh any of these bads to which they might also be subject. Hence, even if they lack autonomy and central elements of their well-being, could we not say that they are at least living in a morally right way? Adorno would reply by objecting, once again, to the consequentialist nature of the argument – it is not that we can simply weigh up the bads we might produce by partaking in and maintaining a guilt context, however inadvertently, against the mitigation or avoidance of bads that we bring about within it. There is something wrong in the idea of weighing these bads, of proposing a calculus of this sort – not least because it overlooks the fact that the social world and its thought forms are so bad that they trump any positive contribution we may make within it. This is not to say that whatever an individual contributes towards avoiding inhumanity is insignificant – just the opposite, such an individual is living less wrongly, even (in the best and rare cases) decently. (I come back to what it means to live less wrongly and decently in later chapters.) Rather, these contributions, however significant, are insufficient for right living – the latter constitutes a higher standard than decency and we cannot achieve it in our modern social world. In this way, the moral landscape is not completely flat – there are differences, albeit 'merely' between living *more or less wrongly*. Taking part in the fight against racism or injustice or environmental degradation is a decent thing to do (as well as an expression of negative freedom, of which Adorno – as we see in Chapter 3 – thinks we are still capable on occasion). Yet, even if one contributed towards resisting these evils, one would still be too implicated in the on-going radical evil of modern society and too powerless to live rightly, partly because any fight against these bads would only be fully successful under radically different social and material conditions which no individual can change on their own.

Ironically, given Adorno's strained relationship with Brecht, it is in the first stanza of one of Brecht's poems ('*An die Nachgeborenen* [To Those Born Later]' [1939]) that we find encapsulated Adorno's view of our guilt context and the impossibility of right living within it. The stanza begins as follows:

> Truly, I live in dark times!
> A guileless word is foolish. A smooth forehead
> Suggests insensitivity. The man who laughs
> Has simply not yet had
> The terrible news.
>
> What kind of times are these, when
> A talk about trees is almost a crime
> Because it implies silence about so many horrors?
> That man there calmly crossing the street,
> Is already perhaps beyond the reach of his friends
> Who are in need?

The first stanza continues by revealing that it is no consolation to the person speaking in this poem that he is lucky enough to earn his living and have access to food and drink, since his luck can run out any moment and comes at the expense of others who lack basic necessities. It also reveals that he nonetheless eats and drinks. The stanza ends with Brecht's enumerating how we should live, according to one theory – the wisdom of the Stoa (retreat from strife; live without fear and violence; free oneself from desires rather than aim to fulfil them), before concluding:

> All this I cannot do:
> Truly, I live in dark times![50]

---

50 Brecht 1967: Vol. IX, 722–3/translation in Brecht 1976: 318–19. See also MM, Aphorism No. 5.

3

SOCIAL DETERMINATION AND
NEGATIVE FREEDOM

One aspect of Adorno's No Right Living Thesis – his thesis that wrong life cannot be lived rightly – is the important claim that in our current predicament, we cannot actively determine our life. In a word, we lack autonomy.[1] I briefly touched upon this claim in the previous chapter, but it calls for more discussion, and in this chapter, I investigate it in more detail, in part by considering a number of objections to it.

I Beholden to (social) externality

In one of his lectures, Adorno said:

> But what appears in Kant as the intertwining of man and nature is also the intertwining of man and society. For in that second nature, in our universal state of dependency, there is no freedom.[2]

In the same year, he wrote:

> the contradiction in which philosophy has entangled itself, that is, that humanity is inconceivable without the idea of freedom while in reality people are neither internally nor externally free, is not a failure of speculative metaphysics but the fault of the society that deprives people even of inner freedom. Society is the true determining factor, while at the same time its organization constitutes the potential for freedom.[3]

And in *Negative Dialectics*, he somewhat enigmatically alludes to the same point:

---

1 See MM, Aphorism No. 17.   2 PMP 1963, 261/176.   3 10.2: 549/CM, 85.

> Human beings are unfree because they are beholden to externality, and
> this externality in turn they are also themselves.[4]

These are stark views. According to Adorno, it is society that threatens
freedom – not what traditional philosophy had seen as a threat to human
freedom: determination according to natural causality. Moreover, it is
not human society as such that is the real threat, but the modern social
world in particular. This seems to fly in the face of the reality. For the
modern social world, many would protest, makes more freedom possible
than any time before in history – in pretty much any conception of
freedom. Not only do individuals now enjoy legal protections and individual rights that slaves in the ancient world or serfs in the Middle Ages
could only dream of, but the average person (at least in the affluent
societies) also has the material and technological wherewithal to realise
their conception of the good to an unprecedented extent. The ideal of
human self-determination might not be fully realised, but Adorno's claim
that there is no freedom is either plainly wrong or relies on a too high
standard that we would do well to reject.

Instead of addressing these objections directly at this point, I would
like to invite the reader to suspend these and other worries for the time
being, and to allow me to put some more of Adorno's views on the table
first. He would be the first to admit that these views do not seem immediately plausible. For even though he thinks society determines us to an
extent that to speak of our having freedom is hollow, he acknowledges
that things seem different to us:

> Society destines the individuals to be what they are, even by their immanent
> genesis. Their freedom or unfreedom is not primary, as it would seem under
> the veil of the *principium individuationis*. For the ego, as Schopenhauer
> explained by the myth of Maya's veil, makes even the insight into its depend-
> ence difficult to gain for the subjective consciousness. The principle of
> individualization, the law of particularity to which the universal reason in
> the individuals is tied, tends to insulate them from the encompassing
> contexts and thereby strengthens their flattering confidence in the subject's
> autarky.[5]

By facing a world populated by different individuals, none of whom
seems to be all-powerful and most of whom seem to have some degree of

---

4 ND, 6: 219/219; translation amended.
5 ND, 6: 218/219, see also ND, 6: 134, 215, 258ff., 271ff., 292/126, 215, 261ff., 275ff., 297;
  MM, 4: 15–16/17; PMP 1963, 182/122–3.

control over their lives (and are often held responsible for the way they exercise it), it becomes difficult, even near impossible, to see the real determining factors. Instead, our experience seems to present us with these individuals as making choices, often against society – and this suggests that they are not determined by it, or at least not to the extent that they lack freedom and autonomy altogether.

Adorno admits that in pursuing one's individual interests, one *feels free*, but he suggests that this feeling of freedom, ultimately, *is largely illusionary*, since the individuals sustain in their behaviour – in following their own interests (and especially in *just* following their own interests)[6] – a society which has its own immanent *telos*, to which it subordinates all human purposes:

> The individual feels free in so far as he has opposed himself to society and can do something – though incomparably less than he believes – against society and other individuals. His freedom is primarily that of a man pursuing his own ends, ends that are not directly and totally exhausted by social ends. In this sense, freedom coincides with the principle of individuation. A freedom of this type has broken loose from primitive society; within an increasingly rational one, it has achieved a measure of reality. At the same time, in the midst of bourgeois society, freedom remains no less delusive than individuality itself. A critique of free will as well as of determinism means a critique of this delusion. The law of value comes into play over the heads of the formally free individuals. They are unfree, according to Marx's insight, as the involuntary executors of that law – the more thoroughly unfree, the more rank the growth of the social antagonisms it took to form the very conception of freedom. The process of evolving individual independence is a function of the exchange society and terminates in the individual's abolition by integration.[7]

Adorno alludes here to society's *telos*, of which we are the mere executioners, in terms of the law of value. As already indicated in Chapter 1, strictly speaking this law within Marxist theory just concerns the equivalence of the value of commodities with the socially necessary labour-time required to produce them. Yet, Adorno seems to use it as a placeholder for the market-mediated drive to maximise surplus-value within capitalism and thereby for a much more general phenomenon: the means-end

---

6 See PMP 1956/7 (unpublished), Vo1333.

7 ND, 6: 259/261–2, translation amended; see also HF, 11–12/5–6. Adorno's claim that individual freedom has only reality as formal freedom is reminiscent of Marx's discussion of rights and freedoms in 'On the Jewish Question' [1844], MEW 1956–90, I: 347–77/ MECW 1975–2005, III: 146–74.

reversal characteristic of our social world. Human purposes, including self-preservation of the species, are only taken care of, if they are taken care of at all, as a by-product of the pursuit of surplus-value maximisation. What developed as a way of securing human needs has become an end in itself, using human needs (both real ones and the artificial ones capitalism creates) for its own purposes (see Chapter 1).

It is important to realise that, on Adorno's picture, society impinges on the freedom of the individual in a double sense. Externally we are restricted by the demands of a totalised exchange society, and the various political forms that go with it. We are in this respect, as Adorno puts it on various occasions, mere 'appendages of the machine'.[8] Concrete ways in which we experience this external restriction are the pressures involved in finding paid employment, or indeed the various other market pressures we face. Moreover, and this is the second sense, society determines the individual also internally. As Adorno puts it in a passage already quoted earlier, 'Society destines the individuals to be what they are, even by their *immanent genesis*.'[9] This social constitution of individuals reaches into the very depths of the self:

> Even where men are most likely to feel free from society, in the strength of their ego, they are society's agents at the same time. The ego principle is implanted in them by society and society rewards that principle although it curbs it.[10]

If Adorno is right about this, then it provides another piece in the puzzle of explaining why individuals do not immediately recognise the way society restricts their freedom: they have internalised this restriction so much, it has become so much their second nature, that they struggle to see it as the alien, heteronomous imposition it is.[11]

Still, it is not the case that these internalisations of domination leave no trace. Just the opposite, the high prevalence of individual patholo-gies (Adorno, following Freud, talks especially of neuroses) and collec-tive pathologies (most notably various forms of racist, anti-Semitic, or nationalist group behaviour) within capitalism are a clear index of the reality of unfreedom.[12] Pathological states indicate that our

---

8 See, for example, MM, 4: 13/15; PMP 1956/7 (unpublished), Vo1378.
9 ND, 6: 218/219; my emphasis; see also 272/276.
10 ND, 6: 292/297; see also 239, 272/241, 276.
11 See, for example, Adorno 1974: 262–3.
12 See, for example, ND, 6: 221–2, 293/222, 298; see also Whitebook 2003: 701.

inner self is not the realm of freedom that we normally suppose it to be.[13] If reflected upon, these states show us that our freedom is, in fact, a form of domination.

Moreover, it is also important to note that Adorno is far from advocating the nominally socialist regimes of his day as a superior alternative to the capitalist West. He either speaks of them in the same breath as both instantiations of domination – such as when he says in one of his lectures that progress towards freedom 'is impossible because of the increasingly dense texture of society *in both East and West*; the growing concentration of the economy, the executive and the bureaucracy has advanced to such an extent that people are reduced more and more to the status of functions'.[14] Alternatively, he emphasises that the capitalist West has at least formal freedoms, which makes it clearly preferable to the direct forms of domination and repression practised in the nominally socialist East.[15] Indeed, it is no accident that Adorno (and Horkheimer) took refuge in the USA (not the USSR) in the 1930s and 1940s, and moved not to East, but to West Germany after the war.

Also, it is worth emphasising that Adorno does not hold a conspiracy theory where small elites direct the self-sustaining society for their benefit. While he would certainly not deny that there are elites that benefit more than other groups from the modern social world – whether it be capitalist or nominally socialist – he would view this as a side-effect of impersonal, structural domination, and reject conspiracy theories, premised as they are on personal domination. Indeed, in one of his lectures, he emphasises clearly an old Marxist point about ruling elites as mere instantiations of functions:

> Mankind has reached a point today where even those on the commanding heights cannot enjoy their positions because even these have been

---

13 As Adorno puts it at one point: 'All truth content of neuroses is that the I has its unfreedom demonstrated to it, within itself, by something alien to it, the feeling that "this isn't me at all"; [demonstrated] there, where its rule over inner nature fails' (ND, 6: 221/222; translation amended).

14 HF, 11–12/5. Much more would have to be said about the nominally socialist regimes. For even if they are also self-perpetuating systems of domination, they fit differently into Adorno's general schema than capitalism – after all, it is less clear that surplus-value maximisation is as ingrained in their social fabric. Still, for Adorno the two types of regime would be structurally similar at least insofar as they are systems of organising human beings in the pursuit of self-preservation that have taken on a life of their own, such that human purposes are subordinated to the system's blind *teloi* (see also here, Chapter 1).

15 See, for example, 'Die UdSSR und der Frieden' [1950], co-authored with Horkheimer, 20.1: 390–3.

whittled away to the point where they are merely functions of their own function. Even captains of industry spend their time working through mountains of documents and shifting them from one side of their desk to the other, instead of ignoring office hours and reflecting in freedom. Were they to pursue the latter course, their business would collapse in chaos.[16]

In this way, even the elites are not actually in control; even their freedom 'is reduced to the possibility of sustaining one's own life' within the narrow confines of a dominating social world.[17]

To summarise, we *feel* free in following what we perceive as our interests, but are *in fact* unfree, and this unfreedom is also experienced in the form of social pressures which narrow down and shape our options of choice. In this way, the antinomy of freedom is not about two opposing theoretical positions – say, as with Kant, between one position that excludes causality of freedom and one that requires it. Rather, the antinomy of freedom is the expression of two ways of experiencing oneself, namely as both free and unfree.[18]

There is another way to bring out Adorno's point that society governs the individual (both internally and externally) to such an extent that individual freedom is radically undermined. Adorno objects to the idea that freedom would be exhausted by choosing within pre-given options or situations.[19] The reason he objects to this is that often such situations have already built-in coercion, as is – ironically – illustrated by some of the famous examples about human freedom. Adorno refers especially to two authors: (a) Kant, with his well-known gallows example, and (b) Sartre, whose examples are often situated in fascism; and he criticises both of them for failing to adequately acknowledge the coercive character of having to choose between the unchosen alternatives in question.[20] It might be unavoidable that elements of our situation of choice are unchosen, but we lose track of an important dimension of freedom (and an important aspect of unfreedom) if

---

16 HF, 12/6.   17 Ibid.   18 See ND, 6: 294/299.

19 See, for example, 6: 225 and n./226 and n.; PMP 1956/7 (unpublished), Vo1332.

20 See ND, 6: 225 and n./226 and n.; for a similar complaint about Kierkegaard, see 2: 56–7, 249–50). Part of what Adorno objects to here is that such examples present the misleading picture that coercive situations are the '*condition humaine*' (ND, 6: 225 and n./226 and n.). While Adorno might accept that currently the state of freedom is mainly characterised by having to act within coercive situations, he denies that this need be true of all human societies.

we neglect to examine the option set and how it was generated. Specifically, the role of coercion and other potentially avoidable vitiating factors have to be reflected upon and we should aim to eliminate them, instead of using examples which contain them as paradigmatic instances of freedom.

Coercion can be built into situations both via external pressures (such as market forces) and via internalised domination (which, for example, might restrict our sense of possibility in such a way that we consider only certain options and not others). Thus, to give an example, a typical Marxist point (which Adorno accepts)[21] is that wage labourers in a capitalist economy do not have a real choice between selling their labour-power and not doing so, since not to do so would threaten their ability to survive (or, at least, make life very difficult for them). While this is a choice of some description, it is not a 'real' choice in that one of the two alternatives is hardly acceptable and the option set is due to social domination.[22] Thus, the question cannot just be how we relate to situations and alternatives, but also how far we can (at least jointly) control them. If one focuses merely on the individual choice, not the conditions of choosing, one has already let unfreedom in, before freedom – which is then merely illusionary – enters. Thus, without the freedom to change situations, we cannot really talk of freedom.[23] According to Adorno, our current society is not allowing us to change our situations (at least not fundamentally), but, rather, is petrifying them via external and internalised domination.

For Adorno, then, we live in an 'age of universal social repression',[24] in a 'state of universal dependency'.[25] Still, however inescapable the modern social world may present itself, the social domain does not in principle exclude freedom. While we can never be completely independent of influences by our social context, in a collectively self-governed society, these influences would not be an obstacle to our freedom – in fact, in such a society, they would be enabling.

21 See S, 8: 14/271–2.
22 The claim that freedom requires a range of acceptable options is defended also in recent literature on freedom and autonomy (see, for example, Raz 1986; Oshana 1998).
23 See: 'A free person would only be one who need not bow to any alternatives and under existing circumstances there is a touch of freedom in refusing to accept the alternatives. Freedom means to criticise and change situations, not to confirm them by deciding within their coercive structure' (ND, 6: 225 and n./226 and n.; translation amended).
24 ND, 6: 262/265.   25 PMP 1963, 261/176.

II Freedom is historical

We have seen that Adorno thinks that the current social world blocks individual freedom by governing us against our own interests behind our backs. Now, while social determination blocks freedom, it is also important to realise that it is *social*, rather than natural determination that stands in freedom's way. Thus, although Adorno conceives the social reality surrounding us as universally deterministic, there is an important difference to determination by nature. If nature is really deterministic, then this is not self-imposed, but something true and independent of our behaviour (individually or collectively).[26] The universal determination by society is, on the other hand, self-imposed, albeit not individually, but rather collectively. It is not a necessary fact about humans that they have to live in an unfree society – or, at least, so Adorno claims. It is not necessary, since freedom depends on objective conditions which can change. The objective conditions for freedom might be missing or blocked at some stage, but they could develop, and what blocks them could be overcome in order to make freedom possible. Thus, even if a society is controlling its members and restricting their freedom, such a society and its determination are still something brought about and reproduced by the people making up this society.[27] The individuals might not realise this, but they sustain the society which subordinates them. Moreover, since society is dependent on the cooperation of its members, they could refuse to offer this cooperation.

Following on from this, freedom – both individual and social – is for Adorno fundamentally historical. If freedom depends on the state of society and certain objective conditions of material production, then it is natural to presume that freedom is historical in that the state of freedom might change. In fact, this is true both of the concept of freedom and its realisation (both individually and socially). In a crucial passage, Adorno writes:

> By no means, however, did it occur to Kant whether freedom itself – to him, an eternal idea – might not be essentially historic, and that not just as

26 Even in the Kantian story, where the universal determination of each event by natural causality is in some sense self-imposed, it is not self-imposed in the sense that we could change it, but a necessary and a priori condition for having experiences.

27 Recall the passage quoted earlier to the effect that the externality to which we are beholden is upheld by ourselves (ND, 6: 219/219).

a concept but in its empirical substance. Whole epochs, whole societies lacked not only the concept of freedom but the thing... Before the formation of the individual in the modern sense, which to Kant was a matter of course – in the sense meaning not simply the biological human being, but the one constituted as a unit by its own self-reflection, the Hegelian 'self-consciousness' – it is an anachronism to talk of freedom, whether as a reality or as a challenge. Likewise, freedom, which without impairment can only be achieved under social conditions of unfettered plenty, might be wholly extinguished again, perhaps without leaving a trace.[28]

Rather than being an eternal idea (as Kant had it), freedom both as a concept and as reality has been absent for much of human history. The concept of individual freedom really came into its own only – at least so Adorno claims here – once the modern self, the self-reflecting individual, had developed. Even then its actualisation, freedom's reality, was rather limited – elsewhere, Adorno speaks of a liberal phase of capitalism, in which 'The individual was free as an economically active bourgeois subject, free to the extent to which the economic system required him to be autonomous in order to function.'[29] In short, it was mainly the freedom of the bourgeois entrepreneur, along with the 'freedom' of the workers to sell their labour-power (which, as Marx pointed out, included both the legal freedom from serfdom and the fact that workers no longer commanded means of production). For Adorno, only in a free society could the individual be genuinely free,[30] but a free society is only possible once certain objective conditions obtain ('under social conditions of unfettered plenty') and once we have collectively taken conscious control of these conditions. In this way, individual freedom had to develop, become partially realised, and could only be fully actualised in a possible society of the future, but could also disappear again.[31]

---

28 ND, 6: 217–18/218; see also ND, 6: 218–19, 259, 293–4/219, 262, 298–9; 10.2: 492–3/CM, 34; PMP 1956/7 (unpublished), Vo1307, 1488.

29 ND, 6: 259/262.

30 As he says about individual freedom at some point, 'It necessarily presupposes the freedom of all, and cannot even be conceived as an isolated thing, that is, in the absence of social freedom' (PMP 1963, 261–2/176, see also ND, 6: 261, 271, 272, 294/264, 275, 276, 299; PMP 1956/7 (unpublished), Vo1336).

31 In both the social and historical rendering of freedom, Adorno's treatment of the issue is clearly influenced by Hegel (see also Dews 2008: 189). For a recent discussion of Hegel's view of freedom that brings out these two aspects clearly, see Pippin 2008.

III The (political) quest for freedom

One consequence of this view is that the full realisation of individual freedom becomes intertwined with the possibility of overcoming the current society. Thinking about freedom leads for Adorno to politics, not merely to a morality for individuals. In this sense it becomes a collective problem.[32] If freedom requires a free society, then the quest for freedom requires the quest for a free society and so becomes a political quest.[33]

Yet, the political quest is beset by problems. The quest to establish the social conditions necessary for freedom seems to be undermined by the lack of freedom at the individual level. Put differently, what is necessary for having individual freedom (social freedom) seems to require individual freedom to bring it about. Adorno seems to have landed himself in an inextricable dead-end.

He is not unaware of this problem. In fact, one finds many statements in Adorno's texts that express pessimism about whether the current society could be overcome. Often, Adorno portrays this society as having total control over individuals[34] – and this would suggest that we are inextricably caught in the web of unfreedom. Moreover, Adorno points out that freedom is so radically restricted by society that the (political) quest for a free society can make things worse.[35] Presumably, it could make things worse because one can overlook the difficulty of the problem and thereby reproduce or even cement what one set out to oppose, while causing suffering in the process. In general, Adorno is worried about how much society overwhelms us, and its ability to integrate even what opposes it. Good intentions alone will not protect against actions misfiring, and this is true also of inaction. As Adorno puts it at one point, 'Whatever an individual or a group may undertake against the totality they are part of is infected by the evil of that totality; and no less infected

32 The problem turns into a collective problem in the sense that it cannot be solved at an individual level. Indeed, not even the negative effects on individuals of society's domination could be removed at an individual level, according to Adorno. He was very critical of Freud's later writings, in which (he thinks that) Freud tended towards accepting the belief that the individuals could actually achieve a well-integrated, reconciled self through psychoanalytic treatment on an individual basis. Adorno does not think that the psyche commands the means necessary for this (see Whitebook 2003: 688).

33 PMP 1963, 262/176; see also ND, 6: 294/299; and Menke 2005: esp. 45–8. Menke also points to the problems of the political quest, on which I comment in the next paragraph and, at greater length, in Freyenhagen 2012 (unpublished).

34 See, for example, ND, 6: 271/274; PMP 1956/7 (unpublished), V01378.

35 See, for example, ND, 6: 292/297.

is he who does nothing at all.'[36] That free action is demanded and yet blocked is the dilemma of our current situation for Adorno.

At the same time, one should keep in mind that Adorno's portrayals of our current social world are meant as exaggerations (in the sense of presenting what are often mere tendencies as fully unfolded reality). One reason for this procedure of exaggerating the state of unfreedom is that Adorno thought that often we can only bring the truth into relief by exaggeration.[37] Presumably, overstating one's case can shake people out of their slumber into which society and its manipulative mechanisms have put them. As Adorno puts it memorably in *Minima Moralia*, 'The splinter in your eye is the best magnifying glass.'[38]

Furthermore, Adorno never ceased to talk about the possibility of a free society, and this is partly because of broadly Marxist considerations.[39] According to Hegel and Marx, freedom is something which can only be realised once certain objective conditions have been established. In Hegel's case, these conditions consist in a highly developed level of rationality achieved both at the level of thought (especially in philosophy) and at the institutional level (state and societal organisation). In Marx's case (and Adorno follows him on this point), the objective conditions of freedom concern much more the development of the forces of production than rationality (although the two are obviously not unrelated: a developed state of rationality comes with, and helps towards, a developed state of the productive forces). Before a certain level of production is reached, freedom is impossible. For Marx and Adorno, the minimum level of production necessary for freedom is not just the point of subsistence economy. Rather, only once each of us is freed from the necessity of material production to a considerable extent, can we become really free (recall the earlier passage about the need for 'social conditions of unfettered plenty').[40] Moreover, Adorno makes the point

---

36 ND, 6: 241/243, translation amended.
37 See, for example, DE, 3: 139/118; MWTP, 10.2: 567/99.
38 MM, Aphorism No. 29.
39 One other reason for this is that he claims that complete or absolute despair is unthinkable (ND, 6: 395–6/403–4). Perhaps, what Adorno means here is that as long as we can still *think* that there is absolute despair, such despair has not yet materialised.
40 However, there is disagreement about when this level has been reached, with Adorno suggesting that, *pace* Hegel and Marx, a free and rational society was possible much earlier in human history (see, for example, HF, 100/67–8). Nonetheless, Adorno admits that the emergence of freedom, even its mere concept, required a stage of unfreedom, coercion, and domination of nature (ND, 6: 150, 262/147, 265; HF, 72, 82, 287–8/47–8, 55, 208; see also here, Chapter 2).

that objectively speaking the development level of the productive forces would allow – here and now – a universal satisfaction of basic needs with a minimum of human labour.[41] Admittedly, this would require a radical re-organisation of society, specifically a change in how the productive forces are used and controlled. This radical re-organisation would signify that human beings had taken conscious control of their fate for the first time, since for Adorno – following Marx – most of human development so far has been quasi-natural [*naturwüchsig*] and blind.[42]

One might wonder, if the objective conditions for freedom exist, why freedom has not been realised yet. It would lead too far here to investigate a full Adornian answer to this question, but an important clue is provided by the following claim: 'There has been as much free will as people wanted to free themselves.'[43] Among other things, this brings out that for Adorno one of the main obstacles to freedom is false consciousness or ideology. False consciousness blocks people from realising that they live in unfreedom and that they have to free themselves. Thinking wrongly about the nature of unfreedom does in fact contribute to making it real in the first place. It is by mistaking social reality for naturally grown and unchangeably fixed reality – by viewing society as second nature – that this reality actually takes on these characteristics for the practical lives of individuals. Just as when a belief in god(s) or one's nation is sufficiently ingrained in social practices and institutions for it actually to have reality in people's life (for example, in terms of punishment for transgression of the religious code, or in having certain feelings when one's national sports team wins), a belief in the inevitability of the modern world can have similarly real consequences, even though it is – at another level – a mistaken belief.[44] False consciousness makes it possible for society to sustain itself by making us believe in the illusion that we are inextricably caught up within it. Unfreedom is human-made; it is not blind fate or nature, much as it might present itself in this way. Reflection upon our predicament would be the first

---

41 See ND, 6: 207, 218, 275, 390, 395/207, 218, 278–9, 398, 403; 7: 55–6/2004: 41.

42 See, for example, 8: 306–7.

43 ND, 6: 262/265, translation amended; see also PMP 1956/7 (unpublished), Vo1487–8.

44 Another way of putting this is by using Hegel's distinction between reality as mere existence and reality as actuality, as the realisation of essence. A three-legged dog is no less real than a four-legged one, but it is less actual in Hegel's sense; believing that one has an interest in avoiding damnation by a vengeful god can have real existence in people's life, even if it is not in the actual interests of human beings.

and crucial step towards full freedom. For while unfreedom is real, we are ensuring its continuation by accepting it as such. It would be grossly oversimplified to say that for Adorno humans would just have to see through 'the spell [*der Bann*]'[45] to get rid of it. However, in realising that their freedom is collectively self-imposed, human beings can at least start resisting what they themselves sustain against their true interests and behind their own backs.

IV The negative freedom to resist unfreedom

This also highlights another aspect of the passage that 'There has been as much free will as people wanted to free themselves.'[46] In effect, what Adorno says is that in the form of negative freedom, as resistance against unfreedom, freedom can already begin appearing in the current social world, just by virtue of our reflecting on our predicament and mobilising our powers against it.[47]

Other passages confirm this. For example, Adorno writes: 'Freedom can be grasped in determinate negation only, corresponding to the concrete form of unfreedom. Positively it becomes an "as if".'[48] Adorno invokes here Kant's distinction between negative and positive freedom, against whom this claim is partly directed. In Kant, negative freedom is the independence from determination by our (natural) impulses, while positive freedom consists in the ability to give ourselves a law, in autonomy.[49] While Adorno does not accept Kant's specification of the two forms of freedom in its entirety, it is a good indication of what Adorno does accept. Negative freedom consists for him in the ability to resist determination, although not by our natural impulses so much as – one

---

45 LCoIS, 8: 370/Adorno 2003a: 125.   46 ND, 6: 262/265; translation amended.

47 This aspect of Adorno's view is rarely, if ever, recognised and appreciated in the secondary literature. One exception is O'Connor 2012, who speaks of 'autonomy as resistance', whereas I would insist (with Adorno) that negative freedom of resistance falls short of autonomy.

48 ND, 6: 230/231; translation amended; see also ND, 6: 154, 222, 231, 239/151, 223, 232, 241; PMP 1956/7 (unpublished), Vo1488. It is noteworthy that even the 'addendum' (i.e., the physical impulses which are a constitutive part of spontaneity for Adorno; see Appendix), is conceived in negative terms as the – in Bernstein's words – 'excrescence of the pure will' (2001: 256). What the addendum points to, a reconciliation with nature, is not yet conceivable and will be only conceivable if we view nature differently, which – as we saw – is connected for Adorno with a different society.

49 See G, 4: 447–8; KpV, 5: 33.

presumes – by society (whether in form of external or internalised pressures). Something of this sort of freedom is available in our modern social world. On the other hand, positive freedom, understood as actively determining one's life (rather than merely reacting to, and resisting, external pressures), is not possible within it. Such freedom could only be realised in a free society – as noted before: individual self-determination would require collective self-determination of a sort impossible in the social world.[50] In fact, Adorno thinks that to talk of positive freedom as existing is to help entrench its non-existence. The reason for this is that the illusion of individual autonomy plays an important part, in the form of ideology, in sustaining the unfree society that Adorno thinks we are in today.[51]

In a sense, Adorno is here making again the point that freedom is historical and social, for whether there is freedom and what kind of freedom there is depends on the socio-historical context and what it enables or blocks. Consider:

> What is decisive in the ego, its independence and autonomy can be judged only in relation to its otherness, to the non-ego. Whether or not there is autonomy depends upon its adversary and antithesis, on the object which either grants or denies autonomy to the subject. Detached from the object, autonomy is fictitious.[52]

Instead of talking about autonomy of human beings as such (as Kant does in his moral philosophy), we have to analyse the concrete forms of unfreedom, to conceptualise freedom 'as the polemical counter-image to the suffering under social compulsion, unfreedom as its mirror-image'.[53] As we have seen, Adorno thinks of the current forms of unfreedom as almost all-encompassing, as leaving no room for positive freedom, for autonomy.

Still, there remain chinks in the armour of the self-sustaining society, and these make possible determinate negations – the negative freedom of resistance, in the first instance, and possibly eventually the freedom

---

50 Indeed, given that positive freedom has never been realised before, our notion of it is seriously impoverished, for we cannot anticipate what this realisation would entail. This is another sense in which to talk of positive freedom is problematic, and we have only access to negative freedom – for we know what unfreedom is and some of the ways to resist it. Adorno is a (substantive and epistemic) negativist also about freedom.

51 See, for example, ND, 6: 218, 231/219, 232.

52 ND, 6: 222/223; see also 262/265.

53 ND, 6: 222/223; Redmond's translation used; see also HF, 243/174.

required for a radical transformation. Despite society's becoming more and more an integrated whole (a totality), it remains in Adorno's eyes antagonistic and characterised by ruptures.[54] The importance of this for the continuing possibility of freedom is expressed very clearly in a letter by Adorno to Horkheimer (dated 31 December 1962), in which he writes that 'As long as the world remains antagonistic and itself perpetuates contradictions, the possibility of changing it will be a legacy.'[55] Moreover, the impetus towards negative freedom also arises from the fact that the individual's material needs are largely unsatisfied by modern society.[56] Indeed, partly as a consequence of this, the full integration of them into society has not yet succeeded.[57]

Admittedly, there is no guarantee that the ruptures within society or the unsatisfied needs will translate into resistance to society's integrating tendencies, rather than into pogroms or other pathologies. Still, the fact that there are these ruptures and unsatisfied needs leaves it at least open that there could be critical individuals capable of reflecting on the society that produces them and of resisting this society at least in some spheres of their lives.

These critical individuals would have to be extremely vigilant and careful in their endeavours to spread the critical spirit and to resist social determination (see also Chapter 6). They would have to be vigilant and careful in order not to accidentally contribute to the reproduction of unfreedom, after all – a danger with which Adorno was very concerned. The critical individuals might not be successful in what they resist, but their becoming conscious of the possibility of freedom would be the first step towards making it actual. In other words, something of the freedom which only pertains to humans in a free society is already anticipated in the actions of those who resist.[58] Specifically, negative freedom – the freedom to resist – seems to be something which we are capable of, at least sometimes and to some extent.

---

54 See, for example, ND, 6: 395–6/403–4; 8: 194; 10.2: 655/CM, 175.
55 Quoted in Wiggershaus 1994: 556.
56 See, for example, ND, 6: 99/92. Here Adorno's materialism comes to the fore. Freedom and hope for a just society rest for him on our material needs. As he expressed it once, 'The metaphysical interests of humanity need the unrestricted recognition of their material [ones]' (ND, 6: 391/398, translation amended).
57 See also 8: 92; and 10.2: 655/CM, 175. Adorno sometimes suggests that the potential for resistance is particularly great in those areas or countries that are least advanced in their capitalist development – such as, in remote mountainous regions (HF, 13/6; see also 8: 92).
58 See ND, 6: 292/297.

v A crisis in moral practice

Morality, Adorno once said in a lecture, depends on the degree of free-dom: in a concentration camp, the claim that there is (positive) freedom is an empty claim; in this context, there is no moral autonomy.[59] As we saw in this chapter, the current state of freedom is, according to Adorno, one largely characterised by unfreedom. Modern society governed by the law of value is so overwhelming and overpowering, that individual freedom is generally undermined and threatened. Freedom turns for Adorno into a 'borderline value'.[60] And this has a crucial implication: morality itself is threatened. However, this implication needs to be under-stood correctly – it is not the case that there are no longer any moral demands, but that the practice of morality has become problematic and to some extent over-demanding for the individual. This is part of what Adorno means in saying that there is no right living in our current social world (see also Chapter 2), and might be dubbed the 'Crisis of Moral Practice Thesis'.

There is a common sense association of freedom with (moral) respon-sibility. Some philosophers deny this link.[61] Still, if someone's freedom is severely impaired (for example, if their brain has been damaged in a car accident, or, arguably, even if they are a drug addict), then we view him or her, at least for the time being, as incapable of moral agency and thereby as no longer responsible.

In a similar way, Adorno is prepared to bite the bullet and say that we are so caught up in a web of unfreedom that what is morally demanded is – at least in part – something that goes beyond what we are individually capable of doing. He writes:

> The individual who deems him or herself to be morally safe fails and participates in guilt, because, being harnessed to the social order, he or she has virtually no power over the conditions which appeal to the ethical [*sittliche*] *ingenium*: crying for their change.[62]

Elsewhere he claims that in the current social world 'no individual is capable of the morality that is a social demand but would be reality only

---

59 PMP 1956/7 (unpublished), Vo1 307. This is not to say that there are no moral choices to be made in the camps. As I go on to say in the main text, moral demands exist for Adorno despite the absence of autonomy, and we should use our freedom of resistance to live as decently as possible.

60 ND, 6: 271/274.   61 See, notably, Frankfurt 1969.

62 ND, 6: 241/243; translation amended.

in a free society';[63] that we must question our moral categories because the current level of freedom is so minimal;[64] that, given the dominion of society over individuals, it is not clear whether moral terms are still meaningful or the moral sphere has not been abolished;[65] that moral practice becomes increasingly problematic with the decline in self-determination in the life of the individual;[66] and that 'morality [*Moral*] is over-demanding' because the individuals are no longer sufficiently independent.[67] He even goes as far as to claim in one of his lectures that humans are, so to speak, beyond morality and immorality;[68] and in *Negative Dialectics* he identifies society, not the individual's choices, as the root cause of the radical evil in the current world.[69]

Adorno laments the fact that moral practice is in crisis – in fact, he thinks it is an objective contradiction of our time that morality is both almost impossible because of radically diminished individual freedom and at the same time required. Basically, Adorno thinks that because of our unfreedom we are not in the position to live a moral life, that is, we are unable to live in such a way as morality would require. The best we can hope for is not (morally) right living, but mere decency (and even that is hard to come by).[70] The difference between the two is that while right living is for Adorno a matter of impossibility because whatever we do we become guilty of sustaining the badness of the current world, he does not deny that there is space for living the wrong life more or less wrongly (see Chapter 2). It is here where decency comes in. Decency is basically *the least bad level of living possible within our radically evil social world*. The details of what is required for decency – adherence to the new categorical imperative and Adorno's ethics of resistance – are discussed later (see Chapters 5–6). The key point here is that avoiding direct participation in any gross misconduct, resisting joining in where we can, and mitigating as much as possible the bads produced by our social world are moral aims individuals can actually achieve in our current social world, albeit that even achieving them is insufficient for right living.

---

63 ND, 6: 294/299.   64 PMP 1963, 147/98–9.   65 HF, 285–6/207.
66 PMP 1956/7 (unpublished), Vo1307–8.
67 PMP 1956/7 (unpublished), Vo1376–7.
68 PMP 1956/7 (unpublished), Vo1378–9.
69 See: 'The trouble is not that free men do radical evil, as evil is being done beyond all measure conceivable to Kant; the trouble is that as yet there is no world in which ... men would no longer need to be evil' (ND, 6: 218/218–19).
70 See PMP 1963, 173, 248/116, 167.

Thus, the claim that we cannot live a morally right life under current conditions of unfreedom is not to say that we cannot fulfil some of what the rules of etiquette demand of us (such as courtesy), or that we cannot have some personal character traits (such as honesty or courage) which were traditionally associated with ethical behaviour. Rather, the point is that such behaviour is *insufficient* for constituting a morally right life. It is insufficient, firstly, because we live in an age of moral catastrophe (or, at least, the constant threat of it), and behaving in a socially acceptable way is just not enough under these circumstances. In fact, following the rules of etiquette (or other social norms) is not only insufficient for moral life, but is to some extent even *contrary* to it. Socially acceptable behaviour is not changing anything about the social setting which undermines the possibility of freedom and thereby moral life. Consequently, such behaviour is – however inadvertently – helping to sustain and cement a countermoral system.

What is clear from these considerations is that Adorno is *not* claiming that there are no longer moral demands, but, rather, that many of these demands cannot be realised any more by individuals. In fact, the explanation of why the individuals cannot live a moral life any more relies on the discrepancy between what is morally demanded (changing the social world) and what the individuals are capable of (limited forms of resistance to it).

To change our current social conditions of unfreedom is a moral demand first of all because this unfreedom undermines individual autonomy and morality, so that a change of society is in fact the necessary condition for morality to become actual.[71] In this sense, the demand for social change is a moral demand to put in place the conditions of morality, and it is the first and foremost moral demand. For without it, there can be no others. Moreover, changing our social world is not only a moral demand because this would realise the conditions for morality, but also because the current state of unfreedom is characterised by other fundamental evils (see Chapters 1–2). In particular, the modern social world produced Auschwitz. More generally, the current social world produces evil continuously, by undermining our freedom, by relying on depersonalisation and exploitation, by neglecting our material needs, and by causing physical and psychological suffering as well as by leading to political and economic crises with their knock-on effects such as war and racism. In this sense, we can see now why we live in conditions

---

71 See also Menke 2005: 46–7.

of a moral catastrophe (and why, hence, socially acceptable behaviour is both insufficient and to some extent countermoral). We live in such conditions in the double way just indicated. Firstly, it is presumably morally extremely problematic to live under conditions where morality itself is blocked, when it would be a real possibility to actualise it under different social conditions. Secondly, the social world which blocks morality also produces evil, sometimes (as in Auschwitz) of a very radical nature. What morality requires today, namely to realise the conditions for it and to change the radically evil world, is something which is largely blocked by the state of morality itself, by our not being capable of leading moral lives. In this sense, morality itself is in what looks like an anti-nomical state: it cannot guarantee that we are capable of fulfilling what it demands.[72]

Adorno's view has two related ramifications. Firstly, not the individuals, but only humanity as a whole stands under moral obligation and can be blamed for failing to meet the demands of morality. Only collectively could we lift ourselves out of the state of unfreedom – only as 'global subject' can humanity make genuine progress and avert 'the most extreme, total disaster';[73] and only collectively can we be blamed for not doing so (I return to this in Section VI and Chapter 6). Secondly, this means that morality is currently over-demanding. What it asks of each of us is something we do not seem to be capable of, at least not as (isolated) individuals.

Thus, while moral demands survive in some form, there is a crisis in the moral practice of individuals. Living a moral life is, as we saw in Chapter 2, not an available option for individuals currently. Now, we can also see better why this is the case. Firstly, the social world – as we already saw in some detail in this chapter – dominates us so thoroughly that it does not leave us much room (if any) to resist it. Most of us are so thoroughly integrated that we have neither the will, nor the opportunity to mount resistance. Those who are able to ward off the pressures to join in, can do so only on few occasions and have to rely on the general context of domination even in trying to withstand it.[74] Thus, at best, we might be able to react to a certain form of repression and attempt to oppose it. Yet, even if this form of negative freedom is still sometimes

---

72 This brings it in conflict with the Kantian idea that ought implies can. I consider this worry in Chapter 5.

73 P, 10.2: 618/CM, 144.

74 The ability to be critical becomes a privilege (ND, 6: 51/41; see also MM, §6; and here, Chapter 6).

available to us, any positive freedom is completely beyond us. It is not up to us to really *lead* our lives in the sense of actively choosing a certain form of living; we are not autonomous. In this sense, there can be no right living, because we always fall short in respect of resisting wrong life and because we lack altogether the capacity for building a life over and above what is involved in resisting wrong life. Thus, while we fail completely on the latter count, we also do so on the former one – for our resistance is always too little unless and until the social world is changed (which is not something an individual alone can achieve).

Secondly, our lack of freedom has a negative effect on the possibility of individual moral practice also in a more indirect way. Our unfreedom does not just manifest itself in our not being able to act in the ways which morality requires. It is also the case, according to Adorno, that what morality requires specifically of the individual in a particular situation is often no longer sufficiently obvious. Beyond the antinomical structure of our lives already described in Chapter 2, the reason for this is that we live in a society which we do not consciously control, but which controls us and our actions in often not very transparent ways. The incentive structures, causal mechanisms, and institutional arrangements are all geared towards the survival of the current social world, and, hence, work against any thinking or acting which would aim at change. We cannot rely on our social life to provide us with the right kind of background for moral actions: neither the right kind of sensitivity, nor the right kinds of information are available to us; and the social roles and responsibilities we are pressed into are morally suspect. Most of our reactive dispositions have been undermined by the collapse of traditional societies. Also, the world has become too complex and opaque for identifying causal factors, likely consequences, and clearly defined responsibilities.[75] Moreover, society has determined us so thoroughly in our constitution that even the way we think and react has been co-opted. We are largely unable to think outside the given social possibilities and options, which are too limited to provide genuine possibilities to act in the way morality requires. Similarly, we are deceived about our real interests and about the way we share these interests with others, undermining further our ability to see things in the right light and react appropriately.

It is worth emphasising once more that Adorno is *not* saying that there is nothing the individual can and should do. Morally right living might

---

75 PMP 1963, 147–8, 173, 232/98–9, 116, 156; see also ND, 6: 241/243; and Menke 2005: esp. 41–3.

not be possible any more, but – as already indicated – it is still possible to lead a decent life, to live, as Adorno put it once, 'so that one may believe oneself to have been a good animal'.[76] What he means here will become clearer in the discussion of these issues in Chapters 5–6, but the basic idea is to avoid acting wrongly as much as possible. Right living might be impossible, but living less wrongly is still open.

This way of conceiving individual morality brings Adorno into conflict with much of modern moral philosophy, suggesting (as it tends to do) that it can provide clear guidance on morally right living and that such living is possible to achieve. Indeed, it is part of the Enlightenment outlook that, at least in principle, everybody has at their disposal the capacities for living rightly – moral rightness and virtue are no longer reserved for only aristocrats, priests, or other elites. Before I discuss Adorno's critique of modern moral philosophy in the next chapter, I want to take up one more issue affected by the loss of autonomy and the crisis of moral practice: individual responsibility.

VI To punish or not to punish: an objective antagonism

On Adorno's view, individuals seem to be absolved from moral or criminal responsibility – after all, they are destined by society to be the kind of persons they are and other than moments of resistance (themselves more due to fortune than individual merit and fortitude) they are incapable of even partially meeting the demands of morality. Yet, this view might seem objectionable for two reasons. Firstly, it seems deeply implausible that no one is responsible at all any more in the modern world. Even if one were to accept that society impinges strongly on our choices, one would want to keep at least a limited notion of responsibility. To take an example pertinent to Adorno's own views, there is a lot of historical evidence that suggests that individual soldiers in the German army or individual police officers could have refused to participate in the mass executions of Jews and Soviet prisoners of war.[77] Hence, when they did participate, they should have been held responsible for it. Secondly, it seems that Adorno's own statements on responsibility and punishment commit him to the view that responsibility is still available in some sense. Hence, there seem to be work-immanent as well as

76 ND, 6: 294/299; translation amended; see also PMP 1963, 173, 248/116, 167.
77 See, for example, the seminal study by Browning 1992.

independent reasons for objecting to the Crisis of Moral Practice Thesis, if it absolves individuals of responsibility.

Let me consider first more closely Adorno's comments on responsibility and punishment. It is true that Adorno sometimes sounds as if he would be willing to accept that responsibility has to be given up. For example, he thinks it is society, not individuals, which is the root cause of radical evil.[78] Similarly, he cautions against accepting individual freedom independently of the social conditions, for doing so might lead to people being unfairly held responsible for what society destined them to do.[79] Specifically, he objects to Kant's conception of freedom on the grounds that it would allow holding psychopaths responsible and punishing them instead of viewing them as not fully responsible agents.[80] In particular, as long as freedom is ascribed to us in virtue of our intelligible character alone, then it seems possible to hold people responsible, and punish them accordingly, however determined they might be as empirical selves.[81] The Kantian construction of transcendental freedom induces people to feel guilty, while their determination by society means that they are not guilty.[82] In this way, the doctrine of the intelligible character is criticised by Adorno for having 'made an essential contribution to the alliance between the idea of freedom and real unfreedom'.[83]

At the same time, Adorno seems to want to hold on to the thought of being able to punish evil-doers. For example, he admits that 'According to every psychological insight even Hitler and his monsters were slaves to their early childhood, products of mental mutilation'. Yet, he also maintains that 'the few one managed to catch must not be acquitted lest the crime ... be repeated ad infinitum'.[84]

---

78 See notably ND, 6: 218/218–19 – quoted in n. 69 of this chapter.
79 See ND, 6: 214, 231, 252/215, 232, 255.   80 ND, 6: 287/291.
81 This criticism is also alluded to in the following, initially perplexing passage: Adorno objects that if one translated Kant's ethics into judgements about real people today, the ultimate criterion of people's moral worth would be 'how someone happens to be, thus their unfreedom' (ND, 6: 291/295; translation amended). His point is, presumably, that the idea of transcendental freedom props up the illusion that people could choose how they actually are, while it is, according to Adorno, society which makes them what they are (see: 'the intelligible character is a conceptual duplication of that second nature in which society casts the characters of all its members anyway' (ND, 6: 291/295); see also PMP 1956/7 (unpublished), Vo1 297). In this way, people are doubly punished: by being unfree and by being held responsible for what they do as unfree agents.
82 ND, 6: 221, 252/221, 255.   83 ND, 6: 290–1/295.
84 ND, 6: 261–2/264–5; see also ND, 6: 282/286.

While 'Hitler and his monsters' could be particularly difficult examples, Adorno wants to make a general point: there is a problem in holding people responsible and yet making allowances for the extent they are determined by society. This general problem becomes only more salient in cases of genocide. The incompatibility between the two elements of the problem is not a consequence of a mistake in thinking, but has its source in an 'objective antagonism'[85] – it reflects the real tension between the serious limitations on our freedom and responsibility, on the one hand, and the nonetheless existing moral norms, on the other.

Let me explain further. The objective antagonism is perhaps best thought of as one of the practical antinomies that make right living impossible (see also Chapter 2). In particular, it is an antinomy between the requirement for punishment and the fact that holding people responsible is unjustified because of the social determination to which they are subject. If it is such an antinomy and more specifically one that expresses our current predicament (not just at the level of theory but also in practice), it cannot be simply finessed away. For example, we could not simply read Adorno as wanting to divorce justification of punishment from talk about responsibility and adopting, for example, a Utilitarian defence of punishment in terms of deterrence.[86] Rather, Adorno's account of punishment must preserve the antinomy to reflect that it is a real one – put radically, any account of punishment that does not express the antinomy gets the facts wrong, specifically the fact of an objective antagonism. Our current social world is such that criminal justice cannot be institutionalised in a way that makes full sense – this is unacceptable and another reason to change this world, but as long as we are in this predicament, theory and practice have to acknowledge its antinomical structure, not pretend it does not exist or hide it.

---

85 ND, 6: 282/286; see also ND, 6: 261–2/264–5.
86 There are also textual grounds which speak against Adorno's having chosen this way out of the antinomy. To say that we should punish 'lest the crime (justified to the unconscious of the masses by the failure of lightening to strike from heaven) be repeated ad infinitum' (ND, 6: 261–2/264–5) might suggest a Utilitarian defence of punishment. Nonetheless, the sentence following on from this one (in the German original the same sentence) goes against this reading. Adorno comments that the apparent contradiction in conceding that 'Hitler and his monsters' were psychologically determined, while at the same time insisting on punishing them, is not something 'to be glossed over with artificial constructions such as a utilitarian necessity at odds with reason' (ND, 6: 262/265). Moreover, in another passage commenting on the same issue, Adorno speaks of the punishments as 'just atonement [Sühne]' (ND, 6: 282/286), which has clear retributivist overtones.

One way of preserving the antinomy that also fits Adorno's text is the following. We might have to read Adorno as saying that moral demands continue to exist, even though individuals are no longer capable of putting all of them into practice – to some extent, there will be oughts without the corresponding ability to adequately carry them out, oughts without cans (see also Chapter 5). If we were to accept this, then there is still a sense in which a wrongdoer has done something wrong. To hold them (or, at least, those who commit the greatest wrongs and evils) to account for this, even though they are no longer fully accountable for it, would be the expression of the continued existence of moral norms, such as, in this case, the norm of avoiding and condemning injustice. One way to see the need for such a view is to consider that not holding people to account would be like saying that no evil or wrong had occurred. This, however, would not be how we would want to describe what happened in the concentration camps; or even what happens in more ordinary cases of grave violations of bodily integrity and autonomy. Also, not punishing would lead to 'the continuation of the torture methods for which the collective unconscious is hoping anyway and for whose rationalization it lies in wait; this much of the theory of deterrence is certainly true'.[87] Not punishing the wrongdoers would thus fail to express that wrong was done, and this failure might lead to more wrong because it would create the impression that there is no justice to be violated any more – that now anything goes. In this sense, punishment is the appropriate response to someone's causing suffering and injustice – it expresses the badness of the act and our condemnation of it.[88] Still, this by itself is insufficient to put punishment on a secure footing, or to ground responsibility. Given that individuals are not sufficiently free to be fully obligated, holding people to account and punishing them is not completely justifiable. As expression of the condemnation of injustice, punishment is an appropriate response, but given our current predicament, appropriateness is insufficient for justification.[89]

---

87 ND, 6: 283/287; translation amended.

88 This point should not be understood to imply that the need to express justice is always going to be the driving motive of prosecutors. In an unfree society, there is no guarantee that the prosecutors operate with the appropriate motive. Yet, punishment could be demanded as expressive of justice, whether or not it is administered with this in mind.

89 This consideration allows us to make some sense of Adorno's claim that it would have been better to have shot the Nazi torturers straight away as well as those responsible for and supportive of them 'than putting a few on trial' (ND, 6: 282/286; see also MM, §33). As an expression of our condemnation of injustice, shooting them would have been the least inappropriate response, given that (1) the institution of punishment cannot be

In this way, Adorno adopts the following account of punishment. Given the unfreedom of the individual and the world as the source of the evil, punishment is not fully justifiable. Rather, and this is the crux of the objective contradiction, injustice demands that there is the institution of punishment (to express its badness and our condemnation of it) while, at the same time, there is no justification for this institution (as the individual is insufficiently free).

While this account of punishment respects the objective antinomy regarding punishment, it clashes with our common sense views about responsibility and punishment. We seem to think that individuals are responsible and blameworthy for most of their behaviour, and it seems doubtful that we would accept a blanket rejection of individual responsibility, even if we admitted that our social context is hugely influential in what kind of person we become.

However, against these views, Adorno would insist on the objective nature of the antinomy to which he points – on the fact that there is both a need to punish people and the impossibility of holding them (fully) responsible within a society dominating its members all the way down.[90] We are largely subscribing to illusions in our claims about individual freedom and responsibility. Moreover, our doing so helps to sustain the current social system, not least because these illusions lead us to lay the blame for much of the evil in the world today at the individuals's feet, while society is the root cause of this evil. Thus, while Adorno's views on responsibility and punishment might not be acceptable to our current common sense thinking about these matters, Adorno could be seen to insist that our ordinary thinking about them is mistaken.

At the same time, Adorno need not be read as subscribing to a blanket rejection of responsibility. In fact, while being aware of how little the

---

justified under current conditions; (2) it was predictable that many perpetrators would either not be prosecuted, or receive punishments insufficient to express adequately the condemnation of the injustices they committed, or even be acquitted; (3) any prosecution would lead to distortions and harms, notably to victims (for example, when required to recollect their ordeals and subjected to fierce cross-examination), not just because of committed advocacy on behalf of the persecutors, but also due to the cold war context (even Hollywood senses something in this in its rendering of one of the Nuremberg Trials, the film *Judgment at Nuremberg*). Another consideration also plays a role here: Adorno refrains from justifying the (legal) right or duty to kill someone (see MM, §33), presumably because he worries about the repercussions (namely, possible misuse by the powers that be).

90 A fuller defence would require examining possible justifications for punishments and showing that none of them is sufficient under current conditions. I cannot undertake this task here.

individual can do about the current conditions, he does not want to excuse us completely, or let the fact of social domination serve as an apologetical instrument.[91] Thus, Adorno's views about responsibility might be more fine-grained than the comments quoted earlier about punishment suggest. Admittedly, he thinks that ultimately whether or not we resist the current social world, or behave decently within it, is largely a matter of luck.[92] It is necessary to have the right conditions or opportunities as well as reactive abilities to resist (or to behave decently and with civility); and it is not completely within our control, whether or not we find ourselves in these conditions, or have these opportunities, or react in the required way to them. Nonetheless, Adorno's view would still leave open the possibility of some differentiation, since these matters are only largely, not completely, out of our hands; it is at least to some extent up to the individual to muster the force of resistance. There could, hence, still be a distinction between those people who do muster this force when the opportunities arise and those who do not (and thereby Adorno's view might allow for a limited notion of responsibility as well as of praise- or blameworthiness).[93]

This distinction is related to the one highlighted earlier – between lesser and more wrong ways of living. In Chapters 5–6, I say more about Adorno's ethics of resistance, which operates centrally with these distinctions. Before then, we need to consider why a more full-blown ethics and ethical theory than Adorno's is not an option – in short we need to consider his critique of moral philosophy.

---

91 Adorno notes that talk about overdemandingness has been often 'an apologetical instrument', not least in post-war Germany (ND, 6: 241/241; translation amended; see also Menke 2005: 41).

92 See, for example, ND, 6: 51/41.

93 Adorno's worries about individual responsibility might also be partly epistemological. We often cannot actually know whether the individual was not at all, partly, or fully responsible. The individual's opinion on the matter might not be decisive either, given how deep-seated social domination and its ideology are. In this way, Adorno might allow that there are still degrees of responsibility, but nonetheless insist that we cannot justify punishment in most cases because we cannot ascertain the exact levels of responsibility.

4

ADORNO'S CRITIQUE OF MORAL PHILOSOPHY

One way to disagree with Adorno's No Right Living Thesis – the thesis, to recall, that there is no right life in our wrong social world – is to argue that moral theory can provide us with guidance on how to live rightly, adherence to which would make such living possible. Adorno anticipates this objection, and replies by criticising moral theory. According to him, it cannot in fact provide such guidance. Instead, moral philosophy (at least within our current social world) should be primarily a critical enterprise:

> On the question of whether moral philosophy is possible today, the only thing I would be able to say is that essentially it would consist in the attempt to make conscious the critique of moral philosophy, the critique of its options and an awareness of its antinomies ... Above all, no one can promise that the reflections that can be entertained in the realm of moral philosophy can be used to establish a canonical plan for the right life [*richtiges Leben*], because life itself is so deformed and distorted that no one is able to live the right life in it or fulfil his destiny as a human being.[1]

Thus, for Adorno there is a legitimate, but negative project in moral philosophy – criticising moral philosophy and alerting us to its antinomies. It seems as if he is saying that we should not go beyond this critical enterprise. However, in fact, the story – I suggest in later chapters – is more complex than this, for while guidance for right living is not an option in our world, there is something we can say about how to live *less wrongly* (as, indeed, Adorno does immediately after the quoted passage). Before we turn to this often neglected aspect of Adorno's work, we have to consider his critique of moral philosophy and whether or not

---

1 PMP 1963, 248/169; translation amended.

it is true that moral theory cannot 'underwrite' right living.[2] If the latter is the case, then his No Right Living Thesis would be confirmed; but, if he fails to mount a convincing attack on moral philosophy, this thesis (and much else in his practical philosophy) would be found wanting.

In his critical engagement with moral philosophy, Adorno concentrates mainly on Kant's theory. The reason for this is that Kant's view is 'moral philosophy par excellence'[3] – it captures not just something about a particular instance of moral theory, but something about the tensions and antinomies of moral philosophy as such. Thus, Adorno's main strategy seems to be the following: by showing what is wrong with this most paradigmatic instance of moral philosophy, we might be able to establish what is wrong with moral philosophy in general. Put differently, if the most consistent and thought-out attempt to do moral philosophy is Kant's, then in demonstrating that it is problematic we call into doubt alternatives to it too. However, Adorno also offers more specific criticisms, albeit mainly in passing, of (some of) these alternatives. In this chapter, the focus is – following Adorno – mainly on Kant's and Kantian moral theory (Section I); followed by a high-altitude sketch of Adorno's critical engagement with non-Kantian moral philosophy (Section II).

I Adorno's critique of Kant's moral philosophy

Adorno advances a great number and variety of criticisms against Kant's moral philosophy, and I cannot here do full justice to either these criticisms or the even bigger number and variety of possible Kantian replies to them. Instead, I present four clusters of interconnected criticisms, which cumulatively both support Adorno's claim that Kant's ethics cannot underwrite right living and present significant problems for Kant's moral outlook more generally (and even for Kantian ethics in its more recent developments) – at least so I argue.

2 This picks up again a passage already quoted in Chapter 2: 'there is no right way of living the wrong life, for a formal ethics cannot underwrite it, and the ethics of responsibility that surrenders to otherness cannot underwrite it either' (PMP 1963, 246–7/166; translation amended). One cautionary comment: the way to read this passage is not that, for Adorno, right life *would have to*, but cannot currently, be underwritten by moral philosophy, but as the negative claim that those who think it can be so underwritten are mistaken. In a Socratic fashion, he aims to show the immanent failure(s) of the underwriting project, without thereby accepting it as necessary or advisable. For his own (sceptical) views of this project, see Chapter 7.

3 PMP 1963, 158/106.

I.1 Moral worth, repression, and happiness

Given Adorno's criticisms of Kant's conception of freedom (see Appendix), it is unsurprising that he objects to Kant's dualism between rational agency and physical nature also in the context of Kant's moral theory. Specifically, this dualism is at issue in Kant's account of moral worth. For Kant we only accrue moral worth for our actions if we act in accordance with duty out of respect for the moral law, with any inclinations and desires playing at most an accompanying role, but not that of supplying the underlying and sufficient motivation (the determining ground). Moral motivation, in this picture, is contrasted with any motivation (any incentives) with which our sensuous nature provides us. While Adorno objects to this picture of moral worth, he also recognises that it is a natural upshot of viewing natural inclination as a threat to freedom (and thereby to morality):

> Kant's every concretion of morality bears repressive features. Its abstractness is a matter of substance, eliminating from the subject whatsoever does not conform with its pure concept. Hence the Kantian rigorism. The hedonistic principle is argued against not because it is evil in itself, but because it is heteronomous to the pure ego. ... As he honors freedom, however, seeking to cleanse it of all impairments, Kant simultaneously condemns the person to unfreedom in principle.[4]

Put differently, Kant divorces moral worth from natural inclination and hedonism (and, more generally, from empirical motivations) because of a combination of two thoughts: (a) we can only get praised and blamed for what is sufficiently in our control and (b) motivation by natural inclination is not sufficiently in our control and not sufficiently aligned with what morality requires us to do. In order to be credited for our (moral) motivations, they have to be independent of our sensible nature (and the empirical world as a whole) – Kant is here taking a typically moral-philosophical thought to its logical conclusion, and

---

4 ND, 6: 253/256; see also PMP 1963, 107–8/71–2. There are at least two kinds of rigorism in Kant's ethics: rigorism in the sense that an agent's ultimate maxim/disposition can be either moral (respect for the moral law) or non-moral (self-love), but not a combination of the two; and, on the other hand, rigorism in the sense of moral absolutism (such as in Constant's famous example of whether we are permitted to lie to someone intent on murdering a friend about the latter's whereabouts and Kant's famous answer that we are never permitted to lie when we cannot avoid to respond to a question, even if put to us by such a would-be murderer). I will come back to the second sense of rigorism in Section I.2, but the issue here concerns the former, motivational rigorism.

Adorno recognises this. In order to save the idea of moral worth, we need the pure, transcendental ego – removed from moral luck, from the contingencies of what our sensuous nature endows us with, and from what the external world makes out of our well-intentioned best efforts in terms of consequences.

However, honouring freedom by cleansing it of everything empirical – Adorno objects – is at the same time to introduce an element of unfreedom into its very heart; specifically, it introduces inner repression into the workings of freedom (see also Appendix). In other words, freedom is purchased at the price of dominating our sensuous nature. The problematic nature of this domination is revealed in the pathologies that result from it – if Adorno is correct, then we are all suffering from such pathologies at least to some extent and do so (at least in part) because of the inner repression we subject ourselves to. What is more, the dualism underlying Kant's motivational rigorism is neither sustainable nor necessary. This latter criticism builds on Adorno's objections to Kant's conception of freedom discussed in the Appendix: the dualism is not sustainable because there cannot be an invention by the pure mind. Physical impulses are not just the expression of rational decision-making (as Kant has it), but constitutive of it. Similarly, the dualism is not necessary because in a free society physical impulses and rational requirements would pull in the same direction. It might be true that after a long history of alienation from our physical impulses and needs, what we take to be rational requirements pull in a different direction to the physical impulses, but this does not mean that they have to do this as a matter of principle.

One way Kantians could reply is to argue that Adorno's worry about inner repression is premised on a misunderstanding of Kant's views. A certain way of reading the examples Kant discusses (such as his famous examples of the shopkeeper who does not cheat his customer and of someone who gladly helps others in need) might suggest that we have to suppress inclinations in order to become morally worthy: it is the fortitude shown in the struggle with inclinations that makes one deserving of moral praise. Kant does, indeed, sometimes sound as if he endorsed such a viewpoint – for example, he says that the action of helping others 'first has its genuine moral worth' when the philanthropist's mind is 'overshadowed by his own grief which extinguishes all sympathy with the fate of others, but he stills helps them'.[5] However, this reading is, all

5 G, 4: 398–9; my emphasis.

things considered, misleading – Kant's point in the examples is merely that we cannot know in cases where motivations other than respect for the moral are present, whether or not the latter was sufficient as a motivation for the act in question, and, hence, we cannot know whether or not the act has moral worth – the moral motive only comes to our attention in cases of conflicting motivations that are overcome.[6] In other words, Kant is advancing an epistemic, not a moral or metaphysical claim in these examples. His full picture of moral worth leaves room for sensuous nature and does not necessarily imply its domination. To be morally worthy, you have to act morally for moral reasons, but doing so is not always possible without the help of our sensuous nature. The latter can prompt morally worthy actions – for example, unless we have certain emotional sensibilities (such as empathy for the suffering of others), we will not recognise the morally salient features of situations and be prompted by this into considering our duties. Kant even says that we have a duty (albeit an indirect one) to develop these sensibilities – say by exposing ourselves to those who suffer from illness and misfortune.[7] Also, the mere presence of motivations with which our sensuous nature equips us (say joy in helping others) does not detract from our moral worth, since these motivations can accompany the morally worthy motivation of acting in accordance with duty out of duty. The key point is merely that respect for the moral law has to be sufficient as incentive for actions in order to gain moral worth for them. Finally, some recent Kantians weaken even this requirement: it would be permissible and accrue moral worth to act on natural inclinations and desires as long as these inclinations and desires have been framed – worked through, if you like – by respect for the moral law.[8] In other words, these Kantians admit that our inclinations, desires, and emotions are not just fixed givens beyond our control, but can be shaped by our rational nature and once this has happened, they are perfectly suitable as moral motivation. In these ways, Kant's dualism between sensuous nature and rational agency is presented as less stark, or even – in the final response just indicated – as something that can be overcome in some instances. Still, if this picture is to be at all a Kantian one, then the dualism has to remain part of it. Otherwise, we would have to give up Kant's central claim that all competent adults have the capacity for rational and moral agency as well as its corollary that we can hold all of them morally and legally responsible for their actions. (This claim illustrates well the way Kant is

6 G, 4: 497–8.   7 MS, 6: 457/575–6.   8 See Herman 2007: esp. Ch. 1.

committed to the egalitarian Enlightenment project of treating all (competent) adults as responsible agents with rights, independently of any arbitrary contingencies.)

In response, Adorno would question the underlying view (partly following Nietzsche). Firstly, he is sceptical that maintaining the idea of universal moral and criminal responsibility is in fact well-motivated. It might seem to be something progressive, but in fact is driven by an urge to punish – such that we hold individuals responsible for what they are not responsible and mask what is really a social problem by individualising blame (see Chapter 3).

Secondly, there is a second kind of Nietzschean worry: if inner repression is necessary to underwrite moral agency (at least initially when the character is formed), then it is worth asking whether or not this sacrifice is worth it. In fact, even Kant recognised that happiness is a kind of constraint on morality – he concedes that there is something problematic in a moral theory, if happiness has no place at all in it. For Kant, happiness does not have a place in supplying the motivation for acting morally (for our actions to have moral worth the incentive we incorporate into our maxims of action cannot be the happiness gained from so acting, even if the action happens to be in conformity with duty); it does not supply the criterion of rightness or wrongness (as in Utilitarianism); but Kant acknowledges that happiness is a constraint insofar as we could reasonably reject morality, if we had not even the hope for happiness (in proportion to our virtue). If we had no rational hope that the highest good (happiness in proportion to virtue) could be achieved, then morality 'must be fantastic and directed to empty imaginary ends and must therefore in itself be false'.[9] There is a rather complicated story at issue here – to underpin rational hope, Kant postulates freedom, the existence of God (who guarantees the hospitability of nature to moral agency and secures the highest good by his grace), and the immortality of the soul (required for the infinite striving towards virtue), albeit only for practical purposes – but we need not enter into it here. The important point is that, as Adorno highlights, happiness is a kind of constraint on morality even for Kant:

> Kant finally concedes that the world would be a hell if it were not possible to achieve – and were it only in a transcendental realm – something like the unity of reason and the impulses it has suppressed.[10]

---

9 KpV, 5: 113–14; see also *Critique of Pure Reason*, A811/B839.   10 PMP 1963, 108/72.

In fact, Adorno goes further:

> The postulates of practical reason which transcend the subject – God, freedom, immortality – imply a critique of the Categorical Imperative, of pure subjective reason. Without these postulates the Imperative would be unthinkable, all Kant's avowals to the contrary notwithstanding. Without hope there is no good.[11]

Put more strongly still, Adorno seems to say that without hope, there is no moral right. His critique then is that if we accept (as Kant does) that happiness is an indirect constraint on morality and if we further accept (as Adorno wants to convince us that we should) that it is possible to reconcile reason and physical nature in the empirical domain (albeit not in our current social world), then a morality that is premised on either postponing happiness to an other-worldly realm or even just relies on the hope of such happiness is guilty of legitimising excessive repression and blocking real reconciliation. By promising happiness beyond the empirical domain, one contributes to people's acceptance of repression in this world, rather than to changing the social setting.

Thirdly, even if one rejected the two Nietzschean worries, there is another rejoinder open to Adorno: Kant cannot underwrite moral agency, even if one granted – for argument's sake – Kant's dualism. This point is connected to the next set of criticisms that Adorno levels against Kant's ethics.

I.2 Pure egos, consequences, and The Wild Duck

The first such criticism is that there are a number of dangers involved in accepting the Kantian view of moral agency beyond the danger of excessive inner repression, such as notably the tendency towards self-righteousness and a rigorism of a second sort (enforcing what one thinks is morally right, no matter what the consequences are). This danger is connected to the Kantian thought that we cannot control the consequences of our actions (but only our willings). As long as I have good intentions, exert myself fully, and rely only on permissible means, then what actually happens cannot be something that affects the moral worth of my actions – in Kant's famous words, my good will would still 'like a jewel, shine by itself'.[12] Indeed, as long as justice is what I aim for by permissible means, I am in the right, even if the heavens should

11 ND, 6: 272/276.   12 G, 4: 50.

fall. Considering the actual consequences of my action might actually distract me from doing what morality requires or lead me astray in my conception of morality – making me overlook the fact that the categorical demands of justice do not depend on consequences either for their applicability or for determining their content.

Adorno thinks that there is something deeply problematic about this view:

> As little as the isolated act can be weighed, so little is there something good which is not externalised in acts. An absolute disposition [*Gesinnung*], devoid of all specific interventions, would be bound to deteriorate to absolute indifference, to inhumanity. Objectively, Kant and Schiller both are preluding the odious concept of a freely suspended nobility which self-appointed elites can later attest to themselves at will, as their own quality. Lurking in Kantian moral philosophy is a tendency to sabotage it.[13]

There is a clear similarity in what Adorno says here to Hegel's worry about 'beautiful souls':[14] if you are only concerned with your intentions (whether they are morally good), then you might become indifferent to the consequences of your intentions and action, eventually eschewing actions all together, even where the world requires an active response. The difference is that Adorno is not so much worried about inactivity as that the Kantian picture of moral worth and agency has the consequence that people become self-righteous. For example, in one of his lectures Adorno makes this point by considering Ibsen's *The Wild Duck*.[15] He takes one of the main protagonists (Gregers Werle) as a kind of exemplary Kantian agent who keeps his promises for the sake of duty and who pursues justice even when it leads to his own unhappiness or misery (a life in poverty instead of a lucrative partnership). In the play, this pursuit of justice mainly takes the form of Gregers's exposing the lies on which the lives around him are built. The two central lies being the betrayal by Gregers's father (Old Werle) of his old friend (Ekdal), which led to Ekdal's going to prison for their shady business deals and then becoming a drunkard, while the father grew rich on the basis of the deals; and Old Werle's fathering a child (Hedwig) with his mistress (Gina), but marrying her to Gregers's best friend (Hjalmar), who takes himself to be Hedwig's (biological) father, while living off the

---

13 ND, 6: 291/296; translation amended.   14 Hegel [1807] 1977: §§632ff.
15 See PMP 1963, lecture 16.

modest living provided by Old Werle for him as photographer (albeit that Gina does all the work). Gregers aims at revealing the truth and how people have been wronged by these lies. The pursuit of justice leads, however, to terrible consequences – the suicide of the only truly innocent person in the play, Hedwig, who cannot live with the change of behaviour by Hjalmar towards her upon his discovery that he is not her biological father. Adorno suggests that the fact that the Kantian pursuit of justice can lead to such bad consequences shows that morality should also attend to the consequences that acting on its requirements can bring about, not just to the intentions and efforts that went into the actions – even (or perhaps especially) if the intentions consisted in the pursuit of justice for its own sake.

There is a complication here. Gregers appears to be an exemplary Kantian moral agent, who acts out of respect for the moral law, and has in this sense a pure will (not one swayed by the impure motivations that our sensuous nature supplies). However, Adorno suggests that what on the surface looks like a moral action for purely moral reasons is actually motivated by rather different incentives and driving forces, many of which are morally dubious: Gregers's feeling of inadequacy; his sense of guilt about the actions of his father and, indeed, his own actions that drives him into taking revenge on his father and prosecuting the faults of others; a general rebellion against his father; the feeling of not fitting in and wanting to destroy the social world that makes him feel like this. The surface impression that he has a pure will is not just an illusion but also functions as a cloak for these dubious motivations. Ultimately, we encounter here an example of the resentment-driven morality about which Nietzsche was writing at the same time as Ibsen's play appeared. Importantly, Adorno's point presumably is not merely that Gregers seems to be a good Kantian agent, but, in fact, is not – then the example would not have been well-picked in the disagreement with Kant (who readily admits that human agents often are not as morally worthy as they seem, that the 'dear self' is turning up as determining ground instead of respect for the moral law, and even that there might never have been a true example of virtue or friendship).[16] Rather, the point is different and more subtle: reality also invades our character, our willing, and Kant's view is not well-equipped to handle the negative consequences of this, despite Kant's awareness of the possibility and high propensity of moral narcissism. In enjoining us to aim for pure willing, it does not sufficiently

16 See G, 4: 407–8.

safeguard against the fact 'that the so-called pure will is almost always twinned with the willingness to denounce others, with the need to punish and persecute others, in short, with the entire problematic nature of what will be too familiar to you from the various purges that have taken place in totalitarian regimes'.[17] In a word, Kant's theory has insufficient resources to deal with the conditional nature of moral action – ironically, the upshot of trying to rescue morality from the contingencies of empirical life (the consequences of our actions; the way reality impinges on our willing) is to deprive us of what is necessary to deal with these.

Kantians would reply to this set of objections in various ways. Firstly, they might take issue with the example Adorno presents from *The Wild Duck*. While Gregers – like everyone else – has a duty to tell the truth when he cannot avoid answering, it is less clear that he has a duty to reveal the lies of others when he could avoid doing so. Also, Gregers turns out – on Adorno's own admission – not to be a purely willed agent, after all, and, thus, is rather limited as counter-example. Still, it is presumably always permissible within Kant's ethics to be truthful, even when not called upon to answer or able to avoid answering and even when being truthful can have bad consequences. Indeed, it is arguable that some people are wronged by the lies at issue – most notably Gregers's best friend Hjalmer – and that this makes it morally obligatory to reveal them, even if this leads to bad consequences. This also means that even if Gregers was not pure willed (but acted, ultimately, on inclinations, such as a desire to take revenge on his father), his actions were nonetheless in accordance with Kantian duty – they would not have moral worth for Kantians (which would also require acting from duty), but nonetheless could not be disowned by them as morally wrong, despite the terrible consequences.

Secondly, Kantians would argue that, even if the example cannot be rebutted so easily, the general objection can be, for there are resources to deal with consequences and self-righteousness within Kantian ethics. As a first step, Kantians would concede to Adorno that it is, indeed, a mistake to focus on individual maxims in isolation.[18] Instead, we should always widen our assessment to other maxims also implicated in the action. While the unit of moral evaluation is rational willing (not state of affairs or consequences) in Kantian ethics, this does not mean we should only focus narrowly on single maxims. Rational willing also includes taking sufficient means for carrying out the action (or at least

17 PMP 1963, 242/163.   18 See Herman 1993: Ch. 5.

all the means and efforts an agent can muster), and, hence, the maxims and practical rules involved in preparation also should be taken into account. Thus, backward-looking considerations play a role in the assessment of the action and the agent. Just sitting in one's study and wanting the world to be different, a better place – having merely a beautiful soul – is mere wishing, and not yet an instance of willing (whether a moral, permissible, or immoral one). In addition, the reaction of the agent to the outcome of the action is also part of rational willing. In particular, it is part of rationally willing an action to show regret in case of failure – when, despite a good will, we fail to produce the intended outcome. Even in cases where the failure is not the agent's fault (but due to causal factors beyond the agent's responsibility, such as interference by others), a set of responses is required of the agent, such as renewing his or her efforts. Otherwise, the agent is not, after all, rationally wiling the action he or she claims to be aiming for in their maxim. Rational willing constitutively includes that one takes adequate means, that one is not negligent in carrying out the action(s), and that one shows a certain set of responses in case of failure and success. Thus, while Gregers should perhaps have gone ahead and revealed the lies affecting his friend's life, Kantians can admit that he has reason for regret – both regarding his preparation of this act (perhaps, he could have broken the news differently) and its effects. Such regret expresses the Kantian commitment of respecting humanity, of concern for persons as ends in themselves. Indeed, this commitment makes the kind of indifference that Hegel and Adorno suggest results from Kant's ethics actually incompatible with that ethics. Furthermore, the constraints of public reason and intersubjective justification – directly flowing from the moral equality that rational agents have as ends in themselves that is central to Kantian ethics – also make it the case that it is not just up to an individual to proclaim that they have done all they could do to further morality, and that all adverse effects were simply out of their control and do not stop their good will shining forth like a jewel. Gregers's acts would not be subject merely to his own conscience, but the moral judgement of all other agents. In these ways, Kantians suggest that their moral system builds in sufficient checks and balances against people's becoming inactive or self-righteous – people might nonetheless become this, but then it is not the fault of the moral system that is structurally constituted to work against such outcomes.

However, by way of rejoinder, one might object that these responses are not fully doing justice to what troubles us about examples such as Gregers's behaviour. They might go a long way in the right direction, but they still do not give consequences the right kind of weight: even if there might be something majestic in the Kantian view that the world may perish as long as justice is served, there are circumstances where taking this line leads to consequences so disastrous (for example, as in *The Wild Duck*, the death of an innocent person) that it should have been renounced and Kantians cannot even countenance this possibility.

In reply, some Rawlsian neo-Kantians go further still in accommodating consequences. They are prepared to drop the rigorism (in the sense of absolutism) of the eighteenth-century founding father. For them, obligations depend on their specific content in the cultural and social context. Most importantly, there can be exceptions to obligations. For example, they think that the nature of one's obligations depends, among other things, on how others behave: if others have already violated their duties, then we are faced with a non-ideal context and this means that what we are required and permitted to do is different from the ideal case where everyone is in compliance with what morality requires.[19] Thus, whether we should lie to a would-be murderer about the whereabouts of the intended victim does not just depend on whether or not lying as such is morally permissible, but also on the fact that we are dealing with a would-be murderer – his/her bad intentions (and evil deeds) might absolve us from our duty to be truthful to him/her. Whether this move is compatible with Kantian ethics might be debatable, but if it were compatible, then this ethics would not be as context-insensitive as it is often believed to be.

In many ways, Adorno might welcome the different ways of adding texture to Kant's abstract morality that I introduced in this section. However, he would doubt that Kantians can actually help themselves to these resources in a way that could actually provide detailed guidance for right living. To see why he would be sceptical in this way, we need to discuss another of Adorno's criticisms.

I.3 Adorno's Empty Formalism Objection

Like Hegel before him,[20] Adorno objects that Kant's formal ethics is unsuitable to provide concrete guidance to right living. In particular, he

---

19 See, for example, Korsgaard 1996: Ch. 5.
20 For a discussion of Hegel's Empty Formalism Objection in the light of recent Kantian replies, see Freyenhagen 2011b.

thinks that the supreme principle of morality within Kant's ethics – the categorical imperative – is unsuitable for deriving specific guidance and even for testing whether independently generated guidance is applicable and morally sound. This is problematic, especially as we are agents that need specific guidance and ends in order to navigate the concrete situations we face in life.

The first reason underpinning this objection is that, according to Adorno, we are not capable of the reflections necessary to judge whether or not one's proposed maxim is universalisable:

> . . . try and become clear in your own mind whether your maxim can serve as the basis of a universal law. If I may apply a Kantian scheme for once, that really would be to assume that the infinite ramifications of social possibilities, an infinite choice then, is actually at my disposal so that I really would be in a position to establish the connection between my maxim and this universal law. In other words, the categorical imperative does indeed exist on paper, but it is not really valid in the strict, internal Kantian sense. This is because it is tacitly assumed that I can verify my judgement, that I can establish whether my maxim is an appropriate basis for such a universal law, whereas in reality my judgement presupposes innumerable reflections, reflections which are beyond the capacities of individual human beings. For a vast amount of knowledge would be called for, something which cannot be claimed to exist as a self-evident moral fact.[21]

Here it sounds as if it is generally impossible for individuals to make use of the testing procedure of the categorical imperative. However, this general point has particular significance in our social world, for in pre-modern times, people did not need to consider the categorical imperative to know what they should morally do – the circumscribed universe in which they lived assigned each person a station in life with clear duties (and even if there was doubt in a particular case, there was a clear arbitration mechanism in matters of morality – for example, asking the local priest). It is our modern social world that both makes it more pressing to have a mechanism for finding out what to do (for it is no longer self-evident within this world) and makes such mechanisms – including the categorical imperative but presumably also consequentialist tests – even more impossible to use, for this world has become so vast and complex in its working that it has become harder to identify causal factors and likely consequences as well as to apportion individual

---

21 PMP 1963, 232/156; see also PMP 1963, 146–7, 173/98–9, 116; ND, 6: 241/243.

responsibility. While using the categorical imperative does not require calculating the goodness of the likely consequences of our actions, its use still requires that we are able to find out about responsibilities of individuals and the causal workings of the social world generally as well as to imagine different social possibilities. Only then can we know what our duties are and how to enact them. If Adorno is right, then social life has become too opaque for any such reflections to take place successfully.

Also, in order to engage in moral deliberation, including on the Kantian understanding of this enterprise, we need to have certain capacities, such as the capacity to recognise the morally salient factors at play – to understand and appreciate what matters morally and what does not.[22] However, having a grasp of moral salience requires that we have been brought up in a way that equips us with it, and, if Adorno is right, then our social world does not so equip us. Just the opposite: our social world trains us to function within capitalist production mechanisms, which includes being cold to each other (rather than sensitive and empathising). Hence, whether or not the categorical imperative could guide right living in a different social setting, it cannot do so in a social context that deprives individuals of the ability to pick out morally salient features and be moved by them. Similarly, we lack the imagination required to think of radically different possibilities of interaction. We are so constrained in our imagination that we just reproduce in different guises the very same social world of which we are part now – we will only rearrange the deck chairs on the Titanic. This also limits, even excludes, the possibility of the kind of critical moral deliberation that Kantians claim is possible under any social circumstances: stepping back from our social world and comparing it to a genuinely moral world (a kingdom of ends). Moreover, according to Adorno, we are for the most part deceived about our real interests and needs, so that recourse to either of these can provide only limited guidance.

However, one might think that Adorno is being unfair to Kant and the Kantians – after all, they make more specific recommendations of how we should act than the mere idea of asking whether or not our maxims can be rationally willed to be a universal law. Perhaps, the latter test would be too abstract to be of much use, whether in past circumscribed societies or our complex modern ones. Yet, this is not all there is – notably, there is the objective end of humanity, and a list of duties for

22 See Herman 1993: Ch. 4.

which Kant argues in the *Metaphysics of Morals* on the basis of this objective end.

Adorno recognises that Kant and Kantians do, in fact, make specific recommendations, but argues that these recommendations are not so much the upshot of Kantian ethical theory, but rather of the way they have been raised and their position within the social context in which they find themselves. It is unsurprising that Kant recommended a life 'in accordance with the model of bourgeois rationality, that is, with the rules of exchange'[23] – a life in which we do not cheat our customers, keep our promises and contracts, pay our loans, and propose reforms but condemn revolutions.

Kantians could, in response, try to show how the specific recommendations of Kantian ethics can, and often do, deviate from the demands of bourgeois rationality, but, ultimately, they need to offer a less piecemeal and more principled answer: even if their recommendations *coincided* with the rules of exchange, this would be a matter of coincidence, for their real basis is the moral law, with the consciousness of its bindingness on us a fact of reason.

I.4 Adorno's critique of the fact of reason

In particular, Kantians could have recourse to the fact of reason to show that moral living is always possible, no matter what the social circumstances may be. There is proof of our having the capacities to act morally just in virtue of our consciousness of the obligatoriness of moral duties (and the nature of this consciousness). Kant's argument runs as follows:[24]

a) If there is a moral law (an unconditionally binding moral principle), it is not (and cannot be) given in experience.
b) For there to be a moral law which is binding on us, we must be capable of autonomous willing [Reciprocity Thesis].
c) We are conscious of the moral law as binding on us as a 'fact of reason'.
d) We are capable of autonomous willing.

In support of premise a), Kant is basically arguing that experience can never generate a principle that holds of necessity. The second premise is meant as an analytic thesis: if we understand what acting from the moral

---

23 PMP 1963, 174/117.   24 See KpV, especially §§1–7.

law requires, then we also see that we need to be autonomous to thus act (where this includes both the negative freedom to be free from determination by sensuous nature and the positive freedom of self-legislating one's principle of action); and *vice versa*: if we understand what it means to give ourselves our own law, then we see that only the moral law is what could be so given to ourselves. As to premise c), it is already clear in the light of premise a) that the facticity (the givenness) of the moral law has to be different from empirical facticity (and givenness), whatever that may be.[25] Also, we are faced here not with a fact *for* reason – a fact that reason apprehends or which is given to it. Rather, it is a fact *of* reason in the sense of reason's form giving itself to itself. The fact of reason tells us something about reason itself, not about something given to it.[26]

Adorno objects that this facticity, while different from an empirical one, is still problematic: givenness is not sufficient for justification, even when it is non-empirical.[27] Admittedly, when something is given, certain sceptical worries can be rebutted: as long as its existence is indeed a fact (not just an illusion), it cannot be questioned. Still, often appeals to givenness are meant to rebut further questions, ascribing to something that exists a certain kind of authority or claiming that its existence consists in providing such authority.[28] Yet, especially within the Kantian framework, we could and should not accept this additional move. Kant cannot appeal to the idea that something just by its very existence has or is an authority that we cannot question further. Kant is committed to a picture where we need reasons for accepting any authority. Specifically, the legitimacy of any authority derives from public reason – each person has to be able to accept its justification in the court of reason. A mere appeal to authority does not suffice for legitimacy – even if it is an appeal to the authority of reason itself. Such an appeal would be unfounded, even irrational:

> The antinomical character of the Kantian doctrine of freedom is exacerbated to the point where the moral law seems to be regarded as directly rational and irrational – as rational, because it is reduced to pure logical reason without content, and as not rational because it must be accepted as given and cannot be further analyzed; every attempt at analysis is anathema. ... The *ratio* turns into an irrational authority.[29]

---

25 See also PMP 1963, 114–16/76–7.   26 See also PMP 1963, 117–20/78–80.
27 ND, 6: 283/287.   28 See PMP 1963, 117/78.
29 ND, 6: 258/261; translation amended.

Still, Adorno also thinks that there is something true in what Kant says. In appealing to a given at this pivotal point in the argument, Kant – inadvertently – attests to the truth that there is a non-discursive element in morality, which any account of normativity has to take into account. There is something in morality that you cannot deduce from any supposedly ultimate principle of morality, or ground discursively in any other way. If one tries to do this, one will just end up in an infinite argumentative back and forth. Kant's recourse to the moral law as given is a typical instance of 'acts of violence performed in the awareness that morality is underivable'.[30]

This is a controversial and complex claim that will require careful unpacking, and I want to start discussing it by considering a Kantian reply to the reasoning leading up to it. Kantians would argue that Adorno misunderstands the authority of reason. This authority is not something that one could question further. Rather than the Kantians failing to question the authority of reason and hiding their unreflective acceptance of it with talk of a fact of reason, this talk acknowledges their insight into the inscrutability of this authority. As noted, the fact of reason is no ordinary fact, but reason giving itself to itself and – going beyond what I noted earlier – thereby validating itself. One way to support this extra step is to ask what else could validate reason other than itself. What could do the deducing other than the very principle on which we are relying already, i.e., reason's principle? The answer seems to be that nothing could. One might then conclude that as nothing else than reason could ground reason discursively, it must be reason itself that validates itself. Put the other way around: reason validates itself since nothing else could validate it.

Adorno rejects this reasoning, and not just because of the earlier discussed worry that a mere self-consistent form is insufficient to guide action. Even if it were true that reason is normally involved in discursive grounding and that one could not have such grounding without reason, this does not show that reason self-validates itself. It might be true that we cannot go beyond reason in discursive grounding and that nothing other than reason could ground its authority discursively, but this does not show that reason is itself grounded, for it might be that reason's demands *cannot* be proven or grounded. Similarly, it might be that we cannot go beyond rational consistency when it comes to discursive grounding, but this does not show that rational consistency is the form

---

30 DE, 3: 104/85; translation amended.

of morality – it might just be that morality cannot be rationally, discursively grounded all the way down. Presuming that morality is whatever is left once we cannot continue in our search for what can be justified all the way down is already to prejudge that there is such a justification. By taking rational consistency as the form of morality because nothing else held up to complete rational justification is 'fatigue in the face of the argument'.[31] It does not answer, but merely presupposes a positive answer to the question as to whether morality can be rationally justified all the way down.

Moreover, Adorno can offer an explanation why the fact of reason, our consciousness of the bindingness of moral obligations, feels inscrutable and seems to hold, no matter what the social situation is – an explanation which debunks rather than validates the authority of the hold of these obligations on us:

> The Kantian turning of the moral law into fact has a suggestive power because in the sphere of the empirical person Kant can actually cite such a datum to support his view. This helps to establish a connection – always problematic – between the intelligible and the empirical realms. The phenomenology of empirical consciousness, not to mention psychology, comes up against the very conscience which in Kantian doctrine is the voice of the moral law. The descriptions of its efficacy, notably those of the 'constraint' it exerts, are not mere brainstorms; it was in the real compulsion of conscience that Kant read the coercive features he engraved in the doctrine of freedom. The empirical irresistibility of the super-ego, the psychologically existing conscience, is what assures him, contrary to his transcendental principle, of the factuality of the moral law – although, for Kant, conscience ought to disqualify factuality as the basis of autonomous morality, as much as it disqualifies the heteronomous drives.[32]

This explanation is broadly Freudian in that Adorno relates our obligations to internalisations during our early socialisation that congeal into a super-ego, perceived by us as the voice of conscience, and endowed with what seems to be irresistible force.[33] Thus, the inscrutability of the fact of reason is not that we have run out of further justificatory grounds and are faced with a self-validating authority, but is rather an expression of the sense of irresistibility that attached to the super-ego as congealed internalised pressure. In this way, our consciousness of the

---

31 PMP 1963, 187/126.
32 ND, 6: 267–8/270–1; translation amended. See also PMP 1963, 122–3/81–2.
33 ND, 6: 267/271.

unconditional bindingness of the moral law is grounded empirically (and thereby unsuitably for what is meant to be an a priori principle). Our conscience is formed by internalising the social norms exemplified and enforced by our parents. It rests not on reasoned grounds, but on the contingent commands of the particular social setting that were internalised by force. The inscrutability of the bindingness of the moral law is due to our not wanting to confront the coercion and pain that went into forming our conscience. In this sense, heteronomy can be found at the heart of (Kantian) autonomy; rather than proving our autonomy, the givenness of the moral law demonstrates our internalised social unfreedom.[34]

One example would be the protestant work ethic often associated with capitalism's development and still operative in perhaps now secular form. For Adorno, people's subscribing to this work ethic is explained by the requirements of capitalist production, and plays a role in sustaining it. Growing up in a capitalist society, we are socialised by our parents and social institutions (such as schools and universities) into assigning work a paramount role in our lives and value systems. The resultant work ethic then contributes to maintaining the very conditions that foster it: for example, it contributes to people's acceptance of long working hours, despite the fact that the long working hours are now only necessary for the survival of capitalism (the maximisation of surplus-value), which has enabled the development of the forces of production to a point where a significant reduction in labour-time would be possible without affecting human needs detrimentally.

Considerations such as these also lend further support to the claim that whenever Kantian (and indeed other) moral theorists make claims to specific guidance about morally right living, it is in fact normally the social background and position of the theorist that comes through, not something that their theory would require independently of this background and position. Admittedly, sometimes the way our upbringing and social context comes through is by way of rebellion to them, but even then they tend to form our moral consciousness decisively. In this

---

34 See ND, 6: 252–3/255–6; DE, 3: 113/94; PMP 1963, 122–3/81–2. What is interesting about Adorno's criticisms of Kant's moral philosophy is that he wants to rescue something from this theory even where he criticises it. This is true also about the fact of reason and conscience, which, according to Adorno, is not just (internalised) 'heteronomous coercion' but also contains a moment of universality, which gestures to 'the idea of a solidarity transcending the divergent individual interests' (ND, 6: 278/282; see also 271–2/275).

context, we can think back to Gregers (from Ibsen's *The Wild Duck*): even the Kantian aim of acting morally for moral reasons alone, is best interpreted as a way of dealing with his bad conscience by crusading for the morality of others and as a form of revenge for the domination we can imagine that he was subjected to by his parents, most notably his father.

In sum, Adorno presents a number of interrelated criticisms of Kant's moral philosophy, including a radical and original critique of the fact of reason – showing how Kant relies on an unwarranted assumption about the need for and possibility of discursive grounding, and offering an error theory of why this assumption arises. This critique is pivotal in the wider argument about justification, which is explored further in later chapters. For now, the key point is that Adorno takes himself to have shown that Kant's attempt to underwrite moral agency and right living has failed, despite the attempts of later Kantians to defend it.

II Adorno's critique of non-Kantian moral philosophy

Even if one accepted the soundness of Adorno's objections to Kant's ethics, one could still insist that Adorno has not shown that it is impossible for moral theory to guide us towards a right life in our social world. In particular, non-Kantian moral philosophy could be seen to provide such guidance – not least because it avoids the problems of Kantian moral philosophy, which (at least according to Adorno) isolates morality so starkly from nature and society. However, one of the objections to Kant's theory already indicates why Adorno is sceptical that non-Kantian moral philosophy could help us out of our predicament – if our social world is too complex and opaque, guidance for right living is also unlikely to come from non-Kantian alternatives. Still, apart from this general worry, Adorno also makes a number of specific criticisms of some of these alternatives, to which I turn now.

Unfortunately, Adorno engages significantly less with these alternatives than with Kant's theory, so that there is less to work with in reconstructing his critiques. Partly as a consequence, the approach taken here is mainly systematic – considering Adorno's stance towards a number of options that would be alternatives to Kantian views, without discussing the works of philosophers who defend these options in detail. Thus, one might think that given Adorno's objections to Kant's ethics, a substantive ethics that takes consequences into account would fare better; or that if the current values are a problem, one should postulate new ones; or that a focus on character traits, on virtues, could make possible what principle-based morality could not deliver; or that concentrating on compassion would be a way to guide us towards right living in a world that systematically engenders suffering. I discuss these options in turn, and in the case of three of them, I follow Adorno to associate them with Hegel, Nietzsche, and Schopenhauer respectively, but even in these cases no conclusive interpretive claims are attempted or required.

II.1 Hostage to existing reality: critique of the ethics of responsibility

We saw earlier in this chapter how Adorno objects to Kant's ethics of disposition by arguing against its indifference to consequences. It might be natural to conclude from this that Adorno advocates an ethics of responsibility, which he attributes to Hegel and summarises as follows:

> What is meant by this is an ethics in which at every step you take – at every step you imagine yourself to be satisfying a demand for what is good and right – you simultaneously reflect on the effect of your action, and whether the goal envisaged will be achieved. In other words, you are not just acting out of pure conviction, but you include the end, then intention and even the resulting shape of the world as positive factors in your considerations.[35]

Also, an ethics of responsibility, especially in the form advocated by Hegel, is not an abstract morality like Kant's, but rooted in social norms and practices. It thereby avoids the Empty Formalism Objection that Adorno (following Hegel) makes against Kantian morality.

However, matters are not so straightforward. Adorno worries – in a Kantian manner – that adopting an ethics of responsibility makes morality hostage to existing reality, especially in Hegel's case.[36] By counting the goodness and badness of the effects of our action towards moral rightness, the latter is made dependent on the way of the world. Similarly, if the norms used to evaluate individual responsibility are rooted in existing practices – say social roles – then again morality is dependent on the way of the world. Indeed, a Hegelian ethics of responsibility seems to make itself wholly dependent on this – for even where it is critical of specific phenomena of the modern world, this is only ironing out internal tensions within this reality. Yet, if this way of the world is morally problematic – as we repeatedly saw that Adorno thinks

35 PMP 1963, 240/162.   36 See PMP 1963, 243–6/163–5.

is the case – then an ethics that is wholly dependent on it cannot provide us with the critical distance required for right living. Indeed, even an account that makes morality partially dependent on what turns out to be good and bad in a thoroughly problematic social world is likely to be infected and thereby unsuitable as a guide. It would condone actions as right that should not be condoned as such, for as long as the effects of the actions are sufficiently significant, almost anything (even torture of innocents) would count as morally right. Thus, whatever the merits of an ethics of responsibility may be in other contexts, in our social world it cannot guide us towards right living. In fact, given its complicity with the social world, it cannot guide us even in our resistance to it.

It is not entirely clear how deep Adorno's disagreement with Hegel runs on this issue. At one point, Adorno accuses Hegel of holding the view that 'existing reality ... is always in the right over against the human subject'.[37] He might here follow a swathe of commentators who read Hegel's famous slogan (from the Preface to the *Philosophy of Right*) – 'What is rational is actual/And what is actual is rational' – as suggesting a conservative apology for whatever is the case. However, not only is this, arguably, mistaken as a reading of Hegel,[38] Adorno himself admits elsewhere that the slogan is not 'merely apologetic', since the actual can be considered rational only insofar as freedom shines through it.[39] Hence, it is more likely that something else is going on.

My suggestion would be to see the disagreement with Hegel in practical philosophy as more historical than principled[40] – in short, as a disagreement about the socio-historical context in which we should base our norms on social reality and can be (legitimately) held responsible for the consequences of our actions. Specifically, Adorno, unlike Hegel, would view the modern social world as not actualising human freedom, but as initially a way-station to such actualisation, and, in later stages, a serious obstacle to it. There is nothing in principle wrong with making ethics dependent on existing social reality, but there is something wrong with making moral rightness dependent on the current social reality. Only in a possible free society would such dependence be innocuous and appropriate.

---

37 PMP 1963, 245/165.   38 See, for example, Stern 2006.
39 5: 288/Adorno 1993b: 44; see also 276/30.
40 This is not to say that the disagreement between Hegel and Adorno is merely historical, and not also principled, in other aspects of philosophy – notably in their respective views of dialectic and art.

One might still think that Adorno is doing Hegel's philosophy injustice. While the historical person Hegel might have endorsed the modern social world, there are resources within his view that provide critical tools, which could even be employed against this social world (and Hegel's endorsement of it). Admittedly, these will not be the tools of an abstract Kantian morality that Hegel and Hegelians (including, as we saw, Adorno) reject. Rather, Hegelians would point to Hegel's conception of rationality as historical. This is a complex issue, but the rough idea is that there is a process of historical learning about human freedom, such that various social forms of achieving human freedom have been tested in history and found unstable, so that the more modern institutions – as long as they heed the lessons of the past – are more rational arrangements than those which preceded them. On this view, our modern social world could either be faulted for failing to heed the lessons of the past, or for nonetheless being subject to too many internal contradictions.

Adorno does not buy fully into this picture. As seen earlier (see Chapter 3), the fact that (in his view) the modern social world is riddled with antagonisms is important for the possibility of overcoming it. As also seen earlier (see Chapter 2), Adorno is not advocating a return to past social arrangements, both because he thinks it is impossible and because he acknowledges that these past arrangements were also build on domination, albeit of a different (more direct, and personal) kind. However, Adorno does not think that we can still maintain the view of history as moving towards more rational social arrangements. Again this is a complex matter, but the following passage summarises his views well:

> Universal history must be constructed and denied. After the catastrophes that have happened, and in view of the catastrophes to come, it would be cynical to say that a plan for a better world is manifested in history and unites it. Not to be denied for that reason, however, is the unity that cements the discontinuous, chaotically splintered moments and phases of history – the unity of the control of nature, progressing in its rule over human beings, and finally over their inner nature. No universal history leads from savagery to humanitarianism, but there is one leading from the slingshot to the megaton bomb. It ends in the total menace which organized mankind poses to organized men, in the epitome of discontinuity. It is the horror that verifies Hegel and stands him on his head. If he transfigures the totality of historic suffering into the positivity of the self-realizing absolute, the One and All that keeps rolling on to this day – with

occasional breathing spells – would teleologically be the absolute of suffering.[41]

Yet, if a Hegelian view of history cannot be constructed other than as an inverted one – as one not of the progress of humanity, but of human suffering and catastrophes – having recourse to historical rationality cannot guide us towards living rightly. At most, a Hegelian view of history can tell us about what bads to avoid – those social forms which have already failed the test of history – but not what we should positively aim for. After all, for Hegelians, philosophy always comes second (famously, the owl of Minerva only flies at dusk) – historical developments, specifically practical innovations, have to precede philosophy before they can become fully rational with the help of philosophical reflections. What philosophy cannot do is anticipate these developments. Any such anticipations would just be abstract ideals, and as such either altogether mistaken or at least unsuitable for guiding our lives and social transformations.

In this sense, Hegel's ethics of responsibility cannot guide us to live rightly now, for any substantive ethical guidance on right living it can offer us is too beholden to a social world that makes right living impossible; and the historical lessons it emphasises can at most tell us what bads to avoid.

II.2 Against (Nietzsche's) new values

One way to respond to Adorno's claim that moral theory cannot guide us towards right living in our social world is to propose that a philosophy that introduced new values – to replace the existing values infected as they are by the wrong world – could be a way forward. Adorno saw Nietzsche as a philosopher who was also deeply critical of contemporary forms of life and morality, but who responded to this by postulating new values, not by denying that there could be right living. I leave it open whether or not this characterisation adequately captures Nietzsche's complex and changing views – even if it does not, it is instructive to discuss the philosophical position at issue.

It is hard to overestimate the importance of Nietzsche for Adorno, including for his practical philosophy. In one of his lecture series, Adorno states 'of all the so-called great philosophers I owe him [Nietzsche] by far the greatest debt – more even than to Hegel'.[42]

---

41 ND, 6: 314/320; see also HF, lectures 2, 9–10.   42 PMP 1963, 255/172.

This debt is apparent throughout the whole of this lecture series. Adorno credits Nietzsche with having seen how the ascetic ideals contained in the concept of morality are expressions of entrenched interests, rather than the result of rational justification.[43] He also thinks that Nietzsche clearly recognised how morality was nurtured on faded theological ideals and how much people try to recreate something like these ideals long after they have faded.[44] Still – from Adorno's perspective – perhaps the most important insight of Nietzsche is the latter's recognition that 'the bad has assumed concrete forms within the positive institutions of society and, above all, in the different ideologies'.[45] Adorno is particularly impressed by Nietzsche's extraordinary understanding of the inner workings of ideologies. Moreover, although Adorno has no sympathy for the brutality he thinks Nietzsche's views license, he agrees that direct violence is more innocent and less dangerous than violence rationalised as good. Specifically the modern 'functionalized and anonymous form of domination' is in Adorno's mind far more brutal as well as less easy to see through and unseat than open tyranny.[46] In these ways, having recourse to Nietzsche's views can aid those repressed by unearthing the power relations behind the moral façade of modern civilisation; but their employment as state religion – Adorno thinks here of the Nazi regime – would lead to the very thing Nietzsche opposes, namely support for the powers that be and resentment.[47]

Thus, Adorno has great sympathies for the critical project contained in Nietzsche's works, yet, he disagrees with their positive content. To some extent, he charges Nietzsche with having failed to think his own critical project through. According to Adorno, the positive norms in Nietzsche's outlook are 'really nothing more than the negative mirror-image of the morality he had repudiated'.[48] It is not possible to read off a true morality from a critique of repressive ideology – we would not yet have a comprehensive view of what else we should avoid, and we often

---

43 PMP 1963, 25–6/13.
44 PMP 1963, 28/15. However, Adorno also thinks that Nietzsche did not really free himself of this theological baggage, since his conception of a higher self 'shows itself to be a desperate attempt to rescue God, who is supposed to be dead' (DE, 3: 135/114; translation amended). Nietzsche aims 'at independence from external powers, at the unconditioned maturity defined as the essence of enlightenment' (DE, 3: 135/114–15), and thereby continues in the tradition of attempting to recreate what was lost with the fading of religion.
45 PMP 1963, 255/172.   46 PMP 1963, 259/174.   47 DE, 3: 121/101.
48 PMP 1963, 256/172.

only know what is wrong with a view, but not yet how to avoid the wrongness in question.

Moreover, the objective contradiction between the need for individual moral practice and the fact that such practice is currently blocked cannot be overcome simply by imposing values. The reasons for this are two-fold. Firstly, such an imposition or positing of new values would be 'the opposite of freedom',[49] i.e., heteronomy, domination. Instead, values have to develop socially and historically through a dialectical process.[50] Secondly, the values Nietzsche proposes – for example, nobility [*Vornehmheit*] or boldness [*Kühnheit*] – may be 'wonderful values in themselves, but in an unfree society they are not capable of fulfilment, or at best can only be realized on Sunday afternoons'.[51] Adorno illustrates this second claim by considering the example of the Nietzschean value 'nobility'. Actualising this value would be a matter of impossibility for those at the bottom, presumably because their concerns are – to re-phrase Brecht – 'food first, then nobility'. Yet, this may not concern Nietzsche very much. What would concern him is that even someone who is closest to his ideal, a go-getter and capitalist entrepreneur, would not survive in a capitalist economy by being noble, but end up being bankrupt.[52]

These two reasons point in the same direction. To think one can impose values independently of social reality is both arbitrary (and thereby potentially repressive if put into practice) as well as futile. This is especially so, since Nietzsche wanted to impose what are basically feudal values on a bourgeois society.[53] The solution cannot be to reject the current values, to tear down the old table of commandments, and simply to postulate new ones (or, worse still, replace the current value with outlived old ones). Rather, what is needed is to build the social institutions and conditions that make individual freedom possible and the concrete norms that encapsulate genuine reconciliation of people's interests.

---

49 ND, 6: 271/275.   50 See also PMP 1963, 259/174.   51 PMP 1963, 256/173.

52 PMP 1963, 257/173. The problems in realising Nietzsche's values just bring out once more Adorno's claim that whichever way we go, or whatever status we hold, there can be no right living (see here, Chapter 2).

53 PMP 1963, 257/173. It is unsurprising that Nietzsche proposed pre-modern values – for, if Adorno is right that we cannot even imagine what positively would go beyond the current social world, we are bound to end up proposing variants of either existing or past values, not genuinely new ones.

In sum, the positive part of Nietzsche's project falls as much victim to the problems of right living today as Kantian morality, and in fact more so, since its critical part should have guarded Nietzsche against this.

II.3 Virtue has grown old

Part of the problem of Kant's ethics is – at least, according to Adorno – that it is too abstract and principle-based to guide us. One might think that an ethics that focused on character traits, on virtues, would fare better. Such an ethics looks to what it is for agents to react in the right way to particular situations, where these reactions are not fully codifiable – indeed they might not even involve deliberation or discursive reasoning. Guidance would be less in terms of rules than paradigm examples of virtuous action or agents. It would also be more concrete, not least because the sets of dispositions to react to situations are linked up with specific historical and social contexts. They are formed by these contexts and express the particular reconciliation between universal and particular interests achieved in them. Moreover, the agent does not act on abstract ideas (not even of his or her virtue), but for particular ends, attachments, and projects which form part of the agent's identity and are infused by his or her set of ethical dispositions. Might not such an ethics provide us with a guide to right living?

The short answer is that for Adorno it cannot *currently* do so. In his lectures, he describes the concept of virtue as 'obsolete' on two different occasions.[54] He is also quite explicit about the reasons for this. Virtue is only possible within a circumscribed universe,[55] and the same is true of being tactful,[56] a successor idea and practice to the ancient Greek conception of virtue. Without a circumscribed universe, the conditions for forming and using the ability to have the appropriate cognitive and emotive reaction to situations are undermined.[57]

Let me expand on this. We already saw that for Adorno the causal nexus, individual responsibilities as well as likely consequences are no longer transparent in our modern social world. This means that there cannot be the kind of learned immediacy of the moral cognition and reaction characteristic of virtuous behaviour. While (ethical) reflection has been able to compensate for this loss to some extent, it has also led to inaction and over the long run contributed to undermining the

---

54 PMP 1956/7 (unpublished), Vo1379; PMP 1963, 146/98.   55 PMP 1963, 147/98.
56 PMP 1956/7 (unpublished), Vo1395; see also MM, Aphorism No. 16.
57 See also Jaeggi 2005: 70–1; and Menke 2005: esp. Sect. 3.

necessary dispositions – not because they are alien to reflection, but because they are alien to too much of it.[58]

Similarly, the close social networks which sustained individual moral practice, for example by educating people in the right dispositions, have also been undermined in modern society. This has affected the practice of virtue, since the number of those who could practice it has increasingly diminished. Without a circumscribed universe the socialisation of individuals has radically changed; in fact, it has changed to the point that socialisation does not produce individuals any more (in the sense of people with stable characters of virtue or vice). It does not lead any more to the right kind of 'fixed sedimentation'.[59]

Moreover, the diversity and complexity of modern society has also weakened our ability to trust in a common way of reacting to events and ethical questions. This makes it more difficult to make judgements which affect other people. A common framework of background assumptions is missing and to impose it would be repressive.

All these developments are heightened by the fact that for Adorno our society is fundamentally delusional in character. Virtuous dispositions are meant to be linked to our actual needs and capacities. Yet, a society which moulds us to its own image for the purpose of maximising surplus-value production has made it extremely difficult to tell what we really need and what our human-specific capacities are. Society has become so overwhelming and has arranged the incentive structures, causal mechanisms, and institutional arrangements in such a way as to assist its survival. Again, reflection might help us, but even critical reflection cannot change the fact that social and individual interests are so far apart that it is almost impossible to mediate between the good for individuals and the good for the species.[60] Consequently, even where reflection does not lead to inaction, it has little to offer us in terms of practical guidance. This means that apart from extreme situations (for example, when we encounter someone being tortured), or lucky circumstances (for example, when we still have the benefit of a decent upbringing), decent behaviour – never mind virtuous or tactful behaviour – is beyond us.

Indeed, it is a mistake to pretend that one could still uphold virtuous practices, even when the background conditions are missing. Thus, in *Minima Moralia* Adorno criticises strongly those who want to maintain the

---

58 See Chapters 3 and 7 as well as the Appendix; see also Menke 2005: esp. 38, 41, 42–3.
59 PMP 1956/7 (unpublished), Vo1395.   60 See PMP 1963, 241–2/142–3.

bourgeois virtues of the early capitalist world (such as independence, tenacity, or prudence), even though the economic and social conditions for their practice are no longer in existence. Such people concentrate their energies on their private spheres, on keeping their homes and gardens proper and immaculate, while reacting with hostility to new, alien, or different situations and people.[61] Instead of the liberality of early capitalism, they narrowly pursue their interests and would deny shelter even to those who flee persecution and certain death.

Similarly, Adorno sometimes associates the term 'ethics' with a certain moral view (predominant in post-war Germany), according to which moral behaviour is a question of character and of fulfilling one's nature, rather than of morality and social norms.[62] He rejects the (exclusive) focus on personality or character as 'a sort of conjuring trick by means of which the decisive problem of moral philosophy, namely the relation of the individual to the general, is made to disappear'.[63] By making moral practice a mere question of individual character, the determination by society – which, according to Adorno, reaches deeply into our character-formation – is largely ignored. It sweeps away the essential question 'whether culture, and whatever culture has become, permits something like right living, or whether it is a network of institutions that actually tends more and more to thwart the emergence of such right living'.[64] Focusing on people's characters as an antidote to ineffectual morality fails to analyse why our mores have become ineffectual, inadvertently reinforcing the social domination that has undermined them. It presents a social problem as if it were a matter which merely requires individual reorientation. In this sense, an ethics of character traits has not only become anachronistic, but can even become misleading.[65]

These considerations lead to another important point: for Adorno, there are no patterns of behaviour or reaction which are good in an invariant or timeless manner.[66] What is good and bad depends to a large extent on the social and historical conditions. For example, being truthful might be good in most societies, but, *pace* Kant, there are

---

61 MM, Aphorism No. 14; see also Jaeggi 2005: 78–9.
62 See PMP 1963, 22–30/10–16.   63 PMP 1963, 23/10.
64 PMP 1963, 28/14; see also PMP 1956/7 (unpublished), Vo1296.
65 However, this need not stop us from using a carefully qualified sense of the term 'ethics' to describe Adorno's own views on how we can and should live in an administered world (see the end of Chapter 6).
66 See also Jaeggi 2005: 70–1.

circumstances in which truthfulness is inappropriate or inapplicable. If one lives in a society that persecutes innocent people (say in post-1933 Germany), then resisting it and protecting those persecuted as best as one can might mean that one should not be truthful in most of one's interactions with people. Similarly, if one lives in a radically delusional society, it might no longer be meaningful to ask people to be truthful.

Hence, while it might be true that Adorno has Aristotelian sympathies,[67] virtue ethics cannot underwrite the possibility of right living in the administered world. This world has undermined the conditions of the practice of virtue, that is, concrete social norms and individuals able to master the thick concepts that issue from these norms. In fact, the focus on virtues and the attempt to cling on to them can even lead to immoral practices, if – as a consequence of such a focus – reflection on the general circumstances of the modern world is shunned.

II.4 Always too little compassion

As we see later, Adorno holds in high regard both identification and solidarity with others (see Chapter 6). Given also his emphasis on human suffering and on impulses generated in response to it, one might think that an ethics of compassion would represent a live option for Adorno. In fact, Schopenhauer's influence on Horkheimer is well-known.[68] It would, therefore, not be very surprising to see Adorno move towards an ethics of compassion along the lines Schopenhauer envisaged. Might such an approach provide guidance for right living?

However, once more this alternative is blocked. Although Adorno has a nuanced view of compassion, he ultimately rejects it as a basis for ethics. There are two main reasons for this. Firstly, there is a Kantian worry about compassion, namely, that it cannot ground moral practice, since doing so would make this practice dependent on the contingency of people's capacity for compassion, which is too unreliable a basis.[69] An ethics of compassion would be completely dependent on how much compassion people are capable of showing, and Adorno observes that people are never compassionate enough,[70] at least in our social world.

---

67 As I argue later, Adorno and neo-Aristotelians share a conception of normativity (see Chapter 9).

68 See, for example, Schnädelbach 1986; see also Früchtl 1991: 1–2, 43 nn. 2, 4.

69 PMP 1956/7 (unpublished), Vo1518.

70 DE, 3: 123/103. Elsewhere, Adorno raises the same doubt about kindness [*Güte*], pointing out that (at least for now) there never is sufficient kindness around (2: 215).

In one of his lectures he points to a reason for this: compassion requires identification, to see oneself in the other;[71] and Adorno thinks that there is insufficient identification in a deficient social world, especially as this world is based on everyone pursuing their self-interest.[72]

Secondly, there is a more far-reaching and important, though not unrelated worry. Adorno objects to an ethics of compassion on the grounds that it sets out only to mitigate injustice, not to change the conditions that create and reproduce it.[73] As he puts it in one of his lectures:

> ... we must admit that Nietzsche's criticism of the morality of compassion has an element of truth. This is because the concept of compassion tacitly maintains and gives its sanction to the negative condition of powerlessness in which the object of our pity finds itself. The idea of compassion contains nothing about changing the circumstances that give rise to the need for it, but instead, as in Schopenhauer, these circumstances are absorbed into the moral doctrine and interpreted as its main foundation. In short, they are hypostatized and treated as if they were immutable. We may conclude from this that the pity you express for someone always contains an element of injustice towards that person; he experiences not just our pity but also impotence and the specious character of the compassionate act.[74]

Rather than challenging the social context that gives rise to suffering, compassionate behaviour takes it as a starting point and, at least, implicitly resigns itself to it. This is unacceptable for Adorno – for this context deserves to be resisted and changed, not treated as if it could not be changed.[75] Moreover, Adorno thinks such behaviour is also an injustice towards the beneficiary of our acts, because the act of compassion cements the injustice and thereby his or her status as beneficiary.

---

71 PMP 1956/7 (unpublished), Vo1518.   72 See also EA, 10.2: 687/CM, 201.

73 See Noerr 1995: especially 17. Recall the example of humanitarian aid from Chapter 2: it is often lamented that giving such aid, at best, mitigates some of the bad effects of structural injustices and, at worst, adds to them (say by eroding local markets and food production).

74 PMP 1963, 257–8/173–4; see also DE, 3: 122–3, 126/102–3, 106.

75 At the basis of Adorno's disagreement with Schopenhauer is that the former, but not the latter, thinks that more than mitigating injustice is possible, at least in principle. In effect, Adorno accuses Schopenhauer of making a virtue out of a bad situation by presenting compassion as the only available and appropriate reaction when it is, in fact, decidedly second-best, even problematic, by entrenching what could and should be changed. See also Cornell 1987: Sect. 4.

These criticisms notwithstanding, there is also another side to Adorno's stance on compassion.[76] What he objects to is the limit of our softness expressed in compassion (both in the sense of the limit of the extent of our compassion and the limited difference compassion can make), not the softness itself. In line with this thought, Adorno criticises the critics of compassion (and amongst those first and foremost Nietzsche and Kant). He objects to their contempt for compassion,[77] both as such and by its contributing – however inadvertently – to repressive practices in totalitarian regimes.[78] Thus, while compassion for Adorno is insufficient for right living, one should not mistake him as rejecting the identification and solidarity with others that is at the heart of compassion. What is missing is the right framework, the just social conditions, for this softness; what is missing is *not* that people are hard or cold. On the contrary, the bourgeois coldness which is the antithesis of compassion played a crucial role in making Auschwitz possible.[79] Compassion might contain an element of resignation and it might not be suited to underwrite right living, but it can still stop people from committing horrific acts. Indeed, as we see in more detail later (see Chapter 6), identification and solidarity with others (and the other in oneself) is of crucial importance for living less wrongly.[80]

---

76 See also Cornell 1987; Früchtl 1991: esp. Sect. 1; and Noerr 1995.

77 See, for example, ND, 6: 257–8/260.   78 DE, 3: 123–4/103; PMP 1963, 257/173.

79 See ND, 6: 355–6/363; EA, 10.2: 687/CM, 201; see also Früchtl 1991: 38.

80 In this way, Cornell might be correct to characterise Adorno's engagement with Schopenhauer's ethics of pity (or compassion) as a 'deconstruction and yet appropriation' (1987: 5). Also, Früchtl points to another area of overlap between Adorno and Schopenhauer: he suggests that Adorno distinguishes between narcissistic and real compassion, mirroring a similar distinction in Schopenhauer (1991: 38–9).

5

A NEW CATEGORICAL IMPERATIVE

So far we have considered why Adorno thinks that there is no right living and how he handles a number of objections to this thesis. Now, it is time to consider Adorno's views of how we can live less wrongly. The first piece in this puzzle is the new categorical imperative – an in-depth examination of which is the topic of this chapter.

I To arrange our thoughts and actions so that Auschwitz will not repeat itself

Adorno introduces the 'new categorical imperative' towards the end of *Negative Dialectics*, in the second of twelve 'Meditations on Metaphysics'. This meditation, entitled 'Metaphysics and Culture', concerns the failure of culture, which the occurrence of Auschwitz is meant to have proved – instead of having made people immune to behaving brutally, culture is implicated in the unprecedented brutality of Auschwitz, which happened in the midst of Western society and despite 'all of the trad-ition of philosophy, art and enlightened science'.[1] Adorno also refers to the new categorical imperative, or the basic ideas it contains, in some of his lectures and writings.[2]

Adorno states the new categorical imperative at the beginning of the meditation:

> A new categorical imperative has been imposed by Hitler upon human beings in the state of their unfreedom: to arrange their thoughts and actions so that Auschwitz will not repeat itself, so that nothing similar will happen.[3]

1 ND, 6: 359/366.
2 See MCP, 181–2/116; HF, 278–9/202; EA, 10.2: 674, 690/CM, 191, 203.
3 ND, 6: 358/365; translation amended.

133

The new categorical imperative consists in the moral demand not to let Auschwitz or something similar repeat itself. Immediately following this statement, Adorno comments further on this imperative:

> This imperative is as refractory to being grounded as the givenness [*Gegebenheit*] of the Kantian imperative once was. Dealing discursively with it would be an outrage, for the new imperative gives us a bodily sensation of the moral addendum – bodily, because it is the now practical abhorrence of the unbearable physical agony to which individuals are abandoned, even after individuality, as a form of mental reflection, has begun to vanish. It is only in the unvarnished materialistic motive that morality survives.[4]

The new categorical imperative cannot be discursively grounded, but then again this is no different from the case of the Kantian categorical imperative – or so Adorno claims (see Chapter 4). In fact, one suspects that Adorno thinks that the purported failure of Kant's attempts to provide discursive grounding for morality is emblematic of the general impossibility of such a project (see also Chapter 7). Moreover, discursive grounding is not just impossible; attempting to undertake it is also inappropriate (an 'outrage'). Finally, Adorno highlights the importance of a physical element to morality ('the now practical abhorrence of the unbearable physical agony'), and claims that it is thanks only to this element that morality continues to exist at all (after Auschwitz).

This passage contains a number of noteworthy points, especially if one compares Adorno's new categorical imperative to Kant's original one. In what follows, this comparison provides an important foil for the discussion.

II Historically indexed

To speak of a *new* categorical imperative is somewhat paradoxical. According to Kant, there can be only one such imperative, albeit in different formulations.[5] Adorno must have been well aware of this, but it is unlikely that he means to offer just a new formulation of the same single imperative.

Admittedly, it is possible to read the new categorical imperative merely as a new formulation of the 'old' Kantian one. After all, one would hope that Kant's categorical imperative also commanded us to

---

4 ND, 6: 358/365; translation amended.   5 See G, 4: 421, 436.

stop another Auschwitz from happening.[6] In this sense, the new categorical imperative might just be a more particularised formulation of what morality, and thereby the categorical imperative, demands of us all along.

However, this reading is misleading. Firstly, it is not clear that Kant's categorical imperative could be as particularised as Adorno's new categorical imperative is. Kant's categorical imperative is meant to be a formal principle, not a substantive norm which refers to a particular event and demands that such an event, or events like it, should never be repeated. Admittedly, for Kantians, any genuine moral duty is a categorical imperative in a (secondary) sense, but even so, it is highly unlikely that any such duty could be particularised in quite the way the new categorical imperative is (on which more shortly).

Secondly, the idea that Adorno merely offers another formulation or a more specific variant is also implausible on textual grounds and does not fit well with Adorno's overall argument in the passage under consideration. The quoted passage lives off the contrast between the new categorical imperative and the Kantian one – its rhetorical and argumentative force would be diminished if Adorno just offered another formulation. This becomes clearer still if we take the wider textual context into account. Adorno's concern in the 'Meditations on Metaphysics' is that we need to break with modern thought forms and culture because they failed to prevent Auschwitz. Hence, it would be surprising if he then suggested the categorical imperative could basically remain the same, but just needed to be formulated or specified differently. The fact that the new categorical imperative is substantive and particularised down to the mentioning of a name is not accidental. It is an implicit critique of the formal ethics of Kant – such an ethics is, after all, for Adorno an instance of failed culture, of the fact that 'spirit [*Geist*] lacked the power to take hold of human beings and work a change in them'.[7] In other words, even if Kant's ethics also condemned what happened in Auschwitz in principle, one of Adorno's points here is that Kantian ethics nonetheless failed to get a foothold for this condemnation in people and, if anything, contributed to the

---

6 One would hope this, but if Adorno is right in his criticisms of Kant's moral philosophy (see previous chapter, especially Adorno's Empty Formalism Objection), Kant's categorical imperative might actually fail to command this (not because it commands us to the contrary, but just because it is unsuitable to command anything).

7 ND, 6: 359/366; translation amended.

fact that morality lost this foothold.[8] As such a critique, the new categorical imperative is best read as a replacement for, not a variant of, Kant's categorical imperative.

This point is reinforced by the following consideration. The difference between Kant's categorical imperative and Adorno's new categorical imperative is not just that the former is a formal principle and the latter is a substantive norm. Rather, along with this change, there is another difference: Adorno brings a historical anchoring (or indexing) into play – both by mentioning a particular event (and, in fact, a particular place, Auschwitz) and by his formulation that Hitler has imposed this imperative.

In particular, one might say that the new categorical imperative is true as a reaction to a particular historical experience – the genocide of the European Jews and Roma and Sinti, the murder and mistreatment of homosexuals, political opponents, civilians, and prisoners of war.[9] This reading fits well with what Adorno says elsewhere about moral demands. For example, he claims that demands, such as that there should be no torture or concentration camps, are 'true as an impulse, as a reaction to the news that torture is going on somewhere'.[10] Adorno thinks of moral demands as dependent on the ethical features of situations and as expressive of our reactions to these features – I come back to this point later in the chapter (and in Chapter 7). For now, the key point is that Adorno's indexing of his imperative (and moral demands generally) stands in contrast to Kant's ahistorical conception of the categorical imperative.

This historical indexing is also the acknowledgement of the fact 'that the content of the moral principle, the categorical imperative, constantly changes as history changes'.[11] If there is a historical, even experience-based index to particular events, then the paradigmatic experiences to which the categorical imperative refers and which it commands us to prevent vary over time – the command to prevent

---

8 One way Kantian moral philosophy contributed to the failure of culture is its denial of the materialistic element of morality, the addendum (discussed in Appendix). Generally, by making morality too abstract and empty, Kantians opened the door, however inadvertently, to people's dressing up their abhorrent behaviour as morally required – famously, Eichmann claimed to have always acted according to Kant's categorical imperative (see Arendt [1963] 1994: Ch. 8; see also MacIntyre 1998: 197–8; and Chapters 1 and 5 here).

9 For a similar interpretation of this aspect of the new categorical imperative, see Bernstein 2001: Ch. 8; and Schweppenhäuser 2004: 344–5.

10 ND, 281/285; see also PMP 1963, 144–5/97.   11 HF, 285/206.

another Auschwitz might still have a foothold in us (one would hope), but the command to prevent another Rwanda might have a more immediate pull on us still.

Interestingly, Adorno does not think that such a historical (or situational) index takes away the categorical character of the demand not to let Auschwitz repeat itself. As with Kant's categorical imperative, this demand is meant to hold for agents independently of any other ends, motives, or inclinations they might have. In fact, one reason why Adorno uses Kantian terminology here is to indicate and endorse this categorical aspect of moral demands. Thus, Adorno is not just subverting an aspect of the miscarried culture – Kant's ethics – in proposing a new categorical imperative that is historically specific and impulse-based, but he also wants to preserve something of the Kantian idea. To wit, that certain requirements have an unavoidable, categorical nature; that the experience of Auschwitz demands a certain reaction of everyone, irrespective of what other purposes they might be pursuing. As Adorno puts it in one of his lectures:

> In other words, it might be said that in view of what we have experienced – and let me say that it is also experienced by those on whom it was not directly perpetrated – there can be no one, whose organ of experience has not entirely atrophied, for whom the world *after* Auschwitz, that is, the world in which Auschwitz was possible, is the same world as before. And I believe that if one observes and analyses oneself closely, one will find that the awareness of living in a world in which that is possible – is possible *again* and is possible *for the first time* – plays a quite crucial role even in one's most secret reaction. / I would say, therefore, that these experiences have a compelling universality, and that one would indeed have to be blind to the world's course if one were to wish *not* to have these experiences.[12]

One difficulty with this passage is that we are given two not quite identical accounts of the compelling universality of the experiences in question – first Adorno says we cannot but have them unless our 'organ of experience has entirely atrophied', then he talks about the blindness of which one would be guilty if one wished not to have these experiences. Still, the two accounts can be rendered compatible: unless one cannot have experiences at all any more, one undergoes the experience that post-Auschwitz the world is no longer the same (and that nothing similar should happen again); and unless one blinds oneself to the

12 MCP, 162/104; original emphasis; see also 170/109.

world completely, one does not wish that one could avoid having these experiences, since – as painful as they may be – they tell us something true and important about the state of the world, including that it should be overcome. The main point, in any case, is that the experiences connected to the new categorical imperative have 'compelling universality', and, hence, although the character of the imperative has changed from formal to substantive, its status as categorical remains. (Whether the change has implications for the way to underwrite the categorical status is a question which I take up later.)

III Imposed on humankind in its state of unfreedom

Adorno informs us that the categorical imperative is imposed on humankind in its (current) state of unfreedom. This is again unusual, not least because according to Kant the categorical imperative is directed at transcendentally free, but not fully rational beings.[13] Indeed, for Kant, it is the principle and expression of our autonomy.[14]

While it might seem odd to have a categorical imperative that is imposed on unfree human beings, it actually ties in well with Adorno's pessimistic views about the possibility of individual moral practice and (positive) freedom (see Chapters 2–3). It brings out one more time how the badness of the current world can lead to moral demands, even if individuals are not actually fully capable of meeting them – the reason why there can be no right living within this world. In a sense, Adorno reverses the order of how the principle 'ought implies can' is customarily understood – the ought comes first, even when we cannot yet fulfil it; and the ability to discharge it then may historically develop, first as the negative freedom of resistance (which we can muster nowadays to some extent) and, hopefully one day, as the positive freedom of actively determining our lives.

It also highlights how moral demands are objective for Adorno, not a matter of contracting into morality or self-legislating its commands (see also Chapter 7).[15] The actions of others change the moral fabric of the world, and whether we endorse this or not, this imposes duties on

---

13 See especially G, 4: 454.   14 See, for example, G, 4: 440.

15 Moral realist readings of Kant's ethics could accommodate the objective element to which I point here to some extent – for them, self-legislation concerns only the obligatoriness of moral demands, not their content (see, for example, Stern 2009: §III.1, with further references). Still, some disagreement remains: for Adorno, even the obligatoriness arises from the situation itself.

us, and does so often not because others acted legitimately (say by helping us in need, so that we have a duty of gratitude to them), but in morally problematic ways (as Hitler and his followers did).

At this point, it might be helpful to briefly discuss an objection to the picture presented by Adorno. It seems that his claim that there exist moral demands without the guarantee of the corresponding freedom is objectionably over-demanding. For it is often thought that we can only be obliged to do what we are able to carry out.[16] Thus, one could argue on the basis of the commonly accepted principle 'ought implies can' that Adorno faces a dilemma:[17] either his moral demands are over-demanding and should be rejected as such; or they are not over-demanding because Adorno has to weaken his thesis about our degree of unfreedom and allow for the possibility of right living.

The first thing to note in this context is that there is a sense in which Adorno would admit that it is problematic to have moral demands without the guarantee that they could be fulfilled: he would be the first to lament that right living is blocked while being so desperately required. However, Adorno would insist that the problematic nature of morality is our actual predicament. Thus, we cannot just infer from the over-demanding nature of moral demands that they are not binding on us. Ought, so to speak, *ought* to imply can, but it does not always actually imply it. This is something which gives us cause to be unsatisfied with the current state of morality, but it is not something which we can simply argue away.

To recall an earlier point, moral demands have for Adorno an objective status – it is the nature of our social world, of the bads it cannot but produce, that demands its abolition. The capacity to address these matters is a derivative consideration – even if this capacity were lost, there would be reason to lament the badness, to demand that the world be different.

One way to think about this is in terms of moral dilemmas (a pertinent comparison, given Adorno's views that our lives are structured by

---

16 As Kant puts it at one point: 'duty commands nothing but what we can do' (R, 6: 47).

17 To be precise, the commonly accepted 'ought implies can'-principle is that we cannot be (morally) obliged to do what we cannot do. What we can do *restricts* what we are (morally) obliged to do. Sometimes, 'ought implies can' is understood differently – here the knowledge that we (morally) ought to do something *enables* us to see (or even know) that we can do it. Surprisingly perhaps, Kant mainly uses the latter (enabling) version, not the former (restrictive) one (see Timmermann 2003; see also Stern 2004; Martin 2009: esp. 111–12).

practical antinomies in the modern social world; see Chapter 2). If there are genuine moral dilemmas, then it is not possible to act in a morally right way, whichever option we eventually take. What is not always recognised is that this makes genuine dilemmas incompatible with the 'ought implies can'-principle (restrictively understood). For on this principle, if we cannot but act in a morally problematic way, then the moral demands in question ought to be revised so that we can avoid this – either by privileging one option or by accepting that whichever option we take we act in a morally right way. Yet, this seems unconvincing, for genuine moral dilemmas are part of the moral fabric of (at least) our social world; and to say that choosing one or either horn is morally right (rather than excusable but tragic) is to do injustice to the idea of dilemma. It is to not acknowledge properly the fact that both sides exert a pull on us, so that taking only one cannot be morally right and should leave us with regret.

Moreover, in one sense it is not true that Adorno's view violates the principle in question: for as a global subject, as humanity, we have the capacity to transcend the social world (and its thought forms) and as individuals we have (sometimes) the negative freedom to discharge our indirect duty to help humanity to exercise this capacity – I come back to this later in this chapter.[18] Indeed, one reason to be sceptical whenever someone insists that something is impossible for them to do and that therefore it is problematic to even ask it of them, is that we are often mistaken about what we can do – for example, our social context has led us to have a constricted sense of opportunities and possibilities. Adorno suggests that something like this is true at the collective level for us – as seen, he thinks we wrongly think of our social world as immutable, whereas in fact we could, collectively, change it (see Chapter 3). In this sense, denying that we are morally required to change this world because we (purportedly) could not, can be ideological and pernicious by cementing the illusion that this world is inescapable. It can also be a self-fulfilling prophecy – for the more we believe that we cannot do it, the less we might actually be able to do it.

Finally, even if something is impossible to achieve, it might still serve as an ideal for our practice and as such have normative pull on us, even

---

18 Adorno is not saying that it is *logically* impossible to discharge our moral demands. It might be true that moral demands cannot require logically impossible things, but this implies nothing of substance for historical situations like ours that limit our ability to discharge these demands. See also Martin 2009: esp. 122.

moral bindingness. For many Christians, a life without sin is both an unreachable ideal for finite, embodied beings, but nonetheless strictly demanded of them.[19] For others, such a life was merely a regulative ideal it was demanded that they should approximate and yet it thereby still served a practical, normative role. Similarly, many moral and political theories propose ideals that their proponents full well know that we can, at best, realise in sub-optimal ways.[20] While it is an interesting question whether this means that we should nonetheless aim for them (or rather for the second best),[21] this often depends on the specific context, and, at any rate, a lot of our moral experience and landscape would be lost if we simply gave up on all oughts that we cannot (fully) realise.

IV Not maxim-centred

Another striking feature of the new categorical imperative is that it focuses on thoughts, actions, and outcomes, not on maxims. This again puts it in contrast to Kant's categorical imperative and his 'ethics of disposition'. However, this shift away from an ethics of disposition makes good sense in the context of Adorno's worries about such an ethics (some of which we discussed in the previous chapter).

Admittedly, it is not that dispositions are dropped completely. After all, the categorical imperative commands us to also arrange our *thoughts* in a certain way, and this might reasonably be interpreted to include the demand to adopt the right kind of dispositions, although it probably extends wider than (ethical) dispositions are often understood (for example, it might also involve a change to our cognitive engagement with the world around us). It is unclear whether arranging our thoughts so that Auschwitz will not repeat itself is a matter of adopting the right kind of maxims for Adorno. Given his disparaging comments about acting on maxims ('a person acting in this way would be more of a monster than a human being'),[22] having the right kind of dispositions might not be best understood in this way. Be that as it may, the main focus of the categorical imperative is on consequences and outcomes: the prevention of a particular event of a certain sort.

---

19 See also Martin 2009.

20 For example, on Sangiovanni's reading, Rawls views justice as a regulative ideal (2010: 221).

21 See, for example, Goodin 1995 for the argument that in political contexts the second best is (often) to be preferred as guiding policies and action.

22 PMP 1963, 232/156.

In a way, the categorical imperative can be more easily compared with Kant's conception of external right than the categorical imperative and the demands of virtue. According to Kant, duties of right enjoin us to behave in a certain way (to keep contracts, not to murder or steal, etc.), but leave it open on which incentive we act; whereas duties of virtue require not just that we try to do the right thing, but also that we do it for the right reasons (i.e., in Kant's case for moral reasons, specifically respect for the moral law).[23] Just as with duties of right, the new categorical imperative has its focus on actions and their outcomes, not on what motivates these actions. Admittedly, it is plausible to think that not any incentive or motive would do to prevent another Auschwitz from happening and that the most reliable and suitable motives would be such that they include a direct reference to the evil of Auschwitz. Still, the new categorical imperative does not *in principle* restrict the range of motives on which we can act to straightforwardly Kantian moral reasons. As in Dietrich Niemöller's famous poem, we might be afraid that we are next in line to be persecuted and that fear would be reason enough to adopt the new categorical imperative.[24]

Consider also the comparison to Utilitarianism, which demands of us to secure the greatest happiness for the greatest number. Although the new categorical imperative is consequentialist in the sense of being outcome-orientated, it is not a maximising principle. Admittedly, we should do our utmost to stop another Auschwitz from happening, but the goal is about not crossing a certain threshold and functions more like a side constraint than a requirement to maximise.

V The materialistic motive

Adorno makes suffering and the physical impulse as reaction to suffering central to the new categorical imperative.[25] In fact, he goes so far to say that it is *only* in 'the practical abhorrence of the unbearable physical

---

23 See, for example, MS, 6: 218–19.

24 There is no authorised source for this poem but various versions, the first of which seems to have appeared in 1946 (see http://www.history.ucsb.edu/faculty/marcuse/niem; last accessed 17 December 2012). One version runs as follows in English: 'First they came for the Communists, / and I didn't speak up, because I wasn't a Communist. / Then they came for the Jews, / and I didn't speak up, / because I wasn't a Jew. / Then they came for the trade unionists, / and I didn't speak up because I wasn't a trade unionist. / Then they came for the Catholics, / and I didn't speak up, / because I was a Protestant. / Then they came for me, and by that time there was no one/left to speak up for me.'

25 See also Schweppenhäuser 2004: 344–5.

agony' that morality survives.[26] This is unlike the Kantian conception of morality, according to which physical impulses cannot be central to morality for fear of turning it into heteronomy. It is, however, in line with Adorno's views on freedom and moral philosophy that we have encountered in earlier chapters.

While I will say more about the materialistic element later in the chapter (and in Chapter 7), I want to note here already that Adorno thinks that only by building the bodily abhorrence of physical agony into the moral outlook does morality have the kind of foothold in human beings that, according to Adorno, Enlightenment culture and Kantian ethics lacked, specifically 'the power to take hold of human beings and work a change in them'.[27] In its very concrete reference to particular events, the new categorical imperative is meant to elicit in us exactly that element that is subordinate in Kantian ethics – the addendum of the physical impulse which is involved in the experiences of these events (and hearing about them). Rather than moving from rational insight and deliberation to action – a model that, in practice, leads to sabotaging action (see Appendix) – we should be guided by the physical impulses expressed in our reactions of abhorrence at suffering.

The contrast to Kant is not just at the level of how moral action and motivation is conceived, but also at the (admittedly related) level of normativity: for Adorno, but not for Kant and Kantians, pain and suffering are intrinsically bad, they by themselves call for remedy.[28] It is not that pain and suffering are bad *only or mainly* because they make living an upright moral life difficult for human beings; or because their intentional infliction in most cases would involve a maxim we could not universalise; or because we view them as bad on rational reflection and thereby 'create' their negative value by rational willing.[29] Such Kantian accounts of the badness of pain and suffering miss something important about them – that they are bad in themselves.[30] Moreover,

---

26 ND, 6: 358/365.   27 ND, 6: 359/366; translation amended.

28 As I comment on shortly, Adorno might hold a more qualified claim – that only certain forms of pain and suffering are intrinsically bad – but the nature of the disagreement would not change fundamentally.

29 The third variant is the one endorsed by Hill (1992: 89).

30 Korsgaard recently attempted to integrate the badness of pain (both of human and non-human animals) within the Kantian moral framework (see Korsgaard et al. 1996: 145ff.), but again it is telling how forced and distorting this addition is. For example, for Korsgaard, it is ultimately not the animal's pain that is the reason for us to help it or

the Kantian denial of the inherent (negative) normativity of pain and suffering is not just problematic at the level of theorising, but with it Kantian ethics also contributed to culture's failure to prevent Auschwitz. The coldness to the suffering of others was instrumental in carrying out the unspeakable acts, and this coldness was also fuelled by the way culture and, within it, Kantian ethics, downplayed the direct normative importance of bodily suffering.

There is much more to say on these issues. I come back to aspects of it later when discussing Adorno's own views on normativity (see especially Chapters 7–9), but let me make a few remarks about pain and suffering already at this point, even though this leads us away to some extent from the discussion of the new categorical imperative.

No one would deny that suffering plays a pivotal role in Adorno's theory. However, there are a number of unresolved matters in this context – concerning both interpretation and philosophical cogency.[31] Firstly, there is a delicate balancing act between acknowledging the significance of suffering for Adorno and not ascribing a monist and reductionist position to him – one according to which only suffering (perhaps, ultimately, only physical suffering) has intrinsic disvalue and all other bads (unfreedom, alienation, misrecognition, etc.) are only bad if and insofar as they lead to (physical) suffering. There are passages where Adorno *sounds* like a hedonist Utilitarian and reductionist materialist – notably, when he writes that 'All pain and all negativity ... are the many times over mediated form of the physical, [which] sometimes has become unrecognizable; just as all happiness aims at sensual fulfilment and garners its objectivity in it.'[32] Still, on my reading of this passage and his work as a whole, he holds a different position from that of a hedonist, reductionist materialism. His view is instead that all negativity, including emotional pain and negativity other than suffering,

---

refrain from inflicting certain treatment on it, but that we could not value ourselves, unless we also valued animal nature (see 152–3). (It is also doubtful that this latter claim is actually true and that anything determinate and significant would follow if it were true; see, for example, Pippin 2008: 89.)

31 Apart from the two issues I discuss in the main text, there is also a mainly interpretive one about the exact relationship between '*Schmerz* [pain]' and '*Leiden* [suffering]' in Adorno's work. Martin Eichler has suggested to me that pain denotes, for Adorno, the pre-conceptual experience, while suffering is the conceptually mediated experience of the same phenomenon. I am not convinced that there is textual evidence for attributing this view to Adorno, but I have no clear alternative proposal. Sometimes, he seems to treat them interchangeably (10.2: 682/CM, 197); sometimes he lists them separately (8: 91).

32 ND, 6: 202/202; Redmond's translation used and amended.

is *modelled on* physical suffering,[33] and *typically accompanied or expressed by the latter*. In other words, we learn about negativity by way of experiencing physical suffering, and this genesis continues to provide the framework – such as, for example, certain patterns of reaction – for experiencing negativity in all its forms (in this sense, all negativity is 'the many times over mediated form of the physical, [which] sometimes has become unrecognizable'). Physical suffering shares with other forms of suffering and negativity the structure of vulnerability, about which we first learn through physical pain and suffering. In addition, Adorno believes that negativity will have somatic manifestations. Whether or not this additional thesis is true in all cases – it might be more plausible for neuroses and emotional stress than other cases, such as having one's legitimate projects thwarted without ever knowing about it – the key point in this context is that what Adorno is saying is merely that physical suffering can be an *index* of the bad even in those cases where it is not the originally inflicted bad itself. Saying this is compatible with understanding normativity pluralistically, as comprising a variety of bads, not just the bad of physical suffering. Indeed, this is how Adorno understands it: for him, negativity is not reducible to or exhausted by physical suffering, not even suffering in all its forms. Rather, it includes also unfreedom, misrecognition, humiliation, alienation, and other forms of disregarding human potential and animality (see also Chapter 9). Thus, for Adorno we typically suffer when we are unfree; and we suffer from the objectification and alienation to which our social world subjects us.[34] Yet, this suffering is not the only thing that is wrong with unfreedom, objectification, and alienation; they are also wrong in themselves. The objective negativity of our social world is experienced subjectively as suffering, but the social world is objectively negative not just because of the suffering it causes, but because of its inhumanity more generally.[35]

Secondly, it is unclear whether Adorno holds that *all suffering* is bad and should be abolished; or only a subset thereof – be it *senseless suffering*; or (as Geuss suggests)[36] *historically superfluous suffering*. There is textual evidence for all of these possibilities, but also reasons to be sceptical about each – interpretive and philosophical reasons. I consider these three possible interpretations and their respective merits in reverse order.

33 Bernstein also suggests that for Adorno valuing is modelled on our animal relation to pain (2001: 406–7; see also 301–6 and Ch. 6 as a whole).
34 See, for example, 10.1: 294; 14: 67.   35 20.1: 253.   36 Geuss 2005: 112.

One clear instance, where Adorno objects to historically superfluous and accepts historically necessary suffering is when he, on the one hand, lambasts our social world because people go hungry although they could be fed; but, on the other hand, rejects criticising past societies, in which the forces of production were insufficiently developed to feed all of its members, for the suffering of those that went hungry in them.[37] Still, I am wary of reading too much into such passages. As I already noted in Chapter 1, Adorno is very aware of the fact that what is presented as historically necessary is often no such thing. In fact, he criticises Hegel and Marx for accepting too easily that domination and hierarchies in past societies were necessary, when they (and the suffering they produced) had, actually, become superfluous.[38] As also noted in Chapter 1, even when the bads of social organisations were necessary for increasing the chances of human survival, Adorno does not think that they are – *pace* Hegel and Marx – redeemed by this.[39] Instead, they leave a (negative) normative remainder. Indeed, Adorno claims that metaphysical longing does not aim just at abolishing existing suffering, but also at revoking the irrevocably past suffering.[40] Impossible as the aim is, this claim suggests that for Adorno historical necessity is not the last word on the normative standing of suffering.

Elsewhere Adorno speaks of 'senseless suffering', and that it could and should be abolished.[41] The contrast here is to meaningful suffering – to those cases where suffering is a (possibly inescapable) part of activities and events which imbue our lives with meaning, either directly (as in relationships, education, achievements, and the like) or as background condition (for example, maintaining one's good health). In some such cases, we could and happily would engage in the activities in question (say dental surgery) without the experience of pain that can accompany them; but, in other cases, the activities and experiences (such as grieving) essentially involve suffering and yet one might still think that they are appropriate within any recognisable human life. Also, suffering can – Adorno admits in the context of discussing Wagner – become 'sweet' in certain instances, such as when relishing in a challenge and enjoying the suspense involved in taking it on.[42]

37 8: 347/Adorno et al. 1976: 62.
38 See HF, 99–100, 249–50/67–8, 181; see also ND, 6: 315–17/321–3.
39 See HF, 72, 82/47–8, 55.   40 ND, 6: 395/403.
41 ND, 203/203; 8: 62; HF, 72/48.   42 See 13: 64.

One problem here is that one person's meaningful suffering is another person's senseless one: is the self-flagellation of a monk senseless suffering or rightful penance? Is the pain experienced by an athlete vindicated by the achievement or a silly sacrifice for an unimportant goal? Is the grief of a severely depressed person appropriate or should they move on since their loved one cannot be brought back by this and would have wanted them to live a happier life? Indeed, a problem arises here which is similar to the one regarding historically superfluous and necessary suffering: ruling elites might proclaim certain kinds of suffering – say that caused by market-driven economic organisation – as inescapable by-products of or otherwise required for certain meaningful activities (say the exercise of an abstractly conceived individual freedom and pursuit of happiness, which purportedly provides people with material wealth, technological innovations, and cultural offerings in a way that allows them to pursue their own projects to the maximal extent possible).

Perhaps because of considerations like these, Adorno sometimes seems to aim for a stronger thesis – the abolition of *all* suffering. Notably, he claims that 'The physical element tells our cognition [*Erkenntnis*] that suffering ought not to be, that things should be different'; that a social change would be to 'abolish suffering or mitigate it to a degree which theory cannot anticipate, to which it can set no limit'; and that the 'telos' of a free society 'would be to negate the physical suffering of even the least of its members, and to negate the internal reflexive forms of that suffering'.[43] Here he seems to view suffering – in particular physical suffering – as something that should be completely abolished. Indeed, elsewhere he goes further and denounces 'every clandestine agreement with the inevitability [*Unabdingbarkeit*] of suffering', adding that 'Solidarity prohibits its justification.'[44] This can be rendered compatible with the earlier quoted passages insofar as one could read Adorno as saying that, given the level of development of the forces of production, all suffering (or at least all physical suffering) has become historically superfluous and senseless suffering, such that

---

43 ND, 6: 203/203–4; translation amended.

44 10.2: 701/CM, 214; translation amended. It is unclear whether 'its' refers to 'suffering' or to 'agreement with the inevitability of suffering'. What speaks for the former is that a few sentences earlier he speaks (critically) of 'suffering and its justification'. Still, for our purposes here, nothing much hangs on it – in the paragraph as a whole he clearly objects to suffering and to accepting that it is inevitable.

objecting to the former can also be framed in terms of the latter, and *vice versa.*

The position that all suffering, or even 'just' all physical suffering, can and should be abolished seems implausible and surprising. It seems implausible, because, as long we are still human beings, suffering, including its physical forms, will continue to exist – surely, even in a free society, accidents will happen and people will get hurt, not to mention unrequited love or grief. Also, even if it were possible to abolish (physical) suffering altogether, making the unqualified abolition of (physical) suffering one's aim would seem one-dimensional insofar as it overlooked that there are other valuable matters (such as love or achievements) which would have to be sacrificed in pursuit of this.[45] The position seems surprising since Adorno must have been aware of these commonplaces about the human condition. It seems even more surprising, given that he was such a close reader of Nietzsche's texts, in which pain and suffering are presented as great teachers, as making us into spiritual animals, such that we can see the world and our place in it lucidly, without self-pity or wishful thinking.[46] Indeed, at least in some interpretations, Nietzsche advocates that pain and suffering are not just contingent conditions of a well-lived life that we should grudgingly accept, but constitutive of such a life and of what makes it desirable, insofar as pain and suffering are part and parcel of overcoming resistance and of enabling greatness.[47]

One way to respond to this would be to admit that pain and physical suffering might be ineliminable, but that we should aim to reduce them as much as we can. While accidents and physical pain might not be completely avoidable even in a free society, it would be possible to reduce them considerably and even to abolish 'the suffering brought on by social coercion'[48] and that produced by our domination of nature – for in a free society, there would be no social coercion and we would no longer dominate nature. Does this mean that such a free society would come at the expense of greatness? For a start, Adorno would criticise the supreme valuation of overcoming resistance and creative production in the Nietzschean alternative as fetishistic, as 'blind fury of activity', deeply shaped by the bourgeois conception of nature and the insatiable productivism of capitalism that we should

---

45 See Geuss 2005: 130.
46 See Han-Pile 2011: 239 (with references); see also Reginster 2006.
47 Reginster 2006: 13–15, 133–5, 186, 188–9, 195–6, 230ff.   48 ND, 6: 222/223.

reject.[49] Beyond this, it is worth recalling Adorno's pluralism about the bad: if ending suffering really came at the expense of avoiding other bads – if, say, the former required forgoing grief at the death of loved ones – then he would accept that some suffering will remain part of human life even in a free society. Whether rightly or wrongly, he would, nonetheless, insist on the tragedy of this, rather than accept it as either redeemed by what it makes possible, or as something we cannot even lament as tragic because we could not have a recognisable valuable human life without such suffering.

Perhaps, this way to respond is, ultimately, best characterised as backtracking and falling back on the view that it is 'only' senseless suffering that Adorno wants to – or, at any rate, can defensibly want to – abolish. The passages in which Adorno seems to say something stronger would then be seen, at worst, as misleading and, at best, as useful exaggerations that remind us that we have a tendency to set a premature limit on how much we can abolish (physical) suffering while preserving meaningful activities and events. This raises the issue noted earlier of how to settle what suffering is senseless and what suffering is meaningful. Given Adorno's suspicion of our common beliefs and values, what he means by senseless suffering would be determined with reference to our objective interests as creatures with a certain potential (see also Chapter 9). Thus, many human achievements might require a certain amount of discipline, and to instil this in our children might be acceptable, even though doing so involves suffering. (Adorno would insist that we were fooling ourselves, if we denied that this involves suffering.) Yet, if instilling discipline became an end in itself, then Adorno would reject it, at least in part because it would then involve senseless suffering. Crucially, he would reject it, even if the person administering the discipline and the person to whom it is administered accepted the suffering as meaningful.

Returning to the discussion of the new categorical imperative, I note that Adorno's view of suffering and pain might need to be qualified or even amended, but the point against the Kantians still stands: whenever pain and suffering are bad, the Kantians either cannot account for this, or only in a way which is tortured and inappropriate (see also Chapter 7). This failure had, Adorno believes, fateful consequences in making Auschwitz possible.

---

49 MM, Aphorism No. 100, 4: 178/156.

VI The absolute moral minimum

The moral demand not to let Auschwitz repeat itself is much narrower in scope than Kant's categorical imperative, which was meant to underwrite a full-blown moral system. This might also suggest that it plays a different role from a supreme principle of morality from which every aspect of morality can purportedly be derived. In fact, the new categorical imperative is to some extent narrower even than the other elements in Adorno's minimalist ethics of resistance (which we consider in the next chapter). One way to explain this is the following: preventing another moral catastrophe like the genocide of the European Jews is for Adorno something like a minimum condition whose fulfilment is absolutely required within his already minimalist ethics – it is the absolute moral minimum. Thus, whatever we do, not letting Auschwitz repeat itself is in any case demanded of us. In this sense, the new categorical imperative inherits the form of what would be a strict duty in traditional morality (to be precise, a prohibition). The idea of the new categorical imperative as a strict, negative duty also fits well with the centrality which suffering and the physical impulse as reaction to it have for the categorical imperative. The prevention of suffering (and of other evils) has traditionally been associated with strict, negative duties.

However, this last element already points beyond the more narrow focus. According to Adorno, Auschwitz stands for the continuation of suffering not only despite the technological, rational, and organisational advances of the modern age, but partly in virtue of these advances. Ultimately to arrange human actions and thoughts so that Auschwitz will not repeat itself is to change the current social world, since in it the objective conditions for Auschwitz to repeat itself continue to exist.[50] Thus, the categorical imperative might be narrower than Adorno's other views about resistance and not joining in. Still, this imperative and these views are also linked in that they share in an ultimate concern, namely, to overcome the current social world (see also next chapter).

In this context, it is also apt to comment on a difficulty thrown up by the new categorical imperative: how would we recognise a repeat of Auschwitz or, indeed, something similar? Is the 1994 Rwandan

---

50 See, for example, EA, 10.2: 674/CM, 190; see also here, Chapter 1.

genocide, which was carried out much less by industrial means than the extermination of the European Jews (and other victim groups) in the 1940s and under different socio-economic conditions, a repeat of Auschwitz? Was it also due to a failure of culture linked to modern capitalism and thought forms? Does what happened in Abu Ghraib count as sufficiently similar to be covered by the new categorical imperative?

These are complex matters which I cannot hope to do full justice here, but let me point to some of the resources Adorno has for dealing with them. Firstly, we should recall that he is sceptical about an ethics, such as Kant's, that bases everything on a supreme principle. Any such principle will be too abstract and general to guide our actions in specific contexts (see also Chapter 4). Moreover, it will divorce morality too much from the non-discursive, materialistic motive, which Adorno thinks is central to morality. For these reasons, it might even seem surprising that Adorno speaks of a new categorical imperative at all – such imperatives are normally at home only in principle-based moral philosophy, which he rejects (see also Chapter 7). If, however, we also recall that Adorno changes the character of categorical imperatives from a formal principle to an experience-based substantive norm, then we can see that talk of a categorical imperative is not so surprising – given the compelling universality of the experiences in question (see earlier). Also, we can see how we should think about the guidance his new categorical imperative offers. Even a principle-based ethics, such as Kant's, does not work on the model of an algorithm, such that whatever the highest principle of morality says can just be computed, without any need for exercising judgement. On the contrary, Kant admits that we 'require a judgement sharpened by experience, partly to distinguish in what case they [the moral laws, FF] are applicable'.[51] In the case of Adorno, the role of judgement would also be important, perhaps more so. Still, the judgement would not be about the application of a principle, but rather about recognising which core features of (the experience of) Auschwitz are present in (our experience of) a situation. Put differently, the events referred to in the new categorical imperative and the appropriate reactions to them function more like *paradigm examples* than principles. Equally, recognising their

---

51 G, 4: 389; see also O'Neill 2007.

reoccurrence or that something similar is taking place should be thought of more along the lines of (Wittgenstein's idea of) family resemblance than in terms of meeting necessary and sufficient conditions. In more Adornian terms: these events and the appropriate reactions to them are less like subsuming instances under categories and more like constellations, such that similar occurrences would share some elements, but not necessarily all or even the same elements in each case. There would be a wide ambit and important role for judgement, and we would have to look to the most critical minds and their assessment of the multidimensional and multifaceted continuum. Presumably, the Rwandan genocide would be closer to Auschwitz in some respects (such as scale, intention, attempt to eliminate an ethnically constructed group, and wide participation of large parts of the population) than the abuses at Abu Ghraib by US military personnel, but in other respects the latter would be closer to Auschwitz than the former (the ways the inmates were deported, torn from their cultural context and stripped of their identities, the use of torture and deprivation for the purpose of breaking them, or the level of bureaucratic-technical machinery at work). Indeed, there is something problematic in thinking about such events as all along one dimension of moral reprehensibility, vying for the top spot. We do better to think of them multidimensionally, and as both unique *and* all too familiar; similar *and* singular; comparable *and* incomparable.

Instead of looking to principles, we should look at core elements of the events and our experience of them – I return to identify some of those in the case of Auschwitz in the final chapter, and the considerations there also speak to the issue at hand here. We have to exercise our judgement – indeed, as we have seen, we do so even in a principle-based ethics, albeit differently – and guidance for this might involve looking to those most skilled in these matters or at least to those whose ability to have unrestricted experiences is least damaged. Thus, as we see in more detail in the next chapter (and return to in Chapter 9), there is a considerable role within Adorno's practical philosophy for the few critical individuals lucky enough to exist in our current social world. They can function as orientating exemplars. Finally, as we also see in the next chapter, Adorno's theory contains other guidance besides the new categorical imperative, and this richer, albeit still minimalist picture can provide additional resources to navigate our ethically challenging world.

VII Addressed at humankind

The new categorical imperative is addressed not, first and foremost, to the individual, but to humankind as a whole.[52] Its very content is such that it cannot be about what individuals could also do in isolation (in contrast to certain duties to oneself, such as the duty not to overeat or drink excessively, or the duty not to kill or maim oneself). It is only at the social level that we could stop Auschwitz from repeating itself. Individuals can at most hope to undermine the subjective conditions for their joining in a second Auschwitz, but this will leave the objective conditions untouched.[53] To change the latter, we would have to radically change our current social world. Adorno speaks of this in terms of 'social morality [*gesellschaftliche Moral*]',[54] presumably referring to what is demanded of us *qua* members of society, not *qua* private individuals. Thus, the new categorical imperative is mainly aimed at humanity as a whole, since only as a collective could we change the objective conditions – only as 'global subject' can humanity make genuine progress and avert 'the most extreme, total disaster'.[55] The content of these demands – not to let Auschwitz repeat itself and to end the bad infinity that is the current social world – is such that only humanity as a whole could fulfil them. This is not to say that it does not have an individual dimension as well – I come back to this soon. The important point for now is that, while individually we cannot change the social world, Adorno seems to think that socially speaking we have all that is required for fulfilling these demands. In this sense, we have both collective responsibility and – in the absence of our changing the world – collective guilt.

One might object that the position I attribute to Adorno requires commitment to agents other than individuals and that this idea is itself implausible, since groups or collectives have neither separate ontological status, nor agency. Moreover, one might also object that any talk of collective agency and guilt will, at least in practice, function to deflect away from individual responsibility and guilt.[56]

---

52 Admittedly, Adorno speaks of the new categorical imperative as 'imposed on human beings [*den Menschen aufgezwungen*]', not on 'imposed on humankind/humanity [*der Menschheit aufgezwungen*]'. However, from what I go on to say in the main text, it should be clear why its addressee – the agent who could discharge the duty – is, first and foremost, a collective subject.
53 See, for example, EA, 10.2: esp. 675–6/CM, 192–3; see also next chapter.
54 ND, 6: 294/299; see also ND, 6: 241/241; PMP 1956/7 (unpublished), Vo1323.
55 P, 10.2: 618/CM, 144; see also here, Chapter 3.
56 For both of these points, see, for example, Narveson 2002.

It is not clear whether Adorno would accept this demand for methodological individualism or, indeed, whether we should accept it.
However, even if one granted that collective agency and responsibility
are problematic notions unless they can be cashed out, expressed, in
terms of individual agency and responsibility, there is a way of thinking
about the collective responsibility in question that avoids the purported
implausibility. Adorno's talk of demands on humanity might be seen in
terms of other collective action problems, such as environmental protection. To take an example, global warming might only be prevented if
the whole of humanity (or at least large parts of it) changed their
behaviour radically. Moreover, the way global warming is produced
might be such (let us assume this for argument's sake) that, whatever
we do as individuals (for example, take the train instead of the car,
reduce our use of electricity, etc.), we cannot escape contributing to it. It
might be the case that modern societies are so organised that it is
virtually impossible to live in a way that does not rely on certain structures (supermarkets, health care, employment, etc.) which add to
global warming. In this situation we might be able to live less wrongly,
but we could never live rightly (at least, as far as global warming is
concerned). If this were the situation, it is not implausible to say that
humanity as a whole has a responsibility to change its ways and stop
global warming because only humanity as a whole can do this. The
individual, on the other hand, may not have a direct responsibility to
stop global warming (this would be beyond them and so too much to ask
of them). What the individual might have is an indirect responsibility,
namely to do what it takes to contribute to humanity fulfilling its
responsibility. This could, for example, mean that the individuals have
the responsibility to gain insight into the nature of the predicament and
the need to address this problem collectively.

Adorno thinks something very similar about the moral demand of
stopping Auschwitz from repeating itself and ending the bad infinity
that is the current social world. Individuals cannot on their own bring
these outcomes about. However, even *qua* individuals we might be able
to minimise our contributions to the worst excesses of the radically evil
social world. The only 'agent' which could do anything final and definitive about the matters at hand would be humanity as a whole, and so this
responsibility rests on its shoulders. However, this does not preclude our
responsibility as individuals, insofar as we are responsible for not setting
the collective 'agent' in motion (which is not an agent independently of
our actions, but just the tendency arising from what we as individual

agents do within the particular structural framework we sustain). Thus, *qua* individuals we are responsible both for minimising our personal involvement in the worst and for taking steps that would enable humanity to take up its responsibility. In other words, there might be an *indirect* duty on each individual to do what is in his or her power to enable humanity to discharge its duty. For example, Adorno speaks of being critical as a moral demand.[57] This demand could be seen as part of the indirect demands on individuals flowing from the direct demands on humanity. For Adorno, we are only able to overcome the current social world, which has become our second nature, by recognising that it is human-made and by seeing through the mechanisms which keep us within this bad infinity (see also Chapters 3 and 6). Hence, for him, critical reflection is a demand on each one of us, flowing from the demand on humanity to rid itself of this second nature.[58] Thus, there is a sense in which what constitutes a life of resistance is demanded of the individual, after all. This means – as we see in more detail in the next chapter – resisting the social world in a way that makes use of, and is expressive of, negative freedom.[59]

The advantage of putting the idea of a demand on humanity in terms of collective action problems is that we need not suppose that humanity is an agent over and above the individuals making it up (thereby avoiding the metaphysical objections to collective responsibility). The point is merely that certain tasks demand a collective approach and that in this respect there exists a collective responsibility. Furthermore, we also do not completely lose a handle on which individuals we can blame, and how much we can blame them, for the failures of humanity.[60] Blame would attach to those individuals who failed to contribute towards putting humanity in a position to fulfil its responsibility, and it would be proportional to their ability to discharge this indirect duty. Thus, to

---

57 PMP 1956/7 (unpublished), Vo1361–2.

58 It is perhaps in this way that we should take Adorno's remark: 'Paradoxically, it is the desperate fact that the practice on which everything depends is obstructed that grants to thought a breathing space which it would be practically criminal ['*praktischer Frevel*'] not to use' (ND, 6: 243/245; translation amended). It would be practically criminal because we would thereby violate our indirect duty to further humanity's duty to change the social world.

59 See, for example, HF, 243/174; on negative freedom, see here, Chapter 3.

60 This is important because Adorno, as seen in Chapter 3, does not want to give up completely on holding individual wrongdoers to account (especially when it comes to the participants in the Nazi regime and the Holocaust), despite his insistence on the problematic nature of individual freedom and morality.

come back to the example of global warming; a politician in an economically developed country might have more responsibility than a
citizen of this country who, in turn, might be more subject to blame
than a subsistence farmer in a developing country. Similarly, I indicated
in Chapter 3 that Adorno might accept that there is differential responsibility, such that those who have the opportunity for negative freedom
of resistance are more responsible than those who are denied even this
opportunity.

Ethical normativity comes in for Adorno both at the individual level
(as we see in more detail in the next chapter) and at the social level (in
the form of moral demands). Moreover, if the considerations about
collective responsibility are correct, then the fact that normativity comes
in at the social level also generates normativity at the individual level (in
the form of indirect moral demands).

VIII The outrage of (attempts at) discursive grounding

There is one more element of the new categorical imperative on which I
have not commented: Adorno's rejection of discursive grounding in
ethics. Adorno, to recall, states that the categorical imperative is 'refractory to being grounded' and rejects any attempts of 'dealing discursively
with it' as 'outrageous'.[61]

Adorno denies both that discursive grounding is possible and that
attempts at providing it are morally appropriate. According to him, it is
the physical impulse which lies at the core of morality's survival. If
Adorno is correct about this, then it is not so surprising that morality
is 'refractory' to discursive grounding. If morality is dependent on a
non-rational, materialist element, a physical impulse, then one would
not expect it to be possible to ground morality on reason alone or,
indeed, to ground it discursively in another way. A purely rational or
discursive grounding would end in a bad infinity of argumentation (as
he calls it elsewhere).[62] Moreover, for Adorno, all the normativity
required is already contained in the badness of what happened in

---

61 ND, 6: 358/365.

62 See ND, 6: 281/285; and here, Chapter 7. This might be the thought behind the claim
that the givenness of Kant's categorical imperative – the consciousness of the moral law as
a 'fact of reason' – proved refractory to grounding (see the passage of the categorical
imperative quoted earlier; ND, 6: 358/365). While Kant does not think that this fact
allows or requires further grounding, this is of no use for defending him against Adorno's
criticism. In fact, the non-deducibility of the 'fact of reason' is exactly the nub of Adorno's

Auschwitz. In this sense, to insist on providing a grounding for the normativity in question would be 'outrageous' (as well as unnecessary), since it would not take sufficiently seriously the claim which the events, for which the name Auschwitz symbolically stands, make on us. (I return to these claims in Chapter 7, showing that they do not imply an objectionable irrationalism and leave a place for vindication, as distinguished from discursive grounding.)

IX Intermediate summary

I have commented on the following seven points in respect to the new categorical imperative (albeit in a different order). Firstly, Adorno, unlike Kant, has a historical understanding of the moral imperative. Secondly, the new categorical imperative is directed at unfree humankind, an idea which fits well with Adorno's views of freedom and the crisis of individual moral practice today, but goes against the original Kantian conception of the categorical imperative (as a principle of autonomy). Thirdly, the new categorical imperative is consequence-sensitive, not purely maxim-centred. Fourthly, suffering and the physical impulse as reaction to suffering are central to the new categorical imperative – it is in them that morality is said to survive. Fifthly, the new imperative does not concern all that is normally covered by morality; it is more limited. It also does not function as a principle, but more like an expression of appropriate response to paradigmatic events. Still, the experience in question (and thereby the new imperative expressing it) has categorical force in the sense of compelling universality. Sixthly, the new categorical imperative is, in effect, a demand on humanity, rather than on individuals, although this also means that demands on individuals flow from it. Finally, I pointed to Adorno's claim that morality, including his new categorical imperative, cannot be discursively grounded and that attempts to do so are not just futile, but also outrageous.

There is much more to be said about the new categorical imperative, including critical questions of various sorts. Some of the issues it raises – such as why Adorno thinks that Auschwitz shows that culture failed, rather than indicating a momentary relapse into barbarism, a deeply

immanent criticism: even Kant's project of providing discursive grounding comes to a point where such grounding is no longer possible, suggesting, at least according to Adorno, that there are non-deducible, non-discursive elements in morality (see also the earlier discussion in Chapter 4).

regrettable anomaly in a not yet fully democratised country – I have already drawn attention to (see Chapter 1). Others I take up later in detail – such as the matter of discursive grounding and what its rejection means for the kind of vindication of Adorno's views that he or we could offer (Chapter 7). However, in concluding this chapter, I want to discuss one other objection.

x Radical evil and moralising

As we have seen, Adorno holds the stark thesis that the systematic persecution and murder of the European Jews (and other victim groups of the Nazi regime) was not accidental to the modern social world and its thought forms, but the result of the inhuman tendency inherent in it. In his view, the worst catastrophe has already happened in Auschwitz,[63] and our social world, by its very nature, is steering towards a repeat of such a catastrophe or even towards its permanent occurrence.[64] Not least for this reason, it is radically evil (see Chapter 1).

One might be surprised by Adorno's use of – what seems to be – moralistic language, especially given how influenced he was by Nietzsche, who submitted talk of evil to scathing critique. 'Evil' is a potentially misleading or even dangerous term in that it is often used to oversimplify matters and create clear-cut oppositions when in fact there is much more complexity. In this way, pursuing even a good cause (such as alleviating suffering) under the banner of fighting evil can create – however inadvertently – greater havoc. For example, the suffering of a population can be used as a justification to wage war against its government, even if the resulting reality will predictably turn out worse, including for the population in question. 'Evil' is an absolutising notion and such notions suggest that no balancing of probabilities of success and failure or harm and benefit is neither necessary nor even appropriate. (Consider, for example, how Tony Blair reportedly reacted to a briefing about the likely problems for a post-invasion Iraq by simply asking 'But Saddam is evil, isn't he?').[65] Appeals to evil are often a form of moral blackmail – if you do not join us in this fight, then you are completely morally depraved and can be counted among the enemies. Moreover, such appeals are often used as justification for punishing or

---

63 See MM, Aphorism No. 33; EA, 674/CM, 191; and MTP, 10.2: 769/CM, 268.
64 See, for example, ND, 6: 355/362.
65 For discussion, with references, see Geuss 2010: Ch. 3.

disciplining individuals. Perhaps, then we would do better not to appeal to such stark, moralising terms.

Adorno is aware and wary of the moralistic tendencies just outlined, but he nonetheless continues to make use of the terms in question. This might seem puzzling, perhaps even ill-advised. I cannot hope to defuse the concerns this raises completely here, but let me at least indicate what his thinking is.

For a start, Adorno's talk of evil reflects the view that the bads we are faced with are so grave that they are beyond any relativistic questioning – they express objective bads and should be acknowledged as such.[66] As little as Adorno wants to cut short debate, he thinks that everybody would and, at any rate, should acknowledge the evils of Auschwitz (delusional prejudice, oppression, genocide, and torture) – that is why the new imperative is categorical. As he says at one point, oppression and lack of freedom are 'the evil whose malevolence requires as little philosophical proof as does its existence'.[67] In fact, thinking that these require discursive grounding or derivation from higher principles is already to misunderstand them and their normative force; thinking this is to react inappropriately (see also Chapter 7). Moreover, Adorno is not alone in taking avoidance of certain evils as the objective background presupposition of moral practice and philosophy.[68] Admittedly, we should be wary to what uses people put appeals to such objective evils. Yet, if we gave up on these notions altogether, we would deprive ourselves of an important moral resource, and even get the nature of our moral situation wrong. Instead we have to make use of other strategies to avoid the moralistic tendencies identified.

In particular, Adorno's talk of evils is not meant to cut short critical scrutiny – as appeals to evil often tend to do. Just the opposite: Adorno

---

66 See, for example, PMP 1963, 260–1/175   67 10.2: 465/CM, 10.

68 See, for example, Hampshire's comment: 'There is nothing mysterious or "subjective" or culture-bound in the great evils of human experience, re-affirmed in every age and in every written history and in every tragedy and fiction: murder and the destruction of human life, imprisonment, enslavement, starvation, poverty, physical pain and torture, homelessness, friendlessness. That these great evils are to be averted is the constant presupposition of moral arguments at all times and in all places … That destruction of human life, suffering, and imprisonment are, taken by themselves, great evils, and that they are evil without qualification, if nothing can be said about the consequences which might palliate the evil; that it is better that persons should be free rather than starving in prisons or concentrations camps – these are some of the constancies of human experience and feeling presupposed as the background to moral judgements and arguments' (1992: 90).

insists on our facing up to the problem of evil much more than has happened in the past. After Auschwitz, we cannot just go on doing philosophy and living our lives as before. Instead, we have to explicate what these evils involved; to investigate how social, cultural, and moral mechanisms were powerless against them; and to adjust, even radically change, our lives and theories according to the findings. In general, he emphasises the importance of (self-)reflection and the avoidance of self-righteousness (see also next chapter); and proposes, at least in my interpretation, an explanation-based account of the ills of our social world (see Chapters 7 and 9).

Indeed, Adorno's use of the term '*Böse*' ('evil') is less moralistic than it might sound. He also uses other terms – such as *Übel* (which could be translated as 'evil', but also as 'ill', 'malady', or even 'trouble'), *Unheil* ('calamity', 'catastrophe'), *Grauen* ('dread/horror'), and '*Horror*'. These terms are equally evaluatively charged, but seem to be referring to a state of affairs rather than to properties of persons. Crucially, the predicates are primarily and mainly ascribed to our social world, not to individuals. As we have seen in Chapter 3, Adorno is wary of the urge to punish and thinks that individual responsibility is radically diminished; and that it is at the level of society that the blame lies. Indeed, he writes in *Negative Dialectics*:

> The trouble [*das Übel*] is not that free men do radical evil, as evil is being done beyond all measure conceivable to Kant; the trouble is that as yet there is no world in which ... men would no longer need to be evil. Evil, therefore, is the world's own unfreedom. Whatever evil is done comes from the world. Society destines the individuals to be what they are, even by their immanent genesis.[69]

An analogy might help here: modern capitalist society is for Adorno like the Stanford Prison Experiment writ large, just that it is not an experiment that was intentionally initiated by anyone or that we could easily stop. The conditions, under which we grow up and live, shape us in such a way that we have a tendency to commit atrocious acts and severely negligent omissions. In fact, even mere decency is an achievement; living a right and good life (going beyond mere decency) is objectively blocked (see also Chapters 2 and 3).

Adorno's claims about the way in which modern society necessarily engenders evil are – without a doubt – controversial. Moreover, for

69 ND, 6: 218/218–19.

Adorno the basic tendencies towards moral catastrophe materialised not just in the 1930s/1940s and then disappeared, but remain in place in the 1960s (or, presumably, the early 2000s too). According to him, modern society and its thought forms present a grave danger from which one should take flight, and his evaluatively charged language owes a lot to his fear that many will fail to recognise this danger. It is used to warn us, to shake us out of our complacency, to alert us to the fact that we perpetuate what ought to be changed. Instead of forgoing strongly evaluative language we need to examine its use in specific instances, to challenge it whenever it leads to more of the very evils it condemns (or, indeed, to other ones). In this way, we do not even need to know what the good or the right is to be vigilant about moralistic uses. It is enough to employ the conception of wrong life and less wrong living that is operative in Adorno's thinking, explored in more detail in the next chapters.

6

AN ETHICS OF RESISTANCE

Adorno notoriously asserted that there is no right life in our current social world. This assertion has contributed to the widespread perception that his philosophy has no practical import whatsoever. And this perception has given rise to the criticism that it would fail its purpose as a theory with emancipatory intent. It was this criticism which discredited Adorno in the eyes of his New Left critics in the 1960s and 1970s.[1] This criticism also played an important role in the reorientation of the Frankfurt School by the second and third generation theorists.[2] Most famously perhaps, this criticism finds expression in Lukács's memorable phrase that 'A considerable part of the leading German intelligentsia, including Adorno, have taken up residence in the "Grand Hotel Abyss"', where they despair at the state of the world and the impossibility of doing anything about it, while enjoying a comfortable, even luxurious life.'[3]

In response to this criticism, defenders of Adorno have tended to emphasise his personal practical engagement, for example, the numerous radio programmes he did in the 1950s and 1960s.[4] However, insufficient attention has been paid so far to the fact that Adorno actually made recommendations and prescriptions on how we should live in our social world. In this chapter, I aim to close the gap between this perception of Adorno's philosophy and the reality of what he is saying. In fact, in the previous chapter, we have already encountered one central element of Adorno's views on how we should live our wrong lives, the new categorical imperative. But there is more to his ethics and in this chapter I discuss these further elements (Section I) and, also, how Adorno thinks

---

1 See, for example, Krahl 1975.   2 See, for example, Honneth 1995: Ch. 3, 95–6.
3 See Lukács [1916] 1971b: 22 (Preface [1962]).
4 See, for example, Pickford 2002: 327ff.; see also Berman 2002.

we might foster their development within a delusional, increasingly over-whelming social world (Section II).

I Resistance and not living wrongly

If the right living is unavailable to individuals, then the question arises, what is available to them? Let me trace Adorno's sketch of an answer to this question by returning to Aphorism No. 18 from *Minima Moralia*.

In Chapter 2, we have already briefly seen that for Adorno certain forms of living would constitute *less wrong* forms of living the wrong life than others. In particular, he recommends a suspended form of life, a private life that does not lay claim to be of particular meaning or substance. This life presumably is better at least insofar as it might involve less ideology – if we do not lay claim to particular meaning in life, then we do not give in to the illusion that such meaning is currently available.[5] In fact, Adorno even goes further than just recommending a suspended form of life in Aphorism No. 18. He also says that one should add to Nietzsche's rejoicing in not being a home-owner by including in morality the demand 'not to be at home in one's home'.[6] Extrapolating from this, the general recommendation is *not* to be or make oneself at home in this world and life, starting with one's living arrangements, though presumably not limited to them. This distancing, this suspen-sion from one's life, might not change anything directly – no individual

5 Similarly, with claims to legitimacy: once we realise that no ethical theories can underwrite right living, the best we can do is not to lay claim to being able to (fully) legitimate our behaviour. Bernstein expresses this point well: 'If his [Adorno's] analyses are true, then there is no morally correct way of acting, even in the intimate sphere, except a suspended one that refuses to claim legitimacy for itself beyond its unwillingness to settle for the choices on offer; the moral choices on offer are themselves "immoral," not consonant with what we take morality to be. And to the degree to which this is the case, to the degree to which we can be neither good wills nor utility maximisers concretely envision the confluence of these two moralities in a new or renewed virtue ethics with its caring voice, then the very idea of morality evades us. By taking a suspended, aporetic stance we affirm the possibility of ethical life by denying its present, empirical and conceptual, embodi-ments' (2001: 56–7).

6 MM, 4: 43/39. The moral demand not to be at home in one's home (and in the world), which Adorno endorses, is different from turning the problem of making oneself at home into a prudential norm, which he criticises (see Chapter 2). To react prudentially in this way would be to overlook that there is something (morally) problematic in the fact that our social world is not a world in which we can and should make ourselves at home; it would be to mistake (a) something which is unfortunate but required as a response to a morally objectionable state of affairs with (b) something which we should use to our own (prudential) advantage.

can change on his or her own the radically evil social system and the wrong life it produces.[7] Nonetheless, such a suspension is the only thing left to work for and a necessary condition for there to be any change.[8] However, it is noteworthy that a life of suspension cannot be one of aloofness and inactivity, since the latter are criticised by Adorno. It is not that we should not do anything – those who do nothing are implicated just as much.[9] Rather, we should do what we can do, in the awareness that whatever we do, we will live wrongly to some extent. A suspended life is one which contains no claim to rightness or to avoiding guilt, but it is not a life of aloof inactivity.

A number of other passages confirm this reading. Whenever Adorno speaks of what the individual can (and should) do, he strongly emphasises reflection and not joining in. Perhaps the clearest passage to this effect can be found in one of his lectures:

> The only thing that can perhaps be said is that the right way of living today would consist in resistance to the forms of the wrong life that have been seen through and critically dissected by the most progressive minds. Other than this negative prescription no guidance can really be envisaged. I may add that, negative though this assertion is, it can hardly be much more formal than the Kantian injunction that we have been discussing during this semester. So what I have in mind is the determinate negation of everything that has been seen through, and thus the ability to focus upon the power of resistance to all the things imposed on us, to everything the world has made of us, and intends to make of us, to a vastly greater degree.[10]

Adorno asserts here that one must reflect on how society shapes us and resist what on reflection shows itself to be forms of the wrong life. This brings out clearly that a life of suspension is an active one, namely, what might be called a 'life of resistance'.

What is crucial about this passage is the idea that only a *negative* prescription is possible and *that* a prescription is possible. There are three things to note about this. Firstly, this idea is consistent with Adorno's No Right Living Thesis. Adorno need not and should not be taken to say

---

7 MM, 4: 42/39; see also here, Chapters 3 and 5.
8 See PMP 1956/7 (unpublished), Vo15 19–20; PMP 1963, 250/168.
9 ND, 6: 241/243.
10 PMP 1963, 248–9/167–8; translation amended; see also ND, 6: 262/265; PMP 1956/7 (unpublished), Vo15 19.

here that the wrong life can be lived rightly after all.[11] When he talks about what resisting bad life consists in, then the only thing he is committed to saying is that there are better or worse forms of living the wrong life and that the better forms involve such resistance. As seen, drawing an evaluative distinction between different forms of life is compatible with the No Right Living Thesis. Moreover, Adorno has the conceptual space for a distinction between living the wrong life *rightly* and living it *not wrongly* – he can affirm the latter, without being committed to the former. As Adorno always insists against Hegel, a determinate negation of something does not amount to a positive thesis about it.[12] Living the wrong life less wrongly does not automatically constitute right living. In fact, what is required to resist wrong living might not be necessary any longer once wrong life and the radically evil social world are overcome.[13]

Secondly, the negative prescription to resist forms of the wrong life is not the only negative prescription to be found in Adorno. Most notably, there is also the new categorical imperative, which commands us 'to arrange our thoughts and actions so that Auschwitz will not repeat itself, so that nothing similar will happen'.[14] The important point to realise is that it is a prescription (even an imperative) and that it is negative. It tells us what we have to avoid (a repeat of Auschwitz), and it is clearly not meant to underwrite a full-blown morality governing all aspects of our ethical life (as, arguably, Kant's categorical imperative was meant to do). In a way, the new categorical imperative is just a more specific variant of the negative prescription to resist all forms of the wrong life which have been seen through. Auschwitz can be recognised as evil, and commands us to resist and prevent its reoccurrence. As we have seen in the previous chapter, we even have a bodily reaction which informs us of this evil and its negative normativity: our abhorrence of unbearable physical suffering has become something practical for us in the course of our development as human animals, and it tells us that such suffering – whether by us or by others – should not be.[15]

11 In other words, Adorno is not entitled to the positive terms with which he begins the passage just quoted ('The only thing that can perhaps be said is that the right life today would ... '). However, what he means can be expressed in the negative terms I suggest in the main text, that is, in terms of living wrong life less wrongly.

12 See, for example, ND, 6: 161–3/158–61.

13 On the historical specificity of Adorno's ethics of resistance, see also Freyenhagen 2011a.

14 ND, 6: 358/365; see also here, Chapter 5.   15 ND, 6: 358/365; see also 203/203.

Thirdly, the idea of a negative prescription to resist wrong life fits well with Adorno's conception of freedom, according to which we are, currently, only capable of negative freedom, not positive freedom or autonomy (see Chapter 3). This prescription, in effect, just consists in the demand to make use of this negative freedom, for the latter is nothing other than the ability to resist external determination (notably by society). It will not be sufficient for living autonomously. Even when we are able to resist determination by society on a particular matter, we are not freely directing our lives, but merely *reacting* to the 'changing forms of repression'.[16]

One important point to note is that Adorno's norm of resisting all forms of life that have been seen through by the most critical minds is largely formal (as he himself notes in the long passage quoted earlier) and only substantive analyses of specific forms of life will make it more concrete. This is not surprising, but fits with his general outlook – specifically, with his claim that moral theory is insufficient to guide us, as demonstrated against the paradigm example of Kant's ethics (see Chapter 4). What is required instead is a careful, detailed, and interdisciplinary analysis of the concrete situation at hand and the dangers it contains. I cannot hope to do this for our times within confines of this study, but what I can do is add to the ethical framework offered by Adorno for this purpose – which is much richer than is commonly recognised.

Let us return then to the longer passage quoted earlier to see how Adorno elaborates further on what it means to resist and to live the wrong life less wrongly. In its final sentence, Adorno recommends 'resistance to all the things imposed on us, to everything the world has made of us, and intends to make of us, to a vastly greater degree'.[17] Thus, one should try as much as possible to resist the pressures that make one conform to and reproduce the current social world. Adorno realises that this cannot be only a matter of external resistance, for society has invaded individuals themselves. Consequently, what is required is also to resist the temptations we have to join in.[18] This starts with products of the culture industry. Entertainment can contribute to our being more ensnared within the repressive social world, and it thereby often goes against, or even undermines, any insights into this society and dispositions to resist

16 ND, 6: 262/265.
17 PMP 1963, 249/168. Adorno particularly gives credit to Kierkegaard for emphasising that one should learn how to resist (rather than how to agree), and for refusing friendship with the world (2: 225–8). However, Adorno is critical of what Kierkegaard makes of this insight. According to Adorno, it leads Kierkegaard to overemphasise interiority.
18 PMP 1963, 249/168.

it we might have acquired. Adorno gives the example of going to the cinema:[19] even a trip to the cinema is, for Adorno, not an innocent act, but a form of joining in, of making oneself at home in the world – perhaps, he is thinking particularly here of mainstream cinema and its recurrent reconciling themes of searching and ultimately finding true love, of the USA as a deeply troubled country but ultimately the best there is, of the person who with hard work can make it to the top, of the need for strong men to save us all from evil, and so on. Similarly, living according to ascetic ideals is one of the ways one might resist the 'madness of profit-economy'[20] – if life has been restricted to a sphere of consumption which itself is under the dictate of ever-expanding production, then resistance might mean to consume less, to not play along with the pressures to acquire all and every consumer good.

Unfortunately, joining in cannot be completely avoided, according to Adorno. However, what we can avoid is joining in with our full heart or blindly;[21] expressed in the terms introduced earlier, what we can do is live a *suspended* life. Having a reflective distance to our joining in might make things a little different – even though Adorno qualifies this immediately by saying that such a hopeful claim 'contains too much vanity'.[22] The reason for Adorno's qualification is that we cannot know whether critical reflection and resistance might objectively change anything about society, or whether it might not at some higher level help to reproduce it (such as by stopping it from becoming too static). By living our wrong lives less wrongly, we can hope to make a difference. However, to assert that we will is already to overstep the bounds of what can be known in the deeply delusional system that is our society. In this sense, such an assertion would contain too much vanity.

Resistance also extends to the way morality presents itself today. Abstract rigorism in ethics should be opposed[23] – we should avoid becoming like Gregers Werle (from Ibsen's *The Wild Duck*), pursuing (what we view as) justice at any cost, even if the world or innocent persons perish along the way.[24] Similarly, we should criticise and protest against specific moral norms that some groups want to impose on the whole society, for example, in relation to sexual behaviour.[25] In this

19 PMP 1963, 249/168; see also MM, 4: 26/25.
20 MM, Aphorism No. 60, 4: 109/97.
21 PMP 1963, 250/168; see also PMP 1956/7 (unpublished), Vo15 19–20.
22 PMP 1963, 250/168.   23 PMP 1963, 250/168–9.
24 See PMP 1963, lecture 16; and here, Chapter 4.
25 PMP 1963, 252–3/170–1; see also PMP 1956/7 (unpublished), Vo1304–5.

sense, moral philosophy can still contribute to avoid some of the pitfalls of a damaged life. As a critique of rigid moral systems and social norms, moral philosophy has still a role to play in what is a situation of moral uncertainty.[26] For Adorno, moral philosophy is possible today essentially as 'the attempt to make conscious the critique of moral philosophy, the critique of its options and to raise awareness of its antinomies'.[27] What it cannot do is give full-blown practical guidance, for the reason just given: moral theory faces antinomies which it cannot resolve, since they reflect the actual practical antinomies that modern society imposes on us.

It is important to note that Adorno does not conclude from the fact that we are in a situation of moral uncertainty that we have to give up all normative and moral talk. On the contrary, we have to hold fast to there being moral demands, to our having a conscience. Still, one consequence of our current predicament is that we should remain open to criticism and scrutiny by others as well as engage in self-criticism. In this sense, the antinomical nature of moral practice also affects the attempt of trying to not live wrongly. We have to cling on to morality, but without pretending to be in a position where all the answers can be given. Thus, it is important to keep our fallibility in mind and above all to remain modest, to avoid self-righteousness. As Adorno puts it:

> Hence to abstain from self-assertiveness ... seems to be the crucial thing to ask from individuals today. In other words, if you were to press me to follow the example of the Ancients and make a list of the cardinal virtues, I would probably respond cryptically by saying that I could think of nothing except for modesty [*Bescheidenheit*]. Or to put it another way, we must have a conscience, but may not insist on our own.[28]

Adorno, ever mindful of how easily good intentions can backfire in the administered world, insists on modesty as the prime and in fact only virtue.[29] One should resist what has been seen through as wrong, but one also needs to keep in mind one's own limitations and be wary of

---

26 A recent example of moral philosophy as such a critique is Geuss 2005.
27 PMP 1963, 248/167.
28 PMP 1963, 251–2/169–70; see also ND, 6: 345/352; MM, Aphorism No. 6 4: 29/27–8; PMP 1956/7 (unpublished), Vo1327.
29 Butler in her Adorno lecture series emphasises and draws out the importance of modesty and fallibility for an Adorno-inspired moral philosophy (Butler 2003, especially, 11, 54ff., 84, 104ff., 116). She summarises this approach – which, according to her, Adorno shares with Foucault – as follows: 'As Adorno as well as Foucault make clear, one need not be sovereign to act morally; rather, one must lose one's sovereignty to become human' (ibid., 11; my translation).

anyone (including oneself) who proclaims that he or she is in the right. Again we encounter here the idea of a suspended form of life in the sense presented earlier, that is, a way of life which eschews any claims to legitimacy or meaning.

It is difficult to overemphasise the importance of critical reflection in all of this. In many ways it is central to a life of resistance and should come first.[30] To recall, only those forms of life which have been seen through as wrong should be rejected. Thus, critical reflection is the starting point for any resistance. Also, for Adorno one of the main obstacles to freedom is false consciousness (or ideology; see Chapter 3). Society has become a second nature for us. We overlook that unfreedom is human-made, not blind fate or nature, as much as it might present itself in this way.[31] This makes it easier for society to sustain itself. Thus, it is also for this reason that reflection upon our predicament would be the first and crucial step for resistance. For while our unfreedom is a fact, we are ensuring that it remains a fact by (mistakenly) accepting the causes of this unfreedom as inevitably given and unchangeable. It would be over-simplified to say that for Adorno we would just have to see through the illusion to get rid of it, that we would just have to realise that we sustain a society that makes us unfree. However, it is true to say of Adorno that for him the first step of resistance is to realise that our unfreedom is collec-tively self-imposed. Thus, in effect, what Adorno seems to think is that negative freedom, resistance against unfreedom, in fact begins just in virtue of reflecting on our predicament and mobilising our powers against it. Such reflection and resistance cannot replace the practical task of changing the current social order and building a new one. Still, critical reflection is both the necessary precondition for such practice and itself a practice – something which Adorno emphasises against his left-wing critics who accuse him of advocating passivity.[32] Moreover, it is a practice which is less problematic than what is normally and more narrowly understood by practice, since the latter is, for Adorno, too instrumentally related to theorising, too consequentialist and results-orientated, and too prone to have counterproductive results even when pursued by well-intentioned individuals.[33]

30 See, for example, ND, 6: 337/344; PMP 1956/7 (unpublished), V01322, 1517–18.
31 PMP 1956/7 (unpublished), V01313–14; see also ND, 6: 219/219; and here, Chapter 3.
32 See Freyenhagen 2012 (unpublished).
33 See ND, 6: 15, 146–7, 240, 242–3/243, 143–4, 242, 244–5; PMP 1963, 13–17/4–7.

Critical reflection often requires, and consists in, exercising what Kant called *Mündigkeit*, the ability (and courage) to think and judge for oneself.[34] This means questioning the whole of social reality as well as particular practices within it – for example, by opposing social or moral norms which people might want to impose on us. In fact, even the mere act of stepping back and questioning the authority of those who want to push something intellectually uncomfortable away is already an example of less wrong living.[35] Such a stance against authority is also crucial to prevent another Auschwitz from happening.[36] Moreover, as seen, one should adopt this critical stance also towards oneself – given the moral uncertainty of our times, one has to be vigilant against *Mündigkeit* turning into self-righteousness. Any aspect of a life of resistance is deeply coloured by the precarious and antinomical nature of moral practice today: on the one hand, we should not just accept what we are told, but make use of our ability to judge for ourselves and form our own conscience; on the other hand, we have to guard against self-assertiveness and against any claims to infallible authority.

As if this were not a sufficiently difficult balancing act, Adorno also goes further. In one of his lecture series, he says we should try, though we will almost inevitably fail, 'to live as one believes one should live in a freed world'.[37] Living in this way would be to try to anticipate those modes of existence, and to create models of them.[38] Such attempts should, probably, take their cue from the purposeless activities of children, who in their games 'Unconsciously rehearse the right life',[39] or from the equally purposeless activities which Maupassant and Sternheim envisaged against the productivist spirit of modern times.[40]

The important thing to realise about this is that these 'anticipations' or 'models' are not meant to constitute (new) norms of behaviour. What Adorno wants to say is rather that it is part of resisting wrong life to try to loosen up its icy grip on us by experimenting with ways of living.[41] Whether or not we actually succeed in anticipating right living, we ought

---

34 'Beantwortung der Frage: Was ist Aufklärung' [1784], 8: 33–42, especially 35–6. On Adorno's commitment to this idea, see also Finlayson 2002: 6–7.
35 PMP 1963, 259–60/175.   36 EA, 10.2: 679/CM, 23.
37 PMP 1956/7 (unpublished), Vo1519; my translation.
38 See PMP 1956/7 (unpublished), Vo1327.
39 MM, Aphorism No. 146, 4: 260–1/228.
40 MM, Aphorism No. 100, 4: 177–9/155–7.
41 There are both parallels and disanalogies to Mill's view of experiments in living: both Adorno and Mill think that such experiments are necessary for innovation, diversity, and the development of individuality, but in Adorno's theory they are part of resisting

to try out something different from how things are and from how one is expected to behave. We ought to break the hold of the immutable social world on us and the hold of its behavioural patterns and norms. Yet, in doing so, we have to remember that we are by no means assured of being released from its icy grip and that self-assertiveness is to be avoided. Once more, vigilance and a suspended life are required.

Beyond the hope that experimentation may loosen the icy grip of modern society on us, we can only 'try to live in such a way that one may believe oneself to have been a good animal'.[42] What Adorno has in mind here is the following. At various points, Adorno speaks of identification with others and their plight, of solidarity with tormentable bodies.[43] It is this thought which might be meant by living as a good animal. In fact, a direct connection between being a good animal and identification with others can be uncovered by drawing on Rousseau's conception of natural compassion ['la pitié naturelle'].

For Rousseau, compassion consists in the 'innate repugnance of seeing a fellow-creature suffer'.[44] Put differently, it is an instinctive reaction that takes the form of recognising one's own struggle for self-preservation in the suffering of others. Animals experience compassion as much as humans do (in fact, it seems to be in virtue of being animals that humans are capable of compassion).[45] Showing compassion might thus be part of what makes a 'good animal'. What is important about this conception of compassion are two elements: firstly, it involves identification with the suffering of another creature to the extent of reacting with the same immediacy and spontaneity to its suffering as to one's own suffering; and, secondly, it is a natural reaction, one that is not rationalised (for example,

the modern social world (rather than defending it) and not justified with reference to Utilitarianism.

42 ND, 6: 294/299; translation amended.

43 See ND, 6: 281/286; see also 203-4/203-4; 10.2: 697; 20.1: 160; PMP 1956/7 (unpublished), Vo1327. Sometimes, Adorno also talks in terms of 'decency [Anständigkeit]' when discussing the least wrong form of living of which we are still capable (PMP 1963, 173/116; see also 248/167). 'Decency' should not be understood as indexed to what is socially acceptable, as the term might be taken to suggest. Rather, decency for Adorno includes solidarity with others in the sense of animal pity, which, if anything, is endangered by socially acceptable norms. This is not to say that, for Adorno, social conventions have no positive role to play. At one point, he suggests that they have educative value insofar as they provide an opportunity for learning to deal with norm-governed demands on us (see MM, Aphorism No. 116, 4: 204ff./179ff.).

44 Rousseau [1755] 1913: 66 [1.35].

45 Unfortunately, neither Adorno nor Rousseau supplies any evidence that animals have such an instinctive reaction of solidarity (other than anecdotal evidence in the case of Rousseau; see [1755] 1913: 66-7 [1.35]).

via thoughts of reward or reciprocity), but prior to reflection of that sort and, if anything, endangered by it.[46]

In these two respects Rousseau's conception of compassion captures well what Adorno has in mind as identification with others and trying to live as a good animal. The solidarity with tormentable bodies arises out of the abhorrence of (physical) suffering, which has direct motivational force for human animals.[47] Insofar as Adorno situates this practical abhorrence within natural evolution, he would accept that other animals are capable of it and that it is a natural reaction, a 'physical impulse'.[48] Similarly, he shares Rousseau's criticism of rationalised forms of pity: thoughts of pay-back undermine identification-based solidarity.[49] Moreover, Adorno thinks that it is one of the problems of modern society, and the pre-eminence of instrumental reasoning within it, that such solidarity is disappearing. Our social context engenders the opposite of the identification-based solidarity, namely, bourgeois coldness. It is this coldness, that is, the ability to stand back and look on unaffected, which made Auschwitz possible.[50] Identification-based solidarity is, therefore, an important element in not living wrongly, since it is essential for counteracting bourgeois coldness and finds its expression in the impulse against suffering.[51]

At the same time, solidarity is again something we can only aspire to live up to, not something which we are currently able to achieve fully. In the absence of a socially institutionalised and fully functioning ethical life, the conditions for the cultivation of this solidarity do not exist. In this sense, Adorno is here not so much putting forward a principle ('try to live like a good animal'), but describing an ethical ideal. In fact, he has so little confidence in our ability to realise this ideal, that he expresses it in a highly qualified and indirect way.[52] As quoted earlier, he thinks that, at most, we can ascribe the quality in question retrospectively to our life, in the light of how we have lived it. This, presumably, reflects the sense of fallibility that Adorno urges on us. As we have seen, it is not that we have to eschew any moral or normative talk, but such talk has to be informed by modesty, and this affects the way we can formulate our prescriptions and ideals. For the most part, they have to be highly qualified and indirect.

---

46 See Rousseau [1755] 1913: 67–8 [1.36–7]; see also Bernstein 2001: 408.
47 ND, 6: 281, 358/285, 365.   48 ND, 6: 281/285.
49 See, for example, MM, Aphorism No. 13, 4: 36/33.
50 See, for example, ND, 6: 355–6/363; EA, 10.2: 687/CM, 30.
51 See, for example, ND, 6: 281, 358/286, 365.   52 See also Früchtl 1993: 994.

Moreover, it would be wrong to say that Adorno favours an ethics of compassion. Despite the importance he assigns to something like Rousseau's natural compassion, an ethics cannot be built on this. There is always too little compassion in the current world, and it ends up just mitigating the evil, not putting an end to it.[53] Thus, being a good animal cannot be all there is to ethics and will not guarantee right living either – in fact, a certain amount of coldness and distancing is necessary both for survival today and even for right living in a free society.[54] Still, we should not dismiss compassion completely (as Adorno thinks that Kant and Nietzsche do).[55] We cannot currently get the balance right between compassion and coldness. This is why we face a practical antinomy when it comes to compassion (see also here, Chapters 2 and 4): neither being compassionate, nor not being compassionate is a path to right living, and while there are better and worse forms of combining them, there is no genuine reconciliation of them available to us in our current predicament.

Living like a good animal is not sufficient for living our wrong lives rightly also for another reason. Personal relationships and the private sphere may allow for solidarity or decent behaviour; and they are often refuges from the demands of modern society.[56] Nonetheless, we should not rest content with focusing on this sphere. For Adorno it is morally reprehensible not to gather the force for critique of the wrong life,[57] and such critique is not merely limited to opposing repressive moral norms and the pressures on us that make us conform. Rather, 'the quest for the right life is the quest for the right form of politics'.[58] In realising that the right life is blocked by the social conditions, moral philosophy goes over into critique of society and the moral quest merges into the political one.[59] Interestingly, Adorno credits Aristotle with having been the first to see the connection between the right life and the right politics and social setting.[60] However, it is noteworthy that the political

53 DE, 3: 122–3, 126/102–3, 106; PMP 1956/7 (unpublished), Vo1518; PMP 1963, 257–8/ 173–4; see also here, Chapter 4; Früchtl 1991, 1993; and Noerr 1995: esp. 17–18.
54 ND, 6: 356–7/364.
55 ND, 6: 257/260; DE, 3: 123–4/103; PMP 1963, 257–8/173–4.
56 See, for example, MM, Aphorism No. 11, 4: 33–4/31–2; PMP 1956/7 (unpublished), Vo1327.
57 PMP 1956/7 (unpublished), Vo1361–2.
58 PMP 1963, 262/176; translation amended.
59 See PMP 1956/7 (unpublished), Vo1313. Butler has also emphasised this link between moral philosophy and critique of society in Adorno (Butler 2003: 9, 20–1, 30–1, 93).
60 PMP 1956/7 (unpublished), Vo1409. Nonetheless, for Adorno the Aristotelian virtue ethics also does not provide a workable picture of right living within this society – without

quest is in certain respects as problematic as private life. The possibility of the political quest is also affected by the fact that the individuals are damaged and lack positive freedom.[61] Hence, it is not the case that Adorno says that the right life can be found in politics. The right way of living cannot be achieved at all, neither in the private, nor the political sphere. However, living less wrongly requires going beyond the private sphere. The quest for the right form of politics involves the fight for making right living possible by trying to put the required social and political conditions for it in place.[62] The private sphere, on the other hand, can, at best, be the refuge which may provide us with the strength necessary for this fight to continue; at worst, it is here that we particularly fall prey to the illusion of still being able to live a good or right life (and in doing so to perpetuate the wrong one). The political sphere has at least the advantage that it would not be wrong to say of this sphere that within it the change to right living could be effected, while it is wrong to say this about the private sphere. Thus, for Adorno it is part of living our wrong lives less wrongly that we try to resist our social world both in the private and the public sphere, with the latter having *ultimately* greater importance. Still, the qualifier, 'ultimately', is crucial. Adorno suggests that social practice is blocked to such an extent for the moment that we ought to concentrate mainly on the private sphere and on doing philosophy, even if ultimately it is through political action that we will change society.[63] More could be said about Adorno's views of politics,[64] but here we need to consider how one can account for the possibility of critical reflection and resistance within an Adornian picture of the world.

---

the backdrop of traditional social practices, virtuous behaviour is no longer possible (PMP 1956/7 (unpublished), Vo1379; PMP 1963, 147/98; see also here, Chapter 4 as well as MacIntyre 1985; Jaeggi 2005; and Menke 2005). The fact that we cannot live rightly is not just due to the fact that we ascribe to the wrong moral theory (say Kantian ethics or consequentialism instead of virtue ethics), but is rooted in objective (social) conditions.

61 See PMP 1956/7 (unpublished), Vo1326.
62 What this requires in detail depends on the specific social and historical conditions. It could, for example, involve opposing restrictions on civil liberties (as when Adorno publicly protested against the introduction of emergency legislation in Germany; or, nowadays, standing up for due process in relation to anti-terrorist legislation) but also pressing for a universal health care system or more funding for education.
63 See, for example, ND, 6: 15–16, 242–3/243, 244–5; PMP 1963, lecture 1.
64 See Freyenhagen 2012 (unpublished).

II Fostering resistance

From what we have seen so far, it seems that at least three elements are required for resistance, for living less wrongly.[65] It is clear that critical reflection plays a central role in resistance; in fact it is often the first and in many ways the most important step.[66] Still, we have also seen that a sense of fallibility or modesty is important to make sure that resisting the forms of life which have been seen through as wrong does not end up producing new forms of the wrong life. This element is to some extent secondary to the first, since it is usually dependent on critical insight. Modesty is also connected to the third element, to the identification and solidarity with others. Such an identification might help us to avoid self-righteousness and might thereby aid our gaining and retaining a sense of fallibility, of not insisting on our conscience come what may. Conversely, a sense of fallibility, modesty, is conducive to being open-minded and understanding of others.[67] In this way, modesty eases the way for solidarity and identification. Moreover, there also can be a mutually reinforcing relationship between identification and critical reflection. Identification results primarily from our experience of physical suffering, which enables us to imagine and develop solidarity with other people's suffering.[68] Still, there might be a role for reflection to guide this sensibility – for example, by widening our horizon beyond what we had immediate experience of, or by critically questioning a specific reaction for its appropriateness. On the other hand, sensibility towards suffering might be important for people to come to question their world in the first place, since it might bring to consciousness that something is amiss in a world that produces this suffering.[69]

---

65 There is an obvious parallel between what I identify as the three elements required for resistance and what Finlayson describes as the three virtues contained in Adorno's ethics of resistance (see Finlayson 2002: especially Sect. 3, 8): (1) *Mündigkeit* (of which I mainly talk in terms of critical reflection); (2) humility (as Finlayson translates '*Bescheidenheit* [modesty]'), and (3) affection (my solidarity and identification with others). While I agree with him that the three elements are both preconditions for and part of a life of resistance, I would not classify them as virtues. Adorno claims that 'the concept of virtue is obsolete' (PMP 1963, 146/98; PMP 1956/7 (unpublished), Vo1379; see also here, Chapter 4); and talk of virtues is misleading insofar as it suggests that right living is possible within this social world – in order to live rightly we 'just' have to exercise the three virtues.

66 See, for example, ND, 6: 337/344; PMP 1956/7 (unpublished), Vo1322, 1517–18.

67 Butler points to this upshot of Adornian emphasis on modesty (2003: 54–6).

68 ND, 6: 203–4/204.   69 ND, 6: 203/203.

While we can thus imagine a virtuous cycle of each element reinforcing the other, there is also a problem of a vicious one where as soon as
one lacks one, the others (if they developed at all) will either disappear
too or become distorted. Indeed, there is real worry that the elements of
resistance are endangered by the very social world in which having them
would be necessary to resist it. As already mentioned, critical reflection,
for example, has preconditions, most saliently perhaps Kant's idea of
Mündigkeit, of being able (and having the courage) to think and judge
for oneself. Yet, given Adorno's bleak views about the current state of
the world, it is difficult to see how he can account even for the possibility
that such preconditions are met and thereby for the possibility of critical
reflection and resistance – a difficulty which Habermas, among others,
points outs.[70]

As Habermas himself notes,[71] Adorno links the possibility of reflection (and thereby of resistance) to the fate of the (bourgeois) individual
who was the product of the liberal bourgeois era. In other words, the
privilege of being able to reflect critically was, according to Adorno, still
possible in case of those now 'fading subjects' that grew up in an earlier
phase of capitalism.[72] In effect, he is saying that those who have been
around before society became totally delusional can still experience
society as such. Habermas concedes that this might be the case with
individuals like Adorno.[73] However, even if this is conceded, the fundamental problem merely changes: what happens when the individuals
who still remain from a not completely closed bourgeois age die out?
Adorno himself mentions the possibility that the critics might die out,[74]
but he does not say who could replace them.

What Adorno does say are three things: (a) he comments on what
made it possible for critical individuals to have emerged in the more

---

70 See: 'If the diagnosis of the age expressed by Adorno and Horkheimer in the dialectic of
    enlightenment is correct, a question arises concerning the privilege of the experience to
    which the authors must lay claim in relation to the withered contemporary subjectivity'
    (Habermas 1987: 101).

71 Habermas 1983: 101–2.

72 Habermas rightly points to the 'Dedication' of *Minima Moralia* as the source of this claim
    (see Habermas 1983: 101; MM, 4: 13–17/15–18), but it can also be found in other
    works – see, for example, *Negative Dialectics* where Adorno speaks of 'a stroke of luck'
    which those people had who can resist the prevailing norms (ND, 6: 51/41). For a
    criticism of this view, see Jay 1984: 92–3.

73 However, Habermas then goes on to object that this response does not help with the
    more important problem of how critical theory can be justified (1983: 106). I discuss this
    latter problem in Chapters 7–8.

74 ND, 6: 265/268; see also MM, Aphorism No. 88, 4: 153/135.

liberal bourgeois era; (b) he makes some limited suggestions as to what we can try to do in the hope of fostering this critical attitude, whether or not this hope is objectively justified; and (c) he presents the current social world as still inherently antagonistic and as failing to satisfy the real needs of individuals, both being characteristics which leave open the possibility that people become alienated from this world and critically reflect on their predicament. Let me explain and comment on these three elements in more detail.

On the first point, Adorno presents a modified Marxist picture in that he takes up the idea that capitalism produces its own 'gravediggers'.[75] The idea at work here consists, basically, in the claim that capitalism produces immanently, i.e., by what is essential to its functioning, the very conditions for overcoming it. Traditionally, this idea was linked to the proletariat, which – as Lukács argued in *History and Class Consciousness* – occupies a special position in capitalism. It is both in the position to see through capitalism and has reasons to do so (their unsatisfied material needs and experience of alienation). Adorno largely divorces the idea that capitalism produces its own critics from the doctrines of the proletariat and class struggle, but retains the structural thought underlying it (at least as far as the liberal phase of capitalism is concerned).

The best example might be the bourgeois family.[76] On the one hand, the bourgeois family is a medium of bourgeois repression, since it socialises the individuals into their roles and instils into them the reigning norms. On the other hand, the family can only function in its role as main socialising unit by following its own logic.[77] This involves two things. Firstly, that the child develops a conception of happiness via experiencing (motherly) love and tenderness. This conception can then function as a contrasting model to existing reality, and it can help in the development of a well-formed ego which is able to oppose the existing reality's demand for the renunciation of present happiness in exchange for (in fact, never delivered) future happiness. Secondly, the family is central to producing individuality. The existence of strong, independent individuals was necessary at least for the development of capitalism (to produce the innovators and entrepreneurs that shaped its early stages). Yet, the development of modern individuality also opens

75 This picture is famously expounded in *The Communist Manifesto* [1848], MEW 1956–90, IV: 459–93/MECW 1975–2005, VI: 477–519.
76 See MM, Aphorism No. 2.
77 On this point, see Brunkhorst's discussion of Aphorism No. 2 from *Minima Moralia* (1999: 14–19).

the door for critical reflection and emancipation. In a similar way, other spheres of bourgeois life – from education to the production process, from the cultural or scientific realms to political life – have their own logic, which in each case both sustains the modern, capitalist world and produces the conditions for critical reflection and opposition to it.

However, with the increasing bureaucratisation of life, the industrialisation of the cultural realm, and the monopolisation of capitalist production, the semi-autonomy of these spheres becomes increasingly restricted and eroded. This also threatens the existence of bourgeois individuals capable of critical reflection. Indeed, as noted already, Adorno fears that soon no such individuals will remain – that they are dying out.

The clearest example of the loss of semi-autonomy is once more the family, which, according to Adorno, is increasingly disintegrating (at least, in its traditional form). The socialisation happens now more outside the family, and it has been transformed, especially in the sense of the disappearance of the father-figure (by which he does not necessarily mean disappearance of the father, but rather disappearance of a normative authority which allows one to form one's norms and individuality, partly in rebellion against it). As Adorno puts it in *Minima Moralia*:

> With the family there passes away, while the system lasts, not only the most effective agency of the bourgeoisie, but also the resistance which, though repressing the individual, also strengthened, perhaps even produced him. The end of the family paralyses the forces of opposition.[78]

With the traditional bourgeois family's breaking up, the chances that critical individuals could emerge are diminished.

It is important to keep in mind that it was always only a possibility that critical individuals would emerge from the semi-autonomous spheres. In other words, even in the liberal era of capitalism not everyone translated the semi-autonomy found in family, economy, and society into critical consciousness.[79] Yet, the more this semi-autonomy is reduced the more 'Criticising privilege becomes a privilege.'[80] The number of people who can escape complete conformism, who can still see through the delusionary system, is falling.[81] Still, with the continued

---

78 MM, Aphorism No. 2, 4: 23/23.
79 Adorno admits that in his own case the development of critical consciousness was partly due to fortunate circumstances (Adorno 1971: 134–5/Adorno and Becker 1983: 104).
80 ND, 6: 51/41.
81 There is also another sense in which Adorno intends his claim that criticism becomes a privilege. Not only are only few (and increasingly fewer) people able to criticise society,

division of labour, especially the division between manual and non-manual labour, there continue to exist those people who are sufficiently exempt from practice to reflect on reality.[82]

One consequence of this for Adorno is that the truth of the critique of the bad forms of life should not be measured by how widely people assent to it, but indexed to the insights of the remaining critical individuals.[83] Adorno is the first to admit the undemocratic nature of this (as, for example, his talks of the 'privilege' of critique indicates). However, he says little about how to identify these remaining critical individuals. In one of his interviews he merely indicates that they are modern and open to the 'logic of what develops in time'.[84] Also, as we saw in Section I, these individuals have to have a sense of their own fallibility and guard against becoming self-righteous. While Adorno seemed to think of the critical individuals on roughly the model of his own life, there is clearly room for extending the ambit beyond white males from a privileged background and educated in modernist high culture – for it might well be that others will be more attuned to the experience of negativity and the denial of human potential that (according to Adorno) characterises our social world. Be that as it may, if Adorno is correct in believing that critical individuals are, if at all, produced only as accidental by-products of the functioning of the system, it is likely that their number is going to be limited.

Still, Adorno claims that he and others among the dying-out critics can bolster the chances that there will be recipients for their 'message in a bottle [*Flaschenpost*]'.[85] To see how this might be possible, we need to turn first to what he says about trying to prevent Auschwitz from repeating itself (which – to recall – is what the new categorical imperative commands). This can function as a model for how it might be possible to foster a critical attitude generally.

In his essay 'Education after Auschwitz', Adorno draws a distinction between the subjective conditions that made Auschwitz possible and

---

this ability often depends on material and social privileges (for example, a relatively care-free, sheltered childhood). In this sense, those who still have the capability of critical reflection literally feed off the bad society they criticise (see, for example, MM, Aphorism No. 86, 4: 151/133).

82 See, for example, ND, 6: 337/343.

83 ND, 6: 51/41; see Adorno and von Haselberg 1983: 97.

84 Adorno and von Haselberg 1983: 98, 100.

85 Adorno and Horkheimer are reported to speak of their theories and analyses as 'messages in bottles' (see, for example, Reijen and Noerr (eds.) 1987).

could contribute to its reoccurrence, on the one hand, and the objective conditions, on the other:

> Since the possibility of changing the objective – namely, societal and political – conditions is extremely limited today, attempts to work against the repetition of Auschwitz are necessarily restricted to the subjective dimension. By this I also mean essentially the psychology of people who do such things. I do not believe it would help much to appeal to eternal values, at which the very people who are prone to commit such atrocities would merely shrug their shoulders. I also do not believe that enlightenment about the positive qualities possessed by persecuted minorities would be of much use. The roots must be sought in the persecutors, not in the victims, who are murdered under the paltriest of pretences. What is necessary is what I once called the turn to the subject. One must know the mechanisms that render people capable of such deeds, must reveal the mechanisms to them, and strive, by general awareness of those mechanisms, to prevent people from becoming so again.[86]

With changes to the objective conditions highly unlikely, Adorno here concludes that we should concentrate on understanding the (psychological) mechanisms which make people commit atrocities. In this sense, he wants education as 'an education toward critical self-reflection'.[87] This should proceed both via encouraging reflection and criticism from early childhood onwards, and by fostering it via public awareness campaigns about the (psychological) mechanisms in question.[88] Adorno also thinks that instilling a sense of distaste for, or shame about, violence into children (and, if possible, adults) would be important to prevent Auschwitz repeating itself.[89] He even makes a few suggestions about the form and content a post-Auschwitz education could have, such as recommending a focus on the concrete forms of resistance against the social horrors committed under Nazism or the opposition to parts thereof (for example, the euthanasia programme) among the German population.[90] On a social level, he also suggests reminding people of the catastrophic results – authoritarianism, war, suffering – which the fascist regimes had for their own populations and reminding them that fascist revivals would come at similar costs, something which might present

86 EA, 10.2: 675–6/CM, 192–3; see also MWTP, 10.2: 566–71/98–102.
87 EA, 10.2: 676/CM, 194.
88 EA, 10.2: 688–9/CM, 193, 202–3; see also MWTP, 10.2: 571/102.
89 See also Adorno 1971: 130–2.   90 EA, 10.2: 689–90/CM, 203.

more of a counterweight than reminders about the (even worse) suffering of others.[91]

What is most important is Adorno's insistence that this subjective dimension can at best improve the chances of people refraining from participating in such atrocities and thereby reduce the number of those carrying out the murders (though not necessarily the number of the people working in the bureaucratic machine behind the atrocities who Adorno calls 'desktop murderers').[92] Encouraging reflection from early on and public awareness campaigns will not transform the objective conditions. Still, it might influence the ease with which people might be led by these conditions to the most barbaric excesses. As Adorno puts it in his conclusion of the essay:

> Even if rational enlightenment, as psychology well knows, does not straightaway eliminate the unconscious mechanisms, then it at least reinforces in the preconscious certain counter-impulses and helps prepare a climate that does not favour the uttermost extreme. If the entire culture really became permeated with the idea of the pathogenic character of the tendencies that came into their own in Auschwitz, then perhaps people would better control those tendencies.[93]

The mere knowledge of how things go wrong may not be sufficient to stop them from going wrong, but it may, so to speak, strengthen the immune system of individuals or even whole societies against the objective tendencies towards depersonalisation, means-end reversal, and disregard of individuals.

What I want to suggest is that something similar applies to fostering critical reflection generally, not just to preventing another Auschwitz from happening. It might be the case that the objective conditions do not encourage critical awareness, but rather form a delusional system. Adorno seems to think this especially with regard to the cultural sphere, which for him is – as the subtitle of the essay 'Culture Industry' in *Dialectic of Enlightenment* puts it – 'enlightenment as mass deception'. The semi-autonomy of the different spheres which produce and encourage individuality might be increasingly under threat. Nonetheless, this does not mean that we cannot try in the 'subjective dimension' to foster critical awareness, for example, by reflecting on the mechanisms of the culture industry within educational frameworks.[94] Admittedly, this

91 MWTP, 10.2: 572/102-3.   92 EA, 10.2: 690/CM, 204.
93 EA, 10.2: 689/CM, 203; translation amended.
94 Adorno 1971: 145-6./Adorno and Becker 1983: 109-10.

presupposes – as does what Adorno says about preventing a repeat of Auschwitz via education and public awareness campaigns – that there still is some room for such effects within the educational sphere (and even within the public culture).[95] Given Adorno's views on these matters, this room for fostering critical awareness is constantly endangered and, hence, needs to be continuously defended. Nonetheless, Adorno remains committed to at least the possibility of installing enlightenment structures in schools and universities as well as running public awareness campaigns.[96] This also commits him to defending the autonomy (or semi-autonomy) of the educational and the public sphere and to work towards maintaining in them the conditions for fostering and strengthening critical awareness. Indeed, many of his efforts – both public and private – in Germany after World War II were focused on rebuilding and protecting the education system and the intellectual climate: be it in the form of his numerous TV and radio appearances, his writings on education, or his engagement in educating and examining prospective teachers – in educating the educators. He did this partly in the awareness that democracies have to at least keep up the impression of allowing free debate and criticism, and the hope that this would ensure that the fostering of critical awareness would survive in them.[97]

Moreover, there is one other reason to think that critical reflection will survive. One way to see this is to recall Lukács's conception of the proletariat as both capable of and required by their interests to see through capitalism. These two elements can come apart. Indeed, Adorno seems to have thought that, even in the liberal phase of capitalism, the capacity in question was largely restricted to bourgeois individuals, who are least necessitated by their material conditions to use it in a critical way. With the subsequent demise of the bourgeois individual, the capacity for critical reflection has come under serious threat. Now, the best we can hope for is that it can still be nurtured in the remnants of semi-autonomous spheres. On the other hand, the reasons which make critical reflection necessary – not only from the point of view of humanity as a whole, but

95 Kluge and Negt took Adorno's thought further by suggesting that critical theory should work towards creating a counter-culture, within which critical reflection could be fostered (see Kluge and Negt 1976).

96 For all his criticisms of the culture industry, Adorno was a lively contributor to the public debates in post-war Germany (especially on radio programmes). He must have thought that fostering critical reflection via the public sphere was still a possibility (see also Berman 1983: 95).

97 See Adorno 1971: 146/Adorno and Becker 1983: 109.

also from the perspective of the individual – could still persist relatively unaffected. If this is the case, then the idea of a 'message in a bottle' begins to make some sense, namely as the hope that somehow people will, eventually, become capable of doing what their situation produces a need in them to do.

That the situation still produces the need for critical reflection has to do with the state of society, which – as already noted in Chapters 1 and 3 – remains antagonistic and fails to meet its members's real needs.[98] Both these aspects give people a reason, even a need, to critically reflect on society, whether or not they are all or always capable of doing so. Admittedly, there is no guarantee that the ruptures within society, or the unsatisfied needs, will produce critical awareness (as traditional Marxists seem to have thought).[99] Still, the fact that there are these ruptures and unsatisfied needs leaves at least open the possibility that there could be critical individuals capable of reflecting on them and on the society producing them. Thus, to a certain extent, the problem of how people are capable of critical reflection in an administered world is less pressing than it first appears. In his more optimistic moments, Adorno seems to have thought that it was a matter of impossibility to integrate each one of us completely into the bad life.[100] While this does not guarantee that people actually will be led to critical reflection and resistance, it does anchor the possibility of this happening.

In sum, Adorno is aware that his conception of society as a delusional system makes it difficult to see how critical reflection and resistance are possible. He tends to tie the possibility of exercising these to individuals brought up in the liberal bourgeois era, but dying out in his lifetime. However, Adorno's account is not limited to this way of underwriting the possibility of resistance and critique. Rather, he seems to suggest that it is still possible to foster critical awareness – something which we should do (and he actively tried to do), both in order to undermine the subjective conditions for Auschwitz's repeating itself and, more generally, to make it possible to resist being co-opted by the radically evil social

98 See, for example, ND, 6: 99–100/92; 10.2: 655/CM, 175; see also ND, 6: 395–6/403–4; and 8: 392–6.

99 The deviation of Frankfurt School critical theory from traditional Marxist optimism about this point is well expressed by the following worry uttered by Marcuse: 'Perhaps an accident may alter the situation, but unless the recognition of what is being done and what is being prevented subverts the consciousness and the behaviour of man, not even a catastrophe will bring about the change' (1968: 13).

100 See, for example, 10.2: 655/CM, 175.

world. Adorno especially pinned his hope on the sphere of education, to which he turned a considerable amount of his attention in the post-war years. Adorno relies on the idea that knowing about the mechanisms of how we conform, or how we commit atrocities, can, so to speak, strengthen our immune system sufficiently for us to resist, at least to some extent. Furthermore, while the capacity for critical reflection is indeed under threat in a delusional system, the need for this reflection continues to exist.

In all this, one has to remember that whether or not critical reflection and resistance might objectively change anything about the administered world, or might not at some higher level help to reproduce it (for example, by stopping it from becoming too static), is something we cannot know. By living our wrong lives less wrongly we might hope to make a difference, but to assert that we will is already to overstep the bounds of what can be known in the administered world – in the words quoted already earlier, to assert this would 'contain too much vanity'.[101]

III Conclusion

In this chapter, I have retraced Adorno's sketch of how we can and should live in our current state of unfreedom. We have seen that, even though right living is impossible, it is nonetheless possible to live our wrong lives more or less wrongly, to make more or less use of our negative freedom to resist. Living less wrongly involves critical reflection, refraining from laying claim to meaning or legitimacy, trying not to join in, experimenting to find new ways of living, showing solidarity with others and their suffering, not focusing on the private life alone, and cultivating a sense of modesty to counteract self-righteousness. Living more wrongly involves violating these ideals, norms, and prescriptions.

In all of this, Adorno's recommendations and prescriptions are *negativist* and *minimalist* in nature. Adorno does not, and cannot, tell us what the right life consists in, or to what we should positively aspire above resisting wrong life. Rather, Adorno's sketch of a life of resisting highlights the pitfalls of such a life. It makes careful and few recommendations. It purposely falls short of a full-blown morality. Hence, Adorno offers us some practical guidance, but in a restrained manner and only on a general level. In this way, he does not paper over the tensions inherent – at least according to him – in moral practice within our social

101 PMP 1963, 250/168.

context, but acknowledges and reflects on these tensions within his theory (see also Chapter 3). Suggesting that more than such limited guidance could be offered, would be to ignore the precarious nature of individual (moral) practice today; suggesting that nothing could be said at all, is to miss what the analyses of the wrong forms of life can uncover (for example, in respect to the subjective conditions of these wrong forms of life, such as self-righteousness, or coldness to the fate of others). Even in an administered and radically evil world, different kinds of living can be evaluated differently, although these evaluations can never add up to more than a *minima moralia*.

It is worth emphasising, however, that what I have reconstructed *does* add up to a *minima moralia*. What we have encountered is a constellation of ideals (such as to have lived like a good animal), recommendations, prescriptions (including a categorical imperative), and other norms, and this makes it justifiable to ascribe an ethics to Adorno.[102] By this I mean to say that Adorno's philosophy contains a 'guide to how one should live'. Ascribing an ethics to Adorno's philosophy *in this sense* is compatible with the spirit and (most of) the letter of his work. It is not called into question by the fact that Adorno was critical of the term 'ethics' in other respects and of the dominant forms of modern moral philosophy.[103] In fact, the ascription of an ethics to Adorno in the sense specified is even compatible with his claim that 'there can be no ethics in the administered world'[104] – what he means here is that there can be no full-blown and solely private ethics of the good or right life.

In *Minima Moralia* Adorno places himself very much in the tradition of trying to provide a guide to right living. He is not optimistic that we currently can offer much substantive guidance on this matter because of the objective conditions of the world.[105] However, he does not deny that we can offer some such substantive guidance. In fact, *Minima Moralia* is rich in content, providing, among other things, exemplary cases of

---

102 I deliberately speak of 'constellation' here to highlight that Adorno's views are neither a merely random collection, nor a deductively worked-through system.

103 See PMP 1963, 22–30/10–16. Adorno was critical of the term 'ethics', partly because he thought that its use (particularly by German post-war Existentialists) masked the social conditions under which we live and focused attention on the individual's character at the expense of critical reflection on (his or her entanglement in) society. However, trying to give an answer to the question 'how should we live?' need not involve such masking or narrow focus, and, hence, ethics *in this sense* is not excluded by what Adorno has to say negatively about the term. On Adorno's critique of the dominant forms of modern moral philosophy, see here, Chapter 4; see also Geuss 2005: Introduction and Ch. 3.

104 PMP 1963, 261/176.   105 MM, 4: 13/15; see also PMP 1963, lecture 1.

how to live and how *not* live in our current predicament – Aphorism No. 18, on which we focused in Chapter 2, is perhaps the most poignant example in this respect, but there are others. Adorno's lectures on moral philosophy, on which I focused in this chapter, are perhaps even richer in their practical guidance on how to live the wrong life. We should not be blinded by the fact that the guidance Adorno does offer is limited and takes the form of negative prescriptions. It is guidance nonetheless. Even if only a negative, minimalist ethics of resistance is possible today for Adorno, the important point is that such an ethics is possible for him and that he subscribes to it. Put in a nutshell, Adorno subscribes to an ethics, since he considers certain forms of living the wrong life to be less wrong than others and prescribes us to strive towards living in these less wrong ways.

7

JUSTIFICATION, VINDICATION, AND EXPLANATION

So far we have seen that – according to Adorno – our modern social world (and its thought forms) are deeply morally problematic, that there is no right living within it, that moral theory cannot change this, and that we can only live less wrongly, for which Adorno provides us with negativist, minimalist guidance. It is clear that this picture is deeply evaluative – containing a variety of ethical claims about what we have reasons to believe, to do, and refrain from doing. As indicated in the Introduction, Adorno's theory has, however, been criticised for not containing the resources to account for these claims. I begin the exploration of Adorno's response by, firstly, returning to his critique of the idea that morality can and should be discursively grounded (already briefly considered in Chapter 5), and then, secondly, to move to general considerations about what it is to account for normativity.

I Against discursive grounding

Recall the passage in which Adorno formulates a new categorical imperative:

> A new categorical imperative has been imposed by Hitler upon human beings in the state of their unfreedom: to arrange their thoughts and actions so that Auschwitz will not repeat itself, so that nothing similar will happen. This imperative is as refractory to being grounded as once the givenness [*Gegebenheit*] of the Kantian. Dealing discursively with it would be an outrage, for the new imperative gives us a bodily sensation of the moral addendum – bodily, because it is the now practical abhorrence of the unbearable physical agony, to which individuals are exposed, even

after individuality, as a form of mental reflection, has begun to vanish. It is
only in the unvarnished materialistic motive that morality survives.[1]

In the context of this chapter, the most important element about this
passage is that Adorno rejects discursive grounding for morality. He
thinks, as we already saw in Chapter 4, that Kant's attempt to ground
morality discursively failed. Kant is the paradigm case for Adorno, and
he presumably judges other attempts to ground morality in this way as a
failure too. It is the importance of physical impulses for morality which
might explain its non-discursive nature. If Adorno is correct about
morality surviving in physical impulses ('the unvarnished materialistic
motive'), then it is not so surprising that morality is 'refractory' to
discursive grounding, since the physical impulse might not be something which can be fully rationalised (see Chapter 5).

Consider a second passage:

> It is not in their nauseating parody, sexual repression, that moral ques-
> tions are succinctly posed; it is in lines such as: No man should be tortured;
> there should be no concentration camps – while all of this continues in
> Asia and Africa and is repressed merely because, as ever, the humanity of
> civilization is inhumane towards the people it shamelessly brands as
> uncivilized. But if a moral philosopher were to seize upon these lines
> and to exult as having caught the critics of morality, at last – caught them
> quoting the same values that are happily proclaimed by the philosophy of
> morals – his cogent conclusion would be false. The lines are true as an
> impulse, as a reaction to the news that torture is going on somewhere.
> They must not be rationalized; as an abstract principle they would fall
> promptly into the bad infinities of derivation and validity. ... The
> impulse – naked physical fear, and the sense of solidarity with what
> Brecht called 'tormentable bodies' – is immanent in moral conduct and
> would be denied in attempts at ruthless rationalization. What is most
> urgent would become contemplative again, mocking its own urgency.[2]

Morality, Adorno tells us here, can be encountered in demands that ask
for the end of torture or concentration camps, but these demands are
not something to be discursively grounded (nor are they to be elevated
to abstract principles). These demands are appropriate as impulses, not
as rationally derived conclusions. And to attempt to rationally ground
these demands would also be unsuccessful. Such attempts would only
lead to 'bad infinities' of argumentation as well as undermine the

---

1 ND, 6: 358/365; translation amended; see also MCP, 181/116.
2 ND, 6: 281/285; see also MCP, 182/116.

practical aspect of our reaction, which is inextricably caught up with the physical impulse.

Adorno seems to think that no rational or discursive foundations (or grounding) for the impulse of resisting torture are possible. Trying to supply such foundations (or grounding) leads to an infinite dialectic of back and forth which is not resolvable one way or another.[3] The arguments on both sides can be made (to look) equally strong – for example, that torture is never justifiable because it involves treating people as a mere means *versus* that it is sometimes justifiable (for example) to prevent a great (moral) catastrophe. In other words, people might reasonably disagree about issues such as the permissibility of torture *at the level of rational deliberation*. As Adorno and Horkheimer remark in the *Dialectic of Enlightenment*, it is a matter of 'impossibility to derive from reason a fundamental argument against murder'.[4] Without the non-discursive physical impulse, there is nothing to stop the bad infinity of argumentation, such that reason could be used either way, for or against torture, for and against murder, without finding a conclusive resting point.

Also, to try to discursively ground the response that there should be no torture would be to take away the urgency to which we respond with an impulse. The interference of reason would cancel out this impulse which is part and parcel of moral conduct, and this would result in not taking the urgency the impulse expresses seriously. This point comes perhaps closest to Williams's famous one-thought-too-many objection, which is meant to bring out that reflection (in the sense of searching for discursive grounding) can lead us to abandon or disregard valid claims and our initial, appropriate response to them.[5] Here, it is supposed to be a certain situation – someone is tortured – which makes a claim on us, and it is not taking this claim sufficiently seriously – 'mocking its urgency' – to contemplate its justification.

Adorno also raises these issues in one of his lectures:

> If we attempt to set up an absolute law and to ask the laws of pure reason to explain why on earth it would be wrong to torture people, we would encounter all sorts of difficulties. For example, the sort of difficulties many Frenchmen have encountered in Algeria where in the course of the terrible concatenation of events in this war their opponents did resort

3 See also PMP 1963, 187–8/126–7.   4 DE, 3: 140/118; translation amended.
5 See, notably, Williams 1981: Ch. 1, 17–19. I discuss the Kantian response to this objection later in the chapter.

to torture of prisoners. Should they follow this example and torture their own prisoners or should they not? In all such moral questions, the moment you confront them with reason you find yourself plunged into a terrible dialectic. And when faced by this dialectic the ability to say 'Stop!' and 'You *shouldn't* even contemplate such things!' has its advantages.[6]

The difficulty of grounding morality in reason is again emphasised here. If when confronted with problems such as whether to torture one's opponents one were to start weighing up all the reasons for and against, one would end up in a 'terrible dialectic'. Compared to this dialectic, it seems better to respond with a moral impulse to such questions. Adorno goes on by providing the following illustration:

> For example, consider the moment when a refugee comes to your door and asks for shelter. What would be the consequence if you were to set up the entire machinery of reflection in motion, instead of simply acting and telling yourself that here is a refugee who is about to be killed or handed over to some state police in some country or other, and that your duty therefore is to hide and protect him – and that every other consideration must be subordinated to this? If reason makes its entrance at this point then reason itself becomes irrational.[7]

Let me expand on the idea that it would be 'irrational' to appeal to reason in this case. An appeal to reason might prolong the contemplation about whether or not to help the refugee to such an extent that the decision is taken out of your hands (after all, the refugee is 'about to be killed or handed over to some state police'). Reason's entrance could be practically self-defeating in the sense that the time taken for contemplation undermines the possibility of enacting what you might well have been required to enact upon contemplation. Moreover, the self-defeating character of contemplation is not merely an issue of time. Rather, reflection might also undermine the reactive, impulse-based component, so that contemplation could lead to having the right insight at the expense of being able to act on it. Thus, it might turn out on further reflection that it would be right to take in the refugee and hide him or her, but such reflection could also highlight how dangerous such a step might be, and this could undermine the person's impulse of solidarity. Consider, for example, the stakes of trying to rescue Jews from deportation and death during World War II – punishment for such action was

---

6 PMP 1963, 144/97; translation amended. See also MCP, 181–2/116.
7 PMP 1963, 144–5/97; see also 10.2: 550/CM, 85.

death, and the risk of discovery high, so that fear and concern for one's own family often prevented people from taking action. Consider the following description of a family's decision not to hide an old friend and his sisters because (the family thought that) the sisters looked too conspicuously Jewish and the old friend refused to be saved alone:

> Had the decision of my family been different, there were nine chances to one that we would be all shot. The probability that our friend and his sisters would survive in those conditions was perhaps smaller still. And yet the person telling me this family drama and repeating 'What could we do, there was nothing we could do!', did not look me in the eye. He sensed that I felt a lie, though all the facts were true.[8]

Indeed, it is part of the problem of the modern social world that the way it is arranged, makes resisting it or preventing atrocities riskier than joining in and standing by – that within this world, it is *in a certain sense* rational not to resist but stand by, so that contemplation of the facts is likely to undermine, not to strengthen, the impulses to help where we should.

The idea of reason's becoming irrational if it makes its entrance in this situation can also be taken to refer to the claim that calling into question the legitimacy of a reaction is in a way to disregard the claim to which it was a response (or, at least, to disregard the seriousness of this claim). In connection with contemplating torture one should say 'stop' to the dialectic of reason not only because it might take too long or because it might undermine one's impulses and ability to act, but also simply because the situation itself lays claim to a certain reaction. Similarly, in the case of the refugee, one should 'simply act', not 'set the whole machinery of reflection in motion'. To ask for further justification or for the foundation of this claim is already to misunderstand the claim and not to see its force. This is the case, whether or not the asking for justification will lead one to uphold the claim. To think that such justification is necessary is to miss the point; it is monstrous because it involves acting in a way that shows disregard for the claims arising directly from the situation and the people involved in it. At the back of this objection is a belief that certain situations, states of affairs, or persons have claims in and of themselves, whether or not they can be discursively grounded. (I come back to this later.)

I have gone to some lengths to expound Adorno's views on discursive grounding because it is a delicate, multifaceted matter, and the force of

8 Quoted in Bauman 1989: 202.

his views depends on accumulating different pieces of evidence, not in providing one knock-down argument. Beyond the material contained in the three passages considered, there are also two further elements that provide support for Adorno's claims. Firstly, as hinted at in the new categorical imperative passage, there are determinate criticisms of strategies to ground morality discursively, such as Adorno's criticisms of Kant's proof of freedom in the *Critique of Practical Reason* which we discussed in Chapter 4. In order to defend Adorno, one would then have to extend such a piecemeal strategy of criticisms to other proposals of discursive grounding – such as Habermas's discourse ethics. These criticisms directed at specific attempts of discursive grounding might not add up to undermining the general strategy of discursive grounding completely, but, if each of them is successful, they cast a dark shadow of doubt over the very project of discursive grounding.

Secondly, there is an aspect that I have not really mentioned before. Adorno sometimes seems to be suggesting that we should give up the idea of discursive grounding because this idea is a hangover from when religion formed the background of morality.[9] Moral philosophy tries to fill the vacuum left by weakened religion with attempts by reason to ground morality.[10] Yet, we would do better to be sceptical about the whole project of searching for first principles. This project is, according to Adorno, unsuccessful, for it ultimately involves disregarding how mediated everything is by everything else by stipulating one element as basic.[11]

Among these multifaceted considerations which Adorno musters against the possibility and appropriateness of discursive grounding of morality, the importance he attaches to physical impulses is particularly significant. According to the passage in which Adorno formulates the new categorical imperative, it is the physical impulse which lies at the heart of morality's survival (and the other two passages considered confirm this). In one of his lectures, he puts it stronger still and claims that 'the true basis of morality today is to be found in bodily feeling, in identification with unbearable pain'.[12]

9 Not unlike what Anscombe says about the law conception of morality in her famous essay 'Modern Moral Philosophy' (1958).
10 DE, 3: 104/85.
11 See 5: 14ff./Adorno 1982: 5ff.; see also 1995: 224, 239ff./148, 157ff.
12 MCP, 182/116; translation amended. This formulation is potentially misleading – if Adorno is serious about anti-foundationalism, then talking of 'true basis of morality [*Grund der Moral*]' is problematic. However, the context of the passage makes clear that what he means by true basis is not (discursive) grounding of morality's normativity, but the materialistic motive as the one motivational force that is still available in our

The importance of the physical impulse for morality relates to Adorno's discussion of Kant's account of spontaneous willing (see Appendix): it is not surprising to find Adorno making a materialist, impulse-based element central to ethics, because he thinks that without such an element, there can be no spontaneous willing, and thereby no agent-directed practice. In the same way as, in Adorno's conception, freedom requires two elements – reason and physical impulse – that have often come apart both in other (philosophical) conceptions and as a matter of fact, thus morality for him does not exhaust itself in reason alone, but always requires a physical impulse as well.[13] Indeed, reason and reflection can even undermine decision-making and acting (as in Hamlet's case: see Appendix).

Thus, according to Adorno, morality requires non-discursive and non-deducible elements to have content and to be efficacious. In this way, Adorno stands in direct opposition to Kant who thought that some ends and all the motivation required for acting morally can be derived directly from the categorical imperative and thereby from reason.

The standard move by Kantians in reply to objections of this sort is to say the following.[14] It is not the case that in the Kantian picture one always has to go through the whole procedure of formulating maxims and testing them. Rather, a virtuous person will normally act immediately for what this test would have shown to be the right course of action. The point is solely that it must be possible to check on each decision and action via the universalisability test, and a virtuous person would be able to justify each of their acts in this way, if called upon to do so. For something to be a moral decision and act, it has to be *justifiable* in this sense (whether or not the justification process is actually carried out). Thus, while it is most often the right thing to provide a refugee with a hiding place, or to save your wife rather than a stranger if one can only save one out of the two (to take Williams's example), it is not always the case: the refugee might be a mass murderer trying to escape justice, and your wife might be intentionally responsible for the shipwreck, but the child next to her not. Without ascertaining that individual cases conform to what reason, and thereby morality, requires, one might be doing

current social world to enact moral demands and the vindication of these demands, where vindication – as I discuss later in the main text – differs from grounding.
13 See PMP 1963, 17–21, 145, 167–8/7–9, 97, 112–13; PMP 1956/7, Vo1306–7; MCP, 182/116.
14 See, for example, Allison's version of this reply (1990: Ch. 10, 196–8).

a great injustice.[15] Better to fail to act in time on a few occasions, or sometimes to act in what might seem alienated and alienating, than to open the door to injustice and arbitrariness.

Adorno would give the following rejoinder. It is true that physical impulses are not always reliable as a moral compass – they can be manipulated and distorted. Indeed, racism and anti-Semitism might operate less at the level of belief and rational deliberation than at the emotional level – say by mobilising certain strong reactions (like disgust, anger, or resentment) against the groups in question. Adorno is very aware of the phenomenon in question – much of what he says about anti-Semitism is about how repression of impulses leads to projection of one's fears and angers on others, which in turn leads to aggression against them.[16] He also admits that we need to respond to these phenomena with reflection-inducing, critical questioning, so as, among other things, to unveil the mechanisms at play in the psychological manipulation and distortions (as already discussed in Chapter 6). Indeed, the physical impulses of the sort that Adorno has in mind are not completely unconnected to critical, theoretical insight.[17] They have legitimacy, but become one-sided and potentially problematic, if there is no reflective scrutiny at any point and they are never 'developed [*entfaltet*]' within a theoretical framework.[18]

Still, we should not throw the baby out with the bathwater: just because physical impulses are not always reliable and can be manipulated does not mean that we can do without them. Just the opposite, they

---

15 Some Kantians might accept exceptions here – issues in relation to which they would not hesitate to judge that the maxim in question is permissible or impermissible, whatever the case may be. Take, for example, the contemplation about whether or not to use torture in order to save a large number of people: while some Utilitarians might need to run a calculation of expected utilities, most Kantians would not even have to consider the issue in much detail, but reject this contemplation outright. However, they would still insist that the ground for this reaction lies in the categorical imperative, which produces an absolute prohibition here, making a case-by-case testing unnecessary (albeit nonetheless possible and successful, if insisted upon). As indicated earlier and discussed further in the main text later, it is objectionable to think that, if there are such absolute bads, they have grounding in something else – it is to miss the normative force they have *qua* (absolute) bads.

16 See his and Horkheimer's essay 'Elements of Anti-Semitism: Limits of Enlightenment' in *Dialectic of Enlightenment* (1972).

17 See PMP 1963, 19–20/8.

18 Adorno 2003b: 149–50/102. In Chapter 9, I suggest that an Aristotelian conception of normativity is part of the theoretical framework in which Adorno develops the impulse-based resistance, but crucially this conception and his framework as a whole are neither principle-based nor an attempt at discursive grounding.

are often the *least bad* guide we have – especially considering how appeal
to general principles is not sufficient to settle what *specifically* we should
do in the current circumstances in which many background conditions
for moral agency are missing (see Chapters 2–4). Indeed, there are
many examples from everyday life as well as from more unusual moral
situations (such as war and atrocity) that suggest that physical impulses
are often better guides to our actions than what we rationally, deliberately, or based on principles think should be the case – they find
expression in the hunches that the chosen career is not really for us
despite our thinking that it is after much deliberation; or in Huck Finn's
acting against his 'best judgement' when he helps Jim to escape.[19] As
Arneson puts it, 'untutored instinct might predictably do better than
tutored reason by reason's own standard'.[20]

Moreover, Adorno sometimes seems to qualify his claim about physical impulses: trusting our impulses is our best option *when faced with
something extremely horrible* such as torture or the Nazi regime;[21] but not
necessarily in all other situations. It is in the extreme situation that we
react directly and aptly by way of a mimetic response of solidarity with
the suffering encountered in it. In these situations, we go wrong when
we begin to rationalise these reactions, or start appealing to principles –
then we get caught in terrible, infinite dialectics of argumentation, in
the difficulties of translating general principles into specific guidance.
Checking our principles either leaves matters undecided (involving us
in an infinite dialectic), whereas the first reaction clearly guided us in
the appropriate direction; or, alternatively, the appeal to principles
brings with it the kind of distance to the situation, which then makes it
easier to rationalise away our first reaction of solidarity and to repress or
divert it. In this way – as pointed out already – rationalisation could
undermine the confidence we started off with and lead us astray.

The fact that it might only be in the especially bad cases where
impulses are still reliable fits well the following consideration: it is in
these cases where the appeal to principle seems least necessary and
thereby least plausible. While the categorical imperative might show
that torture is wrong, our physical impulses already express this and

---

19 See Bennett 1974; Arpaly 2000 and 2003.
20 Arneson 1994: 52. In Chapter 9, I suggest that my Aristotelian reading of Adorno's
   theory can also help to remove the impression of irrationalism that his appeal to physical
   impulses gives rise to – indeed, just in the way Arneson suggests, physical impulses can be
   expressive of (objective) reasons and more so than the results of deliberation.
21 See MTP, 10.2: 778/CM, 274.

insisting on grounding them on principles (or reason) would suggest
that these specific reactions could have turned out to be false or, at any
rate, have only derivate normative value and force – a suggestion that
seems to miss the point (I come back to this later). In this sense,
whenever the impulses might still guide us, appeal to principles is
unnecessary and misguided; and whenever the impulses do not guide
us, appeal to principles typically does not help either, given that the
same conditions which negatively affect our reactive attitudes also
undermine our capacity of judgement and our ability to use rules of
moral salience (the necessary presuppositions for using principles).

In many ways, the disagreement with Kantians comes down to whether
or not they (or indeed anyone) can pull off the trick of a non-impulse-
based morality with discursive grounding. As already indicated, Adorno is
sceptical about the possibility of discursive grounding and a principle-
based morality that relegates impulses to, at most, a secondary role. If this
project is, indeed, an impossible one, then Adorno's view is not lacking
anything in not attempting to offer general principles or a discursive
grounding. In fact, in that case, being unable to offer such grounding is
not a failure – if it really is impossible, then it does not make sense to speak
of failure or lack.

Before coming back to this thorny issue, let me note another aspect
of Adorno's normative outlook, which is also connected to the point just
made about extreme situations in which – if Adorno is right – our
physical abhorrence to suffering (and oppression) provides the least
bad practical orientation available. What I have in mind is the situation-
dependent aspect of his outlook. It already comes out to some extent in
the second passage considered earlier, in which he says that the demand
that torture is to be ended is true as a reaction to the news that torture is
going on.[22] It is expressed even more clearly in another passage, where
Adorno quotes approvingly one of the members of the resistance of
20 July 1944, who says the following:

> But there are situations that are so intolerable that one just cannot continue
> to put up with them, no matter what may happen and no matter what may
> happen to oneself in the course of the attempt to change them.[23]

---

22 ND, 6: 281/286. Recall also his comment to Gehlen quoted in the Introduction: 'Ethics
is surely nothing else than the attempt to do justice to the obligations, with which the
experience of this entangled world presents us' (in Grenz 1983: 246; my translation).
23 PMP 1963, 20/8; see also 10.2: 778/CM, 274; HF, 333/240; and PMP 1956/7 (unpublished), Vo1 306–7.

Situations themselves can give rise to a demand on us (namely, to change them). We should be reacting directly to situations, and we should be reacting to them independently of the prospects of success or the consequences for ourselves (or, at least, this might be the case for certain extreme situations such as living under a murderous regime). Moreover, as Adorno goes on to explain after this quotation, our reactions should even be (largely) independent of (ethical) theory – their normativity and justification derives not so much from principles, but from reacting appropriately to the situation and expressing the physical impulse of morality.[24]

This also suggests a further sense in which Adorno's conception of morality is materialistic – not this time in relation to our bodies, the physical impulses, but as indexed to situations or states of affairs (rather than principles or ideas). Put differently, Adorno's conception of morality is objective: only by recourse to how the world actually is can we arrive at a normative demand.[25] Thus, while for Kant a situation is an instance to *implement* an already given and grounded norm, for Adorno the norms derive from and are indexed to particular situations. In his dispute with Popper, Adorno formulates this point as follows:

> The normative problems arise from historical constellations, and they themselves demand, as it were, mutely and 'objectively', that they be changed. What subsequently congeals as values for historical memory are, in fact, question-forms [*Fragegestalten*] of reality, and formally they do not differ so greatly from Popper's concept of a problem. For instance, as long as the forces of production are not sufficient to satisfy the primitive needs of all, one cannot declare, in abstract terms, as a value that all human beings have to eat. But if there is still starvation in a society in which hunger could be avoided here and now in view of the available and potential wealth of goods, then this demands the abolition of hunger through a change in the relations of production. This demand arises from the situation, from its analysis in all its dimensions, independently of generality and necessity of a notion of value. The values onto which this demand, arising from the situation, is projected are the poor and largely distorted copy of this demand.[26]

24 See also Bernstein's discussion of 'material inferences', and specifically his example that the appropriate response to someone's bleeding badly is to apply a tourniquet (2001: 264–5, 322–3, 356–7, 450).
25 See ND, 6: 241/243.   26 8: 347/Adorno et al. 1976: 62.

These are rather stark claims, and many would dispute that values are derivative phenomena of the historically specific demands that arise directly from situations.

To see the force of what Adorno is saying, we have to return to the case of the new categorical imperative. In arising out of a particular historical context and experience, this imperative epitomises the idea of an objective index to a situation – the events associated with the name of Auschwitz – that places moral demands on us. In particular, the idea comes into view when we return to Adorno's claim that attempting to discursively ground this imperative is to commit an 'outrage'. It is an important, even pivotal thought, worth considering in more detail – something to which I now turn.

There is a weaker claim that might more readily find acceptance: Adorno says at one point that oppression and lack of freedom are 'the evil whose malevolence requires as little philosophical proof as does its existence'.[27] The idea here seems to be once more that grounding at the level of theorising or principle is unnecessary – we know that oppression is bad, even without such grounding. Kantians might accept that there are some evils (such as torture, genocide, and indeed oppression), where it is unnecessary to set the whole machinery of reflection in motion to ascertain that they are, indeed, evil. Still, the thought that to attempt discursive grounding is an outrage is a stronger thesis than the one that such grounding is (occasionally) unnecessary.

One way to support the stronger thesis is to consider that it does, indeed, seem outrageous to suggest that torture is wrong *mainly or solely* because the maxim in question cannot be universalised or because the balance of utility would speak against it in most cases or because it violates the presuppositions of discourse. Similarly, it would be outrageous to demand a justification for saying that what happened in the extermination camps was evil – implying that it could in principle turn out that the actions in question were not evil or that this evil would be merely derivative; rather than seeing these events as paradigmatic and constitutive of evil.[28]

---

27 10.2: 465/CM, 10.

28 To say that it would be outrageous to demand a justification is not to say that we should not *teach and explain* evils to those who do not (yet) recognise them. Recall also the passage by Hampshire quoted in Chapter 5, in which he describes the great evils as 'the *constant presupposition* of moral arguments at all times and in all places', as 'some of the constancies of human experience and feeling *presupposed* as the background to moral judgements and arguments' (1992: 90; my emphasis).

Here one feels drawn to Adorno's view that something goes wrong when one enters into a search for discursive grounds – both because it might well turn out that reason cannot provide such grounds but instead entangles itself in an infinite chain of arguments; and because it is inappropriate to ask for them. To ask for further grounding here is (a) to miss that all the normativity that there is has already been provided as part and parcel of the situation or example facing us, and (b) to fail ethically in overlooking this. In this way, it is not just that a philosophical proof of oppression, lack of freedom, or unbearable human suffering is unnecessary; it is also an outrage. If anything, philosophy should draw on these bads and operate with them firmly in view; it does not and cannot ground them. Indeed, some of the inappropriateness of attempting to ground them is apparent in the torturous nature of such attempts – which, for example, in Kant lead to the conclusion that moral respect for persons is, in fact, 'properly only respect for the law' of which persons (lucky for them!) give us an example and that we should not wantonly destroy nature or non-human animals *only* because it brutalises us which, in turn, is *only* wrong because it makes discharging our moral duties to persons more difficult.[29] By turning to ever higher, more abstract ideas that are meant to finally deliver the elusive discursive grounding of morality, we distort the very experience and access we have to the bads whose existence and justification need no philosophical proof (and can be afforded none).

In other words, what is being missed in many philosophical accounts is that the bads in question are *bad in themselves*; that their negative normativity is primitive in the sense that it is not derived from something else, but rather they provide us with paradigmatic examples to orientate ourselves in other moral matters (see already Chapter 5). To even suggest that the justification or source for negative normativity lies elsewhere or requires external verification (which comes, ultimately, to the same thing) is to miss something fundamental about them, even if a plausible story about why they are bad for such and such a reason then follows – it might give the right answer (say, that torture is morally bad if anything is), but for the wrong reasons (say, that torture's badness mainly or only consists in treating people as mere means, as if the pain involved was merely incidental to it) and to overlook the fact that the right answer does not require such further reasons and that offering them can even be a sign of defective virtue.

29 G, 4: 401; MS, 6: 564.

Still, if Adorno does not want to fall into irrationalism or dogmatism, he should be able to offer something to support his highly contentious claims. To insist on a morality that is impulse- and situation-dependent in a way which eludes discursive grounding would seem to be cutting short the debate, unless more could be offered to vindicate this outlook. As Adorno himself is wary of cutting short debate,[30] it is the case that, *by his own standards*, more needs to be said about the moral demands to which he lays claim. Also, in one of his lectures, Adorno explicitly denies that he endorses irrationalism (and, for that matter, natural law intuitionism).[31] But what other than discursive grounding can Adorno offer to escape the charge of irrationalism and dogmatism? Sometimes, he distinguishes between 'grounding [*Begründung*]' and 'vindication [*Rechtfertigung*]', criticising and rejecting only the demand for the former.[32] To understand why this is and what the difference amounts to, we need to consider – as a first step – what it would be to account for normativity more generally.

II What kind of account of normativity (if any) does Adorno need?

Unsurprisingly, much hinges on how the project of accounting for normativity is understood. It might be understood either (a) as a grounding (or justificatory) project, or (b) as an explanatory project, or (c) one might think that no (general) account of normativity (whether justificatory or explanatory) is necessary or attractive. The Problem of Normativity has normally been put in terms of (a), while Adorno would seem to only accept either (b) or (c). This places certain constraints on any Adornian account of normativity – constraints that, I suggest in the final chapter, are fully and probably best met by ascribing an Aristotelian conception of normativity to Adorno.

What is at issue in accounting for normativity is to account for the standards of judgement (or norms) used in a theory and the reason-giving character of these norms (in particular, the force of the reasons generated by them). Now, one might think that the best way, or perhaps

---

30 See PMP 1963, 187–8/126–7; and also here, Chapters 4–5.
31 MCP, 181–2/116; see also MM, Aphorism no 44.
32 ND, 6: xx/xix; see also MCP, 177, 181–2/113, 116; 20.1: 319. (NB: The respective translators mark this distinction differently from my (more literal) translation – talking of justifying/basing on reason (Ashton in ND) and justifying/founding on logic (Jephcott in MCP).)

even the only way, to do this is to *ground* the norms in something independent or at least to *justify* them on independent grounds – such as in human nature, in (formal) reason, in the presuppositions of communicative action, or in the conceptual structure of our practical identity as agents. Not all of the variants of this view need be foundational in any straightforward sense – for example, some forms of constructivism probably fall into the general category at issue, but they are non-foundational. Yet, whatever differences there might be among the theories within this category, they all share the assumption that an account of normativity is a *justificatory* project.

However, this way of accounting for normativity is by no means the only way. Another approach would be to argue that what is at issue in such an account is an *explanatory* project. Most of the time this view is combined with the rejection of the grounding or justificatory project mentioned first. Hence, the thought is that while it might not be possible (or, indeed, necessary) to ground normativity, we can provide a general explanation of how anything can be normative for us and of what is normative and with what force. Such an explanation might play a clarifying or reassuring role for those who accept the normative practice or theory in question, although it might be unsuitable for convincing a sceptic of this normative practice or theory. This is not to say that such accounts rule out justification altogether; rather, the point is that in this view justifications can be only of an internal and limited kind, not independent and extending all the way down. There is no denial of the fact that we make normative claims and engage in justification, but accounting for normativity is not another, possibly more fundamental instance of this practice, but something different: an explanation of it.

Moreover, one could also take a third line on the question of what an appropriate account of normativity would consist in. One can be altogether sceptical of the possibility or usefulness of a (general) account of normativity, whether of an explanatory or a justificatory nature. While we do, indeed, make normative claims all the time, any (general) theory of this activity will either be uninformative or impossible to construct. The only appropriate account of normativity is either to say that there can be no such account, or at least none of a general and invariant kind (as opposed to a context-specific one).

Let me illustrate these three approaches with examples. It could be said that the normativity involved in the particular conception of moral personhood which supposedly underpins Rawls's theory of justice is meant to be justified in his early work by (a) the fact that the principles derived are in reflective equilibrium with our considered judgements about relevant cases and (b) arguments based on a certain view about the human good which make it the case that the conception of moral personhood has priority over other values. This is an example of the first kind of account of normativity: the conception of person-hood is supposedly justified with recourse to a certain methodology (the coherentism and constructivism of the method of reflective equi-librium) and a certain conception of the good. However, the later Rawls moved away from this view. In his later writings, at least in some interpretations of them,[33] the account is explanatory: it is a fact that citizens of modern democratic societies are committed to a particular conception of moral personhood, and it is this fact which explains why the theory of justice derived from it has normative force for them. Yet, this fact is not used and probably could not be used to justify the normative force of Rawls's theory to those who do not subscribe to the main tenets of the public political culture of liberal democracies.[34] In the writings of the later Rawls (thus interpreted) neither a concep-tion of the good, nor reflective equilibrium as a method plays a role in justifying the theory as a whole (though the latter still has some heuristic and possibly even justificatory function *within* the theory). In this sense, we encounter here an example of an account of norma-tivity in the second sense. Finally, one might argue (perhaps with Isaiah Berlin or Stuart Hampshire) that there are indeed manifold reasons to object to this injustice or another, but that there is no one general justificatory or explanatory story which underpins or explains these reasons – perhaps because a deep value pluralism makes this impossible.[35] We should, hence, neither expect, nor require that the normativity contained in political philosophy is justified or explained by a general account of it. For those who agree on the normative force of a viewpoint, no further account is necessary (but this is not to say that this agreement justifies or explains this force); and for those who do not agree with it, any further account would probably be of no use either (here only a different kind of force would do). This is an example of the third kind of approach to the project of accounting for normativity.

With these more general thoughts in mind, we should consider what sense of accounting for normativity is at issue between Adorno and his

33 See, for example, James 2005.   34 See Scheffler 1994: especially 21–2.
35 See, for example, Hampshire 1992.

critics. The idea that accounting for normativity is aiming to ground or justify the norms employed in a theory (that is, (a), see earlier) might be what most of the critics of Adorno have in mind. This can be seen in the way they formulate their criticisms by, for example, saying that Adorno's philosophy lacks 'normative foundations [*normative Grundlagen*]'.[36] What these critics lament is that Adorno cannot answer the question how critical thought can be justified, that he cannot give 'reasons for the right of criticism'.[37] And they would, presumably, say the same about the possibility of providing reasons for the right of raising ethical demands: within the negativistic confines of Adorno's theory, no such justifying reasons could be given. From the perspective of the critics, Adorno can only be seen to escape into art, aesthetic theory, or philosophical 'gesticulation', and in this way he pays a heavy price for the aporia of the critique of instrumental reason.[38]

However, as we have seen in this chapter, Adorno rejects the need for, as well as the appropriateness and success of, 'discursive grounding'. Trying to ground normative claims discursively or at the level of abstract principles is both unsuccessful and an outrage. It is unsuccessful, since morality, according to Adorno, can have content and practical effects only in virtue of relying on non-discursive and non-deducible elements, namely, our impulse-based reactions to suffering and injustice. To suggest that it is necessary to ground normative claims discursively is to implicitly deny that the particular situation *by itself* contains normativity and to claim that instead the normativity given in it *derives* from some deeper level of theorising or some higher principle. This idea of derivation, however, gets things terribly wrong in Adorno's view. For example, it does not take seriously enough the evil of the events for which the name 'Auschwitz' stands; for to search for discursive grounding implies that it is necessary to obtain reassurance about the negative normativity of these events at a general level abstracted from them. Not only is such reassurance impossible, it is ethically wrong to ask or search for it – 'monstrous'.[39]

Two points emerge from these views of Adorno's. Firstly, it should now be clear why Adorno never explicitly provided what his critics asked for. We have just seen that what the critics demanded is a justificatory account of normativity. Yet, as Adorno rejected this project, this demand

---

36 Habermas 1984: 374; see also Benhabib 1986: especially Chs. 5–6.
37 Habermas 1983: 106.   38 Habermas 1984: 385.
39 EA, 10.2: 674/CM, 191. Adorno's rejection of 'normative foundations' is also discussed in Schweppenhäuser 1992, 1993: esp. 210–11; Schweppenhäuser 2004; and Kohlmann 1997: 152ff.

is (from his perspective) misconceived. While it would have been good to explicitly say so, he probably assumed that his views on the merits and demerits of the justificatory project were sufficiently well-known for him not to comment further on the matter.

Secondly, we can reconstruct from Adorno's sceptical views about 'discursive grounding' some constraints on how Adorno would have approached the project of accounting for the normativity of his views. The account would not be justificatory in the sense outlined. Specifically, this implies two constraints: (a) it should not commit the outrage of disregarding the normativity given in a situation by deriving it from a deeper or higher level; and (b) it needs to be sensitive to the non-deductive, impulse-based elements in Adorno's ethics (and philosophy as a whole).

Are there any further constraints on such an enterprise? It seems to me that the following considerations show that there is at least one more constraint besides the two mentioned before. One important element of Adorno's philosophy is what we might call a kind of 'error theory'.[40] For Adorno, most people relate wrongly to the world and each other. In fact, according to him, we all have distorted reactions and attitudes most of the time because of the way society has constituted, conditioned, and programmed us. We desire things we do not really need and do not respond fully to the neglect of what we do in fact need.[41] In order to make this theory work, Adorno not only needs to have an explanation of why people behave in this way – as just indicated, he seems to think that it is determination by society which explains this – but also needs an explanation of why behaving in this way is wrong or constitutes an error. For example, one way such an explanation could go is to show how states of affairs can give us reasons for action, for believing, etc., and how in most cases people do not respond adequately to these reasons in our current social world – by overlooking them, by letting less weighty considerations override them, etc. As a matter of fact, some such account seems to be at work in Adorno's theory, though it is often phrased more in terms of a contrast between what a few critical individuals who were lucky to escape complete programming by society think about the world and what the majority of uncritical individuals make of it.[42] Admittedly, one might then need further assurance that the

---

40 The concept of 'error theory' was introduced by Mackie 1977.
41 See, for example, 8: 392–6; ND, 6: 99–100/92–3.
42 See, for example, ND, 6: 51–2/41–2.

judgements of the critics provide the right kind of standard for assessing the judgements of the majority (I return to this soon). Still, the first point to note here is that Adorno needs some sort of account of the errors which most of us all the time and all of us most of the time are committing in relating to our (social) world and each other. Moreover, this places a third constraint on any Adornian account of normativity: it has to be suitable to explain the error(s) in question.

My contention is that Adorno meets the three constraints by way of an explanatory account of normativity (rather than by way of a context-dependent one). I have no conclusive proof of this, but in the final chapter I suggest that this interpretation allows us to draw together the various strands of Adorno's (practical) philosophy. Here I want to consider one objection, which applies – albeit perhaps in somewhat different ways – to both of the non-justificatory accounts: how could an error theory run just on the basis of explanatory resources, not justificatory ones?

Adorno is, as far as I can tell, relatively silent about this kind of meta-theoretical issue. However, he would be sympathetic to accounts such as, for example, Taylor has provided (albeit in a slightly different context).[43] Taylor argues that it is impossible to have a fully justificatory account of practical reason, since the only way such an account could go is by abstracting from all our strong evaluations and self-understanding, and doing so would deprive us of any substance with which arguments can be made. Nonetheless, this lack of justificatory account does not mean that anything goes and that nothing could be said to defeat any intellectual positions in support of, for example, the behaviour of the Nazis. In most cases of disagreement, what happens is actually that people start from shared assumptions (which are not further justified) and then justify their behaviour against this backdrop.[44] Thus, according to Taylor, even intellectual support for the behaviour of the Nazis (if any such support were actually offered) accepts the ban on murder, but then goes in for special pleading in order to show that the behaviour in question is not murder after all or is required all things considered. The way to deal with special pleading is not to offer a grounding of the shared assumption, but by showing that the special pleas just do not stand up to any critical scrutiny, since they are absurd and irrational when measured against the standards everyone party to the debate

---

43 See, for example, Taylor 1993. This and the next paragraph draw on this paper.
44 For a similar view see, for example, Rescher 1958.

accepts. In this sense, the error consists in inconsistency, or lack of clarity, and exposing that error does not require a justificatory account.[45] (The game of demanding and giving reasons can be played also within an explanatory account – as noted before, the difference from a justificatory one is rather that justifications do not extend all the way down, and vindication at some point takes on an explanatory dimension instead.)

Yet, what if there is a fundamental disagreement about the basic assumptions – might we not need an independent criterion or ground in this case? Again, Taylor argues that this need not be so. Different sets of assumptions or theories can be compared in terms of explanatory power, such as that the one of the two theories can explain why people might hold the other theory (and why they are, by the light of former, mistaken in doing so); or one theory might be able to explain the success of the other theory in its own terms, but the same is not true *vice versa*; or one of the two can be shown to be internally incoherent. Thus, error would here be cashed out in terms of lack of explanatory power.

Admittedly, the story presented by Taylor is somewhat optimistic – perhaps, more than one theory is sufficiently flexible to adjust to objections that call into question their explanatory power, so that, ultimately, disagreement about which theory has the greatest explanatory power are bound to remain (and perhaps there are also problems of commensurability of the radically different frameworks). Hence, it is best to concede that even when it comes to explanatory power, there is no silver bullet available that puts all matters beyond debate; rather comparing explanatory power is an additional resource, a way of increasing the costs of rejecting a theory in favour of an alternative despite the former's debunking explanation of this alternative and its powerful account of the phenomena at issue.

What we would get here is then not an a priori or infallible defence of a proposed view, but only a comparative judgement that the view in question is the best account (in terms of explanatory power) constructed so far. Yet, unless we already believe in the possibility of a stronger, justificatory account, this fallibility should not trouble us too

45 Adorno's way of dealing with the spectre of a relativist challenge also proceeds either (a) by way of appealing to something which presumably all would accept: the badness of inhumanity (PMP 1963, 261/175); or (b) by pointing out that in respect to any concrete situation, the relativist can be defeated by way of immanent critique (ND, 6: 45–8/35–7).

much. In cases of disagreement about who is in error, we either will find common ground with which we can settle this question, or invoke the greater explanatory power of one of the views. Failing either of these strategies, the individuals or groups will then have to find ways of tolerating each other, or, if this is not a viable option, to defend them-selves, even if no justification or explanation acceptable to the other side can be given.[46]

In a similar way, an Adornian error theory could be cashed out in terms of differential explanatory power (instead of requiring an appeal to the idea of ultimate justificatory grounding). The only authority which the critical individuals can and need to claim for themselves is the authority of having a clearer and fuller grasp of the modern social reality. This also reveals how he understands '*vindication*' – in a nutshell, if his critical theory succeeds better than rival theories in explaining certain social phenomena and developments (such as the high inciden-ces of paranoia and neurosis or modern anti-Semitism), then it is as redeemed as anything could be.

Let me take stock of what I have said in this section. I have suggested that there can be three kinds of approach to the project of accounting for normativity: a justificatory, an explanatory, and a sceptical one. The critics of Adorno ask for the first of these, while Adorno, on the other hand, rejects the demand for and possibility of a justificatory approach. This leaves it open whether Adorno would prefer an explanatory or a sceptical approach to the project of accounting for normativity. While I did not explicitly argue one way or the other on this matter, I proposed three constraints on any Adornian approach to this project: (a) it should not commit the (putative) outrage of disregarding the normativity given in a situation by deriving this normativity from a deeper or higher level; (b) it needs to be sensitive to the non-deductive, impulse-based ele-ments in Adorno's ethics (and philosophy as a whole); and (c) it needs to provide support for Adorno's error theory about how most of us react

---

46 See also Lenman 1999. One consequence of rejecting the justificatory project (and of the emphasis on ethical sensibility) is, at least for Adorno, that we have to write differ-ently. Instead of taking a logical proof or deduction as our model, we have to rely fundamentally on examples and aphorisms; we have to present matters in such a way that people see them in a different light; we have to provoke people into thinking for themselves and engage in an *éducation sentimentale*. If what I argue in this chapter and the study as a whole is correct, then doing this is perfectly legitimate and appropriate and neither discursive grounding nor a philosophical system is missing.

to the world and to each other.[47] I have also argued that none of these constraints, not even (c), commits Adorno necessarily to a justificatory account of normativity.

This is, however, only the beginning of the defence of Adorno – for I have not yet demonstrated that negativism is coherent, or added sufficient texture and detail to Adorno's version of it. It is to these tasks that I turn in the next two chapters.

---

47 I return to these constraints in Chapter 9.

8

NEGATIVISM DEFENDED

It is now time to return to the Problem of Normativity that I summarised in the Introduction as follows:

A Adorno's philosophy contains normative claims.
B In order to justifiably make normative claims, one needs to provide an account of the normativity in question.
C Accounting for normativity requires appeal to (and knowledge of) the good.
D Within Adorno's philosophy no such appeal (or knowledge) is possible. [Adorno's Epistemic Negativism.]
E From (B), (C), and (D), Adorno cannot justifiably make normative claims.
F From (A) and (E), Adorno is not entitled to make the normative claims his philosophy contains.

In earlier chapters we have seen that Adorno clearly makes normative claims, albeit of a minimalist, negativist nature. We have also seen in the previous chapter that in some sense Adorno accepts that an account of normativity is required – not in the sense his critics have in mind (a justificatory account), but as an explanation-based vindication of his views. In the Introduction, I have already discussed Adorno's commitment to Epistemic Negativism, and the later discussion of his views on freedom, ethics, and moral philosophy has remained within its strictures. Thus, only premise C is left to contest if one hopes to defend his views without giving up its core tenants. As indicated in the Introduction, it strikes me that we should – quite independently of a defence of Adorno – reject this premise, and it is in this chapter that I aim to make good on this claim.

In a nutshell, I argue that we need not appeal to or know the good (or the right)[1] to account for the normativity inherent in Adorno's critical theory and ethical claims – both for reasons internal to his theory and because of independent considerations. In order to show this, I distinguish between the different objections which have been, or could be, made against a negativistic approach (both in general and to Adorno's philosophy).[2] I argue that none of these objections is successful, although the reasons for this will differ in each case. For example, we see that some of them rest on implausible views in value theory, while others merely highlight the limitations which are the inevitable consequences of a negativistic philosophy, but which are not by themselves a reason to abandon it

There are the following five ways in which one might think that Adorno's philosophy would fail in the task of accounting for its normativity if it were purely negativistic: (1) an appeal to the good is necessary to show why badness has (negative) normativity for us, and insofar as Adorno's philosophy relies on the normativity of badness, it relies on an (implicit) appeal to the good; (2) we are automatically committed to a conception of the good whenever we criticise something as bad (or put forward the ethical demands that it ought to be changed), and, hence, Adorno's critical theory cannot but contain a conception of the good; (3) unless we bring in knowledge of the good, Adorno's philosophy cannot be constructive in the sense of offering positive alternatives (and any theory ought to be constructive in this sense); (4) without appeal to the good, Adorno's philosophy could not have the practical import to which it lays claim as critical and ethical theory; and (5) without knowledge of the good, we cannot recognise the bad, and, hence,

---

1 From now on, I speak only about 'the good', not 'the right' as well. The two may well differ in a number of important ways, but the kind of worries that Adorno faces are actually upstream than any of these differences – the real issue is whether Adorno can do without an appeal to a positive normative standard, be it that of the good or the right. The reason I run the argument in terms of the former is that the textual evidence would, if at all, point rather to the good than the right as a positive core in Adorno's work, but nothing really hangs on this for the purposes of the overall argument. Similarly, while Adorno uses a number of other locutions, such as 'reconciliation' and 'utopia', I will simply assume in this paper that they refer to the good (or its realisation).

2 Surprisingly perhaps, the replies I advance on Adorno's behalf are neutral between a justificatory and an explanatory account of the normativity of Adorno's philosophy. Thus, even those unconvinced by Adorno's rejection of the justificatory project (discussed in the previous chapter) are given reasons why the various specific guises in which the Problem of Normativity presents itself do not defeat Adorno's theory.

Adorno's philosophy could not get started, even if its normativity derived solely from the bad. I will discuss these five charges in turn.

The initial plausibility of the Problem of Normativity derives, I submit, at least in part from the fact that it has these different guises. If the problem is shown to be unconvincing in one guise, the others rear their heads and a sense of a problem lingers. Unless a systematic and complete discussion is provided – of the sort offered here – this multifaceted problem will continue to cast a dark shadow over Adorno's theory. The Problem of Normativity is a dragon with many heads, and one must make sure that each of them is decapitated – otherwise they all tend to grow back.

I The normative force of the bad

It might be said that accounting for normativity involves justifying the normative force of the standards of judgement used in a theory. Thus, any critique needs a standard or contrast – a norm – with which to justify its critical stance towards the object of its critique, and we have to underwrite these norms. Similarly, ethical claims make use of norms – be it principles (such as Kant's categorical imperative), or ideals (such the life of Jesus), or virtues (such as modesty). If accounting for these norms consists in justifying their force, then the question arises whether or not a conception of the bad would be sufficient for this task. One answer might be that the fact that something is bad does not by itself give us a reason to change or criticise it. The bad, it might be thought, is not independently normative; we only have reasons to act (or to criticise) if we also appeal to the good.

However, such a view is implausible. It seems superfluous to ask for a reason to avoid the bad; its badness is reason enough. If someone said that a certain action would be bad to do, but that this is not a reason to refrain from doing it, we would think that he did not understand what he was saying, or was talking nonsense.

Consider the example of pain; when we feel pain, we want it to go away: its badness signals us that – as Adorno puts it – 'things should be different. "Woe speaks: 'Go.'".'[3] In this sense, the badness of pain

---

3 ND, 6: 203/203. This view is not restricted to Adorno. For example, Sussman writes: 'Insofar as the experience of pain has any content, it seems to be that of a pure imperative. To feel pain is to confront something like a bodily demand to change something about one's condition, to do something to silence this very demand. ... like someone incessantly

(its painfulness) gives us a reason to avoid it and no appeal to the good seems to be necessary for this.[4] It might be that not all forms of pain and suffering give rise to reasons to avoid them (see Chapter 5); but those that do, give rise to such reasons without appeal to the good. It might also well be the case that the reason which a particular pain or a particular instance of suffering gives us to avoid it could be outweighed by other considerations (such as the avoidance of more pain and suffering later), but this does not change the fact the there is such a reason.

The same can be said of badness generally: it gives us a reason to avoid it, albeit one which is sometimes defeasible. Thus, it might make sense to ask of a particular bad whether one should avoid or endure it, since it might be the case that enduring it is the best policy, all things considered. However, this does not take anything away from the negative normative force of badness, that is, from the fact that to deny this force would be to fail to recognise the reasons which the bad gives us. For even reasons which are outweighed or trumped on some occasions are reasons; and even when they are outweighed or trumped, a normative remainder persists and we should conduct ourselves accordingly (such as renew our efforts or make amends). Similarly, sometimes the best policy is to be rid of the desire whose frustration causes pain (rather than to satisfy it) – think, for example, of someone whose desire to torture others is unfulfilled and who is miserable because of that. Still, pain and badness more generally give us even here a reason for action, although not necessarily a reason to satisfy the frustrated desire (but, say, a reason to change the society that brings about desires such as these; or to undergo therapy).

Admittedly, I explicated this response in terms of a particular conception of reasons, according to which certain states of affairs give rise to defeasible reasons. Still, this conception is not specific to Adorno or his negativism, but has more general support. Moreover, denying it is of no use to his critics. Thus, one might think that there is no such thing as defeasible (or *prima facie*) reasons, but only all-things-considered reasons. Accordingly, badness would not always have negative normative force, but only if it outweighed other considerations. However, the same

---

screaming "Shut me up!"' (2005: 20). He also claims that pleasure 'does not have the same kind of imperatival quality as pain, the same self-referential demandingness' (ibid.).

4 Ascribing to Adorno an Aristotelian conception of normativity makes it possible to offer a rationale for his view that pain by itself gives us a reason to avoid it (see Chapter 9; on the badness of pain, see Aristotle, NE, VII.13). However, this view is not limited to Aristotelians (see, for example, Hume [1748, 1751] 1975: 293; Nagel 1986: 156–63).

would be true of the normative force of goodness. Hence, appeal to the good would not in all cases be necessary (nor would it always be sufficient), even if one took this alternative view of reasons. As long as it would not be denied that the bad had sometimes sufficient normative force to carry the day (and it would be implausible to deny that), the view that there are only all-things-considered reasons would not lend support to the attack on negativism.[5] Similarly, Adorno's critics could adopt anti-realism about reasons, but even this would not vindicate their particular worries about normative negativism. For example, they might claim that to say that the bad gives us a reason to avoid it is to state nothing else than that we have a corresponding desire to do so (the Humean view) or self-legislated a suitable principle to this effect (a particular kind of Kantian constructivism). While Adorno's critics could deny in this way that badness is directly normative, this would again not really help against the negativistic defence strategy of Adorno, since on the anti-realist view an appeal to the good would not by itself give rise to reasons either. Anti-realism is not scepticism about the negative normative force of the bad in particular, but about normative force as such. On this view, neither the good, nor the bad give us reasons by themselves. In other words, whatever might be wrong with the conception of reasons I invoked in Adorno's defence earlier, it is not the fact that it can be used to give a purely negativistic account of the normative force of the bad.

In sum, it is plausible to think that badness has normative force by itself (at least in some instances). While this idea might be best cashed out in terms of a particular view of reasons, any controversy surrounding this view has nothing to do with negativism in particular.

Before moving to the discussion of the next objection, I should note a linguistic upshot of negativism, partly because it relates to a lingering doubt the reader might still have relating to my response to this (first) objection. Would negativists say that avoiding bads is 'good' or 'better' than not doing so? Yes, *in a certain sense*, negativists would say this, and can do so without violating negativism, as long as we understand the meaning of such statements in the appropriate way (which does not necessarily

---

5 It is true that the badness which Adorno's philosophy uses as his standard of critique and for its ethical claims would have to be such that it generates sufficiently strong (negative) normativity for no appeal to the good to be necessary to carry the day. However, it is not implausible to think that the badness in question is of such strength, given that Adorno mainly appeals to the great evils and other significant bads, such as a shortfall from basic human functioning (see Section II and Chapter 9).

coincide with our everyday understanding of them): for the negativists, these statements indicate an acknowledgement of the reasons we have and that we should act on them, but do not refer to the good. Put differently, for negativism, saying 'it is good/better to avoid the bad' (and the like) amounts to saying that we live less wrongly when we act in this way, that we act as we should by discharging the reasons we genuinely have in virtue of the bads we face. In a social world without access to the good, even what we are *entitled* to say is reduced compared to a social world in which the good is realised and accessible – 'better' can only be short-hand for 'less bad'; 'good' for 'avoidance of the worst'.[6] This narrowing might be lamentable, but it is not the fault of theory which acknowledges the restricted normative and linguistic resources (i.e., negativism), but the fault of the world which affords us no other resources.

II A negative characterisation of the good underdetermines it

Another reason why a conception of the bad might be thought to be insufficient to underwrite norms might be the following. When we criticise something as bad, we thereby imply that its absence is good, and in this sense we are automatically committed to a conception of the good. Hence, it is a major oversight to claim (as Adorno does claim) that one could operate with a conception of the bad without operating with a conception of the good, or that one could know the bad without knowing the good.[7]

Again, it is not clear that we should accept this reasoning, and it is certain that Adorno would not have accepted it.[8] Let us concentrate on

---

6 This is not meant as a description of what we ordinarily *take* ourselves to refer to (which might well be the good), but a disclosure of how negativism would constrain what we could *legitimately* refer to (only the bad).

7 Adorno explicitly makes the claim that we can know the bad (or, at least, the inhuman) without knowing the good in the following passage: 'We may not know what absolute good is or the absolute norm, we may not even know what man [*der Mensch*] is or the human [*das Menschliche*] or humanity [*die Humanität*] – but what the inhuman [*das Unmenschliche*] is we know very well indeed' (PMP 1963, 261/175; see also 8: 456; 2003b: 49/28–9). The thought that knowledge of the bad is impossible without knowledge of the good might be one reason why both critics and some defenders of Adorno have argued that he must be making use of the good after all, either illegit-imately (as the critics suggest) or legitimately (as those defenders think who ascribe a positive core to his philosophy). If the argument in the main text is successful, then this major motivation to deny Adorno's negativism falls away.

8 For example, Adorno always insists on the fact that, contrary to what Hegel thought, a negation of the negative does not yet amount to something positive (see, for example, ND, 6: 161–3/158–61). Finlayson summarises Adorno's position well: 'Moreover, this

the former. It is hard to deny that when we criticise something as bad we are implying that its absence would be good. However, this need not commit us to a conception of the good or knowledge of it in any strong sense. The reason why it would be good that a particular bad is overcome, could simply be that the bad demands to be overcome – in other words, we are back to the preceding point that the bad gives us reason to avoid it; that we do not need to know the good to know what we have reason to do (or to welcome). Thus, there need be no reference to a positive conception of the good in saying that it is good that a particular bad has been overcome.

The critics might respond by saying that surely any conception of the bad tells us something about the good. However, this can be admitted without giving up Adorno's negativism. It is true that once I know what is bad, I will also know what the good is *not* like. It is, however, not obvious that it is sufficient for knowing the good that I know what it is not like. Knowledge of a particular bad at most negatively characterises the good to some extent; it underdetermines the good both insofar as it only partially characterises it and insofar as it does not tell us what the good is like in itself.[9] If we only had a negative characterisation of the good available, then too much would be left open. The practical orientation offered – while important in its own right – would not suffice to hone in on the good. Consider a central example from Adorno, namely, his new categorical imperative (see Chapter 5). Aiming to stop Auschwitz from repeating itself clearly commits one to a positive attitude towards a world without the objective conditions for the occurrence of such moral catastrophes. Yet, this says rather little about what such a world would look like. There might, for example, be more than one social order which prevents events like Auschwitz from reoccurring, and even if there is only one such order, we have not learned much substantially about it from knowing what it will *not* be like in this *one* respect.

Nonetheless, the critics could press on. What about complete knowledge of the bad? Would such knowledge still underdetermine the good? First of all, it is not clear that Adorno thinks that we could have complete knowledge of the bad. He merely claims that we know what 'inhumanity'

knowledge that the world is radically evil is not contrastive: it does not presuppose knowledge of what a correct or good world would be, in much the same way that our immediate knowledge that pain or suffering is bad presupposes no antecedent knowledge of what is pleasurable' (Finlayson 2002: 8).

9 Jaeggi also points out that the only characterisation of the good required by Adorno's theory underdetermines it (2005: 75).

is, where this might refer to what is often called 'the great evils' (such as torture, murder, enslavement, etc.) as well as certain other significant bads (such as loss of self).[10] It seems fairly uncontroversial to say that knowing what the great evils and certain other significant bads are, does not add up to knowing what the good is.

Moreover, even if we had complete knowledge of the bad, it is not obvious that this would give us knowledge of the good. We are, for example, familiar in the everyday context with saying that some state of affairs is 'not bad, but not good either'. What we mean by saying this, is that the absence of badness is not the same as the presence of goodness. Instead, the absence of the bad just indicates a *neutral* state of affairs. Thus, on this view of the good, this concept functions unlike other concepts, such as 'valid'. That an argument is 'not invalid' means that it is valid; in contrast, that something is 'not bad' does not automatically mean that it is good.[11] The bad is the good's contrary, not its contradictory.

Admittedly, we might speak imprecisely in everyday context, and the weight of some of the philosophical tradition is behind the view that the good consists in nothing but the complete absence of badness.[12] Consequently, those defending Adorno might do better to fall back on the first point: it might well be true that complete knowledge of the bad would yield complete knowledge of the good, but the normative claims of Adorno do not even imply or require complete knowledge of the bad. Rather, it is sufficient for his purposes if we have knowledge of many of the bads (in particular, knowledge of the great evils), and such knowledge is independent of knowledge of the good (knowledge of the former neither entails knowledge of the latter, nor is knowledge of the latter required to have knowledge of the former).

However, perhaps this is giving in to the critics too easily. We will see in the next chapter that what Adorno is saying can be cashed out in terms of a shortfall from a basic state of human functioning – the bad would then not be related to the absence of the good, but, instead, to the absence of even the minimum level of human functioning.

Still, whichever of the two replies is used, the objection at hand can be answered.

---

10 Recall the passage quoted earlier (in n. 7 of this chapter), in which Adorno says that 'what the inhuman is we know very well indeed' (PMP 1963, 261/175).

11 Finlayson raises a similar point about the usage of 'not wrong' and 'right' (2002: 10).

12 For example, Aquinas seems to have thought that the goodness of an act consists in its being in no way bad ([c.1265–73] 1947), First Part of the Second Part, Question XVIII; see also Foot 2001: 76).

III No need to be constructive

Even if a conception of the bad does not commit one by itself to a conception of the good, one might still object that Adorno needs to appeal to the good for a different reason. In particular, one might think that any critique and any ethics require a positive basis. Without a contrast of what it would be for something to be good, we cannot say of anything that it is bad, or worthy of critique, or that there is an ethical demand to change it. One way to take this objection is to say that it is not very constructive to criticise something (or to characterise it as ethically objectionable) without also offering a positive alternative. To this, one would have to add the claim that non-constructive criticism would invalidate itself (and that the same is true of ethics).

Again, this view would not have been acceptable to Adorno. For example, he squarely rejects the demand to be always constructive whenever one criticises something.[13] He rejects this demand, since meeting it would require subordinating critique to the *status quo* and to what is conceivable within it. Yet, not every *status quo* deserves such primacy. It is certainly Adorno's view that our current social world does not deserve it, but should be subjected to unrestricted critique. In general, we should leave it up to the critical enquiry itself to determine whether it stays within the confines of the *status quo* or not. Similarly, what is conceivable within a given situation should also not be a constraint on critique, or, at least, it should not be a constraint, when what is conceivable is limited in an illegitimate way. For example, if Adorno is right in his claim that socialisation and mass culture have produced in us a constriction of our sense of possibility and our ability to imagine a different world,[14] then it is inappropriate to make the adequacy of critique conditional on the conceivability of alternatives. For these reasons, we might well want to agree with Adorno that the demand to be constructive is a way of suppressing or blunting critique and thereby mainly serves the function of sustaining a *status quo* which ought to be changed.

Yet even leaving aside what Adorno thinks about this matter, we can easily see that we should reject the demand to always offer positive alternatives in our critical enterprises or whenever we make ethical claims. For example, it is common and accepted practice to criticise,

13 See, for example, S, 8: 19/275; 10.2: 793/CM, 287–8.
14 See, for example, ND, 6: 345/352.

say, a philosophical argument without providing a positive alternative to it. Similarly, we often justifiably object to the behaviour of others by simply telling them to stop doing certain things. In fact, the demand to be constructive could be very inappropriate in some cases. At least when it comes to great evils (such as torture), we normally do not think that to criticise that these evils are happening (or to demand that they are stopped) requires offering constructive, positive alternatives of how the person in question could proceed to reach their objectives. To certain things we can object, no matter what.[15] For example, when faced with a group of youths who are pouring petrol over a cat and are about to set it on fire, I do not need to make positive suggestions about how they could spend their afternoon in order to intervene and to criticise them for what they are about to do.

Crucially, if one is saying that a certain state of affairs is bad, then one is committed to not accepting something as bad or worse in its stead (for example, it would be no good if one objected to setting the cat on fire, but would be perfectly prepared to accept the youths' pulling out its limbs one by one). Yet, this does not imply anything beyond a conception of the bad, since such a conception can be used to evaluate both the state of affairs criticised and any alternatives to it (both setting a cat on fire and pulling out its limbs one by one are horrendous actions, while not inflicting any harm on it would not typically be horrendous). To return to the new categorical imperative: presumably the very bads that give rise to it also constrain what we can do in implementing it.[16] If we

---

15 Some might disagree with this statement, since they would insist on a disaster or supreme emergency clause to the effect that certain normally impermissible acts (such as killing civilians or torture) can be acceptable in certain very limited situations. However, even they would accept that these acts are, as just said, normally impermissible and that we can object to them in most cases, whether or not a positive alternative can be provided. In fact, allowing for such an emergency clause in one's ethical theory is not so much insisting on the need to provide positive alternatives, but trying to take account of tragic situations, that is, situations in which whatever we do, we do something wrong (or, at least, allow something bad to happen). To reject a critique of a chosen course of action (say killing civilians) in such a situation (say in the context of World War II) is compatible with a negativistic outlook, since this rejection would merely insist that refraining from acting in the proposed way leads to a still worse outcome (say Hitler's winning the war). Generally, tragic conflicts (as well as difficult questions about the aggregation of moral claims) neither relate specifically to a negativistic outlook, being instead a problem for every outlook, nor imply the demand to be always constructive – if we are faced with a genuine dilemma, there is no positive alternative.

16 What implementation requires in detail depends on a careful study of the original events, other atrocities, and our current context, but there is no reason in principle why this could not stay within negativistic strictures.

jump out of the frying pan into the fire, negativism has the resources to criticise this – indeed, the whole metaphor relies on this fact.

Moreover, even if we granted that critique is constitutively meant to induce change, the demand for constructiveness does not follow from this. Non-constructive criticism could be aimed at inducing change and even achieve it. For example, when creative directors of advertising companies reject a proposed campaign and tell their employees to rework it completely, they might often not give any indication of how it could be done better or be constructive in any other way. We might think that this is rude or not a good way to treat one's employees, but this criticism might still be effective in achieving the change in the campaign. In fact, there is a point in teaching contexts, where being constructive is counterproductive and where a comment like 'this is not good enough; go and redo it differently' is appropriate, perhaps because saying anything more constructive would prevent the student from learning to do things on his or her own.

All of this is not to deny that it is often a good thing to be able to point to a positive alternative when one criticises something (or when one makes an ethical demand to change a state of affairs). To be able to do so is good in a number of ways. It makes it clearer what needs to be done to improve the situation and this increases the chances that the situation is, indeed, improved. Also, being able to point to a positive alternative banishes the worrying possibility that whatever one did, the evil in question might not be avoidable. If one is unable to point to a positive alternative, then perhaps this is evidence that there is no better alternative and then perhaps the current situation is the best available one.[17] Still, just because it is good to be constructive does not mean that we can only criticise something if we offer a positive alternative.

Finally, while there is no guarantee that the current social world can be transformed and that things will be less bad, we have no reason to believe that things would be worse and every reason to support such a transformation. According to Adorno, the objective conditions for a different society are given 'here and now',[18] and the current world only appears to be unchangeable, but, in fact, it is we who sustain this world

17 For example, Knoll seems to think that a positive reference point (and possibly a conception of the good) is necessary to underwrite the possibility of a different world (see Knoll 2002: 178, 186, 196).
18 See, for example, ND, 6: 203/203.

and we who could change it.[19] We have every reason to try do so, since (a) the current social world realises the bad and (b) it is difficult to see how any social world could be worse, since this would be to suggest that the events associated with Auschwitz were merely 'an interlude and not the catastrophe itself'.[20] Admittedly, the alternative could be as bad, but – as it need not be worse and our world is so problematic – it is worth finding out. Moreover, it is, at least to some extent, in our own hands how the alternative turns out.

In sum, it is unreasonable to make it a requirement of any critical enterprise or ethical framework that it must enable us to offer positive alternatives. It may well be *desirable* to be constructive, but failing to be constructive does not invalidate critique or ethical demands.

IV A negativistic philosophy can have practical import

One might think that the problem with negativism is not so much that it is not constructive enough (in the sense of offering positive alternatives); but, rather, that it cannot provide the constraints on action and the guidance for living which any theory with the hope of practical import should provide.[21] Admittedly, Adorno always denied that we

---

19 See, for example: 'But ultimately, what has taken on a life of its own are the relations between humans that are buried beneath the relations of production. Hence the over-powering order of things remains its own ideology and is thus virtually impotent. Impenetrable though its spell is, it is only a spell' (LCoIS, 8: 369–70/Adorno 2003a: 125; translation amended).

20 MM, 4: 62/55; see also MTP, 10.2: 769/CM, 268. See also Levi [1958] 1996: 32–3: 'Then for the first time we become aware that our language lacks words to express this offence, the demolition of a man. In a moment, with almost prophetic intuition, the reality was revealed to us: we had reached the bottom. It is not possible to sink lower than this; no human condition is more miserable than this, nor could it conceivably be so.'

21 See, for example, Finlayson 2002: 9. Finlayson also objects that the three virtues which he ascribes to Adorno would only be instrumentally good on a negativistic reading of his work and thereby 'part of the very context of universal fungibility that they are supposed to resist' (ibid., 10). In reply, the defender of the negativistic reading could make use of the standard move taken by Aristotelians when charged with objection that they reduce the virtues to instrumental goods: the virtues are not just instrumental to, but *constitutive* of the form of life that is ethically demanded, that is, constitutive of the good life (in case of Aristotelians) or of what might be called a 'life of resistance' (in Adorno's case). Finlayson, even in his defence strategy (according to which we have to and can ascribe a positive core to Adorno's theory), needs to make the same move in order to be able to save the three virtues from being merely instrumentally good: for him, they are con-stitutive of the good gained from the experience of attempting but necessarily failing to have ineffable insights. See also Freyenhagen 2011a.

should insist on direct practical application of his theory,[22] and he would probably also reject practical applicability as a criterion for judging theories more generally. However, even if he was right about this, he ought not to foreclose the possibility of practical import completely or in principle. Yet, a purely negativistic philosophy would do so – at least, this is what those objecting in this way claim.

The first thing to note in response is that one can disagree about what level of practical guidance a theory needs to offer for it to still be normative for practice. Take the ethical case; does an ethical theory have to be a full-blown and systematic theory? To say so would surely beg a lot of questions about what kind of ethical theory is possible and desirable. Adorno certainly thought that we could not offer a full-blown and systematic ethical theory in our current predicament – in fact, depending on the interpretation one takes, he either denies the possibility of any such theory altogether, or thinks that it would only be possible to provide such a theory in a free and consciously organised society in which we would know the good. This does not mean, however, that no constraints on practice or no practical guidance on how one should live is available. For example, the new categorical imperative lays down a moral minimum; and there are other ethical demands and practical considerations in Adorno's philosophy that make it possible to ascribe a minimalist ethics to him – as we saw in Chapters 5–6.[23] It is true that such a minimalist ethics will leave many matters undecided; its guidance will be incomplete when compared to a full-blown morality. This might be undesirable insofar as it places a heavy burden on each of us, namely, the burden of exercising our judgement on the basis of only a minimalist set of practical guidance within a world that places us constantly in ethically precarious situations. Yet, Adorno would insist that this upshot of his theory is not speaking against it, but, rather, is a true reflection of the state of ethical life in our current society (if anything, the fact that his theory acknowledges this state of affairs makes it superior to those theories (such as Kant's), which mistakenly suggest that moral certainty and a full set of practical guidance are available).

Secondly, while it might well be true that a negativistic philosophy would not be able to underwrite a full-blown morality (or a system of

---

22 See, for example, ND, 6: 146–7, 242–3/143–4, 244–5.

23 Finlayson accepts that Adorno's philosophy contains an ethics (2002: 6–8), and he would probably also accept that it is merely minimalist in nature; what he denies is that we can account for it purely negativistically.

practical guidance for every situation), there is no reason to think that it could not underwrite a normative theory with practical import which fell short of this.[24] In fact, especially when it comes to constraints on action, a negativistic philosophy would be very suitable – it seems possible to cash out all of the necessary constraints in terms of avoidance of some bad or other. If anything, it is this area of ethics that a negativistic account is best suited for, as the long tradition of negativist moral minimalism shows: to require that people should not murder, rape, torture, or enslave others is something for which we need not appeal to the good. Here, the negative normative force of the intrinsic badness of such actions suffices. Moreover, the particular constraints on action and the practical guidance which Adorno offers can be cashed out in this way, for they are negative prescriptions, they tell us how we ought not to live. Even on the rare occasions where Adorno uses more positive language (such as when he recommends modesty as a virtue), he is still just concerned with avoiding something bad (such as, in this case, self-righteousness).[25] This is how it should be, since his negativism does not entitle him to say anything else.

Just because Adorno's negativistic philosophy cannot offer us the level of practical guidance that we might hope for in a normative theory is not a reason to abandon it. Adorno gives a principled reason for why he cannot offer more (the nature of current society and the fact that we do not know what the good is). Moreover, since the constraints on action and limited practical guidance he does offer can be fully accounted for within the negativistic confines of his theory, there is no need to appeal to the good in this context either.

However, the critics might come back here with the following rejoinder: without appeal to or knowledge of the good, moral demands – even the prohibitions arising from the badness of certain acts and thoughts – are insufficiently *motivating*.[26] Only if we see how the demands fit together into one overall whole – the good, or the ideally

---

24 I am ignoring here the question whether any theory is required for underwriting ethical demands – as we have seen in Chapters 5 and 7, Adorno thinks that underwriting (specifically discursive grounding) is impossible, unnecessary, and inappropriate; but my argument here is independent of whether or not he is right about this.

25 See PMP 1963, 251–2/169–70; see also ND, 6: 345/352; and here, Chapter 6.

26 This objection would rest on a kind of motivational externalism – insofar as it would involve saying that we have (all things considered) reasons to avoid the bad, but might not be sufficiently motivated to act on them. Fortunately, we do not need to consider the protracted debate about externalism here to reject the objection.

just society, or the like – are people moved to act on them. Telling them that they should avoid this bad or the other is insufficient, unless you give them a vision of the good that they thereby make possible. It is the shortfall from this vision that motivates dissatisfaction and thereby action.

While there is some truth in this objection (to which I come back), it is, ultimately, unconvincing. It just is false that bads by themselves are insufficiently motivating – if I am in a burning house, I need no vision of a just society to know that I should extinguish the fire or, if this is by now impossible, leave as quickly as I can.[27] Admittedly, *a contrast* might be required (this is the truth in the objection) – yet, the contrast to the absence of concrete bads (not burning to death) is quite sufficient on its own. Indeed, if anything, the opposite thesis (that focusing merely on the good does not motivate people) might be closer to the truth, partly because the good is – if it has not been realised yet – likely to be more abstract than the concrete bads with which people are often too well acquainted. As Margalit writes:

> the sense of justice is a faint passion unlike being incensed by injustice which is a passionate one. It is not justice that hurts us into action but injustice … There is a moral asymmetry between resisting injustice and pursuing justice; the former is both more urgent and more important, but on top of it there is an immense psychological asymmetry. Fighting injustice is much more of a driving force and much more concrete than pursuing justice based on abstract principles: abstract principles do not make people fight for justice any more than they make martyrs sing in the flames.[28]

One might argue that the matter is different with visions of the good, rather than abstract principles – with Martin Luther King's 'I have a dream'-speech rather than Rawls's two principles of justice. Be that as it may, the key point is that bads can be sufficiently unbearable to jolt us into action on their own. Indeed, on Marx's account, it is the unbearableness of the proletariat's condition under capitalism that would trigger a revolution, not any positive vision of communism (which, anyway, could not be a genuine vision before its actual realisation) – the proletariat would be motivated by the fact that they have 'nothing to

---

27 Once more, one is reminded here of a Brecht poem, '*Gleichnis des Buddha vom Brennenden Haus* [The Buddha's Parable of the Burning House]' (1939); in 1967: vol. 9, 664–6/ translation in 1976: 290–2.
28 Margalit 2011: 178–9.

lose but their chains', not 'fantastic pictures of future society', 'castles in
the air', and 'ideas or principles that have been invented, or discovered,
by this or that would-be universal reformer'.[29] Rather than positive
visions, constructive criticisms, promises of happiness, or words of consolation, what is required for motivation is a clear sense of the negativity
of our situation – as Adorno was fond of saying, 'For nothing but despair
[*Verzweiflung*] can save us.'[30]

One might object to this by arguing that we need hope to be motivated, and that rather than leading to active resistance and change,
negativism will sap people's hope and thereby lead to ascetic withdrawal,
despair, and devaluing whatever small positive elements life might still
hold. In reply, let me raise four points. Firstly, we need to be mindful of
an important distinction – between a situation of objective despair,
where all resistance to negativity is futile, on the one hand, and a
situation of uncertainty, where we do not know that resistance to the
bads to which we are subjected is futile, on the other. Even if it were true
that negativism would lead to ascetic withdrawal in an inescapable
situation, this need not mean that it would do so under conditions of
uncertainty. Secondly, it is not even clear that negativism would be
debilitating in the way suggested in a situation of inescapable negativity.
We sometimes act even when there is no realistic hope of achieving what
we set out to do – instead, we act because we (psychologically or physi-
cally) cannot but do so or because we want to express a value or belief,
such as indignation at injustice. This might be true only when situations
have become intolerable, but what matters in this context is that in such
cases negativity can suffice to motivate a response, as futile as it may be.
Thirdly, the situation in which we are is, even on Adorno's pessimistic
assessment, *not one of knowing* that negativity is inescapable, that resistance is futile. What we can do might be severely restricted, and we might
not know positively that social change can be effected; but we also do not
know for certain that it cannot be and, as discussed earlier (especially in
Chapters 5–6), Adorno thinks that we are obliged, even categorically
required, to make use of whatever negative freedom we have to resist

---

29 Marx and Engels, *The Communist Manifesto* [1848], MEW 1956–90, IV: 474, 490, 491,
   493/MECW 1975–2005, 498, 515, 516, 519. It seems misleading to suggest that
   negativism – appeal to evils as normatively and motivationally sufficient on their own – is
   '*intrinsically* conservative' (Badiou [1998] 2001: xiii; my emphasis). It can be conservative,
   but it can also be revolutionary, as the example of Marx's theory shows.
30 Adorno attributes this sentence to (the German nineteenth-century dramatist) Grabbe
   (see 10.2: 405/2002: 17; 17: 273; in Grenz 1983: 251).

wrong life and prevent another Auschwitz from happening. It might well be that some will, nonetheless, react with ascetic withdrawal. Still, negativism does not by itself imply or necessitate this – just the opposite: Adorno's negativistic ethics would regard such a response as typically worse than active resistance guided by critical theory. Also, suggesting that we can know the good (when we cannot) is more likely to lead to a failure to resist than negativism would – for the former involves not facing up to the situation, and may have the consequence that people ignore its urgency and pursue what they (wrongly) believe are instances of good and right living instead. Finally, and related to the previous point, there is even a sense in which hope can be maintained within negativism – albeit the hope for making things less bad. If action requires some hope, this hope of minimising the wrong can supply this allegedly missing ingredient. Indeed, it is not hope of this kind that Adorno wants to forgo; but rather the hope that makes us overlook the real despair of our social world and remain in the burning house because things are bound to get better. It is the latter hope that saps the motivation to resist, not negativism.

V We can recognise badness without knowledge of the good

One might think that a negativistic philosophy is insufficient for underwriting normativity for yet a different reason. Even if badness is normative in giving us a reason to avoid it, we need to first recognise something as bad in order for this reason-giving force to have an effect on us.[31] It might be that knowledge of the good is necessary in order to recognise the bad, at least under certain conditions. In particular, this applies to Adorno's negativistic views. If he is right that badness, but not goodness, is actualised in our social world, then the question is how we can come to be aware of this.[32] For if all were bad, then we might lack the contrast which would put this badness into focus; we might not recognise the badness for what it is, and criticism of this state of affairs, or ethical demands for its change, could not arise. This problem is one of (moral) epistemology.

31 In fact, one might object that my reply in Section I implicitly relied on knowledge of the good as a background condition that enables us to identify what states are bad. Without this background condition, the bad could not have normative force for us and I could not have argued for its having normative force on its own.

32 This is the nub of Theunissen's influential objection to Adorno's negativistic philosophy (see his 1983). See also Seel 2004: 22.

In reply, despite Adorno's negativism, he is not saying that people can never undergo positive experiences or attain goods. Rather, his claims are fourfold: (1) that such positive experiences are merely localised and often fleeting; (2) that we could not reliably tell which ones are genuine and which ones are not; (3) that they do not add up to either a good life or to knowledge of what the good life would consist in; and (4) that to say otherwise is to succumb to an illusion. Thus, we should, indeed, try to live as happily and decently as possible in our modern social world. In fact, we might not always be mistaken to think that we can be happy or act decently on a particular occasion. Instead, the problem consists in the thought that being happy and acting decently does in fact amount to living rightly and well. The best we can do in our current predicament is living less wrongly. This involves (a) realising that a right and good life is currently not possible; (b) resisting wrong life as much as we can; and (c) refraining from making any claims to the effect that our life is right and free of guilt (see Chapters 2, 3, 5–6).

Moreover, Adorno's scepticism about the possibility of right living does not imply that positive experiences and goods do not fulfil an important function. It might well be that without them we would not be able to develop a critical distance to our radically evil social world and to resist it at least in some instances. For example, Adorno claims that those who did not have a sheltered and happy childhood will be much less likely to have developed the strength of ego that is required to stand up to this social world.[33] Without such a background, they might also lack a contrast with which to recognise the badness of this world. They might be already so damaged that they cannot even see their predicament for what it is. However, Adorno is not saying that a sheltered and happy childhood, or positive experiences more generally, tell one what the right life consists in. What he is saying is that such an experience makes one less likely to uncritically accept a social reality that falls short of the indeterminate promises that these experiences instilled in one.[34] These positive experiences may make one question whether things could not be such that experiences like them occur more frequently. They may make one more open to the negative normativity of badness taking a root in one's bodily

---

33 MM; 4: 22–3/22–3; see also ND, 6: 51/41.

34 In other words, a full and correct conception of goodness is not the only contrast we can employ to despair over the badness of a state of affairs – it might be sufficient to have a *sense* that the current state just cannot be all there is, even if it is not possible to cash out what it would take to satisfy this sense. For a similar reply strategy to the one employed here, see Jaeggi 2005.

reactions and consciousness. Still, just because one's childhood might have settled one with some longing for utopia which plays a role in being dissatisfied with the *status quo* does not imply that it provided one with knowledge of the good – for our experience as children did not make us acquainted with utopia or the good.

Similarly, Adorno allows that art, theology, and metaphysics have a positive function to play.[35] They remind and promise us that things could be different, that what we have now need not be all there could be. Yet, at the same time, it is an illusion to think that they, or the experiences involved in them, bring us in touch with the good. It is not that we can actually transcend the totality of our current evil world in our experiences of engagement with art, theology, or metaphysics. Rather, their claim to transcendence enables us to see this totality for what it is: something which only *seems* to be unchangeable and without real alternative, but is, in fact, sustained by our action and both possible to and in need of change.

Moreover, there is also the materialistic element which accounts for our recognition of the bad. Adorno seems to think that somehow people will be capable of doing what their situation produces a need in them to do, even if we cannot necessarily anticipate how this will be possible. In this sense, the possibility of recognising the bad depends on whether people will continue to have a need to recognise it or not. Given that the current social world is the realisation of the bad and that this causes misery and suffering, the need to recognise the bad persists. In fact, despite Adorno's general pessimism about what the administered world makes out of people, he does not think that people's needs could ever be fully captured and mastered by such a system.[36] In this sense, the continuing disregard of these needs will remain a source for critical questioning, for asking whether this world is really the best there can be. Hence, there is also a further, a materialistic explanation why people might develop the indeterminate sense that things should be different and, as I have suggested earlier, it is this indeterminate sense which might provide enough of a contrast to recognise the bad for what it is. Admittedly, there is no guarantee that people will recognise the badness of the current social world. Still, the fact that it is impossible to integrate them completely into the administered world leaves it, at least, open that such recognition could happen (see already Chapters 3 and 6).

35 See, for example, ND, 6: 207, 396–7/207, 404–5.
36 See, for example, ND, 6: 99–100/92; and 10.2: 655/CM, 175.

Finally, there are different levels of badness – from the extremes of the great evils (like torture) to lesser bads (such as not fully developing one's musical skills). Even if we might not recognise all forms of badness to which we are subjected, this differentiation allows us to recognise the greater ones. Even in a world in which we would be in constant pain, we could experience different intensities and qualities, and those of greater intensity and quality would be what in this world we would see as bads. Thus, we are mistaken if we think that the relief we experience when we escape the greater bads means that we live a good life – our life might still contain too much badness and wrongness for that. Still, we can recognise at least these greater bads even in a world that is radically evil.

In these ways, Adorno does have an answer to the problem of how we can recognise the badness of the current state of affairs, despite not being acquainted with the good. Positive experiences, instances of decency and solidarity, and the experiences involved in art, theology, and metaphysics as well as the dissatisfaction of materialistic needs and the variety of bads to which we are subjected enable such recognition – they are the only foil that we need. However, they enable this not because they provide us with conceptions or images of the good, but because they make it possible for us to see that things ought to be different and because they provide us with the strength to do so. In other words, these experiences do not play a justificatory role in Adorno's theory; they play an explanatory role – they are part of his account of how it is possible for people to remain critical and act decently (albeit not rightly) in our current social world (on this issue, see also Chapter 6).

However, there are two final worries that may arise in this context. The first is that my defence of negativism has relied at key junctures on appeal to great evils. Critics might concede that negativism is at its strongest in cases that involve grotesquely bad states and actions. Yet, even if this rescues negativism, it does so at the price of limited applicability. Many everyday decisions concern cases within a vast moral grey area, not the kind of clear-cut cases involving great evils. One might object further that this shows that negativism is either not sufficient to defend Adorno's theory (because this theory is meant to cover not just situations in which the great evils suffice to settle what we should do and think); or if it is so sufficient (say because Adorno thinks that our current social world really is a grotesquely bad state of affairs), then it is so only because this theory paints an exaggerated, even false picture of the moral state of affairs we are in.

In reply, one could, firstly, deny the idea that (defensible) negativism is quite so limited in its applicability as just presented. In particular, negativism might be – in Adorno's case, is – a pluralistic view, comprising a number of different bads of different strengths and importance. In this way, negativistic resources might be more plentiful and could be successfully deployed even to navigate complex cases and grey areas. Secondly, Adorno would admit that compared to a full-blown moral system, his negativistic theory might seem to offer too little to cover the whole range of moral situations, but he would question that such moral systems can actually be made to work, and reject them as standards for assessing alternatives. He would also concede that it would be advantageous if we could know the good (and the right), and that this would enable us to provide wider and more fine-grained guidance. Indeed, it is part of his complaint about our social world that it leaves us with impoverished moral resources (see Chapter 3). Still, he would insist on the fact that we do not have knowledge of the good, and maintain that instead of shooting the messenger we should make the most out of the limited tools at our disposal. Thirdly, it is not clear that Adorno's theory is directly about providing ethical guidance for everyday decisions. His theory is, first and foremost, about the ethical decisions in respect to our social world as a whole, and this world is, he thinks, a grotesquely bad state of affairs – currently perhaps not in its absolute worst form (that might have been when fascism and Stalinism reigned supreme), but nonetheless one dominated by great evils. Fourth, what I just said about Adorno's theory and everyday decision-making is not the complete picture – for the social world forms a totality for Adorno and so at least *indirectly* even everyday decisions are not separable from it and our conduct implicates us in its radical evil (see Chapters 1–2). Hence, the guidance he does offer has implications for everyday decisions (such as whether or not to go to the cinema; see Chapter 6). If we really do live in a grotesquely bad social world, then just going about our daily business of trying to navigate what we see to be merely the grey areas of everyday existence would be to act wrongly – just as it would be grossly negligent if going about our daily business came at the expense of responding to a situation where someone is tortured.

As a second worry, one might think that Adorno's theory relies on a too absolute sense of what the good life would be, and that it is, hence, both unsurprising that we cannot positively determine what this standard consists in and that he rejects our social world as falling short of it. Put differently, both his epistemic and substantive negativism are due to an over-inflated sense of what the good, if we could know and realise it, would be.[37] This has the practical consequence of an ascetic ideal (in Nietzsche's sense) – just as being free of sins is an impossible ideal for human beings and is bound to lead us to devalue human life, so Adorno's formal requirements on what would count as truly good for human beings are impossible to meet and bound to lead to devaluation of what we have got.

In response, Adorno would insist that it is not a subjective, idiosyncratic longing for the world to meet an impossible standard that he brings to bear on this world. Rather, the standards at play in his critical theory are, so to speak, inscribed in our nature: we and our social world are ill when they are not met. The standards are a central part of an explanatory project which explains these ills, and they derive their validity and legitimacy from the success of this explanatory project (see also Chapters 7 and 9). Naturally, this means that the cogency of these standards, ultimately, depends on the success of this project, and this study is only clearing the philosophical ground for evaluating this success, not actually doing it (not least because such an evaluation would require a lot of comparative work, which would require at least a book-length treatment in its own right). Moreover, as repeatedly emphasised in this study, Adorno suggests that a different social world, in which human capacities could finally unfold, is *materially* possible, given the development of the forces of production – if he is right about that, then it is not an impossible ideal that he is hankering after. In these ways, Adorno thinks that he is just expressing what our current social world reveals in its negativity and has made possible in accelerating the expansion of human productive powers. Many of us will be so badly off, that they would clearly object to the suggestion that asking for a different social world is based on an over-inflated sense of the good. Indeed, this objection is likely to come from those who are privileged and lucky enough to escape the extreme bads to which this world subjects many others. Yet, in their case, we might also be suspicious that this worry is an instance of ideology – specifically, a case of someone's protesting when others rock the boat in which they have made themselves at home. Life-affirmation can be a good thing, but in some contexts it is inappropriate, and life in the modern social world is one such context

---

37 Indeed, even to talk of 'the good' might be misleading, not just because there might be a plurality of human goods (Adorno could accept that), but because there might be no one overarching framework of human goodness (or rightness) at all.

for Adorno. It does not deserve to be affirmed, but only to be resisted and overcome.

VI Conclusion

In this chapter, I have unpacked the Problem of Normativity into five different worries and shown that none of them defeats the negativistic response strategy to this problem. While in some ways the defence of Adorno is thereby completed; in other ways, further substantiation of this defence would be desirable. In particular, it would be good to cash out the key idea that the bad (or part thereof) can be characterised as shortfall from minimal human functioning, and that this shortfall suffices for criticising badness, for recognising it for what it is, and for demanding that it should be overcome. This idea would be compatible with ethical outlooks other than Adorno's, such as negative Utilitarianism and certain forms of liberalism. However, instead of using these theories for the task of substantiating Adorno's views, I argue in the next chapter that we need not look further than his own work to find such a substantiation – for there is an Aristotelian conception of normativity at work in Adorno's theory.

9

ADORNO'S NEGATIVE ARISTOTELIANISM

As a final step, I want to add further depth and substance to the negativistic defence strategy by unearthing an Aristotelian conception of normativity in Adorno's work. I first give a very brief summary of the Aristotelian conception. Then I will show how this conception is the deeper rationale operative in Adorno's thinking.

I The Aristotelian conception of normativity

While there are a number of differences between Aristotle's own views, traditional accounts of his philosophy, and modern adaptations of it, the following core ideas largely cut across these differences.

The basic idea of the Aristotelian conception of normativity is that the evaluation of human actions and dispositions is structurally similar to the evaluation of other things. For Aristotelians there is a grammar of goodness (and badness) which cuts across different contexts of evaluation. What is good (and bad) depends on what kind of thing the something to be evaluated is, on its *ergon* (its purpose, function, or characteristic activity).[1] Good and bad are understood in terms of what it is for a particular thing to function well, that is, which properties or capacities it needs to have to work in the way in which the things, of which it is a particular example, do work. A good knife is one which cuts well; a good fish is one which swims well; a good sunflower is one which turns well with the movement of the sun; and so on. In this way, goodness and badness are indexed to the essential functions, to what is called the 'form' of a thing – its teleological organisation which makes something the kind of thing it is.

1 See, for example, the much discussed 'function argument' in NE, I.7.

In the case of living beings, Aristotelians often speak of 'life form' to denote the *genus* to which an individual specimen belongs. All life forms share a general purpose – they are geared towards survival, that is, to the self-maintenance of the life form. In virtue of this purpose, there are some general categories of functioning for all life forms (such as the need for nourishment, or for protection from the elements). However, life forms differ from each other in how exactly they strive towards the purpose of survival and in which way they fulfil these general functionings (for example, whether they rely on feathers or fur as their protection from the elements). Each life form has a specific way of functioning which is appropriate to it, given its essential characteristics, possible development, and typical habitat. In this way, the life form sets the parameters of how an individual plant or animal should be (although what is required can vary within these parameters, depending on the particular specimen and its circumstances). If members of a particular life form lack any of the capacities appropriate to its life form, then this is bad for them *qua* member of this life form. It might not be the case that they experience it as bad (inasmuch as the life form in question is capable of such experiences). Still, probably they would *typically* experience it as bad, or they would be less well off in other ways (live less long, not reproduce, etc.). The requirements which arise from the functionings appropriate for a life form are, hence, objective requirements; they depend on what the life form is like, not on the particular state of any one specimen. Moreover, these requirements are not meant as mere statistical normality.[2] Rather, the objective requirements faced by a particular life form are indexed to its teleology (its *ergon*). They are norms, albeit norms built on facts about what a life form is like (or what it would be like, if it actualised its potential). In this way, there is a direct link between knowing what a life form is, on the one hand, and knowing what is good and bad for it (what it would take for it to flourish and languish), on the other.[3]

2 For example, even if suddenly – perhaps because of a nuclear accident – *all* kittens were born with five instead of four legs, we would, nonetheless, speak of an abnormality (or, if this change was not reversed in later generations, we would be faced by a new species). Similarly – as Lichtenberg is said to have remarked – it would be odd to marvel at the fact that cats have two holes in their fur at precisely the spot where their eyes are. This also suggests that the norms in question are not statistical.

3 Knowledge of the life form is more complex than a mere empirical generalisation – it involves, in the words of Thompson, a 'natural historical judgement' (2008: 20 and *passim*; see also 2004). Instead of a mere report of what is the case, such a judgement might be

The human life form is no different in this respect. Knowing what it consists in (and what its *ergon* is) tells us about our vulnerabilities and potentialities, and thereby about the objective requirements we have, requirements to avoid what goes against our flourishing and to promote what furthers it.[4] The only notable difference is that the purpose of the human life form is not exhausted in mere survival. Human beings are language-using and rational animals, and this means that they are capable of functionings beyond those needed for mere self-preservation – such as cultural and intellectual endeavours. To live up to their full potential *qua* human life form, they would have to make use of their capacities not only for the survival of their life form (as other life forms do), but also beyond this purpose. Nonetheless, the structural parallel remains: what is good and bad for human beings is still cashed out in terms of what kind of life form they are. It is just that the human life form is more complex in terms of its objective requirements of functioning than other life forms. This complexity does not change the fact that goodness and badness are linked to the human life form, to what humanity and inhumanity consist in. Nor does this complexity change the fact that knowledge of the human life form gives us knowledge of its goodness and badness.

There are three further features of the Aristotelian conception of normativity which are important in this context. Firstly, it is central to this account that goodness and badness constrain rationality (what we have reason to do), not *vice versa*. To say that something is good for a thing or a life form is to say that there are objective reasons for it to be in this way (similarly with the bad, there are objective reasons for it not to be in this way). Thus, the Aristotelian conception of normativity comes with a substantive conception of rationality: it is not just that rationality, say, involves the avoidance of inconsistencies, but rationality itself is informed by goodness and badness. This is particularly relevant in the case of humanity. We are used to the idea that prudential considerations constrain rationality (it is, for example, often said that it is irrational to damage your health, meaning to say that it is imprudent). Yet, for many Aristotelians it is not just prudence, but human goodness in general

compared to Weber's ideal types – models which are based on empirical observations, but also at work in making empirical observations; falsifiable by observations only in complex ways; and characterised by a distinct status and grammar, such as the unusual temporality involved in explications of life forms.

4 See, for example, NE, I.8.

which fulfils this function.[5] If it turned out that acting morally was part
of the human good (as Aristotle and his successors argue), then we
would have objective reasons to be moral and would act irrationally
when we go against the prescriptions and recommendations of morality.

Secondly, there is a certain kind of realism about reasons connected
to the Aristotelian conception of normativity. The objective reasons
which we have *qua* members of the human life form are part of the
fabric of the world in a certain sense.[6] A particular situation has ethical
features in virtue of its non-ethical properties and in virtue of how these
properties relate to our functioning as a life form. For example, the
conjunction of (a) the pain of someone's being tortured and (b) the
requirement of the human life form to avoid pain if possible, gives
the tortured person (as well as those responsive to reasons generally)
an objective reason to end the torture. This point illuminates one aspect
of why Aristotelians speak of objective reasons; the requirements we face
are not figments of the imagination, projections, or constructions; but
actual features of states of affairs or situations.

An interesting upshot of this conception of reasons is that recognising objective reasons involves being receptive and responsive to these
features of situations. This receptivity and responsiveness need not
involve conscious awareness in all cases. Instincts or even reflexes are,
to a certain extent at least, also covered. If I touch something burning
hot, then I perceive an objective reason for me to avoid it (the pain it
gives me and the threat of injury it carries) and respond by withdrawing
my hand – none of this need be conscious or involve going through a
reasoning process. In fact, for Aristotle, even animals ('brutes') can have
practical wisdom (*phronēsis*).[7] Seeing the world in a particular way
enables us to perceive the objective reasons we have to take certain
actions (or refrain from doing so). This requires that we develop and
acquire the right sensibility to see the world in this way. It is a feature of
the virtuous agent that he or she has the necessary receptivity to the

---

5 See, for example, Foot 2001: Ch. 4, esp. 62–3. Not all contemporary Aristotelians agree
   with this view of reasons (in fact, the early Foot is one such example; see her 1978: Ch. 11).
6 At least, they are part of the fabric of the world, if this fabric is not understood too narrowly
   (as modern scientific naturalism tends to do), but also includes 'second nature', our
   human reactions to our environment (see especially the work of J. McDowell, such as
   'Values and Secondary Qualities' [1985] and 'Two Sorts of Naturalism' [1996], both
   reprinted in his 1998: Essays 7, 9; see also 1994: Lecture 4). This point is also more
   contentious among contemporary Aristotelians. For example, Williams clearly does not
   share this realism about reasons (see, for example, Williams 1993: esp. Chs. 6, 8).
7 NE, VI.7.

ethical features of the world and is responsive to the objective reasons thus recognised.[8]

Finally, the Aristotelian conception of normativity involves scepticism about the justificatory project in ethics, mentioned in Chapter 7. For Aristotelians, there is neither the need for, nor could there be an independent justification of normativity, that is, an independent justification of what for them are the objective requirements we face in virtue of being members of the human life form.[9] It is not *necessary* to ground these requirements, since they are by themselves reason-giving, normative, for us – it is constitutive of our humanity that they are. Attempts to ground or rationalise the objective requirements would be *unsuccessful.* For example, aiming to ground the objective requirements we face *qua* human beings in rationality would require severing the link between rationality and goodness. Yet, it is this link which underpins these requirements. Once this link is severed, it is no longer possible to explain how reasons and normativity have a footing in us. This is not to say that Aristotelians can say nothing about normativity. They can explain and elucidate how something is normative for us *qua* creatures who are responsive to reasons (or, at least, they can do so as long as appeal to human teleology or Aristotelian biology is possible and defensible).[10] However, such explanation cannot at the same time function as a justification of normativity.[11] Moreover, if one responded to the Aristotelian account of what we have reasons to do *qua* human beings by asking for such grounding (for example, asking questions such as 'why act on our objective interests?' or 'why be human?'), then one would miss the point. It would be to overlook that all the normativity which is required is already given and accounted for, that all what can and needs to be said has been said. It is no longer clear what those who ask for further grounding are asking for, and they would cease to be

---

8 See, for example, NE, III.4; and J. McDowell, 'Are Moral Requirements Hypothetical Imperatives?' [1978], reprinted in his 1998: Essay 4, esp. 85ff.

9 See, for example, NE, I.4, where Aristotle states that his theory is addressed to those already on the way to virtue, so that he can argue from moral values, rather than derive them (which is anyway excluded, since the fundamental values and principles are intuited, not demonstrable; NE, VI.6; see also VII.8).

10 Contemporary Aristotelians are divided about whether or not such an appeal is still possible and defensible, with the later MacIntyre and perhaps Foot as examples of theorists who seem to think it is (see MacIntyre 1999; Foot 2001), and Anscombe, Williams, and the early MacIntyre as sceptics (see Anscombe 1958; Williams 1993: Ch. 3; MacIntyre 1985).

11 See Williams 1996: especially 213; and Raz 1999.

people with whom we can engage in rational conversation.[12] Finally, it is also noteworthy that demands for an independent justification of ethical normativity are often motivated by what, according to Aristotelians, is a mistaken picture of ethics, namely, one according to which this domain is populated mainly by moral obligations. By rejecting this picture, the motivation for the grounding attempts falls largely away.[13]

II Adorno's negative Aristotelianism

I would like to propose that a variant of this Aristotelian conception of ethical normativity is in the background of Adorno's views. Admittedly, he never explicitly says that he adopts such a conception. Moreover, the source of it might be the Aristotelianism of Hegel or Marx, rather than Aristotle directly – although with the publication of some of Adorno's lectures there is also evidence that Adorno engaged directly with Aristotle's thought and did so in some depth.[14] Be that as it may, ascribing an Aristotelian conception to Adorno makes good sense of what he says – as I show now.

Any Aristotelianism which can be ascribed to Adorno needs to be compatible with his negativism. As it turns out, this conception can actually offer further elucidation of the negativism. In order to show that this is the case we need to look briefly at Adorno's conception of humanity.

According to Adorno, humanity is not something which we actually instantiate in virtue of being born as human animals, but it is a potential which we have and which is yet to be actualised.[15] For the most part, what we are now is just natural beings with animal needs and the potential to rise above these needs.[16] We have not, *qua* species-beings,

---

12 See, for example, Foot 2001: 64–5; MacIntyre 1999: Ch. 13.

13 See Williams 1993: especially Ch. 1; Williams 1996: 210–11; see also Anscombe 1958.

14 For example, ten of the eighteen metaphysics lectures which Adorno gave in 1965 are on Aristotle (see MCP, lectures 4–13).

15 See, for example: 'Without exception, human beings have yet to become themselves. By the concept of the self we should properly mean their potential, and this potential stands in polemical opposition to the reality of the self' (ND, 6: 274/278; translation amended; see also ND, 6: 61, 254–5/51, 257–8; P, esp. 10.2: 618–20/CM, 144–6; HF, lecture 16).

16 I say 'for the most part', for Adorno would presumably not deny that our way of being animals differs significantly from other species, not least because of the role science and technology play in it. What he suggests is rather that these differences, while otherwise significant, do not yet add up to our coming into our own as a species. For all the qualitative differences to animals on some level, there has not really been a qualitative

come into our own. Given that human beings have not actualised their species-being yet, what we view as human history has ultimately still been natural history only.[17] It has been the story of self-preservation driving history, even where human beings *thought* that they had emancipated themselves from this drive.[18] Indeed, Adorno likens human development to 'a giant who, after sleeping from time immemorial, slowly bestirs himself and then storms forth and tramples everything that gets in his way'.[19] Human history proper can only begin, once we really have emancipated ourselves from the dominant influence exerted by the drive for self-preservation – once the giant awakes and 'human beings become conscious of their own naturalness and call a halt to their own domination of nature, a domination by means of which nature's domination is perpetuated'.[20] The mistake so far has been to think that this emancipation has to take the form of renunciation or domination of our material drives and needs. The idea that we could emancipate ourselves in spirit alone is where things went wrong. We should indeed free the spirit from its material and physical requirements, but by meeting these requirements.[21]

In particular, our development has misfired insofar as our attempts to emancipate ourselves have mainly led to inhumanity. They have led to inhumanity in the sense of involving a disregard of our animal nature, of our material needs. They have led to inhumanity also in the sense that we have developed social systems which – while trying to further the aim of human emancipation – erected obstacles to realising our humanity.

jump of the sort which would move us beyond a still ultimately blind pursuit of self-preservation.

17 This idea of history so far being only natural history (or prehistory) is a Hegelian Marxist idea. On Adorno taking it up see 8: 231–4, 373–4/2003a: 93–4; and HF, lectures 13–14. See also Tiedemann's editorial afterword to HF.

18 See, for example: 'All activities of the species point to its continued physical existence, even if these activities may be based on misconceptions of it, may become organisationally independent of it and may carry out this business only by the way. Even the steps which society takes to exterminate itself are at the same time, as forms of absurd, unleashed self-preservation, unconscious acts against suffering' (ND, 6: 203/203; translation amended).

19 HF, 213–14/151: see also P, 10.2: 625/CM, 150.

20 HF, 214/151–2: see also P, 10.2: 625/CM, 150.

21 See, for example: 'The perspective vanishing point of historic materialism would be its self-sublimation, the spirit's liberation from the primacy of material needs in their state of fulfillment. Only if the physical urge were quenched would the spirit be reconciled and would become that which it only promises to be, just as spirit refuses under the spell of material conditions the satisfaction of material needs' (ND, 6: 207/207; translation amended; see also MTP, 10.2: 776/CM, 273; Adorno 1974: 277).

This is especially true of modern capitalist society. While this society is also the outcome of our striving for self-preservation and emancipation, this striving has produced in capitalism a system which has its own dynamic, the pursuit of surplus-value, and this dynamic has usurped the place of human teleology. At the same time, given the objective conditions furthered by capitalism, we actually could move beyond being subservient to self-preservation for the first time. However, due to the deeply delusional nature of our current social world, we do not realise that this is the case, but instead go on sustaining our own conditions of servitude. Thus, according to Adorno, we find ourselves in a precarious predicament: the current social world is evil because it realises inhumanity rather than humanity, and it is so deeply delusional that we cannot even conceptualise or imagine what realised humanity would consist in.[22]

We are now in a position to see how ascribing an Aristotelian conception of normativity to Adorno is compatible with his negativism. In this conception, the good and the bad are indexed to humanity and inhumanity respectively. It is this indexing which we can find at work in Adorno's negativism: it is because we cannot know what realised humanity is, that we cannot know what the good is. In fact, this indexing of the good to humanity makes it more plausible to claim (as we have seen Adorno claims) that we cannot even conceptualise or imagine what the good is. By indexing the good to the realisation of humanity, it is not something which we could derive independently of knowing what this realisation would consist in, and knowing the latter is not just a conceptual matter. We would need some empirical knowledge about how human beings who realised their humanity lived, to know what this realisation consists in. Thus, Adorno's disagreement with the Aristotelians would not be about the basic outlook, the indexing of the good to humanity (and of the bad to inhumanity). Rather, it would be about whether humanity is realised already or not, and thereby about whether we are in the position to say what humanity and its goodness consists in. In this way, Adorno's negativism is compatible with an Aristotelian framework. In fact, it makes more sense within such a framework – for from within this framework, we can say that it is because the current social world blocks the realisation of humanity that the good is unavailable and unknown to us.

22 See, for example, ND, 6: 345/352.

The claim that Adorno's negativism makes more sense against the backdrop of an Aristotelian conception of normativity is also confirmed when we consider another aspect of this negativism. Adorno thinks that we can know the bad (or, at least, the inhuman), even without knowing the good.[23] Ascribing an Aristotelian conception of normativity to Adorno means we can elucidate how such asymmetrical knowledge is possible. To gain knowledge of the bad in this conception, we need to find out what is bad for us *qua* animal beings and what obstacles there are to the realisation of our potential as human beings. To find this out, it is not always necessary to know what the realisation of humanity (and thereby the good) substantially consists in. Rather, at least when it comes to the most extreme forms of the bad, it suffices to speak in terms of what people lack to achieve *basic functioning* (as differentiated from living well, where the latter involves the full realisation of the human potential). As noted in the previous chapter, securing this would be to achieve a state between the great evils and realising the good – a *neutral* state of affairs, not (yet) a good one.

This then is how we should take Adorno's claim about our asymmetrical knowledge of the bad and the good: we can know what a minimum level of human functioning is without knowing what the full realisation of the human potential is, and life in our social world is so deformed and damaged that even this minimum level is impossible to attain (at least for the majority of people). In this sense, it is the widespread shortfall from basic functioning which indicates that things are seriously amiss in our social world, and it is in virtue of this shortfall that we can object to it without invoking a positive conception of the good.

Thus, the key point is the idea that the bad or, at least, the worst can be cashed out in terms of shortfall not from the level of living well, but from the level of basic human functioning. Insofar as we can know what basis human functioning requires (and what a shortfall from it would involve) without having (positive) knowledge of the human potential, we can know the bad without knowing the good. And it is very plausible to think that we can know about basic human functioning without this further knowledge. For what is required for knowing the former is some

---

23 Recall this important passage: 'We may not know what absolute good is or the absolute norm, we may not even know what man [*der Mensch*] is or the human [*das Menschliche*] or humanity [*die Humanität*] – but what the inhuman [*das Unmenschliche*] is we know very well indeed' (PMP 1963, 261/175; see also 8: 456; 2003b: 49/28–9).

basic understanding of our animal nature and of what is bad for us *qua* animals – such as lack of food and shelter, illness, and physical suffering. In fact, physical pain and suffering are good examples. In virtue of our animal nature, pain and suffering are bad for us; we have reason to avoid them.[24] This objective interest is expressed in the direct reason-giving nature of our physical impulse against suffering. In other words, the force of the negativity of pain, while *not being derived* from desires, principles, or the faculty of reason, is *expressive of* our having objective interests in virtue of the kind of situated creatures we are. Hence, the Aristotelian conception accounts well for the badness and direct-reason giving aspect of suffering, to which Adorno is committed.[25]

To find out about the elements of basic human functioning which go beyond mere animal survival is to undertake the kind of theorising in which Adorno constantly engages, namely, using social theory and psychology to investigate and explain how human emancipation has failed. These investigations begin from the (often repressed) experience of misery (physical suffering and psychological distress), and then Adorno tries to get to the bottom of what causes this misery. The investigations reveal that certain minimum conditions need to be met for us to achieve basic functioning, and these minimal conditions are not exhausted by the kind of things we need to have in order to survive as animals. Rather, basic human functioning also requires at least a minimal level of actively choosing how to structure one's life, of developing a sense of the self with an extended life story, of having meaningful relationships with others, etc.

Hence, there is a breadth of requirements involved in achieving even just minimal human functioning, and in the light of this variety, it becomes more plausible to claim that our social world undermines the possibility of attaining this level. Not only does our social world fail to provide almost half of humanity with even the basics for avoiding shortfalls from our minimal animal functioning, but also, at least if Adorno is right, even those living in the capitalist centres with access to an ever-expanding array of consumer goods lack other dimensions of basic human functioning. For example, according to Adorno, our social

---

24 This is not to deny that, in an *instrumental* sense, pain and suffering can be good for animals (including us, human ones), namely, when they fulfil a useful signalling function about what we should avoid. Yet, they only fulfil this function by being experienced as bad, by having intrinsic negative normativity (which is, however, defeasible and can be permissibly overridden in the pursuit of certain goals – as noted in Chapter 8).

25 ND, 6: 203/203.

world reduces everyone to their functions in the reproduction of society and in the course of this gives rise to experiences of being replaceable and expendable, of having to completely adapt to a heteronomous social world in order merely to survive. This experience causes immense suffering (both directly and indirectly in fuelling aggression towards and repression of others), and analysing the causes of this suffering would suggest, at least from an Adornian perspective, that human beings have a basic need to be recognised as individuals, as centres of irreplaceable uniqueness.

In this context we can also draw methodological parallels. The kind of interpretive social theorising in which Adorno engages is also typical of many contemporary contributions to ethical, political, and social theory in the Aristotelian tradition.[26] Like many Aristotelians, he begins with certain social or psychological phenomena (say anti-Semitism), then shows that the best explanation for people's behaviour is in terms of their lives' being deficient in one way or another, and that the best explanation for their lives' being deficient is that they lack those things which by this analysis turn out to be the minimum conditions of basic human functioning.[27] Admittedly, many would not agree with Adorno's explanations. For example, they might not accept that each human being is capable of self-directing their lives and that the denial of this negatively affects their well-being and happiness – they might turn to other explanations of social phenomena, including human suffering, that they do recognise.[28] However, my point here is merely that the methodology itself seems sound: phenomena such as the widespread occurrence of neurotic behaviour are in need of explanation, and explaining these phenomena in terms of shortfalls from (basic) human functioning is a promising strategy. Such theorising – even once backed up with concrete evidence and detailed critical engagement with alternative explanations – might not be fully conclusive, but would present the best attempt at making sense of what conditions are adverse or beneficial for human development and

26 See, for example, Taylor 1993 and also 1985. Another similarity here is to Durkheim's approach in sociology – particularly to his work on suicide ([1897] 1989).
27 Adorno is, perhaps, most explicit about this procedure in his discussion with Gehlen (see in Grenz 1983: 246–7; see also here, Introduction).
28 For example, Gehlen is much more sceptical than Adorno about the importance of human self-determination and the effects of its denial on human well-being, seeming to suggest rather the opposite explanation of the malaise of modern society (that it allows people too much freedom and they cannot cope with it; see in Grenz 1983: 249–50).

flourishing.[29] Yet, once we leave the project of searching for a priori grounds of normativity behind, this lack of conclusiveness need neither surprise nor worry us.

This methodological parallel might help to ease the following worry that Aristotelians would have about Adorno's negativism: if we live prior to the realisation of the human potential and virtue, then how could we develop a conception of humanity at all, given that this conception would have to be partly based on observation of fully functioning specimens? After all, while Aristotelian judgements about life forms are not mere empirical generalisations, they are not completely divorced from empirical reality either, but, so to speak, condensations of its actually observable specimens. In reply, one could highlight the empirical component of Adorno's theory. Admittedly, we cannot yet observe fully developed and functioning specimens (for there are none yet), but some basic functioning is available to view, and the nature and scope of the problems that we can observe human beings to experience in capitalism (and its nominally socialist rivals) indicate that even this functioning is often hampered by these social structures. Also, the misery that we do experience is best explained – at least this is what Adorno would argue – by attributing to human beings some not yet developed and, thus, not yet specifiable potential which is also inhibited and repressed by our current social world. In a sense, the unfulfilled potential to which Adorno points functions like a postulate within his theory – he proposes that we cannot make sense of the world without postulating that there is this potential, despite the fact that we cannot currently know anything positive about it. This postulate of a blocked human *telos* is meant to be vindicated by the strength of the overall theory to explain the social world.

Moreover, this methodology also avoids committing Adorno to the sort of top-down reasoning based on transhistorical claims about human essence and needs that he squarely rejects.[30] Any legitimacy that does

---

29 Such a fallibilist account of philosophical history (and of what it teaches us about human flourishing) can also be found in the writing of contemporary Aristotelians (see, for example, MacIntyre 1985: Ch. 19).

30 See ND, 6: 61, 130/51, 124. Interestingly, Adorno claims that inhumanity and misery [*Unglück*] are historically invariant (see, for example, ND, 6: 346/352). Note also his intriguing comment that 'Every image, of humanity [*Menschenbild*], other than a negative one, is ideology' (8: 67; my translation). Nothing in the Aristotelian conception of normativity commits one to a teleology of the sort that Adorno rejected (and Hegel might have affirmed) – i.e., the view that human history is an overall progress story and that any potential *necessarily* will become actual at one point. To say that human beings

exist for his conception of inhumanity derives solely from the explanatory power of his overall theory: if this theory succeeds better than rival theories of society in explaining certain social phenomena (such as anti-Semitism, or the fact that there is such a high incidence of paranoia and neurosis in the modern social world) and also why rival theories fail to explain these phenomena adequately, then its underlying conception of inhumanity is as redeemed as it could be. In other words, the conception of the bad and inhumanity derives from the successful analysis and critique of our social world, not from a metaphysical or teleological account of human nature. This approach relies on the claim that any theory (or, at least, any theory of society), will – whether it is acknowledged or not – contain normative presuppositions, whose legitimacy is directly tied up with its explanatory power.[31] This fits well with Adorno's view of theorising: understanding a phenomenon and criticising it are one and the same project.[32] The approach also reduces the problem of how we come to know the conception of the bad: it is not a transcendent standard but – to use a formulation by Horkheimer – 'grounded on the misery of the present'.[33]

In this way, we can know what inhumanity and the bad are, and the Aristotelian framework helps us to see how it is possible to know this without violating the strictures of Adorno's negativistic outlook. In addition, the Aristotelian framework also helps us to uncover that there are two aspects to Adorno's conception of the bad: the denial of our animal nature, on the one hand, and the denial of other elements of basic human functioning, on the other.[34] With the help of these two aspects we can elucidate and clarify what Adorno objects to in the modern world as well as show that these objections need not require

have a yet-to-be-realised potential and that the current social world is bad because it blocks this potential is not to say that this social world will necessarily be overcome or, indeed, that it will be overcome by something that realises this potential. At most, it is a statement about what – *barring catastrophes* – will happen under the right conditions, but according to Adorno we have not had the right conditions, might never have them, and instead at least one catastrophe (Auschwitz) has intervened and more threaten to do so in the future. If anything, for Adorno, the tendency towards permanent catastrophe is stronger than the one towards freedom and human realisation.

31 Other Aristotelian thinkers, such as Taylor (see his 1985, especially Ch. 2), would also endorse this view of theorising.

32 See, for example, MCP, 102/64; see also Horkheimer 1972: 216.

33 Horkheimer 1972: 217; translation amended.

34 These two aspects are paralleled in Aristotelian accounts, which tend to distinguish between the vulnerabilities we share with other animals and those vulnerabilities specific to our human form of functioning which go beyond our general animal nature (see, for example, MacIntyre 1999: esp. 72).

knowledge of the good. For my contention is that these two aspects of the bad could be used to account for all the badness and evil to which Adorno objects.

As an example, consider a case which is central to Adorno's philosophy, the evil of Auschwitz. What Adorno objects to is, firstly, the 'unbearable physical agony' to which the victims were subjected.[35] The suffering involved was so large that it 'burned out, without any consolation, every soothing feature of the mind and its objectification, culture'.[36] It was suffering beyond solace. On the proposed model, this badness would be (an extreme) form of disregard of our animal nature. Yet, the badness of Auschwitz is not exhausted in the badness of the (physical) suffering involved, unbearable as it was. What happened in Auschwitz, according to Adorno, was the attempt to destroy completely everything individual or particularised about the victims, even before they were killed.[37] This destruction went so far that 'it was no longer the individual who died, but a specimen [*Examplar*]'.[38] While each individual, according to Adorno, had already lost some of his or her particularity in the development of modern unified self, the inmates of the extermination camps were deprived even of one final element of individuality – of being able to relate to their life as their own. The way they were treated completely destroyed the possibility of their seeing any sense in their life,[39] and thereby of relating to death as the coming to an end of a life-story. The treatment to which they were subjected made it impossible for them to view themselves as agents with a specific life history and attachments and projects, as individuals. Thus, the point

35 ND, 6: 358/365.   36 ND, 6: 358/365; translation amended.
37 The victims were subjected – to use Bernstein's way of characterising it (2001: 381) – first to spiritual death and then to physical death (see also Levi [1958] 1996: 47, 57, 60, 127–8, 156).
38 ND, 6: 355/362.
39 Consider Levi's way of making comprehensible what is incomprehensible in the unspeakable treatment he and others suffered: 'We know that we will have difficulty in being understood and this is as it should be. But consider what value, what meaning is enclosed even in the smallest of our daily habits, in the hundred possessions which even the poorest beggar owns: a handkerchief, an old letter, the photo of a cherished person. These things are part of us, almost like the limbs of our body; nor is it conceivable that we can be deprived of them in our world, for we immediately find others to substitute the old ones, other objects which are ours in their personification and vocation of our memories. Imagine now a man who is deprived of everything he loves and at the same time of his house, his habits, his clothes, in short, of everything he possesses: he will be a hollow man, reduced to suffering and needs, forgetful of his dignity and restraint, for he who loses all often easily loses himself' (Levi [1958] 1996: 33).

Adorno is making is that reducing the victims to mere specimens – in Bernstein's words, to merely a 'meaningless organism, walking bits of flesh and bone with a number attached'[40] – is actually a complete denial of individual agency. In this way, Adorno objects also to the attempts by the perpetrators of the *Shoa* to extinguish in the victims any sense of self, any sense of meaning, and any sense of actively leading a life.[41] All of these can be connected to a denial of our human potential and even, if the suggestions made earlier are correct, of our basic human functioning. To repeat, whatever the full realisation of humanity substantially consists in, in order for humans to even achieve basic functioning, they would have, at least, to be able to acquire (and live according to) a minimum sense of self, a sense of meaning in their lives and relationships, and a sense of actively leading a life. Without these, humanity can neither come into its own, nor can human beings even achieve basic functioning; and in this way the treatment of the victims in Auschwitz was also a radical attack on their humanity in a broader sense than just an attack on their lives and physical well-being.

This way of elucidating the evil of Auschwitz is not guilty of the outrage of which Adorno accuses those who think it necessary to discursively ground this negative normativity. The claim is not that the evil of Auschwitz could not be justified as evil or recognised as such without the Aristotelian conception of normativity. Rather, the idea is that attempts at understanding it as an event will provide us with a better, more detailed conception of the kind of things which human beings should not lack and about how our modern society is at fault for systematically denying them to us. It functions as a paradigmatic example with the help of which we can elucidate and better understand the bad. In this sense, the evil of Auschwitz remains primary in the analysis, rather than being derived or deduced from some higher or deeper level of theorising.

The Aristotelian framework also elucidates a further aspect of Adorno's thought. As seen, for Adorno the bad has its own negative normativity insofar as it demands to be mitigated or overcome and it demands this irrespective of the content of the good.[42] My proposal to ascribe an Aristotelian conception of normativity to Adorno allows us to

---

40 Bernstein 2001: 382.   41 See, for example, ND, 6: 355/362.

42 Adorno, to my knowledge, never *explicitly* states that negativity demands its own abolition, but he, for example, does say this about suffering (see ND, 6: 203/203) and this might serve as model for negativity more generally (see also Chapter 5; and Bernstein 2001: Ch. 6, Sect. 6).

see why this is the case: the bad demands its own abolition by itself (that is, without the need to mention the good) because whatever realised humanity is, inhumanity is bad for us in virtue of the kind of beings we are and could become. *Qua* members of the human life form we have objective reasons to avoid the bad, the inhuman. In fact, this also helps to explain why it is worse that human beings, who are capable of recognising and acting on objective reasons, bring about badness, than that it is caused by accidents or illnesses (that is, to explain why Auschwitz is more problematic and objectionable than the occurrence of the plague): the badness is compounded because human beings could have responded otherwise, but failed to do so, adding the badness of the use of their agency to the badness of the consequences. In both these ways, the deeper rationale for the negative normativity of the bad operative in Adorno's theory becomes visible, if his views are placed within an Aristotelian framework.

Similarly with other aspects of Adorno's theory: ascribing an Aristotelian framework to Adorno makes better sense of much of what he is saying, including some of his most controversial views. Recall the need within Adorno's philosophy for an account of what it is to be mistaken in one's reactions to the world and the reasons it presents us with (that is, the third constraint on an Adornian account of normativity; see Chapter 7). It is a noticeable feature of the Aristotelian framework that normativity is not directly dependent on our feelings, attitudes, and reactions, while, at the same time, it is not completely independent of them either. Certain feelings, attitudes, and reactions are the *adequate* and *typical* expression of, for example, the negativity of pain, but not all experiential or affective states are constitutive of it. Thus, the badness of the pain is not dependent on whether all people actually show a negative reaction to it all the time. Take, for example, people who engage in self-harming activities and willingly inflict pain on themselves; such people, we would say, have distorted, pathological reactions to pain – they are not responsive in the right way to the objective reason to avoid pain. (It might not be their fault that they are not so responsive – it might be due to the fact that their dysfunctional surroundings have left them little other room for expressing their agency – but the fact that it is excusable does not show that they have no such reasons, or that nothing is going wrong here.) This feature of the Aristotelian view can be seen at work in Adorno's theory. If Adorno is right, then we all have distorted reactions and attitudes most of the time because of the way society has constituted, conditioned, and programmed us; we desire things we do not really need and do not respond fully to the neglect of what we do, in fact, need. In this sense, he uses an objective account of normativity built around our vulnerabilities and potentialities to criticise how most of us all the time, and all of us most of the time, react to the radically evil social world we live in (and to criticise this world for making us react in these ways).

Indeed, the Aristotelian methodology also extends further into how Adorno proceeds in this critique of modernity (not least in relation to the culture industry): he has recourse to the experience of a few critical individuals and rejects the way most people view their surroundings.[43] Only these critical individuals have been lucky enough to develop the ability for genuine and unrestricted experience. Structurally similar to the virtuous agent within the Aristotelian framework, these critics are best placed to see the world in the right way and have higher chances than others of responding to the objective reasons thus perceived (including the ethical features of situations). It is from the standpoint of the critics that society can be criticised, and it is in comparison with them that those who are less critical can be seen to be in error, to live more wrongly.

Admittedly, there is something in this account about which we might feel uncomfortable – it seems to imply a certain kind of deference to authority, specifically the authority of the remaining critical individuals. However uncomfortable it might be for us who were raised in (formally) democratic, (purportedly) consensus-oriented societies, it is a fact that Adorno's writings are not premised on widespread consensus and agreement. He would be inconsistent if he said otherwise: if what most of us all the time and all of us most of the time think and experience is distorted, then it is not really an option to rely on general assent and plausibility, rather than on agreement among those few who have been lucky and privileged enough to develop and maintain their critical faculties. It is not that the truth of a critical theory of society is in principle a matter to be judged only by the informed few – Adorno admits, even insists on the fact that, within a different social world, it would be comprehensible to all. His point is rather that the current world makes this impossible by distorting people's consciousness. As he once put it:

---

43 See, for example, ND, 6: 51–2/41–2.

Emphatic reconstructability [*Nachvollziehbarkeit*] is a potential possessed by mankind and does not exist here and now under existing conditions. ... Probably a change in the whole would be required – that whole which today, in terms of its own law, deforms rather than develops awareness.[44]

No appeal to people's intellect or even to constructs of ideal deliberation can help here. As committed as Adorno is that in a free society, each and every human being could achieve self-determination and lead an undirected life, in the state of immaturity that humanity is in now, we have to make do in following the most progressive minds – not uncritically, to be sure, but nonetheless ultimately taking our direction from them. Still, even these authorities, to which we ought to defer, are only genuine authorities, according to Adorno, if they are open to, and constantly engage in, reflexive, critical scrutiny and do all they can to remain modest (see already Chapter 6). Also, they presumably can license only acts of resistance appropriately tailored for the specific social-political context – within democracies, these would be mainly consciousness-raising and immunisation activities.[45] A revolution, a transformation of the social world (and its thought forms), would require recognition among the vast majority that this world (and thought forms) can and ought to be changed, and thereby the development and intervention of a self-conscious global subject.[46] In the absence of the latter, resistance and critical thinking has dwindled to 'small minorities who even have to suffer being castigated for an élitist stance'.[47] While in a free society, each and every human being could be *phronimoi*, the closest we get to this today is the few critical individuals lucky enough to have escaped social determination more than the majority.

An Aristotelian outlook can also be seen at play in Adorno's view that moral or ethical demands are indexed to particular situations (as discussed in Chapter 5). To return to an example quoted earlier, Adorno claims that the demand that no one should be tortured is 'true as an impulse, as a reaction to the news that torture is going on somewhere'.[48] Elsewhere, he argues that the simple fact that someone is a refugee 'about to be killed or handed over to some state police in some country or other' should move us into helping him or her.[49] Similarly, it is

44 8: 327/Adorno et al. 1976: 45.   45 See Freyenhagen 2012 (unpublished).
46 P, 10.2: 618/CM, 144; HF, 202–3/143–4.   47 8: 327/Adorno et al. 1976: 45.
48 ND, 6: 281/285.   49 PMP 1963, 144–5/97.

plausible to think that the new categorical imperative is true for Adorno as an exemplary reaction to a particular historical experience, Auschwitz and the events for which this name stands (see also Chapter 5). Thus, in all of these cases, the truth of the moral demands is linked to the ethical features of the situation, to which the agent shows (or should show) the appropriate reaction. The appropriateness of this reaction, Adorno would say, consists in responding mimetically to the situation and the suffering experienced by others in it. This view of moral demands seems to be a version of the Aristotelian realism about reasons mentioned earlier. It presents reasons as objective insofar as they arise from the features of a state of affairs and the relevance of these features for the human life form; and it suggests that the appropriateness of the response depends on a receptive element (perceiving the objective reasons embodied in situations) as well as an active element directly connected to it (acting on these reasons).

Moreover, Adorno even accepts, as Aristotelians do generally,[50] that both these elements (the perception of and the action on reasons) need not be at the level of deliberation or discursive interaction, but might well take the form of impulses (or, as with animals, instincts). In this way, my interpretation of Adorno as a negativistic Aristotelian remains sensitive even to the impulse-based elements in his view (see Chapter 7 and Appendix). Indeed, we can now see why Adorno is right in thinking that, when he claims that morality survives in the materialistic motive – the physical abhorrence of suffering and repression – and rejects discursive grounding he is not appealing to irrationalism. In the Aristotelian view at work in his thinking, the untutored physical impulses exemplify and express the objective interests of us as the life form we are and could become, and thereby the standards of substantive rationality. In contrast, modern reason, in its formal, mostly instrumental nature has become irrational – abstracted as it is from our material interests – and cannot but get entangled in infinite dialectics of argumentation even on the most basic matters. Within this overall Aristotelian framework, there is even a sense in which the immediate physical impulses are also mediated – by our objective interests, which they embody (sometimes in undistorted form). This also means that there is a way to reflect on the validity of individual impulses – not by hard and fast rules, not in

---

50 See, for example, MacIntyre 1999, Chs. 1–7; see also Foot 2001; and Section I of this chapter.

an absolutely fool-proof way, but by looking at whether or not they would be part of the best explanation of our world and its ills.

In Chapter 1 we encountered Adorno's thesis that we do injustice to objects in the way we impose certain conceptual schemes on them. This claim can be made less puzzling in the light of the Aristotelian conception of normativity that I have unearthed in Adorno's theory. As already noted in Chapter 1, the key point is that objects have – at least potentially – their own organisation and unity; that this organisation and unity is non-purposive in the sense that it is not oriented by instrumental reason; and that such organisation and unity deserves recognition. This recognition can only come from us, but is premised on our acknowledging our own status as natural beings. As such, we bring an affinity with objects to our cognition of them. Indeed, without this affinity, no cognition would be possible at all.[51] The thought seems to be that since we (uniquely) have the capacity to recognise the unity and obligation inherent in objects, we have the obligation to do so. We have this obligation not in virtue of its being derived from a higher principle, but because we cannot unfold our full human potential unless we exercise this capacity. Human beings have the capacity to recognise the organisation inherent in objects (and the aesthetic form of this unity); and it is because human beings, and only human beings, have this capacity that its exercise is part of what it is to fulfil their potential – although we cannot in advance say what it would positively involve to exercise this potential. In our wrong state of affairs, any anticipation of the realisation of this potential would be tainted. The only characterisation we have is negative: such a realisation would mean *not to disregard* the non-identical. This can be well accounted for in Aristotelian terms. We have objective reasons not to disregard the non-identical, since doing so goes against the realisation of the kind of life form we are. It goes against this realisation, firstly, in the sense that such a disregard will often involve destroying nature, which, in turn, makes human life and the unfolding of human nature difficult or even impossible. Secondly, it is bad to disregard the non-identical because it is part of the distinctive potential capacities of our life form to recognise objects (and nature as a whole) for what it is; and this capacity, whatever it involves exactly, can be *negatively* characterised as not doing injustice to the non-identical.

Finally, ascribing an Aristotelian outlook to Adorno also fits well with his worries about discursive grounding of morality. Again, the ascription

---

51 See ND, 6: 267/270; and Chapter 1.

would reveal the strength of his position, since this outlook contains a reasoned explanation for why the justificatory project in ethics fails. An independent justification of normativity is neither necessary, nor possible, nor appropriate. Normativity is constitutive to humanity as a life form; the self-preservation of humanity and the realisation of human potential constrain the content of rationality (which is, hence, conceived in substantive, not merely formal, terms).[52] Each particular normative requirement can be accounted for within this framework. Any further grounding would both (a) involve a disregard of the fact that normativity has already been accounted for in this way and (b) embark on a project of which we cannot even make sense. Hence an Aristotelian Adorno can provide all that can be reasonably demanded of an account of normativity, namely, an explanation of the structure of normativity. This general framework would need to be completed by a specific account of the particular normative claims which Adorno makes, but if my overall argument is correct, then there is no obstacle in principle to carrying out this task within the confines of Adorno's negativistic Aristotelianism. (Indeed, I earlier provided the beginnings of how such a specific explication would run regarding the paradigmatic evil of Auschwitz, while remaining within these confines.)

All of this is not to say that there are not also tensions between an Aristotelian outlook (at least as it is often presented) and Adorno's critical theory of society. For example, it sometimes seems as if Aristotelians lack critical distance to the traditional social practices and institutions which allegedly underwrote the exercise of the virtues in pre-modern times – something which Adorno is not guilty of.[53] Also, it is unclear whether Aristotelians can acknowledge that needs have a historical and cultural dimension to the same degree as Adorno does acknowledge this.[54]

However, these tensions could be of a productive kind. Realising that there is an Aristotelian core to Adorno's thought means that we could take it as a starting point for the challenge of combining the Aristotelian line of thought with a critical analysis of modern societies. In this way, it might be possible to show that Aristotelianism is a live option even in the

---

52 See MTP, 10.2: 775/CM, 272–3; see also 8: 348/Adorno et al. 1976: 62.

53 Williams recognises that Aristotelian accounts of traditional societies may have downplayed the extent of domination and ideology within these societies and that such accounts require supplementation by a critical theory of society of the kind provided by Adorno and the Frankfurt School (see Williams 1993: 166).

54 However, see Wiggins 1991; for Adorno's views on this issue, see, for example, 8: 392–6.

context of large-scale, impersonal forms of interaction, not just in the circumscribed universe of the Ancient Greek *polis*, monasteries, or Renaissance city states. Thus, Aristotelians could also have something to gain from my reading of Adorno. In general, the common ground and tensions between Adorno's theory and various neo-Aristotelian theories could be productively explored – be it in relation to Adorno's conception of nature[55] or in developing a robust defence against attacks on ethical naturalism.[56]

This indicates something which is also true of this whole study: Adorno's critical theory is *not a completed project, but a research programme.* Even if the reconstruction and philosophical defence of Adorno's position presented in this study are cogent, they merely make room for renewing this programme. Only if the practical philosophy presented in broad brushes in this study is linked with sociological, historical, and economic studies, could its merits and shortcomings as a part of an overall explanation of the ills of our world come fully into view. The purpose here was to contribute towards enabling such developments by clarifying and defending this (philosophical) part of his thinking – by showing that it is not the dead end which many friends and foes have taken it to be since the late 1960s. I am all too aware that I could only touch on many important aspects and make only small, if any, advances. For example, we have seen that Adorno proposes what might be called a philosophical anthropology – admittedly, an unusual one in that it is meant to be vindicated by making sense of the ills and wrongs of a particular historical social setting (our modern social world), rather than by comparing different human societies across different historical-social contexts; and also unusual insofar as it is negativist, telling us only about inhumanity and postulating a yet-to-be-realised and yet-to-be-specified potential. Largely in virtue of this anthropology, Adorno is an objectivist, a realist, when it comes to normativity and ethics. There is much in this that people would take issue with, and little I could do in this study to address their concerns. Similarly, the defence I have offered of the idea of a purely negativist philosophy is strongest in respect to extreme circumstances, and many would disagree with Adorno that we are faced with these. Moreover, I have argued that vindicating Adorno's theory would consist in showing that it provides the best explanation of

---

55 See Fink 2006; and Cook 2011.
56 For a crisp, recent statement of the criticisms of Aristotelian naturalism, see Lenman 2005.

our modern social world and its ills, but I have not done the kind of comparative work required to substantiate this explanatory superiority. A fuller defence would have to take these and other challenges on by *carrying out the research programme* that it has been my purpose here to renew and make viable as an alternative worth pursuing and taking seriously.

I end in the way I started – with Gehlen's challenge and Adorno's answer to it. The difference is – I hope – that Adorno's answer makes now more sense and can be seen to indicate the negativistic, Aristotelian conception of normativity that, I have proposed, can be unearthed from his works:

> GEHLEN: How do you know what potential undirected human beings have?
> ADORNO: Well, I do not know positively what this potential is, but I know from all sorts of findings – including the particular findings of the [social and human] sciences – that the adjustment processes, which human beings are subjected to nowadays, lead to an unprecedented extent – and I think that you would admit this – to the crippling [*Verkrüppelung*] of human beings. ... And I would also say that just the psychological observation of all of those uncounted, defective human beings – and defectiveness has become, I would almost say, the norm today – this [observation alone] justifies us in saying that the potential of human beings is being wasted and suppressed to an unprecedented extent by institutions.[57]

---

57 Adorno and Gehlen 1983 in Grenz 1983: 246–7; my translation.

APPENDIX

The jolt – Adorno on spontaneous willing

Adorno takes a particular stance on spontaneous willing which brings him into conflict not just with Kant (his main interlocutor in practical philosophy), but also with most of the philosophical tradition. In this Appendix, I discuss this stance, which is an important background consideration for a number of the arguments in the main text (see Chapters 3–5 and 7).

Among a great number of criticisms of Kant's conception of freedom, Adorno advances one which is particularly telling for his own conception of freedom and morality. This criticism is part of a wider cluster of criticisms to the effect that agency cannot be transcendental, but has to be bodily, temporal, and involve more than a formal sense of the self. I here concentrate on the first and most important point: the inextricably bodily nature of free agency.[1]

I The jolt in freedom: impulses and spontaneity

Adorno argues basically as follows:

a Initiating an action (understood widely to include decision-making) *constitutively* requires a non-rational, somatic element (a physical impulse).
b The transcendental self is not capable of physical impulses.[2]
c Therefore, the transcendental self is not capable of initiating an action.

---

1 For the criticism of the inconceivability of non-temporal agency, see ND, 6: 251/253: see also 201/201; 1995: 238–9, 322/157, 213; and Freyenhagen 2008. As to the criticism of the formal sense of the self, see especially ND, 6: 239, 288/241, 293.
2 ND, 6: 213/213.

The crucial and controversial premise is (a). Kant might agree to premise (b), but he would not accept that transcendental freedom – and, as a consequence, practical freedom – requires bodily impulses. Accordingly, my discussion focuses on the contentious premise (a).

Adorno supplies the main arguments for premise (a) in a passage from *Negative Dialectics*, entitled 'The Addendum [*Das Hinzutretende*]'.[3] In it, Adorno analyses the phenomenology of decision-making (the experience of it).[4] His claim is that our decision-making does not run smoothly, but involves a jolt or leap [*Ruck*].[5] In other words, decision-making involves *experientially* a rupture in the causal chain: we do not experience decision-making like we experience the fall of an individual domino in a giant chain of falling domino pieces, tripped over by the piece before it and its fall, in turn, triggering the fall of the next, all of which in a smooth transition. Rather, according to Adorno, we experience decisions as something that comes over us – specifically, we experience it as a rupture with what might have been a long and laborious deliberation, which seemed inconclusive until we find ourselves with having made a decision, at least sometimes to our own surprise. Such a rupture, or jolt, signals that there is a fundamental difference between willing and merely intellectual thought processes,[6] and this, in turn, shows that willing cannot be exhausted by consciousness, but requires the presence of physical impulses (I return to this final step).

Let me expand briefly on the point about willing and thinking. It might be that willing involves intellectual thought processes, but willing is not just considering premises and drawing conclusions in the same way. I can intellectually entertain various positions, including those that stand in opposition to each other, and reason within each of these positions, but doing so is not the same as adopting one of them as a course of action. Instead, practical deliberation yields a different sort of result. Indeed, according to Aristotle, the conclusion of a practical syllogism is always an immediate action.[7] While this might be too strong a thesis, many of Adorno's critics accept a weaker version. Notably,

---

3 ND, 6: 226–30/226–30; however, some of the same ideas are also found elsewhere (see, for example, ND, 6: 234–5, 237, 240/235–6, 238, 241; HF, lectures 24–6). For a similar reconstruction of the arguments to the one offered here, see Bernstein 2001: 150 ff. and Whitebook 2003: 698–9.

4 See Habermas 2005: esp. Sect. 1; Menke 2005: 39.   5 ND, 6: 226/226–7.

6 See also HF, 317/228. Still, as we see later, there is also an intimate connection between the two for Adorno: to begin thinking processes requires (bodily) willing.

7 NE, 1147a25–30.

Kantians accept that a practical conclusion is the adoption of a maxim, a disposition to act, which, unless other factors interfere, results in taking active steps as soon as a suitable occasion presents itself.

Returning to the phenomenology of decision-making presented by Adorno, one could object that, while we might all have had experiences of decision-making involving jolts or ruptures, many of our decisions – perhaps especially our everyday, mundane decisions – do not involve them, but are experienced as part of a smoothly unfolding world (just like the falling dominos). While Adorno, to my knowledge, does not comment on such habitual decisions and actions, it seems to me that he could concede that they exist and even that they are widespread. Admittedly, one would have to reconfigure his objection to Kantian spontaneity as concerning only certain decisions, specifically those where we reflectively endorse our habitually taken decisions or decide on an aspect of our lives after (possibly protracted) deliberation. Moreover, it does seem plausible that we experience these decisions as something like a rupture in our experiential world; that we are startled and surprised by having come to a decision after what can be a long process of deliberation; and that they exhibit a special kind of temporality and passivity, such that the decision changes from *something yet to be made* to *something that has happened to us*, without our ever being conscious of actively making it. This phenomenon is what we might have in mind when we recommend to people who face a difficult decision that they should 'sleep on it' or tell them that their conclusion 'will come to them'.

The factual element of the jolt in a free action is ascribed by traditional philosophy, Adorno claims, to consciousness. Yet, doing so begs the question about what it is, since whether consciousness could effect such a jolt is part of the issue under consideration. In fact, Adorno does not think that consciousness by itself can account for this jolt. He is deeply sceptical that consciousness could fulfil this role because 'intervention by the pure mind' seems inconceivable.[8] This is not to deny that consciousness plays a role in our experience of decision-making. Without

---

8 ND, 6: 226/226–7. While I focus in the main text on the bodily aspect that Adorno thinks is missing in Kant's and other intellectualist views of the will, intervention of the pure mind is also inconceivable if and because – as with Kant – the mind (the transcendental free subject) is meant to be non-temporal, while the intervention is temporal. Bennett puts it well, 'When Kant says of a noumenon that "nothing happens in it" and yet that it "of itself begins its effects in the sensible world" (B569), he implies that there is a making-to-begin which is not a happening; and I cannot understand that as anything but a contradiction' (1984: 102; see also n.1 of this appendix.).

consciousness there would be no identity of the self in one's decision and action. As a result, there would be no experience of freedom, presumably because such experience requires that we can ascribe an action to ourselves, as a subject. Yet, the experience of decision-making is not exhausted by the presence of (self-)consciousness.[9] The latter might be a necessary condition for the experience of freedom and even for freedom itself, but, according to Adorno, something else, something physical and non-rational (a somatic impulse), is also required.[10] Freedom, according to Adorno, needs rational insight, but also an 'injection of irrationality'.[11] He identifies this moment of irrationality with the physical impulse,[12] and, hence, freedom for Adorno requires a somatic or physical element.

The importance of physical impulses is often overlooked in the analysis of freedom. This might be in part because, at least in Kant's case, freedom is conceptualised in terms of rational agency (and as such contrasted with bodily impulses). Still, another reason for this is that physical impulse and theoretical consciousness are not always experienced separately.[13] According to Adorno, in the case of the archaic, not yet unified self, there is no – as Bernstein puts it – 'sharp distinction between what is somatic in character and what belongs to the domain of consciousness'.[14] It is only in the process of the self's becoming increasingly unified and ordered that the archaic self is split up into two components, consciousness and physical impulses. This process involves a restriction of the self, such that it is no longer the case that both of these components are viewed as belonging to it.[15] In particular,

---

9 See ND, 6: 226/227; see also HF, lectures 25–6.
10 ND, 6: 228/229; see also HF, 333/240. Adorno speaks here from within the position criticised – as emerges soon, he does not think that the impulses are irrational, but his opponents (those that narrow reason down to mindedness) do think of it as bodily and therefore non-rational or even irrational.
11 PMP 1963, 168/113.   12 ND, 6: 228/228–7.
13 See: 'The two moments [consciousness and the impulse] are by no means separately experienced; but philosophical analysis has tailored the phenomenon in such a way that afterwards, in philosophical language, it simply cannot be put otherwise than as if something else were added to rationality' (ND, 6: 228/229).
14 Bernstein 2001: 254.
15 Similarly, our (philosophical) conception of the will as separated from the impulses might have only arisen once the energy of the physical impulses had been increasingly diverted into reason which thereby took on more of an independent existence vis-à-vis them (see ND, 6: 229/230; see also ND, 6: 240/241). We can see from this account that the will for Adorno, in contrast to Kant, is not merely formal in nature (see PMP 1963, 185/125).

the process of developing the unified, modern self results in the self's being conceived as distinct from its impulses, so that the latter becomes an 'inner foreign world' (as Freud would have put it)[16] – something which we have to disown in order to become our own. As a consequence, impulses are now seen – from the perspective of the unified self (and the prevailing perspectives in philosophy) – as involuntary phenomena, broadly on the model of bodily reflexes. Consciousness, on the other hand, is seen as completely independent of bodily impulses – as 'the self's ability to set thinking in motion'.[17] Philosophers have played a part in this process by separating consciousness and the physical impulse in their various analyses of decision-making, and have often (as in Kant's case) ascribed spontaneity and practical freedom to consciousness alone and viewed physical impulses as extraneous to the will (and reason).[18] Thus, there has been a split between self and bodily impulses, and, at least sometimes, this has gone along with excluding these impulses from spontaneity, practical freedom, reason, and the will.

However, as seen, the phenomenology of decision-making reveals that it requires physical impulses. Indeed, Adorno thinks that even setting thinking in motion requires the intervention of the embodied will,[19] let alone moving from insight to action. Thus, physical impulses cannot be eliminated totally, or the will (and thereby thinking) ceases; what is required for freely willed actions (and thinking) is that the 'hand twitches'.[20] Moreover, it is not the case that Adorno just means that free action requires an injection of energy on top of a decision to act. Rather, without the physical impulse *the will does not will*.[21] The impulses are *constitutive* of practical freedom, of the will; not just necessary for translating it into action.[22] To put it in Kantian terminology, adopting a maxim, not only its subsequent execution, involves for Adorno a physical impulse. The adoption is for him an act, and consciousness alone is insufficient to bring it about.

II Towards a different view of nature, the self, and agency

So far we have seen that ascribing spontaneity only to consciousness is in tension with our experience of decision-making (which involves a jolt at

---

16 See Whitebook 2003: 698–9.   17 Whitebook 2003: 699.
18 ND, 6: 228–9/229–30; see also 226/226–7; and Bernstein 2001: 252.
19 See ND, 6: 230/230.   20 ND, 6: 229/230.
21 See ND, 6: 228–9, 240/229–30, 241.   22 See HF, 328/236.

least in important cases). Adorno suggests that it thereby distorts the relationship between freedom and nature as one of opposition between two wholly separable poles (mind and bodily impulses). In a way, the very attempts to reconcile freedom and nature widen the gap between them, which neither was there originally nor need be there at all.[23] In other words, by abstracting spontaneity from all its somatic impulses, we cannot but view nature as hostile to freedom in the way and to the extent that Kant does. Then, it does, indeed, appear to be the case that we have to embark on something like the Kantian quest of finding a way for freedom to have its own domain where nature does not restrict it. However, instead of pursuing this impossible and misguided quest, we should change our perceptions of nature and the self; we should reflect on nature within us.[24] In particular, we ought to realise that for there to be spontaneity and practical freedom, we need not exclude nature, but have to rely on it. (As I discuss in more detail shortly, this is not just a matter of taking a different perspective on life, but would require a social change, for – according to Adorno – the distorted views about freedom and nature have taken root in and partly derive from our way of life, with its long history of the partial distancing and suppression of inner nature for the sake of control over external nature and other human beings.)[25]

Admittedly, nature determines us in a certain way – namely, to pursue our self-preservation. However, our domination of nature has just continued this pursuit by different means. We remain – this is one of the central claims of *Dialectic of Enlightenment* – actually under the spell of nature in our attempts to rid ourselves of it. However, nature's determination of us need not be seen as necessitation in any strong sense. For all we know, nature in itself is not deterministically structured. Rather, we mistake the constraints it places us under – its orientation towards preservation of the species – as causally deterministic. Part of the reason for this is that we have continued to follow the natural drive for self-preservation in blind and unconscious ways. (The sophistication in technology and social organisation we have reached along this path would seem to belie this, but is, in fact, part of the same, ultimately unreflective process.) Put differently, we think of nature as deterministically limiting us mainly because we have made the pursuit of self-preservation so much

23 ND, 6: 228/228–9.   24 See DE, 3: 57/40; ND, 6: 389–90/397.
25 For Adorno's view of this long history, see especially his (and Horkheimer's) discussion of the Odysseus myth in *Dialectic of Enlightenment*.

our own that everything else in our lives has become subordinated to it, instead of reflectively taking it up and putting it in its proper place.[26] Yet, were we to realise this and begin to actively determine our fate, nature would not hold us back.[27] In particular, we would not need to think of nature as deterministically necessitating us.

By recognising that willing requires impulses, we can think differently about spontaneity and practical freedom, and their relation to nature. Specifically, such a reflection points us to a 'concept of freedom as a state that would no more be blind nature than it would be oppressed nature'.[28] To see how this would be possible, we need to realise first that reason itself 'has genetically evolved from the force of human drives, as their differentiation'.[29] In this sense, impulses are not actually 'as alien to reason as it would seem under the aspect of the Kantian equation of reason with the will'.[30] We would have recognised the affinity between reason and impulses, and would restore their natural bond. As a consequence, the state of freedom could be one in which impulses need not be suppressed in order for us to act freely (in this sense it would not be 'oppressed nature'). At the same time, the realisation of the natural origin of reason and the acknowledgement of nature in us would lift us out of the natural realm (the state of freedom would not be 'blind nature'). By virtue of having the capacity for attaining self-consciousness about our being part of nature, 'the human subject is liberated from the blind pursuit of natural ends and becomes capable of alternative actions'.[31] In this sense, it is the acknowledgement of, and positive

---

26 See ND, 6: 266/269; see also PMP 1963, 154/103–4; Günther 1985: 245. In a perhaps surprising appeal to the natural sciences, and in an even more surprising agreement with neo-positivism, Adorno supports the thesis that nature itself might not be a closed system by claiming that the natural sciences have abandoned this idea in the twentieth century (see notably ND, 6: 262–6/265–9).

27 See: 'If the social process of production and reproduction were transparent for and determined by the subjects, they would no longer be passively buffeted by the ominous storms of life' (ND, 6: 260/263; see also 6: 219/219). Obviously, we would have to ensure our survival, but Adorno's point is that self-preservation would not need to be the dominant pursuit that it is today. We would be free from necessitation, even if we still had to care for the necessities of life.

28 ND, 6: 228/229.

29 ND, 6: 229/230; see also 201–2, 262, 285/200–2, 265, 289; PMP 1963, 190/128; Whitebook 2003: 700; Cook 2011: esp. 64–5; and O'Connor 2012: Ch. 5. For Kant's own natural history of reason, see his 'Conjectures on the Beginning of Human History' [1786], 8: 107ff.

30 ND, 6: 228/229; translation amended.

31 PMP 1963, 154/104; see also ND, 6: 266/269.

engagement with, our natural impulses, *not* their subordination, which leads to (genuine) freedom.

The form of agency resulting from a change of perspective would be different from the archaic form, which contained perhaps too little on the side of consciousness and rational insight.[32] Yet, just because the original co-existence and interdependence of insight and impulse was unbalanced, does not mean that physical impulses have to be excluded altogether. It is here where enlightened reason goes too far and becomes irrational. The point is not to cleanse us of our impulses, but rather to create the conditions in which impulses and rational insight need not pull in different directions, but are reunited and can work in tandem. (There is a clear echo here of Schiller's views and, arguably also, of Aristotle's work.)

However, to change our perceptions of nature, the self and agency, we would have to change our social world as well. These perceptions are intimately linked with our current social world – so to transform the former, we need to transform the latter. Specifically, this social world is not organised in such a way that our impulses are properly catered for – in fact, we are alienated from them and they are subordinated to the maximisation of profit, rather than, as it should be, society and production processes serving our material needs.[33] It is thus not surprising that we view our impulses as obstacles, as alien forces to be controlled. Only when we collectively come to control our social destiny – in a possible free society of the future – will they seem different. Still, this point is often overlooked, partly because we tend to misattribute any restrictions on our freedom by impersonal forces to nature, rather than to society (see Chapter 3). This tendency reinforces social unfreedom by presenting it as a matter of metaphysics and thereby as not open to change.[34]

---

32 See HF, 327–8/235–6.   33 See, for example, S, 8: 13/270–1.

34 The tendency 'extends the rule of the status quo metaphysically' (ND, 6: 261/263; translation amended). There is one passage which seems to speak against my interpretation. Here, Adorno writes: 'The chance of freedom increases along with the objectiveness of causality; this is not the least of the reasons why he who wants freedom must insist upon necessity' (ND, 6: 247/250). Adorno seems committed here to the objectivity of causality and necessity. In reply, I would suggest that we read this passage with a view to social compulsion, not natural necessity: the real necessity we face is social, not causality of nature; but to get social necessity into view, we have to insist that its causality is objective. Only then can it be resisted and (negative) freedom take on a concrete form (ND, 6: 262/265). It is in this sense that insisting on necessity is required for freedom. Admittedly,

In the absence of a change in our perception of nature and its social background, the consciousness of freedom feeds off the memory of the archaic impulse.[35] It reminds us of how consciousness and body worked together as spontaneity, however imperfectly, and of the possibility of reuniting them in a more appropriate way, for which the material conditions are now ripe (due to capitalism's exponential expansion of the forces of production).

These considerations also explain another aspect of Adorno's criticisms of Kant. For Adorno, Kant's strategy of situating freedom in the intelligible self achieves practical freedom only at the cost of domination over one's inner nature.[36] Kant's idea of freedom as cleansed from all impulses, and as controlled from the transcendental self's lawful rational agency, encourages the super-ego to usurp a position of domination in respect to impulses and drives. In this way, we experience freedom as a repression of our inner nature, as external control over our empirical selves. While one might reply that we need to restrict our inner nature in order to have any freedom at all and that it is not a too heavy price to pay, we can now see why Adorno could not agree with this. He accepts that some sort of restriction of the drives and impulses is necessary. Still, this should not be done by thinking of them as the other of reason that we can and must stand back from, so as to strike them down whenever they conflict with the upshot of conscious deliberation. When this is done (as in the case of Kant), we undermine freedom in the very act of trying to make it possible. Instead of free agency, we are settled either with indecision and inaction (as encapsulated in the figure of Hamlet before the final scene);[37] or with compulsive and neurotic behaviour (in short, with pathologies)[38] – for this sort of control is impossible, and the impulses will break through anyway at some point, but now with a vengeance and in distorted ways (as, arguably, happens to Hamlet in the final scene).[39]

Adorno does not explicitly spell out in the original passage that the necessity he is talking about is social, but there is evidence elsewhere that this is what he means – indeed, he speaks elsewhere of the 'total social necessity' of capitalism (ND, 6: 259/262). Also, Adorno concedes that coercive civilisation was to some extent necessary for freedom to emerge (first as a concept and hopefully eventually as genuine reality; see already Chapters 2 and 3).

35 See ND, 6: 221/221–2; see also HF, lecture 25.
36 I consider a Kantian reply (and Adorno's rejoinder) in Chapter 4.
37 See ND, 6: 227/228; see also PMP 1963, 167/112; and especially HF, 320–6/231–5.
38 See ND, 6: 268ff./271ff.
39 See HF, 324–6/233–5. There is a clear Freudian strand to Adorno's thinking here.

Crucially, Adorno does not think that we need to control our impulses in this way, or even need to aspire to do so. The danger involved is avoidable, since the possibility of freedom does not, in Adorno's judgement, rely on such an absolute separation from and subordination of the impulses. On the contrary, as we have seen already, willing cleansed of all impulses would be impossible.[40] In a free world, our impulses would not pull in a different direction to our rational insights or be beyond our control to change. In a society more consciously controlled by its members and more tailored towards catering for their material needs, the impulses could be rejoined with reason in such a way that they would not need to be seen either as alien or subordinated to it, but could be shaped to overcome any opposition that a (derailed) natural history and philosophical abstractions might have produced. Hence, this would make domination of the impulses obsolete. Admittedly, this is a yet unfulfilled promise – for such a society has never existed and, even if possible, might never do so.[41]

I should comment briefly on the way Adorno proceeds in his immanent critique of Kantian spontaneity and practical freedom. As seen, this critique relies on a phenomenological analysis of the experience of decision-making – on trying to understand what is involved in our experience of making a choice. This way of proceeding might seem illegitimate – after all, it at most tells us how we experience spontaneity, not how it is in itself. However, at least in the context of an immanent critique of Kant, it is quite acceptable. Kant also proceeds phenomenologically in respect to practical freedom (at least according to Adorno).[42] Especially in Part III of the *Groundwork*, Kant seems to think that the way we experience decision-making can tell us something about its nature. Moreover, any account of decision-making would consider making sense of the phenomenology at least among the desiderata, if not the requirements, it aims to meet.

One could reply on Kant's behalf as follows: 'even if we grant to you, Adorno, that you are right that the experience of decision-making can involve a jolt of the sort you describe, and even if you are right that this means that physical impulses are a part of spontaneous willing, they are, ultimately, only a derivative part of it – i.e., they are just the mechanical enactment of the decisions taken by pure consciousness and any jolts in experience are just the appearance of these decisions'. To explain

40 See also Whitebook 2003: 700–1.   41 See ND, 6: 217–18/218.
42 See PMP 1963, 80–1/52.

further, let me make explicit some of the details of the Kantian picture that so far have remained merely in the background: for Kant, decisions involve either accepting an already given desire as an end for action (but then the desire or inclination is still secondary, because what matters is that we take it to constitute a reason); or the decision involves pure practical reason's giving rise to a feeling, in which case the feeling is again secondary. Thus, either a desire or feeling (and their motivational force) is accepted by reason and then channelled into the decision, or the decision itself creates the feeling in order for it (the decision) to become actual in the empirical self, to appear. In neither scenario do desires, inclinations, or feelings play a primary role. In fact, were physical impulses a constitutive part of willing, then – according to Kant – willing would not be spontaneous any more and there could be no practical freedom. The reason for this is as follows. We ultimately cannot control our impulses for Kant. Consequently, if these impulses were constitutive of our willing something, we could not control our willing. Our willing would rather be pre-determined by causes beyond our control (our genes, upbringing, psychological make-up, etc.). Hence, either impulses are secondary to spontaneity and practical freedom, or there is no spontaneity and practical freedom.

This particular reply depends on making Kant's account of pure practical reason work – something, we saw already (in Chapter 4), Adorno calls into question. Still, I want to leave this particular dispute aside here, since one might think that the opposition to Adorno's view of spontaneous willing would extend further than Kantians – i.e., there is a general worry that physical impulses could not be constitutive of freedom, for if they were, it is unclear in which sense we would still be in control of the actions in question (and freedom is, the proponents of this general worry would insist, a matter of being so in control). If free actions constitutively involved physical impulses, then they would be indistinguishable from bodily reflexes or merely instinctual behaviour. For example, if I strike someone because I suffer from an epileptic fit, then this behaviour would be based on a physical impulse, but it does not seem to be a free action – I could not have acted otherwise; I would not be in control of my bodily movement; I might deeply disapprove of what happened; and even though my body was causally linked to the blow a person received, we would not view me as morally responsible for what this blow (at least in the absence of certain untypical background facts, say that I engineered the situation so that this person would be struck if I were to have a fit). If, on the other hand, I decided to strike the person in question, then my bodily doing of it should be seen as merely an outward manifestation of this decision, not constitutive of it; and freedom and responsibility attach only to the mental event.

As far as I know, Adorno never explicitly addressed this general worry. Still, the following is what he could say in response to it. The objection relies on two key assumptions – both of which he would deny or at least qualify. The first assumption is that freedom is about *ex ante* conscious control, such that this control effects the action in question – in short, it is assumed that we should provide a *prospective* and *causal* account of freedom. The second assumption is that physical impulses *on their own* can never be reasons for action or reason-responsive – at the very least, they need to be taken up in judgement as reasons for action (incorporated into a maxim, as Kantians would have it). Both of these points have some intuitive force, but one might still ultimately reject them and instead adopt a model of freedom that is (a) non-causal; (b) retrospective (at least in part); and (c) allows physical impulses to be reason-responsive (and, in that sense, reasons for action) on their own without *prior* endorsement by the conscious mind. I believe that Adorno subscribes to this alternative model and would, hence, reject the objection in question.

Let us consider briefly the causal model. Proponents of it disagree which psychological states have the causal force in question – whether it is merely desires, or a belief-desire combination, or even beliefs on their own – but they are united in thinking that freedom requires an antecedent psychological state, embodying the intention which then, all being well, gets enacted. There is much to be said about this, but one key problem is that this account does not seem phenomenologically accurate about much of our behaviour we nonetheless consider as actions – it does not capture well our experience of this behaviour. Thus, there is a great part of our engagement with the world that is habitual and, at any rate, does not involve consciously settling on a clearly defined intention in advance – for example, I see a friend and spontaneously greet him in a certain way that is neither arranged nor otherwise the result of a prior decision; or when going for a run, I start with my right leg; or when making breakfast, I first put on the kettle before peeling a piece of fruit. Indeed, some such behaviour – for example, the running – can be sabotaged by our trying to plan and control them consciously in any detail. Like with Hamlet, too much antecedent reflection *can* be inhibiting, rather than enabling.

Moreover, there are cases where it is natural to conclude that what we sincerely felt was our intention – say to be polite to a relative or acquaintance – was in fact not our intention at all, *as our actions reveal* – which, to stay with the example, are far from polite. As much as the intervention of external forces or other contingencies might prevent us from realising what genuinely are our intentions, there, arguably, comes a point where the best interpretation of the displayed behaviour is that we were mistaken about our real intentions – that what we engaged in consciously was merely wishful thinking or self-deception. Indeed, the existence of the latter phenomena might make one adopt a model of agency, according to which there is not first a clearly formed intention and then an action which – barring weakness of the will or other interfering factors – executes the latter, such that the intention and the action are in principle separable from each other; but rather that the intention is only really formed in the action and is thus not separable from its expression. (Hence, philosophers sometimes talk of an *expressive* theory of freedom in this context.)[43]

Such processes of learning about one's intention from one's actions need not undermine one's sense of responsibility for what has happened. Responsibility might then no longer be about whether or not a certain psychological state was present and played a causal role – such a view anyway has problems in accounting for cases of negligence. Instead, responsibility will be about *taking* responsibility for the way one has acted, where this will sometimes involve taking responsibility for something that one did not consciously bring about or even for something which was different or contrary to what one (mistakenly) thought one was intending to do. Thus, to return to the earlier example, I might accept blame for the impoliteness that I now acknowledge to have intended, even though prior to my acts I had mistaken my mere wish to be polite for a genuine intention.

In these ways, it becomes more plausible to think that freedom is something we retrospectively, not prospectively, ascribe; something that

---

43 One need not take this as far as saying that actual behaviour and intention can never come apart. There might be intervening contingencies, such that what actually happens does not reflect the agent's will – think back to the example of the epileptic fit or cases where a sudden gust of wind diverts an arrow from the harmless trajectory intended by the archer, so that someone gets hurt. Still, on the expressive account, we then cannot be sure what the intention actually was and only by looking at the wider behaviour of the agent might we be able to settle the issue. For discussion of this and similar issues in relation to Hegel, see Pippin 2008.

is intimately connected to who we actually are and want to be as these matters are revealed in our actions; but not necessarily something that we consciously control prior to our actions. It also becomes more plausible to think that what our real intentions are, might actually be better expressed by our bodily reactions on occasion than by our conscious deliberation or psychological states. While facial expression and body language can mislead, sometimes they 'speak' the truth, while our own sincere reports on our intentions are mistaken – for example, while I genuinely hold the considered view that going to a particular event is what I want, my bodily demeanour tells a different story and might disclose on this occasion what I really want.

This also relates to the third point – reason-responsiveness. One might be tempted to think of bodily impulses as completely alien to reason, but this is, arguably, a mistake (and not just because of the evolutionary account Adorno gives of reason mentioned earlier). Consider how a bodily reflex such as drawing back from burning heat is well-described as reason-responsive: at least in typical situations, I have a reason *qua* sensible creature to avoid burning heat and to do so with some urgency, and while the bodily reflex in question is not conscious or deliberate, it can still be responsive to the reason in question. Indeed, an evolutionary account for it would presumably make reference to its function in preserving the life and health of those animals which develop this reflex.

Consider also reports of people who experienced how their body took over in situations of danger, such as descending a mountain in treacherous weather or with an injury, both by adopting certain protective postures and gestures without consciously deciding to adopt them and by releasing adrenaline such that the person remains 'energized, pain-free, and fear-free throughout the ordeal'.[44] Their body's taking over was in their interest, accorded with their wishes, and was not regretted by them. Just the opposite, they were thankful for having the bodily impulses in question; identified with these impulses; and even felt empowered by them (and, in that sense, free). Indeed, they were grateful for the spontaneity of these impulses – for the fact that they did not operate via deliberation and reflective endorsement, which might well have led to inactivity and freezing up.

One danger of this view is that almost anything can now count as free action as long as there is retrospective endorsement and a fit with one's interests (or some other form of reason-responsiveness), but this

---

44 Meyers 2004: 55.

is implausible for a range of cases. Thus, the operation of my digestive system is normally seen as something that is a bodily happening, but not a free action; and yet its operations are typically in my interest (and reason-responsive in that sense) and I am glad of their occurrence.

One response would be to say that not all physical impulses are constitutive of freedom. It might be that some of them are beyond our control in a different sense than was at issue so far, and as such are not suitably understood as part of freedom. Perhaps, having a fit or digesting food are such that it would take fairly extraordinary means to stop them (say stopping my digestive system by killing myself); but the same is not true of the body's taking over in the mountaineering example. In the latter case, reflection could have kicked in and stopped the actions – for better or for worse. Again, it might be that Adorno is right that resisting or suppressing a physical impulse on a particular occasion is not the end of the matter and that it will raise its head again on another occasion, possibly with a vengeance. Yet, even Adorno accepts that we could prevent these impulses from unfolding in particular instances (and do so without taking extraordinary means). After all, he is worried that we stop them on those occasions when they actually are reason-responsive and when stopping them is detrimental to the plans we go on to adopt consciously (as in the Hamlet case). It will be a difficult matter to decide which physical impulses are such that they can be compatible with, even constitutive of, freedom, but this by itself does not suffice to show that no such distinction can be drawn at all. Moreover, the boundary might not be fixed forever, but might depend on social and historical circumstances – perhaps what in certain contexts are completely automated physical processes, are more amenable to interruption or training in other contexts. For example, it might be that with modern chemistry and medicine, more of our bodily processes become subject to possible interference, so that people begin to take responsibility for their occurrence (say, accepting that they were negligent in not preventing an epileptic fit because they did not take their medication).

Finally, recall the discussion of the normative, ethical import of physical impulses from Chapter 7. There I noted that for Adorno, it is important that these impulses are subjected to critical scrutiny. Prior to such scrutiny, they might only be the best guide in extreme situations (where they are often more reason-responsive than modern reason), not in all cases. Put in terms of the expressive model of freedom, whether or not the physical impulses are constitutive of freedom does not so much depend on prior conscious control, but on whether we can reflectively take them up and come to own them.[45] This, in turn, will not depend on the individual's perspective alone – in fact, it might be more a question of whether the most critical minds among us could own them or not.

None of this is conclusive as it stands. However, it fits in well with Adorno's general outlook – not least his Aristotelianism (see Chapter 9) – and with the way he chips away at the 'inner citadel' of Kantian freedom, criticising Kant's account of pure practical reason (see Chapter 4), objecting to the repercussions of Kant's account of freedom in moral philosophy (see Chapter 5), and showing that at the heart of Kantian principle-based freedom, there cannot but be an unprincipled choice.[46]

45 See also Jütten 2012.   46 See Freyenhagen 2006: 434–5.

BIBLIOGRAPHY

Works by Adorno

Adorno, T. W. 1966. *Negative Dialektik*, Frankfurt am Main: Suhrkamp. Repr. in 1970–: Vol. VI, 1–412; trans. E. B. Ashton as *Negative Dialectics*, London: Routledge and Kegan Paul, 1973. Alternative translation used: http://www.efn.org/~dredmond/ndtrans.html, last accessed 3 December 2012.

1970–. *Gesammelte Schriften*, 20 vols., ed. R. Tiedemann, Frankfurt am Main: Suhrkamp.

1971. *Erziehung zur Mündigkeit: Vorträge und Gespräche mit Hellmut Becker 1959–1969*, ed. G. Kadelbach, Frankfurt am Main: Suhrkamp.

1974. *Philosophische Terminologie: Zur Einleitung*, Band 2, ed. R. zur Lippe, Frankfurt: Suhrkamp.

1977. 'The Actuality of Philosophy', *Telos* 10, 1: 120–33.

1978. *Minima Moralia*, trans. E. F. N. Jephcott, London: NLB, [1974]; repr. London: Verso.

1982. *Against Epistemology: A Metacritique: Studies in Husserl and the Phenomenological Antinomies*, trans. W. Domingo, Cambridge, MA: MIT Press.

1984. 'Essay as Form', trans. B. Hullot-Kentor and F. Will, *New German Critique* 32: 151–71.

1989. 'Society', in S. E. Bronner and D. M. Kellner (eds.), *Critical Theory and Society: A Reader*, New York: Routledge, 267–75.

1993a. *Einleitung in die Soziologie*, Frankfurt am Main: Suhrkamp. Trans. E. Jephcott as *Introduction to Sociology*, Cambridge: Polity Press, 2000.

1993b. *Hegel: Three Studies*, trans. S. Weber Nicholson, Cambridge, MA: MIT Press.

1995. *Kants 'Kritik der reinen Vernunft' (1959)*, ed. R. Tiedemann, Frankfurt am Main: Suhrkamp. Trans. R. Livingstone as *Kant's Critique of Pure Reason*, Cambridge: Polity Press, 2001.

1996. *Probleme der Moralphilosophie (1963)*, ed. T. Schröder, Frankfurt am Main: Suhrkamp. Trans. R. Livingstone as *Problems of Moral Philosophy*, Cambridge: Polity Press, 2000.

1998a. *Critical Models*, trans. H. W. Pickford, New York: Columbia University Press.

1998b. *Metaphysik: Begriff und Probleme (1965)*, ed. R. Tiedemann, Frankfurt am Main: Suhrkamp. Trans. E. Jephcott as *Metaphysics: Concepts and Problems*, Cambridge: Polity Press, 2000.

2001. *Zur Lehre von der Geschichte und der Freiheit (1964/65)*, ed. R. Tiedemann, Frankfurt am Main: Suhrkamp. Trans. R. Livingstone as *History and Freedom*, Cambridge: Polity Press, 2006.

2003a. *Can One Live after Auschwitz? A Philosophical Reader*, ed. R. Tiedemann, trans. R. Livingstone et al., Stanford University Press.

2003b. *Vorlesung über Negative Dialektik: Fragmente der Vorlesung 1965/66*, ed. R. Tiedemann, Frankfurt am Main: Suhrkamp. Trans. R. Livingstone as *Lectures on Negative Dialectics*, Cambridge: Polity Press, 2008.

2004. *Aesthetic Theory*, trans. R. Hullot-Kentor, London: Athlone, [1997]; repr. London: Continuum.

Probleme der Moralphilosophie (1956/7), unpublished manuscript, Adorno Archiv Vo1289–1520, Frankfurt am Main.

Adorno, T. W. and Becker, H. 1983. 'Education for Autonomy' [1969], *Telos* 56: 103–10.

Adorno, T. W. and Gehlen, A. 1983. 'Ist die Soziologie eine Wissenschaft vom Menschen?', repr. in Grenz 1983: 225–51.

Adorno, T. W. and Haselberg, P. von 1983. 'On the Historical Adequacy of Consciousness' [1965], *Telos* 56: 97–103.

Adorno, T. W. and Horkheimer, M. [1944, 1947] 1972. *Dialectic of Enlightenment*, trans. J. Cumming, New York: Herder and Herder.

Adorno, T. W. et al. 1976. *The Positivist Dispute in German Sociology*, trans. G. Adey and D. Frisby, New York (etc.): Harper & Row.

General bibliography

Allison, H. 1990. *Kant's Theory of Freedom*, Cambridge University Press.

Anscombe, G. E. M. 1958. 'Modern Moral Philosophy', *Philosophy* 33: 1–19.

Aquinas, St Thomas [c.1265–73] 1947. *Summa Theologica*, trans. Fathers of the English Dominican Province, New York: Benziger Brothers.

Arendt, H. [1963] 1994. *Eichmann in Jerusalem*, London: Penguin.

Arneson, R. J. 1994. 'Autonomy and Preference Formation', in J. L. Coleman and A. Buchanan (eds.), *In Harm's Way: Essays in Honor of Joel Feinberg*, Cambridge University Press.

Arpaly, N. 2000. 'On Acting Rationally against One's Best Judgment', *Ethics* 110, 3: 488–513.

2003. *Unprincipled Virtue: An Enquiry into Moral Agency*, Oxford University Press.

Badiou, A. [1998] 2001. *Ethics: An Essay on the Understanding of Evil*, trans. P. Hallward, London: Verso. [French orig., *L'Éthique: Essai sur la conscience du mal*, Paris: Éditions Hatier, 1998.]

Bahr, E. 1978. 'The Anti-Semitism Studies of the Frankfurt School: The Failure of Critical Theory', *German Studies Review* 1, 2: 125–38.

Barnes, J. (ed.) 1984. *The Complete Works of Aristotle: The Revised Oxford Translation*, 2 vols., Princeton University Press.

Bauman, Z. 1989. *Modernity and the Holocaust*, Ithaca, NY: Cornell University Press.

Benhabib, S. 1986. *Critique, Norm, and Utopia: A Study of the Foundations of Critical Theory*, Guildford, NY: Columbia University Press.

2009. 'From "The Dialectic of Enlightenment" to "The Origins of Totalitarianism" and the Genocide Convention: Adorno and Horkheimer in the Company of Arendt and Lemkin', in W. Breckman, P. E. Gordon, A. D. Moses, S. Moyn, and E. Neaman (eds.), *The Modernist Imagination: Intellectual History and Critical Theory*, Oxford: Berghahn Books, 299–330.

Bennett, J. 1974. 'The Conscience of Huckleberry Finn', *Philosophy* 49: 123–34.

1984. 'Kant's Theory of Freedom', in A. W. Wood (ed.), *Self and Nature in Kant's Philosophy*, Ithaca, NY: Cornell University Press, 102–12.

Berman, R. A. 1983. 'Adorno's Radicalism: Two Interviews from the Sixties', *Telos* 56: 94–7.

2002. 'Adorno's Politics', in Gibson and Rubin 2002: Ch. 5.

Bernstein, J. M. 2001. *Adorno: Disenchantment & Ethics*, Cambridge University Press.

Bloch, E. 1978. *Tendenz – Latenz – Utopie*, Frankfurt am Main: Suhrkamp.

Bolton, G. 2008. *Aid and Other Dirty Business: How Good Intentions Have Failed the World's Poor*, London: Ebury Press.

Brecht, B. 1967. *Gesammelte Werke*, 20 vols., Frankfurt am Main: Suhrkamp.

1976. *Poems*, ed. J. Willett and R. Manheim with the co-operation of E. Fried, London: Eyre Methuen.

Breuer, S. 1985. 'Adorno's Anthropology', *Telos* 64: 15–31.

Browning, C. 1992. *Ordinary Men: Reserve Police Battalion 101 and the Final Solution in Poland*, New York: HarperCollins.

Brunkhorst, H. 1999. *Adorno and Critical Theory*, Cardiff: University of Wales Press.

Butler, J. 2003. *Kritik der ethischen Gewalt*, Frankfurt am Main: Suhrkamp.

Canguilhem, G. [1966] 1989. *The Normal and the Pathological*, trans. C. R. Fawcett with R. S. Cohen, New York: Zone Books.

Cohen, G. A. 1988. *History, Labour and Freedom: Themes from Marx*, Oxford University Press.

Cook, D. 2011. *Adorno on Nature*, Durham: Acumen Press.

Cornell, D. 1987. 'The Ethical Message of Negative Dialectics', *Social Concept* 4, 1: 3–38.

Dews, P. 1995. 'Adorno, Poststructuralism and the Critique of Identity', in *The Limits of Disenchantment: Essays on Contemporary European Philosophy*, London: Verso, 19–38.

2008. *The Idea of Evil*, Oxford: Blackwell.

Durkheim, E. [1897] 1989. *Suicide: A Study in Sociology*, ed. G. Simpson, trans. J. A. Spaulding and G. Simpson, London: Routledge.

Easterly, W. 2006. *The White Man's Burden: Why the West's Efforts to Aid the Rest Have Done So Much Ill and So Little Good*, Oxford University Press.

Elster, J. 1985. *Making Sense of Marx*, Cambridge University Press.

Fink, H. 2006. 'Three Sorts of Naturalism', *European Journal of Philosophy* 14, 2: 202–21.

Finlayson, J. G. 2002. 'Adorno on the Ethical and the Ineffable', *European Journal of Philosophy* 10, 1: 1–25.

Foot, P. 1978. *Virtues and Vices*, Oxford: Blackwell.

2001. *Natural Goodness*, Oxford: Clarendon Press.

Frankfurt, H. 1969. 'Alternate Possibilities and Moral Responsibility', *Journal of Philosophy* 66, 23: 829–39.

Freyenhagen, F. 2006. 'Adorno's Negative Dialectics of Freedom', *Philosophy &
Social Criticism* 32, 3: 429–40.

2008. 'Reasoning Takes Time: On Allison and the Timelessness of the
Intelligible Self', *Kantian Review* 13, 2: 67–84.

2009. 'No Easy Way Out: Adorno's Negativism and the Problem of Normativity',
in S. Giacchetti Ludovisi (ed.), *Nostalgia for a Redeemed Future: Critical Theory*,
Newark, DE: University of Delaware Press.

2011a. 'Adorno's Ethics Without the Ineffable', *Telos* 155: 127–49.

2011b. 'Empty, Useless, and Dangerous? Recent Kantian Replies to the Empty
Formalism Objection', *Bulletin of the Hegel Society of Great Britain* 63: 163–86.

2012. 'Adorno's Politics: Theory and Praxis in Germany in the 1960s',
unpublished.

Früchtl, J. 1991. '"Moral begründen ist schwer": Die Rolle der Mitleidsethik bei
Adorno und Habermas', *Schopenhauer Jahrbuch* 72: 36–44.

1993. '"Leben wie ein gutes Tier" Ethik zwischen Mitleid und Diskurs', *Deutsche
Zeitung für Philosophie* 41, 6: 981–94.

Gerth, H. H. and Wright Mills, C. (eds.) 1948. *From Max Weber*, London:
Routledge.

Geuss, R. 2005. *Outside Ethics*, Princeton University Press.

2010. *Politics and the Imagination*, Princeton University Press.

Gibson, N. and Rubin, A. (eds.) 2002. *Adorno: A Critical Reader*, Oxford: Blackwell.

Goethe, J. W. von 1964. *Selected Verse*, trans. D. Luke, Harmondsworth: Penguin
Books.

Goodin, R. E. 1995. 'Political Ideals and Political Practice', *British Journal of Political
Science* 25: 37–56.

Grenz, F. 1983. *Adornos Philosophie in Grundbegriffen: Auflösung einiger Deutungsprobleme*,
Frankfurt am Main: Suhrkamp.

Günther, K. 1985. 'Dialektik der Aufklärung in der Idee der Freiheit: Zur Kritik des
Freiheitsbegriffs bei Adorno', *Zeitschrift für philosophische Forschung* 29: 229–60.

Habermas, J. 1983. *Philosophical-Political Profiles*, trans. F. G. Lawrence, London:
Heinemann.

1984. *The Theory of Communicative Action*, Vol. I: *Reason, and the Rationalization of
Society*, trans. T. McCarthy, Cambridge: Polity Press.

1987. *The Philosophical Discourse of Modernity: Twelve Lectures*, trans.
F. G. Lawrence, Cambridge: Polity Press.

2005. '"Ich selber bin ja ein Stück Natur" – Adorno über die Naturverflochtenheit
der Vernunft: Überlegungen zum Verhältnis von Freiheit und Unverfügbarkeit',
in A. Honneth (ed.), *Dialektik der Freiheit: Frankfurter Adorno-Konferenz 2003*,
Frankfurt am Main: Suhrkamp, 13–40.

Hampshire, S. 1992. *Innocence and Experience*, London: Penguin Books.

Han-Pile, B. 2011. 'Nietzsche and Amor Fati', *European Journal of Philosophy* 19, 2:
224–61.

Hegel, G. W. F. [1837, 1840] 1975. *Lectures on the Philosophy of World History:
Introduction*, trans. H. B. Nisbet, Cambridge University Press.

[1807] 1977. *The Phenomenology of Spirit*, trans. A. V. Miller, Oxford University Press.

[1821] 1991. *Hegel's Philosophy of Right*, ed. A. Wood, trans. H. B. Nisbet,
Cambridge University Press.

Herman, B. 1993. *The Practice of Moral Judgement*, Cambridge, MA: Harvard University Press.

2007. *Moral Literacy*. Cambridge, MA: Harvard University Press.

Hill, T. E., Jr, 1992. *Dignity and Practical Reason in Kant's Moral Theory*, Ithaca, NY: Cornell University Press.

Honneth, A. 1995. *The Fragmented World of the Social: Essays in Social and Political Philosophy*, ed. C. Wright, Albany, NY: State University of New York Press.

Horkheimer, M. [1937] 1972. 'Traditional and Critical Theory' (including 'Postscript'), trans. M. J. O'Connell in *Critical Theory: Selected Essays*, New York: Herder and Herder, 188–252.

Huhn, T. (ed.) 2004. *Cambridge Companion to Adorno*, Cambridge University Press.

Hume, D. [1748, 1751] 1975. *Enquiries Concerning Human Understanding and Concerning the Principles of Morals*, ed. L. A. Selby-Bigge, 3rd edn, rev. P. H. Nidditch, Oxford University Press.

[1739, 1740] 1978. *A Treatise of Human Nature*, ed. L. A. Selby-Bigge, 2nd edn, rev. P. H. Nidditch, Oxford University Press.

Ibsen, H. [1884] 1960. *The Wild Duck: A Play in Five Acts*, trans. J. W. McFarlane, Oxford University Press.

Jaeggi, R. 2005. '"No Individual Can Resist": *Minima Moralia* as Critique of Forms of Life', *Constellations* 12, 1 (March 2005): 65–82.

James, A. 2005. 'Constructing Justice for Existing Practice: Rawls and the Status Quo', *Philosophy & Public Affairs* 33: 281–316.

Jarvis, S. 1998. *Adorno: A Critical Introduction*, Cambridge: Polity Press.

Jay, M. 1980. 'The Jews and the Frankfurt School: Critical Theory's Analysis of Anti-Semitism', *New German Critique* 19: 137–49.

1984. *Adorno*, London: Fontana.

Jütten, T. 2012. 'Adorno on Kant, Freedom and Determinism', *European Journal of Philosophy* 20, 4: 548–74.

Kant, I. 1900–. *Gesammelte Schriften*, ed. Deutsche (formerly Königlich-Preussische) Akademie der Wissenschaften, Berlin: Walter de Gruyter (and predecessors).

1996. *Practical Philosophy*, trans. and ed. M. J. Gregor, Cambridge University Press.

1998. *Religion within the Bounds of Mere Reason and other Writings*, trans. and ed. A. Wood and G. di Giovanni, Cambridge University Press.

Kennedy, D. 2004. *The Dark Sides of Virtue: Reassessing International Humanitarianism*, Princeton University Press.

Kluge, A. and Negt, O. [1972] 1976. *Öffentlichkeit und Erfahrung*, 4th edn, Frankfurt am Main: Suhrkamp.

Knoll, M. 2002. *Theodor W. Adorno: Ethik als erste Philosophie*, Munich: Wilhelm Fink.

Kohlmann, U. 1997. *Dialektik der Moral: Untersuchungen zur Moralphilosophie Adornos*, Lüneburg: zu Klampen.

Korsgaard, C. 1996. *Creating the Kingdom of Ends*, Cambridge University Press.

Korsgaard, C. et al. 1996. *The Sources of Normativity*, Cambridge University Press.

Krahl, H. J. 1975. 'The Political Contradiction in Adorno's Critical Theory', *Sociological Review* 23, 4: 831–4.

Lenman, J. 1999. 'Michael Smith and the Daleks: Reason, Morality, and Contingency', *Utilitas* 11, 2: 164–77.

    2005. 'The Saucer of Mud, the Kudzu Vine and the Uxorious Cheetah: Against Neo-Aristotelian Naturalism in Metaethics', *European Journal of Analytic Philosophy* 1, 2: 37–50.

Levi, P. [1958] 1996. *If This is a Man*, in *If This is a Man, The Truce*, trans. of 1958 reprint by S. Woolf, London: Vintage. [Ital. orig., *Se questo è un uomo*, Turin: F. de Silva, 1947; repr. Einaudi,1958.]

Lukács, G. [1923] 1971a. *History and Class Consciousness*, trans. R. Livingstone, London: Merlin Press.

    [1916] 1971b. *The Theory of the Novel: A Historico-Philosophical Essay on the Forms of Great Epic Literature*, trans. from the German by Anna Bostock, Cambridge, MA: MIT Press.

McDowell, J. 1994. *Mind and World*, Cambridge, MA: Harvard University Press.

    1998. *Mind, Value and Reality*, Cambridge, MA: Harvard University Press.

MacIntyre, A. [1981] 1985. *After Virtue: A Study in Moral Theory*, 2nd edn, London: Duckworth.

    [1967] 1998. *A Short History of Ethics: A History of Moral Philosophy from the Homeric Age to the Twentieth Century*, 2nd edn, London, Routledge.

    1999. *Dependent Rational Animals*, London: Duckworth.

Mackie, J. L. 1977. *Ethics: Inventing Right and Wrong*, London: Penguin.

Marcuse, H. [1964] 1968. *One-Dimensional Man*, London: Sphere Books.

Maren, M. 1997. *The Road to Hell: The Ravaging Effects of Foreign Aid and International Charity*, New York: The Free Press.

Margalit, A. 2011. 'Why Are You Betraying Your Class?', *European Journal of Philosophy* 19, 2: 171–83.

Marrus, M. R. 1989. *The Holocaust in History*, London: Penguin.

Martin, W. 2009. 'Ought but Cannot', *Proceedings of the Aristotelian Society* 109, 2: 103–28.

Marx Engels Collected Works [MECW]. 1975–2005. Moscow: Progress Publishers.

Marx Engels Werke [MEW]. 1956–90. Berlin: Dietz.

Menke, C. 2004. 'Genealogy and Critique: Two Forms of Ethical Questioning of Morality', in Huhn 2004: Ch. 12.

    2005. 'Virtue and Reflection: The "Antinomies of Moral Philosophy"', *Constellations* 12, 1: 36–49.

Meyers, D. 2004. *Being Yourself: Essays on Identity, Action, and Social Life*, Lanham, MD: Rowman & Littlefield.

Moyo, D. 2009. *Dead Aid: Why Aid is Not Working and How There is Another Way for Africa*, London: Allen Lane.

Müller-Dohm, S. 2005. *Adorno: An Intellectual Biography*, Cambridge: Polity Press.

Nagel, T. 1986. *The View from Nowhere*, Oxford University Press.

Narveson, J. 2002. 'Collective Responsibility', *The Journal of Ethics* 6: 179–98.

Nietzsche, F. 1979. *Philosophy and Truth: Selections from Nietzsche's Notebook of the Early 1870s*, trans. and ed. D. Breazeale, Sussex: Harvester Press.

    1980. *Sämtliche Werke*, Kritische Studienausgabe in 15 Bänden, ed. Giorgio Colli and Mazzino Montinari, Munich: Deutscher Taschenbuch.

Noerr, G. Schmid 1995. 'Adornos Verhältnis zur Mitleidsethik Schopenhauers', in G. Schweppenhäuser and M. Wischke (eds.), *Impulse und Negativität: Ethik and Ästhetik bei Adorno*, Hamburg: Argument, 13–28.

Nozick, R. 1974. *Anarchy, State, and Utopia*, New York: Basic Books.

O'Connor, B. 2004. *Adorno's Negative Dialectics: Philosophy and the Possibility of Critical Rationality*, Cambridge, MA: MIT Press.

2012. *Adorno: Routledge Philosophers*, London: Routledge.

O'Neill, O. 2007. 'Normativity and Practical Judgement', *Journal of Moral Philosophy* 4, 3: 393–405.

Oshana, M. 1998. 'Personal Autonomy and Society', *Journal of Social Philosophy* 29, 1: 81–102.

Pickford, H. W. 2002. 'The Dialectic of Theory and Practice: On Late Adorno', in Gibson and Rubin 2002: Ch. 13.

Pippin, R. B. 2008. *Hegel's Practical Philosophy: Rational Agency as Ethical Life*, Cambridge University Press.

Pogge, T. [2002] 2008. *World Poverty and Human Rights*, 2nd edn, Cambridge: Polity Press.

Rabinbach, A. 2002. '"Why Were the Jews Sacrificed?" The Place of Antisemitism in Adorno and Horkheimer's *Dialectic of Enlightenment*', in Gibson and Rubin 2002: Ch. 5.

Rawls, J. 1971. *A Theory of Justice*, Cambridge, MA: Harvard University Press.

[1993] 1996. *Political Liberalism*, New York: Columbia University Press.

Raz, J. 1986. *Morality as Freedom*, Oxford University Press.

1999. 'Explaining Normativity: On Rationality and the Justification of Reason', *Ratio* 12, 4: 354–79.

Reginster, B. 2006. *The Affirmation of Life: Nietzsche on Overcoming Nihilism*, Cambridge, MA: Harvard University Press.

Reijen, W. van and Noerr, G. Schmid (eds.) 1987. *Vierzig Jahre Flaschenpost: 'Dialektik der Aufklärung' 1947–1987*, Frankfurt am Main: Fischer.

Rescher, N. 1958. 'Reasoned Justification of Moral Judgements', *Journal of Philosophy* 55, 6: 248–55.

Rieff, D. 2002. *A Bed for the Night: Humanitarianism in Crisis*, London: Vintage.

Rosen, M. 1996. *On Voluntary Servitude*, Cambridge: Polity Press.

Rousseau, J. J. [1755] 1913. *The Social Contract and Discourses*, ed. and trans. G. D. H. Cole, London: J. M. Dent & Sons Ltd.

Sangiovanni, A. 2010. 'Normative Political Theory: A Flight from Reality?', in D. Bell (ed.), *Political Thought and International Relations: Realist Themes*, Oxford University Press, Ch. 12: 219–39.

Scheffler, S. 1994. 'The Appeal of Political Liberalism', *Ethics* 105, 1: 4–22.

Schnädelbach, H. 1986. 'Max Horkheimer und die Moralphilosophie des deutschen Idealismus', in *Max Horkheimer heute: Werk und Wirkung*, Frankfurt am Main: Fischer, 52–78.

Schweppenhäuser, G. 1992. 'Zur kritischen Theorie der Moral bei Adorno', *Deutsche Zeitschrift für Philosophie* 40, 12: 1403–17.

1993. *Ethik nach Auschwitz: Adornos negative Moralphilosophie*, Hamburg: Argument (Argument-Sonderband Neue Folge AS 231).

2004. 'Adorno's Negative Moral Philosophy', in Huhn 2004: 328–53.

Seel, M. 2004. *Adornos Philosophie der Kontemplation*, Frankfurt am Main: Suhrkamp.

Sen, A. 1981. *Poverty and Famine: An Essay on Entitlement and Deprivation*, Oxford University Press.

Stern, R. 2004. 'Does 'ought' imply 'can'? And did Kant think it does?', *Utilitas* 16, 1: 42–61.

2006. 'Hegel's Doppelsatz: A Neutral Reading', *Journal of the History of Philosophy* 44: 235–66.

2009. 'The Autonomy of Morality and the Morality of Autonomy', *Journal of Moral Philosophy* 6, 3: 395–415.

Sussman, D. 2005. 'What's Wrong with Torture?', *Philosophy & Public Affairs* 22, 1: 1–33.

Tassone, G. 2005. 'Amoral Adorno: Negative Dialectics Outside Ethics', *European Journal of Social Theory* 8, 3: 251–67.

Taylor, C. 1985. *Philosophy and the Human Sciences*, Cambridge University Press.

1993. 'Explanation and Practical Reason', in M. C. Nussbaum and A. Sen (eds.), *The Quality of Life*, Oxford: Clarendon Press, 208–31.

Terry, F. 2002. *Condemned to Repeat? The Paradox of Humanitarian Action*, Ithaca, NY: Cornell University Press.

Theunissen, M. 1983. 'Negativität bei Adorno', in L. von Friedeburg and J. Habermas (eds.), *Adorno-Konferenz 1983*, Frankfurt am Main: Suhrkamp, 41–65.

Thompson, M. 2004. 'Apprehending Human Form', in A. O'Hear (ed.), *Modern Moral Philosophy*, Cambridge University Press, 47–74.

2008. *Life and Action: Elementary Structures of Practice and Practical Thought*, Cambridge, MA: Harvard University Press.

Thyen, A. 1989. *Negative Dialektik der Erfahrung: Zur Rationalität des Nichtidentischen bei Adorno*, Frankfurt am Main: Suhrkamp.

Timmermann, J. 2003. 'Sollen und Können: "Du Kannst, denn du sollst" und "Sollen impliziert Können" im Vergleich', *Philosophiegeschichte und logische Analyse/Logical Analysis and History of Philosophy*, 6 (Geschichte der Ethik/ History of Ethics): 113–22.

Waal, A. de 1997. *Famine Crimes: Politics & the Disaster Relief Industry in Africa*, Bloomsbury, IN: Indiana University Press.

Wellmer, A. 2007. 'Adorno and the Difficulties of a Critical Reconstruction of the Historical Present', *Critical Horizons: A Journal of Philosophy and Social Theory* 8, 2: 135–56.

Whitebook, J. 2003. 'Theodor W. Adornos Interpretation von Kant und Freud', *Psyche: Zeitschrift für Psychoanalyse und ihre Anwendungen* 57, 8: 681–707. English version: 'Weighty Objects: On Adorno's Kant-Freud Interpretation', in Huhn 2004: 51–78.

Wiggershaus, R. 1994. *The Frankfurt School: Its History, Theories and Political Significance*, trans. M. Robertson, Cambridge: Polity Press.

Wiggins, D. 1991. 'Claims of Need', in *Needs, Values, Truth: Essays in the Philosophy of Value*, Oxford: Basil Blackwell, Ch. 1.

Williams, B. 1981. *Moral Luck*, Cambridge University Press.

1993. *Ethics and the Limits of Philosophy*, rev. edn, London: Fontana Press.

1996. 'History, Morality and the Test of Reflection', in Korsgaard et al. 1996: Ch. 8.

2002. *Truth and Truthfulness: An Essay in Genealogy*, Princeton University Press.

2005. *In the Beginning was the Deed: Realism and Moralism in Political Argument*, Princeton University Press.

Wolff, J. 2002. *Why Read Marx Today?* Oxford University Press.

Wood, A. W. 1981. *Karl Marx*, London: Routledge & Kegan Paul.

INDEX

41387235R00169

Made in the USA
Middletown, DE
10 March 2017